Is Socialism Feasible?

To Vinny, with love and solidarity

Is Socialism Feasible?

Towards an Alternative Future

Geoffrey M. Hodgson

Institute for International Management, Loughborough University London, UK

 Edward Elgar
PUBLISHING

Cheltenham, UK • Northampton, MA, USA

Published by
Edward Elgar Publishing Limited
The Lypiatts
15 Lansdown Road
Cheltenham
Glos GL50 2JA
UK

Edward Elgar Publishing, Inc.
William Pratt House
9 Dewey Court
Northampton
Massachusetts 01060
USA

A catalogue record for this book
is available from the British Library

This book is available electronically in the **Elgar**online
Economics subject collection
DOI 10.4337/9781789901627

ISBN 978 1 78990 161 0 (cased)
ISBN 978 1 78990 163 4 (paperback)
ISBN 978 1 78990 162 7 (eBook)

Typeset by Columns Design XML Ltd, Reading

Printed and bound in Great Britain by TJ International Ltd, Padstow, Cornwall

Contents

Preface   vi

Introduction   1

PART I SOCIALISM, MARKETS AND DEMOCRACY

1 What does socialism mean?   25
2 Small socialism requires frugality or markets   50
3 Big socialism brings stagnation and despotism   72
4 Knowledge, complexity and the limits to planning   101

PART II TOWARDS A FEASIBLE ALTERNATIVE:
         LIBERAL SOLIDARITY

5 Social knowledge and freedom to choose   126
6 The limits and indispensability of states and markets   141
7 Varieties of capitalism: the realms of the possible   163
8 The making of liberal solidarity   180

References   211
Index   259

Preface

One of the greatest rivalries of our age is between socialism and capitalism. Despite the undemocratic and oppressive nature of self-described 'socialist' regimes, support for some form of *socialism* seems remarkably buoyant and it has risen further since the global economic crash of 2008.

Many people believe that a humane socialism is possible, and that it would be much better than capitalism. Socialists propose a rational ordering of society, based on human solidarity and cooperation, rather than on self-seeking individualism. They attack capitalism as wasteful, inegalitarian and driven by greed. For such reasons, the idea of socialism attracts many millions. But is socialism feasible?

This book establishes that the word *socialism* remains irretrievably associated with widespread common ownership. Revisionist attempts to change the definition of the word have largely failed. The original meaning endures in the DNA of socialist political parties. It typically connotes a preference for public ownership and an aversion to private enterprise and markets.

We must distinguish *socialism* from what is often described today as *social democracy*. Unlike *socialism*, the term *social democracy* has successfully changed its meaning. Unlike classical socialism, modern social democracy accepts a dominant private sector. Social democratic experiments in Nordic countries have been remarkably successful, as outlined in the second part of this book. Modern social democracy embraces a form of capitalism, not socialism.

The word *socialism* has been in existence for about 200 years, while experimentation with forms of common ownership has been going on for much longer. Socialism has a moving and heroic history, involving millions of men and women who have tried to create a better system. There is much that is wrong with the existing world, and we are right to search for improvements and alternatives.

Socialists aim to create a caring society where people can fulfil their potential and the needy are given support by society at large. I share this aim. But socialists make the wrong assumptions about the kind of system that can sustain such goals.

After two or more centuries of experimentation, socialists should be able to point to an alternative system that works, rather than comparing the actual world with an idealized system of their imagination. Unfortunately, the history of socialist experiments has largely been one of catastrophic failure. The cost has been tens of millions of deaths, by famine or state repression.[1] Economies managed by self-described socialists have been successful only when they have embraced widespread market exchange and allowed a viable private sector.

Imaginary utopias are fine for novels and movies, but they often make bad politics. We need to learn from past experience. Using theory and evidence, this book shows that a humane classical socialism on a large scale is unviable. The history of socialism is as much about tragedy as it is of heroic idealism. Some say that socialism is OK in theory but not in practice. The truth is that both theory and practice show that socialism on a large scale is economically impeded and incompatible with democracy.

In theory, partly because of the irretrievable dispersal of much knowledge to individuals and local organizations, modern, large-scale complex economic systems cannot completely be planned or controlled from the centre. The complexity and dispersed nature of knowledge in a modern economy means that much vital information cannot be gathered or processed by central planners. Comprehensive central planning works neither in theory nor in practice.

Market economies help to resolve this problem through decentralized coordination mechanisms based on contracts and prices. Thereby much information is processed locally and not from the centre. Markets can also provide devolved incentives that are lacking in centralized systems. In one form or another, and to a greater or lesser extent, all large-scale complex economic systems must fall back on decentralized coordination mechanisms involving relatively autonomous mutual adjustments of some kind between local actors.[2]

---

[1] For estimates of the number of deaths under self-declared *socialist* regimes see Rummel (1994) and Courtois et al. (1999).

[2] The term 'decentralized coordination mechanism' was suggested to me by János Kornai in April 2018. Sometimes I substitute 'system' for 'mechanism'. By necessity, both science and modern economies are decentralized coordination systems operating by mutual adjustment among devolved agents. Both these systems rely on dispersed tacit and fragmented knowledge. Consequently, they cannot be adequately planned from the centre. But they differ in other crucial respects. In particular, science is not a market (Hodgson, 2019c) and it relies more on reputational over pecuniary motives. The major contributor to the study of both kinds of decentralized coordination system was Michael Polanyi (1940, 1941, 1945, 1948, 1951, 1957, 1958, 1962, 1967, 1997). Polanyi was a critic of both socialism and unrestricted markets. In another volume on heterodox economics (Hodgson,

In no case has democracy endured within large-scale socialism. Both theory and evidence suggest that (what I call) *big socialism* and democracy are ill-matched. To avoid such major pitfalls, feasible socialism must accept a major role for markets that many socialists reject. If decisions are decentralized, then markets are essential.

In *small socialism*, decentralized coordination of worker cooperatives can be achieved through markets. This has never been tried in full. In Yugoslavia the implementation was incomplete because of the prevalence of *big socialist* ideology with its agoraphobic suspicion of markets. Cautious experimentation in this small-scale direction is the only viable route left for any feasible and democratic socialism.

Supporters of socialism believe that 'another world is possible'. It magically avoids the socialist disasters of the past: 'it will be better next time'. But past socialist calamities cannot simply be put down to bad or ruthless leaders or to aggression from hostile forces, despite these factors being present. Theory and history show that catastrophic defects are inherent in the socialist project itself, at least when it involves strong economic and political direction from the central state. This book explains why.

We are left with the option of working toward major reforms within democratic capitalism, to pursue sustainable economic growth, to provide care for the needy, and to reduce inequality. Within that broader strategy it is also possible to experiment with worker-owned cooperatives and other small-scale socialist ventures.

My previous book – *Wrong Turnings* – showed how the term 'Left' had changed its meaning several times since its inception in the French Revolution of 1789. In several steps, the Left moved away from the positive achievements of the Enlightenment.

Wrong Turnings was drafted before Bernie Sanders established a remarkable public following in the US Democratic Party primary elections of 2016. The book had gone to press before June 2017 when, against a widespread view among pollsters that he was unelectable, Jeremy Corbyn dramatically increased the Labour Party's share of the vote in a snap UK general election.

These two astonishing political campaigns demonstrate that, in post-crash capitalism, candidates who openly proclaim themselves as *socialist*,

---

2019b), I build on Polanyi's application of the notion of decentralized coordination systems to scientific communities. I use it to reveal the strategic difficulties for heterodox economics.

and envision a big expansion in the economic role of government, can gather millions of votes, despite strident opposition from the conservative media.

This book is written for those millions who describe themselves as socialists, and for anyone who is interested in the rivalry between socialism and capitalism. While capitalism has exacerbated inequality and abandoned many to poverty, it has also led to a massive increase of global wealth per capita, and much greater human longevity. In recent decades, extreme poverty throughout the world has been reduced dramatically. Existing capitalism is far from perfect, but these unprecedented historic successes should be acknowledged.[3]

Karl Marx and Frederick Engels famously acknowledged in their 1848 *Communist Manifesto* that capitalism 'has created more massive and more colossal productive forces than have all preceding generations together'. But capitalism then was far from exhausted. In the following 160 years, despite two devastating world wars, numerous other conflicts, famines and other disasters, capitalism multiplied its productive capacity many times over. Global average GDP per capita increased about tenfold in real terms. In the same period, GDP per capita increased 17 times in the USA. Even in colonized and exploited Africa, GDP per capita quadrupled in the 160 years since 1848.[4]

We need to understand the reasons for capitalism's productive success and to devote our energy to minimizing its substantial shortcomings. We already know how to alleviate many of its problems. The experience of the last two centuries shows that the most progressive option is a reformed and judiciously regulated capitalism. It is also the only viable option to deal with the urgent problem of climate change. Claiming that socialism is the only solution to global warming is an argument for postponement of the urgent measures required in the next few years. Generally, instead of chasing unicorns of our imagination, it would be better to tame the beast we have, using tried-and-tested methods and cautious institutional experiments.

This book is critical of the naive view of capitalism as an individualistic utopia where freedom can always flourish alongside a minimal state. The state has always been necessary to make capitalism work. Our problems cannot be overcome by moving towards an impractical, extreme, deregulated system where everything is traded on markets.

---

[3]   For data and references see the beginning of Chapter 7 below.

[4]   Quote from Marx (1973, p. 72). The GDP per capita data are from Maddison (2007). From 1848 to 2008, Japan's GDP per capita has increased by a factor of 33, in Germany and France by a factor of 15, and in the UK by a factor of 10.

Instead we need a reformed and regulated democratic capitalism that serves human needs and minimizes our despoliation of our planet.

Political debate is plagued by purists on all sides. Many socialists see public ownership as a solution to every economic problem, just as market fundamentalists propose privatization and markets as universal panaceas. They are seductive versions of populism: they both propose simple solutions to complex problems.

Reality is more complex. Socialists should understand why sizeable markets and private ownership are necessary, just as libertarians and market fundamentalists should appreciate why some state intervention is indispensable, at least to sustain the institutional infrastructure of a market economy. The way forward involves pragmatism, not purism.[5]

The most obvious and well-tried progressive option available to us is a reformed capitalism with an effective welfare state. Despite the huge and growing economic inequality in major capitalist countries, there is sufficient variety within capitalism to learn from real-world examples with lower inequality and highly developed welfare states. These progressive cases have all been guided by liberal-social-democratic ideologies.

Liberal ideology is huge in its scope and contains many possible variations and internally contested positions. We should explore these copious territories in search of realistic, humane, solidaristic and peaceful policies, rather than sailing off on a demonstrably hazardous voyage toward an imagined, unreal and un-navigated socialism.

This work has benefited greatly from the help and interactions of many friends and colleagues. Among them I wish to thank Sebastian Berger, Paul Canning, János Kornai, David Levi-Faur, Vinny Logan, Joan Martinez-Alier, Hugo Montesinos-Yufa, D. Mario Nuti, Carlota Perez, Aleksandar Stojanović, Mehrdad Vahabi, Matt Vidal and anonymous referees. Their help has been invaluable.

---

[5]   In this book I use the word *pragmatism* in its everyday sense of stressing practical applications and their importance for the evaluation of theories or beliefs. *Pragmatism* has a more specific and technical meaning in philosophy (Joas, 1993; Putnam, 1995).

Introduction

> These are the times that try men's souls.
> Thomas Paine (1776)

> The difficulty lies, not in the new ideas, but in escaping from the old ones.
> John Maynard Keynes (1936)

In 1977 the 'neo-conservative' (and former Trotskyist) journalist Irving Kristol famously declared: 'The most important political event of the twentieth century is not the crisis of capitalism but the death of socialism.' At that time, about 35 per cent of humanity – mostly in China and the Soviet bloc – lived under self-declared *socialist* governments, where the bulk of the economy was in public ownership. Kristol foretold the demise of these regimes and pointed to a rising intellectual tide against socialist ideas.[1]

Kristol seemed vindicated when, late in the following year, Communist China turned away from decades of Soviet-style central planning and began to introduce widespread markets and private enterprise, albeit within a state-dominated economy. Subsequently it enjoyed decades of spectacular growth, raising hundreds of millions out of extreme poverty.

Then, in 1989–91, came the fall of the Berlin Wall and the collapse of the Soviet bloc, which seemed to offer further confirmation of Kristol's claim. Afterwards, all that remained of the former Soviet-style economies were beleaguered Cuba and isolated North Korea. These two made up less than 1 per cent of the world's population. Capitalism was triumphant elsewhere.

For many, socialist ideology seemed dead. The political theorist John Gray wrote in 1993: 'The intellectual hegemony of the New Right in economic theory, and the collapse of socialism in both Eastern and Western Europe, rule out any doctrinal survival of socialism.'[2]

The dramatic events from 1978 to 1991 did not simply undermine hard-line *socialism* or *communism*. The Socialist and Social Democratic

---

[1] Kristol (1977, p. 30). The near-interchangeability of the terms *socialism* and *communism* is discussed in Chapter 1 below.

[2] Gray (1993, p. 278).

parties in Europe were founded on tacit alliances between the organized working class and socialist intellectuals. Both partners in that coalition faced problems. The abandonment of the former big socialist experiments in Russia and China put the intellectuals at sea. Some of them stuck to their previous views, as if the world had not changed. Others differed in the degrees and directions of their revisionism.

Buffeted by relentless globalization, the working class had already splintered into countless occupational specialisms, and their communities had become ethnically segregated. A large segment of the working class became unemployed, disengaged or socially excluded. Many blamed immigrants for their problems, and this group became prey to racism and extreme nationalism.

Both Marxism and social democracy saw the organized industrial working class as the driver of social transformation. But this view of a unified proletariat as the motor of change had become ever more remote from reality. Increasingly, the working classes in major capitalist countries have become occupationally, culturally, ethnically and politically fragmented. Because of these fissures in guiding ideology and social base, both socialism and social democracy foundered.

At the dawn of the new millennium, it seemed that nothing had undermined Kristol's claim: socialism was in its death throes and capitalism was triumphant. Then, in 2008, capitalism suffered its biggest crisis since the 1930s. Banks had to be bailed out and governments had to rescue financial markets from destruction. There had already been decades of real-wage stagnation in the US. This torpor spread to other developed countries. Widely discussed studies revealed growing economic inequality and its deleterious consequences for society as a whole. Millions became disillusioned with the existing economic system.[3]

The faltering of capitalism aroused socialist ideology from its slumber. After the financial earthquake of 2008, the spectre of Marxism also returned to haunt the Western corridors of political power. Sales of Marx's works including *Capital* enjoyed a dramatic rise. People in their millions turned to *socialism* – whatever that was taken to mean.[4]

This revival of Marxism did not correlate with any substantial growth in the militancy of the working class, which was supposed to be the motor of socialist transformation. Instead, many activists behind the revival of socialism and Marxism were drawn from the increasingly insecure middle class, particularly from professional positions in state or

---

[3] Wilkinson and Pickett (2009), Piketty (2014).
[4] Jeffries (2012).

academic institutions. Socialism and Marxism today are not the ideologies of an advancing proletariat; they are more the doctrines of middle-class professional employees, many of whom rely on public funds.[5]

According to a 2017 survey of American adults, 37 per cent preferred (what they described as) *socialism* to *capitalism*. Among millennials (meaning those reaching adulthood in the early twenty-first century), 44 per cent preferred *socialism* over *capitalism*. This survey broadly confirmed previous American polls from about 2015, which showed a surge of support for *socialism*, especially among younger people. In 2015 *socialism* was the seventh-most-consulted entry in the Merriam-Webster online dictionary. *Communism* and *capitalism* were not far behind.[6]

Polling in the UK found that 39 per cent of adults have an unfavourable view of *capitalism*, while 33 per cent were favourable. Yet 36 per cent of this UK sample viewed *socialism* positively, compared to 32 per cent negatively. Germans were reported as even more upbeat about *socialism*, with 45 per cent being favourable and 26 per cent unfavourable.[7]

Although several major socialist parties have been in retreat – including in France and Italy – 2015 saw the election of the traditional socialist Jeremy Corbyn as Leader of the British Labour Party. In the 2017 general election Corbyn led an energetic campaign, increasing Labour's vote share to 40 per cent, up from 30 per cent in the 2015 election (when the Labour leader was Ed Miliband).

Corbyn is the most radically socialist leader of the Labour Party, at least since Clement Attlee. His advance moved the Labour Party away from decades of moderate policies. Labour returned to its classical socialist roots. Corbyn appointed the self-proclaimed Marxist John McDonnell as his Labour Shadow Chancellor of the Exchequer, who

---

[5]   Gray (1993, p. 94) claimed perceptively that Marxism can flourish among 'a radical intelligentsia which perceives its social status to be lower than that of business, which is accordingly estranged from the dominant values of its parent culture, and which is substantially marginalized from the political process'. It 'has attempted to legitimate its interests by the adoption of an anti-market ideology'. A 2016 survey (ESRC, 2016) found that 77 per cent of UK Labour Party members were professionals, managers or similar (from the 'ABC1' middle classes that make up about 56 per cent of the total population) and that 57 per cent of Labour members were university graduates (compared with 42 per cent in the overall population). Labour's 2017 upturn in the UK was not associated with any increase in the strength or organization of the traditional working class. Social class has become a poor predictor of voting intention in the UK and US, where political inclinations increasingly correlate with education and age. In both countries the older, less-educated and rurally located are more likely to vote for Conservative candidates (*The Guardian*, 2017; Tyson and Maniam, 2016).

[6]   American Culture and Faith Institute (2017), Merriam-Webster (2015), Meyerson (2016), Moore (2015).

[7]   Dahlgreen (2016).

listed in his entry in *Who's Who* that one of his hobbies is 'generally fermenting [*sic*] the overthrow of capitalism'. Unlike Attlee, Corbyn has pronounced an 'anti-imperialist' foreign policy including opposition to NATO.[8]

The long-declared socialist Bernie Sanders campaigned for the Democratic presidential nomination in the US in 2015–16. In the primary elections he received over 13 million votes. He won 23 primaries and caucuses and approximately 43 per cent of pledged delegates, compared to 55 per cent for Hillary Clinton. Polls taken in 2017 found Sanders to be the most popular politician in the US.[9]

Sanders was endorsed by the Democratic Socialists of America (DSA), which has its roots in the Socialist Party of America – the party of Eugene Debs (1855–1926). The DSA embraces a version of traditional socialism in its aims. The DSA is today the largest socialist organization in the US and the largest ever there in over a century. It has a young and rapidly growing membership, reaching 50,000 in 2018. In late 2017, the median age of its membership was 33, compared to 68 in 2013. In November 2018, two DSA members – Alexandria Ocasio-Cortez and Rashida Tlaib – were elected to the US House of Representatives.[10]

Socialist ideas have made such an advance in the US that in 2018 the Council of Economic Advisors to the US President was alarmed enough to report: 'Coincident with the 200th anniversary of Karl Marx's birth, socialism is making a comeback in American political discourse. Detailed policy proposals from self-declared socialists are gaining support in Congress and among much of the electorate.'[11]

Like many of the self-declared *socialists* it criticized, the report made no distinction in kind between *socialism* and Nordic-style *social democracy*. This widespread error is fuelled by a commonplace conviction, held by supporters and opponents of *socialism*, that both terms amount to different doses of the same medicine – more state intervention and less

---

[8]   Corbyn (2014), Hodgson (2018, pp. 121, 170–71, 199, 235), Bolton and Pitts (2018).

[9]   Sainato (2017).

[10]   Heyward (2018). The DSA has adopted 'a vision of a humane international social order based both on democratic planning and market mechanisms'. But they also argued that 'widespread worker and public ownership will greatly lessen the corrosive effect of capitalists [*sic*] markets on people's lives' (Democratic Socialists of America, 1995). This vision amounts to a combination of market (small) socialism with state (big) socialism. While it notably accepts a role for markets, its agoraphobic bias is revealed by the failure to mention the corrosive effects of bureaucracy on people's lives.

[11]   Council of Economic Advisors (2018, p. 1).

markets. Using the same conflated terminology, one side promotes and the other rejects the prescription.

Clearly, rumours of the death of socialism have been exaggerated. With hindsight we can see that Kristol and others had underestimated the durability of socialist ideas. Crises-ridden and increasingly inegalitarian capitalism gave socialism a big boost.

SOCIALISM HAS INVADED THE MORAL HIGH GROUND

Socialism seems to have recaptured the ethical high ground, despite the poor record of self-declared socialist regimes in terms of human rights. Socialism raises the moral flag because it claims to be the creed of love, care and cooperation. By contrast, it is argued, capitalism and markets encourage selfishness and greed. Socialists point to defenders of capitalism such as Ayn Rand, who – like the fictional Gordon Gekko in the 1987 movie *Wall Street* – promoted the view that greed is good, and altruism is evil. Many mainstream economists are tainted too: they often favour markets and generally assume individual self-interest as an axiom.[12]

Socialism will replace the system based on profit and avarice. Common ownership will encourage people to cooperate and act unselfishly. So it is claimed. But theory and evidence tell a different story. The socialists, the 'greed is good' defenders of capitalism, and the believers in our total selfishness are all wrong.

Consider human nature. Evolution has provided humans with a mixture of selfish, cooperative and moral capacities, which can be stunted or developed according to different cultural and institutional settings. Small-scale societies have relied on sentiments of cooperation and moral solidarity that have evolved within groups over millions of years. Solidarity within tribes or bands helped them survive in competition over resources with their rivals, undermining the view that we are naturally or entirely selfish.[13]

Marxist anthropologists Eleanor Leacock and Richard Lee published abundant evidence of cooperation in small-scale band societies. They argued that these foraging bands can teach us to end the 'capitalist

---

[12]   Rand (2009), Badhwar and Long (2016), Hodgson (2013, 2019b).
[13]   On the evolution of cooperation see Darwin (1871), Leacock and Lee (1982), Sober and Wilson (1998), Henrich (2004), De Waal (2006), Bowles and Gintis (2011), Boehm (2012), Haidt (2012) and Hodgson (2013).

economy of waste' and help 'all humanity to achieve a cooperative world system'. But this casual projection from small societies to the global system ignores the problem of scale. The mechanisms of cooperation, typically involving familiarity and face-to-face contact, cannot be expanded to thousands, let alone billions.[14]

Consequently, integration in large-scale societies and the avoidance of war require institutions additional to customary small-scale cooperation. The modern world has built up citizen loyalty to nation states, but the downsides have been hostility to foreigners and belligerent nationalism. In the modern world, further institutions are needed to encourage mutual understanding and reciprocity on a global scale.

One of these necessary institutions is the market. But this does not mean that markets are proposed as a solution to every problem. Markets also have downsides. They have weaknesses when dealing with externalities, social costs, positional goods and ecological sustainability (Pigou, 1920; Kapp, 1950; Hirsch, 1977). Both markets and state planning have their benefits and limitations.

The notion that markets always make people greedy, selfish and amoral has been refuted. There is strong evidence that trading relationships can enhance sentiments of inclusiveness and reciprocity. As Herbert Gintis put it: 'The notion that the market economy makes people greedy, selfish, and amoral is simply fallacious.' Rose-tinted socialists and greed-is-good individualists are both rebutted by the reality of markets and their consistency with forms of cooperation.[15]

Of course, the complete commercialization of family and community life would undermine trust, altruism and the vibrancy of civil society. But in large-scale societies, market relations are nevertheless necessary to coordinate millions of enterprises, where billions of decisions are unavoidably devolved.

There is evidence that, on balance, international trade can reduce the risks of war between nations. In larger-scale systems, despite market competition, trade can build bonds and reduce conflict. Wider trade on a larger scale increases mutual interdependence. As Thomas Paine, Richard

---

[14] Leacock and Lee (1982, p. 19). For models that illustrate the problems that increasing population size impose on cooperative mechanisms such as reciprocity see Bowles and Gintis (2005, 2011) and Nowak (2006).

[15] For a small fraction of the huge amount of evidence on these issues see Berggren and Nilsson (2013, 2015), Henrich et al. (2001, 2004, 2010), Gintis (2012), Zak (2008, 2011a, 2011b), Hodgson (2013). See also the brilliant account of rival views of the market in Hirschman (1982).

Cobden, John Hobson and several others argued, markets can help to build solidarity within and between nations.[16]

Yet, despite evidence to the contrary, socialism still clings to the high moral ground. For socialists such as Jeremy Corbyn, socialism is an 'obvious' response, where caring for one another supersedes the greed and profit-seeking that is always fostered by capitalism. Little further detailed evidence is deemed necessary.[17]

If socialism is 'obvious', then how do we explain the failure of other intelligent people to get on board? If they are not stupid, then they must be acting out of personal malice or greed. They must have sold out their principles. When socialism is seen as 'obvious', its opponents are regarded as stupid or evil. There is no need to look at evidence, to experiment, to seek wise counsel, or to listen to critics. Those that deny the self-evident are deluded, corrupt, or in the pay of those that gain from the existing system.

Modern economies are highly complex. To pose any system or solution as 'obvious' is a dangerous populist naïvety. Socialists compare an imaginary 'obvious' socialism with the real world, with all its poverty, inequality and other problems. They decline to explain the workings of their socialist utopia in detail. They simply assume that their imaginary world of love and cooperation will work. They propose that much can be decided democratically, ignoring the fact that it is impossible to process more than a small fraction of day-to-day decisions through meetings or votes. They ignore the problems of incentivizing work and innovation, and of ensuring functional autonomy without private property.

All these problems became apparent in real-world socialist experiments in the past. But these too are ignored, to focus instead on an imaginary socialism that is somehow free of all previous and serious defects.

BERNIE SANDERS AND HIS 'DEMOCRATIC SOCIALISM'

Given his exceptional popularity, Sanders is worthy of discussion. He has made few attempts to explain what socialism means. We must rely on scarce morsels of evidence. As a young man in Chicago in the 1960s, Sanders was a member of the Young People's Socialist League, which was the youth wing of the Socialist Party of America. Founded in 1901,

---

[16]   Hirschman (1982), McDonald (2004), Gartzke (2007).
[17]   Nelson (2015).

this party went through several splits and ruptures, but it was generally clear what it meant by socialism. The following words appeared in its constitution:

> [The] Socialist Party is to bring about the social ownership and democratic control of all the necessary means of production – to eliminate profit, rent, and interest, and make it impossible for any to share the product without sharing the burden of labor – to change our class society into a society of equals, in which the interest of one will be the interest of all.[18]

As established in Chapter 1 below, this formulation – involving widespread common ownership of the means of production – is in line with the original vision of socialism, as promoted by a number of major figures, both Marxist and non-Marxist.

Eugene Debs was a leader of the Socialist Party of America and four times its presidential candidate. In his 1920 campaign, conducted while he was in prison for sedition, he reached a peak of 913,693 votes. He adopted the militant Marxist language of class struggle and supported the 1917 Bolshevik Revolution in Russia, which overturned a democratically elected national assembly in early 1918. He also praised the attempted armed insurrection in 1919, led by Karl Liebknecht and Rosa Luxemburg against the incipiently democratic German Republic.[19]

In 1977 Sanders made a 30-minute documentary about Debs and his ideas. Sanders never recanted the version of socialism promoted by Debs and the Socialist Party of America.[20] For Sanders, democracy itself implied socialism and substantial public ownership. In a 1987 interview he explained: 'Democracy means public ownership of the major means of production, it means decentralization, it means involving people in their work. Rather than having bosses and workers it means having democratic control over the factories and shops to as great a degree as you can.'[21]

Nineteen years later, Sanders was still repeating this argument that extended democracy implied a greater economic role for government.

---

[18]   Socialist Party of America (1922).

[19]   Debs (1919). In fact, Luxemburg initially opposed the 1919 German insurrection, arguing that their party should first participate in the planned elections. She was overruled by Liebknecht and others. A few days later, Liebknecht and Luxemburg were murdered by counter-insurrectionary forces (Watt, 1969).

[20]   In 1980 Sanders served as an elector for the (US) Socialist Workers' Party, in an attempt to put this Trotskyist group on the presidential ballot, although apparently, he was never a member of that organization (Goldberg, 2016). During the 1980s, when he was mayor of Burlington in Vermont, Sanders promoted a twinning programme with Yarolslavl in the USSR. He and his wife spent their honeymoon in the USSR in 1988.

[21]   Ben-Meir (2015). See also Burlington Free Press (1976).

But he then side-lined the question of public ownership. When asked in 2006 what democratic socialism meant, he responded:

> [The] government has got to play a very important role in making sure that as a right of citizenship, all of our people have healthcare; that as a right, all of our kids, regardless of income, have quality child care, are able to go to college without going deeply into debt; that it means we do not allow large corporations and moneyed interests to destroy our environment; that we create a government in which it is not dominated by big money interest. I mean, to me, it means democracy, frankly.[22]

Given his engagement with the US electorate, which has not normally been sympathetic to socialist ideas, it is understandable that Sanders played up democracy and played down public ownership. But there is no evidence that he has abandoned his support for widespread common ownership.

Sanders is not alone in sometimes hiding his socialism behind the word *democracy*. Michael Moore did it in his ironically titled 2009 film *Capitalism: A Love Story*, where he argued that 'capitalism is an evil, and you cannot regulate evil. You have to eliminate it and replace it with something that is good for all people, and that something is democracy.' But democracy is a system of government: it is not a type of economic system. Moore was too timid here to admit that he meant socialism, but in his public promotion of the film he was more candid.[23]

Like Moore, Sanders in recent years has been economical with the truth. He has left the details of his socialism vague. Does Sanders still adopt its original radical meaning of widespread common ownership? Or is he now promoting a version of social democracy, as found in Denmark, Norway or Sweden? Sanders said in 2015 that 'we should look to countries like Denmark, like Sweden and Norway, and learn from what they have accomplished for their working people'.[24]

We certainly should learn from these Nordic countries, but we should not dupe people into believing that they are socialist. A few days after Sanders' comment, the Danish Prime Minister Lars Løkke Rasmussen attacked the misconception that the Nordic model is a form of socialism: 'I would like to make one thing clear. Denmark is far from a socialist planned economy. Denmark is a market economy.'[25]

---

[22] Elliott (2016).
[23] Moore (2009).
[24] *Washington Post* (2015).
[25] Yglesias (2015).

The Nordic countries have relatively high levels of taxation and relatively low levels of income inequality. They have strong welfare states. But they have not achieved anything close to socialism in its original sense. The private sector is still dominant. The whole economy is guided much more by financial markets than by state planning.[26]

Many American opponents of socialism see every economic intervention by the state as socialist – from public enterprise, to US Obamacare and the UK National Health Service.[27] In this context, Sanders has accepted a vague socialist label without much further explanation, knowing that for millions of Americans this is taken to mean even the mildest level of government economic intervention. Sanders has allowed this imprecision to prevail, thus establishing a wide following among liberals, social democrats and radical socialists. He may have told the truth, but not the whole truth. This plasticity in meaning among the politically uneducated may help to explain why so many people these days say that they prefer *socialism* to *capitalism*.

As they have both got closer to the pinnacles of power, Sanders has accepted a place for small-scale private enterprise, and likewise Corbyn has acknowledged the reality of a mixed economy.[28] But crucially, *neither Corbyn nor Sanders have elaborated a positive defence of a private sector.* They may tolerate it for now, but they offer no positive argument as to why its existence in the future must be guaranteed.

Genuine advocacy of a mixture requires making the case for more than one type of ingredient. As well as their support for the public sector, they could have argued, for instance, that a substantial private sector is necessary for a viable civil society. They could have endorsed some market competition in places where it can help to sustain innovation and technological advance. As far as I am aware, Sanders and Corbyn have failed to ratify such arguments.

The absence of a firm defence of the private sector speaks as loudly as their calls for government intervention or common ownership. It suggests that a private sector is being reluctantly tolerated, and it would be swept

---

[26]   As Schumpeter (1934, p. 126) put it, 'money markets' are 'the headquarters of the capitalist system'. This is true for the Nordic countries as well as for other varieties of capitalism. By contrast, the headquarters of a big socialist system are the central bureaux of the state planning authority. By Schumpeter's criterion, most countries in the world today are capitalist, but China is more difficult to classify. Markets and private enterprise have become dominant in China since the 1980s, but financial and some other markets are heavily controlled by the state. China is no longer socialist. If it is capitalist, then it is a member of a sub-species with extensive state controls.

[27]   Williamson (2011).

[28]   Weissmann (2015), BBC News (2016).

up into public territory if the opportunity arose. A mixed economy with markets is to be accepted for now, as the system makes its transition toward full-blooded socialism and the abolition of most private enterprise.

True to form, in 2018 some supporters of Corbyn launched a campaign within the Labour Party to restore the original 1918 wording of its 'Clause Four: Aims and Values' in its *Rule Book* when it advocated 'common ownership of the means of production, distribution and exchange'. This reversal would restore the party's pledge to 'end capitalism and bring about the socialist transformation of society', as the 2018 campaigners put it. Although Corbyn does not see the restoration of the original wording as a priority, he has not declared his opposition to the move in principle.[29]

There is a further problem with the elusive notion of *democratic socialism* that is adopted by Sanders and Corbyn. They promote a vague vision of extensive democratic control in the economy. Neither of them explains in detail how this extensive democratic decision-making is going to work. Would employees and consumers have a say on everything? Or some things? If so, which? Who would decide? How would they decide? How would the hierarchy of decision-making be structured?

The adjective *democratic* is deliberately kept as vague as the noun *socialism.* Questions concerning the details and feasibility of such arrangement are simply ignored. If votes were held on every important question, then the population would be overburdened with a myriad of decisions. Our lives would be taken up with meetings, questionnaires and voting. It is impossible for anyone to gain expert knowledge on anything but a small number of technical and scientific issues. It would be counter-productive to put these technical issues to the vote.

Real-world experiments with worker-managed cooperatives, and with employee participation in decision-making in some private firms, have shown that some degree of involvement is possible and effective. But in these cases, for practical reasons, relatively few daily decisions are put to the vote. Elected or appointed managers are given powers over detailed, day-to-day decisions. Managers often have to act quickly or follow expert advice: extensive discussion and voting in such cases can sometimes be dysfunctional.

In summary, Sanders has tapped into legitimate discontent about inequality and poverty in the US, but he has failed to explain how his version of socialism will work. He has kept the meaning vague, thus

---

[29] Kentish (2018).

providing himself with radical appeal with limited long-term practical substance, other than the adoption of some measures of reform within a capitalist economy.

Sanders is not alone in using the s-word in this vague manner. But, by contrast, Chapter 1 will show that for well over a century, *socialism* had the radical meaning of widespread common ownership that both Sanders and Corbyn originally adopted and promoted. Subsequently, some thinkers tried to shift its meaning, but without consensus or permanent effect.

ISMS: IDEOLOGIES AND SYSTEMS

'Ism' words – like *socialism* and *capitalism* – carry problems and ambiguities. It is important to distinguish between doctrines (including ideologies) and (actual or proposed) systems in the real world. Although they can interact with one another, doctrines and real-world systems are different.

Words like *positivism*, *materialism*, *liberalism* and *conservatism* refer to doctrines or ideologies. Words like *feudalism* or *despotism* usually refer to political or economic systems, or to features of them.

Some 'isms' – notably *socialism* – have a double life. They refer to both ideologies and actual or proposed types of socio-economic system. Some people have difficulty distinguishing between ideologies and systems.

A system is not simply a prevailing ideology. It is a common misconception that social systems are no more than ideologies rooted in people's heads. Social systems are not merely collections of individuals with ideology added. Systems also involve rules and structured relations. Furthermore, an ideology that promotes a social system can never correspond exactly to that system, because no ideology can capture all its complex and covert relations and rules.

Many rules and roles involve tacit understandings that we often take for granted but are difficult to analyse. For example, we all understand money enough to use it. But the precise nature of money is still highly controversial among philosophers and social scientists.[30]

Of course, all social systems rely on ideologies for reinforcement and acquiescence. But that does not mean that those ideas or ideologies are accurate or adequate pictures of the systems themselves. Modern economies are extremely complex. So, if *capitalism* were an ideology, it

---

[30]   Knapp (1924), Keynes (1930), Searle (1995), Smithin (2000), Ingham (2004), Wray (2004), Forstater (2006), Graeber (2011), Hodgson (2015a).

would probably involve false claims and certainly be an inadequate depiction of the complex politico-economic system to which it was related.

The ideology *socialism* advocates a system called *socialism*, but without entailing all the rules and structures involved. But while *socialism* is often used in both senses, *capitalism* is used less frequently to refer to an ideology – it is primarily a label for a specific type of politico-economic system.

Capitalism comes in a large variety of forms. Its governments can be democratic or despotic. They can have small or massive budgets. Its markets can be constrained or subject to minimal regulation. Corruption can be widespread or limited. The degree of economic inequality can vary enormously. Widely different ideologies, such as *liberalism* and *fascism*, relate to forms of capitalism that vary greatly, but share the common prominence of markets, private property, wage labour and financial institutions. One species – many variants.

Capitalism itself nurtures a range of possible ideologies. Consider the role of religion, particularly Christian paternalism, in the early development of capitalism.[31] As another example, an extreme form of individualism has held sway, particularly in Anglo-American capitalism since the 1970s. Some possible meanings of *individualism* are discussed in the next section.

(ATOMISTIC) INDIVIDUALISM

It was no accident that the word *individualism* came into use at about the same time as *socialism*, and in the same general context. *Individualism* appeared in its French form in 1820 and in English in 1840. *Socialism* and *individualism* were regarded as opposed ideologies.[32]

Individualism has a complex history and has taken several (often very different) meanings.[33] Enlightenment thinkers proclaimed the rights of the individual, with strict limitation of coercive power, and emphasized individual autonomy and responsibility. For good reason, not least the history of the twentieth century, we should respect that legacy, and

---

[31] Tawney (1926), Weber (1930).
[32] Bestor (1948, p. 282), Gide and Rist (1915, p. 263 n.), Hayek (1948, ch. 1), Lukes (1973, p. 4).
[33] Hayek (1948, ch. 1), Lukes (1973).

uphold individual rights against actual or potential tyranny. Individualism, in the sense of upholding legitimate individual rights and freedoms, is vital and worth defending.

Individual rights do not necessarily deny rights to groups. Groups have rights to organize and protest peacefully, partly because individuals have such rights. Trade unions have rights. So do corporations, under law. But individuals require vital protection from coercion and injustice found in groups, states and other organizations.

Some versions of individualism are socially corrosive and self-defeating. They can undermine the social fabric upon which individual liberty depends. We need to separate the valuable Enlightenment emphasis on individual rights from the atomistic notion that the individual can and should be treated separately from the social world and from the social institutions that are necessary to sustain life and liberty.

Atomistic individualism neglects the social conditions of individuality. For Milton Friedman, for example, 'the country is the collection of individuals that compose it, not something over and above them'. This overlooks relationships and interdependencies between individuals, which are not reducible to individuals alone. Just as a house is more than a pile of bricks and materials, society is more than a collection of individuals: it involves structures and means of interaction and communication.[34]

Atomistic individualists downplay these connections and interdependencies. They treat people as if they were separable atoms of desire. Individuals are seen as complete in their wants and preferences and formed independently of their interaction with others. Individuals and their preferences are seen as the only objects of concern and analysis, disregarding the ongoing importance of relations between individuals as well.

As well as socialists, some prominent liberals have criticized atomistic individualism. The Scottish philosopher David Ritchie complained that Herbert Spencer and others saw the individuals in isolation from their social context: 'The individual is thought of ... as if he had meaning and significance apart from his surroundings and apart from his relations to the community of which he is a member.' The English liberal economist John A. Hobson wrote similarly of 'the protean fallacy of individualism, which feigns the existence of separate individuals by abstracting and

---

[34]   Friedman (1962a, pp. 1–2) – this statement is an example of ontological individualism. Methodological individualism is a different matter, involving explanation rather than being. There are different versions of methodological individualism, with varied evaluations (Hodgson, 2007b).

neglecting the social relations which belong to them and make them what they are'. The twentieth-century liberal Michael Polanyi developed the concept of *public liberty* to refer to the institutional conditions that were necessary to sustain individual freedom. He complained that other liberals, including Friedrich Hayek and Ludwig Mises, had an overly narrow view of liberty, understood merely as the absence of coercion.[35]

Atomistic individualists often assume that the individual is always the best judge of his or her interests – an idea promoted by Jeremy Bentham and others. Often the individual is wrongly treated as entirely egotistical and self-seeking, neglecting the existence of cooperation in all human societies.[36]

In recent years, several prominent economists have accepted that individuals are not entirely self-seeking. There are strong theoretical and empirical grounds to assume that people, to some degree, have altruistic and moral propensities as well. But much of the theory used by economists to address matters such as public provision and the size of government still assumes that all individuals are entirely self-regarding and selfish.[37]

MARKETS AND NEOLIBERALISM

Atomistic individualism is often allied with what has been described as *market fundamentalism* – the belief that unfettered markets bestow welfare and prosperity, and that state interference with market processes generally decreases human well-being. Market fundamentalists some-times overlook the fact that markets themselves are social institutions. Markets involve rules and norms that involve social relations as well as individuals. These norms and rules have to be built up and sustained, through structured interaction and cooperation with others. Furthermore, states and their legal systems are necessary to constitute or sustain some of these rules and institutions, such as those concerning property and contract. Markets always operate as systems of rules, and hence they can

---

[35] Ritchie (1891, p. 11), Hobson (1901, p. 67), M. Polanyi (1951), Jacobs and Mullins (2016). Unfortunately, the writings of several important thinkers including Hobson and Marx are marred by anti-Semitic remarks.

[36] Altruism, cooperation and moral sentiments are strong evolutionary outcomes: they have aided group survival in humans and our primate ancestors (Darwin, 1871; Sober and Wilson, 1998; Henrich, 2004; De Waal, 2006; Bowles and Gintis, 2011; Boehm, 2012; Haidt, 2012; Hodgson, 2013).

[37] On the evidence see Lane (1991). Stretton and Orchard (1994) provide a forceful critique of policy approaches that assume entirely selfish individuals.

never be absolutely free of regulation or constraint. Terms such as 'free' or 'unregulated' market can thus be misleading.[38]

Atomistic individualism is often associated with *libertarianism*. These days this often refers to the maximization of market arrangements and the minimization of the role of the state. The focus is on individual choice and responsibility, as long as it does not undermine the freedom and rights of others. The context and causes of individual choices are sometimes neglected. The need for the state to protect and sustain markets is underestimated and the practical or ethical limits to markets are downplayed.

I now try to avoid the word *neoliberalism*, except sparingly and with extreme caution. Once it might have been confined to an extreme form of individualism that eschews state regulation, promotes economic austerity and a minimal state, opposes trade unions and vaunts unrestrained markets as the solution to all major politico-economic problems. But today the widespread usage of the word *neoliberalism* is no longer so restricted. Anyone defending a role for markets now risks dismissal as a *neoliberal*.

A wide range of politicians, from Margaret Thatcher and Ronald Reagan at one extreme, to Bill Clinton, Hillary Clinton, Emmanuel Macron and Tony Blair at the other limit, have all been described as *neoliberals*, despite, for example, hugely varied policies on taxation, government expenditure and the role of the state. Some describe the US President Donald Trump as a *neoliberal*. Yet, although he supports significant deregulation of the US economy, he is a supporter of protectionism and he has imposed import tariffs: he does not believe in free trade. The word *neoliberal* is now stretched beyond credence and coherence.[39]

The Marxist academic David Harvey wrote that neoliberalism 'proposes that human well-being can best be advanced by liberating individual entrepreneurial freedoms and skills within an institutional framework characterized by strong private property rights and free trade'. On this basis, the term *neoliberal* might be applied to anyone who supports a private sector or markets.

---

[38]   On market fundamentalism see Soros (1998, 2008), Stiglitz (2008) and Block and Somers (2014). On the role of the state in constituting and sustaining markets see Hodgson (1988, 2015a) and Marshall (2011). Mirowski (2013, p. 16) wrote astutely: 'Appeals to "free markets" treat both freedom and markets as undefined primitives, largely by collapsing them into one another.'

[39]   Cahill and Konings (2017, pp. 48, 144–5), stretch the *neoliberal* label to include both Blair and Trump, despite Blair's substantial increase of government expenditure on health and education and Trump's opposition to free trade.

Sure enough, Harvey described Deng Xiaoping as a neoliberal. From 1978, Deng supported the reintroduction of markets into the Chinese economy. But he still proposed a strong guiding hand by the state, including centralized management of finance and of the macro-economy. Harvey admitted that Deng's policies led to strong economic growth and 'rising standards of living for a significant proportion of the population' but he passed quickly and grudgingly over this achievement.[40]

In fact, Deng's Marxist-revisionist 'neoliberal' reforms lifted more than *half a billion people* out of extreme poverty. That was about one-twelfth of the entire world population at the time. Consequently, China halved the global level of extreme poverty. The bulk of the poverty reduction in China came from rural areas. This achievement is unprecedented in human experience, even if we acknowledge the growth in inequality that followed. If Deng's extension of markets is *neoliberalism*, then *neoliberalism* is the most beneficial economic policy in human history.[41]

Other guardians of socialist purity have discovered earlier contenders for the title of 'the first neoliberals'. In her book *Markets in the Name of Socialism: The Left-Wing Origins of Neoliberalism*, the sociologist Johanna Bockman found roots of *neoliberalism* in the experiments in so-called 'market socialism' in Yugoslavia from the 1950s and in Hungary from the 1960s. There is no stopping this neoliberal treachery – infiltrating socialism as well as capitalism![42]

Adopting the methodology of Harvey and Bockman, I would like to nominate Vladimir Ilyich Lenin as the first neoliberal, for his abandonment of socialist central planning and his introduction of the New Economic Policy (NEP) in Soviet Russia in 1921. In this admitted 'retreat' from socialism, Lenin reintroduced markets and profit-seeking private firms. Crucially, in support of this nomination, there is evidence that Deng's post-1978 reforms drew a strong inspiration from Lenin. Like his Russian predecessor, Deng introduced markets and private enterprise into an economy still dominated by the state.[43]

Of course, I am being ironic. My point is that, thanks to Harvey, Bockman and others, *neoliberalism* as a term has become virtually useless. As Philip Mirowski and Dieter Plehwe put it, *neoliberalism* for some has become 'a brainless synonym for modern capitalism'. Mirowski also complained that opponents 'often bandy about attributions

---

[40] Harvey (2005, pp. 1–2, 120–22).

[41] Ravallion and Chen (2005).

[42] Bockman (2011). In fact, in both Yugoslavia and Hungary, the use of market mechanisms was highly restricted (Stokes, 1993; Woodward, 1995).

[43] Pantsov and Levine (2015, p. 373).

of "neoliberalism" as a portmanteau term of abuse'. But Mirowski did not drop the term. On the contrary, he headlined it, and tried to link it to the Mont Pèlerin Society.[44]

But Angus Burgin's superb history shows that the Mont Pèlerin Society was originally a broader liberal forum and only later evolved into a narrow vehicle under the leadership of Milton Friedman. Burgin commented critically on the term *neoliberalism*: 'It is extremely difficult to treat in a sophisticated manner a concept that cannot be firmly identified or defined.' The word is no longer sound currency. Bad usage has driven out the good. It has become a swear-word rather than a scientific term.[45]

Part of the impetus behind the excessive and ultimately destructive use of the word *neoliberal* is the Marxist belief that *neoliberalism* is a strategy serving the interests of the capitalist class. Following the post-war settlement of 1945–70, which conceded greater power and shares of income to organized labour, rising *neoliberalism* allegedly rescued the capitalists. Consequently, in several major countries from the 1970s, trade unionism declined in strength and the shares of national incomes going to the top 5 per cent increased.[46]

But levels of public welfare expenditure did not decrease in most countries after the 1970s. In some (but not all) countries standards of living have increased, at least up to 2008, even for the lower income deciles. It is questionable that capitalist interests are best served by declines in real wages, given the powerful Keynesian argument that capitalist prosperity depends on effective demand in the economy as a whole. Higher real wages can increase prosperity across the board and serve the interests of capitalists as well as workers.

SOCIAL DEMOCRACY AND LIBERAL SOLIDARITY: REFORMING CAPITALISM

While the term *social democracy* was originally embraced by Marxists and other socialists, generally it has a different interpretation today. Social democracy now refers to a form of market economy, with

---

[44]   Mirowski and Plehwe (2009, p. xvii), Mirowski (2013, p. 29).

[45]   Burgin (2012, p. 57). Burgin (2012, p. 82) also pointed out: 'The "neoliberalism" that became paradigmatic in the Anglo-American policy arena in the 1970s and 1980s looked very different from the "neoliberalism" of the late 1930s and 1940s.' See also Boas and Gans-Morse (2009), Venugopal (2015), Birch (2017) and Hodgson (2019c).

[46]   For an example of this Marxist view see Harvey (2005).

democracy, a welfare state and some redistributive taxation of income and wealth.[47]

This version of social democracy is close ideologically to the wing of Anglo-American *liberalism* that rejected atomistic individualism and supported a welfare state. This stream of liberal thinking goes back to Thomas Paine and was developed by John A. Hobson, David Lloyd George, John Dewey, John Maynard Keynes, William Beveridge and Michael Polanyi. I use the alternative term *liberal solidarity* to describe this line of thought. Liberal solidarity criticizes the atomistic individualism that promotes the self-seeking individual. It advocates a greatly reformed capitalism, with democratic government, reduced inequality, sustainable growth and a viable welfare state.

Socialism is incompatible with these goals. From the 1840s, socialism has been associated with large-scale public ownership and central planning of the economy. All experiments with this kind of big socialism have moved toward dictatorship. This is no accident. The outcome is a consequence of the centralization of politico-economic power.

In some imagined, fictional appearance, socialism might seem superior. But in both theory and practice, socialism does not provide a viable and attractive alternative. At least for the foreseeable future, we need to work toward greater solidarity and less inequality *within capitalism*. We can also experiment with elements of *small socialism* within this market economy, particularly by the development of numerous, autonomous worker cooperatives.

Ultimately, the promotion of small socialism within a capitalist economy is the only feasible socialist option that is consistent with democracy and freedom. I applaud experiments in that direction. But I underline the word 'experiment'. It all depends on what works. No one form of organization or ownership works best in all possible circumstances. Hence any support for (small) socialism must be pragmatic and conditional within a mixed economy.

Supporting a mixed economy means that common ownership is no longer the solution to all problems. It becomes neither an end in itself nor a supreme maxim. Socialism as part of a mixture must be subject to higher principles (which are not themselves socialist) governing the mixture itself. One principle might be the experimental and evolutionary pursuit of diversity. Any practical socialism along these lines should arguably become subservient to some version of pluralist and democratic liberalism in pursuit of human flourishing and solidarity.

---

[47]   See, for example, Martin (1982).

Marxists are fond of posing the choice: 'socialism or barbarism?'[48] I argue in this book that, at least in its heavily statist forms, socialism itself brings a measure of barbarism. Another danger is of nationalist and autocratic capitalism. The progressive alternative is a reformed, liberal-democratic capitalism, with a welfare state and effective measures to reduce inequality. The true choice is thus between liberal-democratic capitalism, on the one hand, and forms of nationalism, big socialism and barbarism, on the other.

THE CONTENTS OF THIS BOOK

Part I of this book is devoted to socialism. The first task is to pin down its meaning. Although there is some understandable variation in its usage, it is shown that the idea of common ownership has been prominent since its inception. Although there were several attempts to modify the meaning of socialism in the twentieth century, by and large they have not caught on.

A distinction is made between small socialism and big socialism. Small socialism was pioneered by Robert Owen, among others. It refers to small-scale socialist communities or worker cooperatives. Chapter 2 relates the experiences of small socialism in its several forms. Nineteenth-century socialist communities in the US did not last for long. A key problem was to establish social cohesion and governance in the group. The Israeli kibbutzim originally received substantial external support. When this diminished, the majority of them were forced to abandon many of their socialist goals. The worker-managed enterprises in Yugoslavia were relatively successful for a while, but they were always hindered by state restrictions on their autonomy and by a flawed and overbearing legal framework. It is argued that any viable small socialism requires a major role for markets, which many socialists have been reluctant to admit.[49]

---

[48]   This dilemma was popularized by Luxemburg (1916) who, while writing in prison, attributed it from memory to Engels. The true source was probably Karl Kautsky (Kautsky, 1910; Angus, 2014).

[49]   I use the term *big socialism* rather than *state socialism* because many socialists believe that a 'democratic' or 'decentralized' system of nationwide public ownership is possible without much state centralization. Such a view was taken by G.D.H. Cole, Karl Polanyi, Tony Benn and others. I argue below that this view is untenable, because it denies decentralized collectives the legal rights to own property and trade on markets. Without those rights, considerable power remains in the hands of the state. Hence *big socialism*

Chapter 3 turns to the experience of big socialism, where the bulk of the means of production is owned by the state. Such systems have several major defects, all of which are confirmed by historical experience. On a large scale there are problems with incentivizing individuals to work with due effort and diligence. Another major difficulty is that a large concentration of political and economic power in the hands of the state undermines the economic foundations of countervailing power and empowers totalitarian forces. These problems are illustrated by two contrasting case studies of Soviet Russia and Chavismo Venezuela. The principal conclusion is that democracy and human rights require the countervailing power, made possible by a market economy without an overwhelming public sector.

Chapter 4 addresses the problem of accessing and using knowledge under big socialism. Socialism is typically infused by an optimistic rationalism, believing that resources can be planned comprehensively and judiciously from the centre. But the ubiquity of tacit and context-dependent knowledge makes it impossible for the planners to gather together all the information for an all-embracing plan.[50] A further problem under big socialism is that in the absence of markets it is difficult to establish meaningful prices to make planning decisions. Another difficulty is establishing effective incentives for managers in the absence of markets and profits.

Crucially, demonstrations that a humane and democratic big socialism is unfeasible do not come from the Austrian school economists – including Friedrich Hayek and Ludwig Mises – alone. Other important contributors to this critique included the German historical school economist Albert Schäffle and the Keynesian liberal Michael Polanyi. The political views of Schäffle and Polanyi differed from those of Hayek and Mises. Although I add little that is original to these arguments, I bring them all together for (what I believe is) the first time.

Other writers have noted the importance of scale: I give it foremost emphasis. Humans have evolved to deal with small-scale interpersonal interactions. Much evidence suggests that inter-personal cooperation can work with small numbers of people, relying on face-to-face interaction and trust-building. But when our ancestors began to agglomerate in cities

---

implies *state socialism*. But I do not build this conclusion into the terminology at the outset. Instead of *small socialism*, Barkai (1972) used the term *microsocialism*.

[50] One of the few attempts to outline a feasible socialism is by Devine (1988). In attempts to rebut those who questioned the feasibility of socialism, Adaman and Devine (1996) mistakenly proposed that all tacit knowledge can be converted into codified knowledge, which rather misses this key point. See my criticisms of their proposal in Hodgson (1998, 1999, 2005).

and other larger units, incentives and monitoring mechanisms that relied on familiarity could not be applied to large-scale communities. New institutions were required to deal with the systemic coordination problems over a more complex division of labour. The state was needed, as well as markets.

This emphasis on scale overturns the view that successful socialist experiments in smaller communities can simply be scaled up to apply to society as a whole. In his defence of socialism, G.A. Cohen attempted a flawed argument along these lines. Cohen used the example of a camping trip to illustrate the virtues of cooperation and sharing. He wrongly assumed that this could apply without further elaboration to a large-scale economy.[51]

In his powerful critique, Jason Brennan showed how Cohen had contrasted the real and grubby world of capitalism with an imaginary world of socialism. Reversing this, Brennan wittily compared the ugly experiments in what is described as socialism with an idealized view of capitalism. He then developed a more realistic case for private property and markets.[52]

Both Cohen and Brennan used small-scale examples. But arguments for private property and markets are stronger in a large-scale context. Brennan's vision of capitalism lacks an employed workforce, a financial sector and a legal system to enforce property rights. He won the argument on points, but his libertarian utopia is as unfeasible as the socialist one. As discussed later in this volume, this failure by libertarian critics of socialism to emphasize the problem of scale dovetails with their reluctance to accept a major economic role for the state.

Part II of this book looks at alternative ways forward. It addresses the limitations of modern market economies and their potential for reform. It also argues for a *liberal solidarity* that addresses the realities of modern complex economies, including the limits to markets themselves.

Chapter 5 shows that the nature of knowledge creates problems for a market system as well as for big socialism. Because the acquisition of knowledge depends on interaction with others, it is socially conditioned and it depends on social cues. This challenges the notion that the individual can be generally the best judge of his or her own interests. Just as the state cannot often know better, the individual does not know independently of his or her social context. This suggests a third approach, where neither the individual nor the state always knows best. This

---

[51]   Cohen (2009).
[52]   Brennan (2014).

argument retains a major role for markets and also for state regulation: in general terms it would transcend the traditional state–market dichotomy.

Chapter 6 brings further arguments concerning the limits to markets under capitalism. In particular, there cannot be complete futures markets for labour. Economic theory tells us that, as a consequence, we are always dealing with second-best solutions: extending markets does not necessarily improve economic performance. The state also has a major role in regulating the financial sector. The chapter continues by considering arguments for and against state intervention in particular situations. It proposes an experimental approach, within a mixed and largely decentralized economy.

Chapter 7 considers the existing diversity of capitalist systems. It examines the huge variations in tax levels, in social spending by public authorities, and in inequalities of income and wealth. It also focuses on the Nordic countries as exemplars of relative egalitarianism and welfare provision. These should be the starting point for those wishing to improve social and economic conditions in the real world. Keeping capitalism does not mean that we are obliged to replicate its US variant.

The final chapter addresses the politics of liberal solidarity. The aim is not to elaborate on detailed policies but to point in the general direction of advance. It becomes clear that liberalism is an extremely broad church with many very different types. Unlike versions of liberalism based on atomistic individualism, liberal solidarity puts stress on the interdependence and moral motivation of individuals and it admits a substantial role for state regulation, redistributive taxation and a welfare state. The book finishes with a discussion of some of the big challenges for democratic liberalism in the twenty-first century.

PART I

Socialism, markets and democracy

1. What does socialism mean?

> Under capitalism, man exploits his fellow man. Under socialism it is
> precisely the opposite.
>
> Eastern European joke from the Communist era[1]

The word *socialism* is modern, but the impulse behind it is ancient. The idea of holding property in common goes back to Ancient Greece and is found in the *Bible*.[2] It has been harboured by some religions and it has been the call of radicals for centuries.

In his 1516 book *Utopia*, Sir Thomas More imagined a system where everything was held in common ownership and internal trade was abolished. Unlike most other proposals for common ownership before the 1840s, More's *Utopia* envisioned cities of between 60 000 and 100 000 adults. It is the first known proposal for what I call *big socialism*.

Before the rise of Marxism, the predominant vision of common ownership was small-scale, rural and agricultural. It was often motivated by religious doctrine. In Germany in the 1520s the radical Protestant Thomas Müntzer proposed a Christian communism. From 1649 to 1650, during the English Civil War, the Diggers set up religious communes whose members worked together on the soil and shared its produce. There are other examples of socialism before the word was coined.[3]

This chapter is about the origins, meaning and evolution of the words *socialism* and *communism*. They are virtual synonyms, both largely referring to common ownership of the means of production and to the abolition of private property. It is also argued that revisionist attempts to change the definition of *socialism* have largely failed. This is unlike *social democracy*, which changed its meaning since the nineteenth century.

---

[1] Len Deighton (1964, p. 177) quoted a version of this subversive joke in his novel *Funeral in Berlin*, where it was told by a fictional KGB colonel, who added: 'we arrested a man for telling that this morning'. Others say the joke was Polish in origin. Like all good witticisms, it probably spread fast. I first heard it in the Soviet Union in 1979.

[2] Erasmus (1977), Pipes (2001).

[3] Manuel and Manuel (1979), Hodgson (2018, ch. 1).

ORIGINS OF THE WORDS *SOCIALISM* AND *COMMUNISM*

The early nineteenth century saw a flowering of utopian ideas, designed to avoid the ills of industrial capitalism and to create social harmony. Among the most famous proposals were by Claude-Henri de Saint-Simon (1760–1825) and François Marie Charles Fourier (1772–1837). They planned utopian communities using what they believed to be scientific principles of social organization and human psychology. But neither proposed the abolition of private property or the installation of common ownership of the means of production. Neither used the words *communism* or *socialism* to describe their schemes. When Frederick Engels labelled these two individuals as 'utopian socialists' he was misinformed or stretching the truth. But many followers of Saint-Simon and of Fourier did eventually promote communities based on common ownership.[4]

Pierre Leroux was one of Saint-Simon's disciples and he claimed to have coined the French word *socialisme* in about 1832. In English, *socialism* seems to have emerged earlier. It appeared in November 1827 in the *Co-operative Magazine*, published in London by followers of Robert Owen, where a writer referred to 'Communionists or Socialists'. It was used in the *Poor Man's Guardian* in 1833 and moved into more frequent usage thereafter. 'By 1840 socialism was virtually synonymous with Owenism.'[5]

For Owen and his followers, socialism meant the abolition of private property. It also acquired the broader ideological connotation of cooperation, in opposition to selfish or competitive individualism. Communal property was seen as its defining institutional foundation. As Owen argued in 1840, 'virtue and happiness could never be attained' in 'any system in which private property was admitted'. He aimed to secure 'an equality of wealth and rank, by merging all private into public property'.[6]

In 1840 in Paris, the word *communiste* appeared in an article by Étienne Cabet and in a pamphlet by Théodore Dezamy and Jean-Jacques

---

[4] Marx and Engels (1962, vol. 2), Manuel and Manuel (1979, pp. 641–75), Hodgson (2018, pp. 62–7).

[5] Harrison (1969, p. 45). On the history and meaning of the word *socialism* see Gide and Rist (1915, p. 263), Beer (1940), Bestor (1948) and Landauer (1959). Honneth (2017, p. 607) noted that *sozialistisch* was used in German in the late eighteenth century with a very different meaning. It referred to a doctrine in jurisprudence that gave natural law a secular foundation.

[6] Owen (1991, p. 362).

Pillot. Influenced by Owen, Cabet was a Christian advocate of utopian communist communities. Dezamy and Pillot were admirers of the French revolutionary Gracchus Babeuf, who plotted the revolutionary abolition of private property and the installation of common ownership, before his execution in 1796.[7]

Carrying a letter of introduction from Owen, John Goodwyn Barmby went to Paris in 1840 to meet the advocates of *le communisme*. On his return, Barmby founded the London Communist Propaganda Society in 1841 and established the *Communist Chronicle* newspaper. Despite his close working links with the Owenites, Barmby criticized socialism because 'it wants religious faith, it is too commercial, too full of the spirit of this world, and therefore is rightly damned'. Communism for him was less materialistic and more divine. With the investment of these idiosyncratic spiritual connotations, Barmby imported the word *communist* into English. It spread in the UK and the US, where the term *socialist* was already prominent. The word *Kommunist* had appeared in German by 1842, when Marx noted its usage.[8]

Barmby's attempt to align *communism* with religion proved unsuccessful. But he was influential for a while. He alerted Engels to the French *communiste* movement. In 1843 Engels reported to the Owenite journal *The New Moral World* that there were 'more than half a million Communists in France' and that 'Communist associations' and individuals describing themselves as communists were plentiful in Germany, Italy, Switzerland and elsewhere. Engels addressed his Owenite readers as 'English socialists' and saw them as having very similar aims to the Continental communists.[9]

In the second (1849) and later editions of his *Principles of Political Economy*, John Stuart Mill noted another early difference of meaning between *socialism* and *communism*. For followers of Saint-Simon or of Fourier in France, *communism* meant 'the entire abolition of private property', whereas *socialism* was 'any system which requires that the land and the instruments of production should be property, not of individuals, but of communities or associations, or of the government'. Unlike *communism*, this meaning of *socialism* would allow for individual ownership of personal possessions. Hence Mill described Owenism as

---

[7] Bestor (1948, p. 280), Hodgson (2018, pp. 37–8, 40, 43–4, 227).

[8] Bestor (1948, p. 280), Harrison (1969, p. 175), Marx and Engels (1975a, pp. 215–21), Taylor (1983, pp. 172–82, with the Barmby quote on p. 174). The Communist Propaganda Society was later renamed the Communist Church, but that folded in 1849. Barmby and his wife Catherine campaigned for female suffrage. Barmby later abandoned communism and became a radical Unitarian minister.

[9] Marx and Engels (1975a, pp. 392–408, 414).

communism, because it upheld the abolition of all private property. But this particular distinction in meaning between the two words was forgotten after the Saint-Simonian, Fourierist and Owenite experiments faltered.[10]

Perhaps more influentially, the 1848 edition of Webster's *American Dictionary* defined *socialism* as a 'social state in which there is a community of property among all the citizens', and defined *communism* as 'a new French word, nearly synonymous with ... *socialism*'.[11]

Hence both *socialism* and *communism* referred to the abolition of (most or all) private property and the establishment of common ownership of the means of production. Slight differences of meaning were proposed by Barmby (who made *communism* more religious and spiritual) and Mill (who understood *communism* to mean the abolition of all – even personal – private property). But these early nuances of difference did not endure. Henceforth the two terms became entwined within Marxism, there to perform an entirely different dance of meaning.

MARXISM, COMMUNISM AND SOCIALISM

Marx and Engels often treated the terms *socialism* and *communism* as interchangeable. But occasionally they gave them different nuances. In 1845 they used the new word *communism* as their label for their movement: 'Communism is not for us a *state of affairs* which is to be established, an *ideal* to which reality [will] have to adjust itself. We call communism the *real* movement which abolishes the present state of things.' When they henceforth started setting up political organizations they adopted and promoted the term *communist* rather than *socialist*. But their ultimate goals were the same as most socialists at the time.[12]

In 1888 Engels explained why he and Marx had chosen the word *Communist* for their famous *Manifesto* of 1848. Engels claimed that the word *socialism* was then too 'respectable' and too 'middle class'. He wrote:

> Yet, when it was written, we could not have called it a 'Socialist' manifesto. By 'socialists', in 1847, were understood, on the one hand, the adherents of the various utopian systems: Owenites in England, Fourierists in France, both of them already reduced to the position of mere sects, and gradually dying out; on the other hand, the most multifarious social quacks ... in both cases

---

[10]   Mill (1909, pp. 205–206, 772).
[11]   Bestor (1948, p. 263).
[12]   Marx and Engels (1976a, p. 49).

men outside the working-class movement ... Whatever portion of the working class had ... proclaimed the necessity of a total change, that portion then called itself communist. ... Thus, socialism was, in 1847 a middle-class movement, communism a working-class movement.[13]

Engels omitted to note that the self-described *communists* in the 1840s also had more than their fair share of middle-class devotees, quacks, bizarre utopians and radical clerics. Engels himself had noted in 1843 that the 'half a million Communists in France' were led by the Catholic priest Cabet, who promoted his own dream of a communist utopia.[14]

It is possible that Marx and Engels adopted the term *communist* partly because it had become more popular in a Continental Europe on the eve of the 1848 revolutions. While *socialism* remained more widespread in Britain, the Owenite movement, with which it was largely associated, had already passed its peak by 1847. While the younger term *communism* had already attracted several oddballs in the seven years of its use, *socialism* had the additional negative legacy of numerous failed utopian experiments in the 1820s and 1830s, in the UK and the US.[15]

Instead of small-scale utopian experiments, Marx and Engels favoured a global insurrectionary strategy. As Engels observed in 1843, the French communists understood the need for 'meeting force by force ... having at present no other means'. Marx and Engels chose the word *communism* in the 1840s, not because their goal was different from socialism, but partly because many self-described *communists* in Continental Europe promoted armed insurrection. The penultimate section of the *Communist Manifesto* attacks various strands of socialism, not for their collectivist goals, but for their impractical strategies and their failure to countenance the use of force. The final paragraph of the whole work drives the point home: 'The Communists ... openly declare that their ends can only be attained by the forceful overthrow of all existing conditions.'[16]

But a few decades later, the word *socialism* was again in the ascendant. In 1880 Engels published *Socialisme utopique et socialisme scientifique* in the French *Revue socialiste*: notably he put *socialisme* rather than *communisme* in the title. By 1890 a number of parties describing themselves as socialist or social-democratic had taken root in Germany, France and elsewhere. In 1895, Engels wrote approvingly of 'the *one* great international army of Socialists, marching irresistibly on and

---

13 Marx (1973, pp. 64–5).
14 Marx and Engels (1975a, pp. 392, 397–400), Erasmus (1977, pp. 111, 201, 205–19, 264).
15 Harrison (1969), Hodgson (2018, pp. 70–73) and Chapter 3 of this book.
16 Marx and Engels (1975a, p. 398), Marx (1973, p. 98).

growing daily in number'. The earlier emphasis on physical force
was also reduced: the possibility of achieving their goal by democratic
means, rather than by insurrection, seemed greater than before. One of
the major reasons for using the term *communism* rather than *socialism*
had disappeared.[17]

William Morris was an artist, craftsman and writer, and one of the first
English intellectuals to embrace Marxism. Writing in a 1903 Fabian
Tract, he saw *socialism* and *communism* as virtual synonyms: 'between
complete Socialism and Communism there is no difference whatever in
my mind'. They assert that the means of production and the resources of
nature 'should not be owned in severalty, but by the whole community'.[18]

Whether they used the term *socialism* or *capitalism*, their fundamental
aim was clear. In the *Communist Manifesto*, Marx and Engels echoed
Owen and called for the 'abolition of private property'. They proclaimed
an economic order in which 'capital is converted into common property,
into the property of all members of society'. Engels repeated in 1847:
'The abolition of private ownership is the most succinct and characteristic summary of the transformation of the entire social system ... and ...
is rightly put forward by the Communists as their main demand.' In 1850
Marx and Engels again declared: 'Our concern cannot simply be to
modify private property, but to abolish it'.[19]

This meant the complete abolition of markets. They wanted an end to
the 'free selling and buying' of commodities. As Marx wrote in 1875:
'Within the cooperative society based on common ownership of the
means of production, the producers do not exchange their products'.
Engels argued in 1884 that 'no society can permanently retain the
mastery of its own production ... unless it abolishes exchange between
individuals'. The abolition of markets was seen as necessary for social
control.[20]

By emphasizing national ownership, Marx and Engels went much
further than Owen and most other early socialists or communists. Marx
and Engels welcomed efforts 'to centralize all instruments of production
in the hands of the state' and looked forward to a time when 'all
production has been concentrated in the hands of a vast association of the
whole nation'.[21] Engels explained in 1847:

---

[17]   Marx and Engels (1962, vol. 1, p. 125).
[18]   Morris (1973, p. 234).
[19]   Marx (1973, pp. 80–81, 324), Marx and Engels (1976b, p. 348).
[20]   Marx (1973, pp. 81–2), Marx (1974, p. 345), Marx and Engels (1962, vol. 2,
p. 267).
[21]   Marx (1973, pp. 86–7).

[The] new social order ... will have to take the running of industry and all branches of production in general out of the hands of separate individuals competing with each other and instead will have to ensure that all branches of production are run by society as a whole ... according to a social plan and with the participation of all members of society.[22]

Described as either *communism* or *socialism*, this utopia of national ownership and 'social' control persisted in their writings. It appeared, for example, in the second volume of *Capital* in which Marx wrote of the planned system of 'social production' where 'society distributes labour-power and means of production between the various branches of industry'. In one of his last manuscripts, written in 1880, Marx remarked that in the society of the future 'the "social-state" will draw up production from the very beginning ... The scope of production ... is subject in such a state to rational regulation.'[23]

In his *Critique of the Gotha Programme* of 1875, Marx used the term *communism* to describe his goal. He considered 'the first phase of communist society as it is when it has just emerged after prolonged birth pangs from capitalist society'. Eventually a new order would follow:

In a more advanced phase of communist society, when the enslaving subjugation of individuals to the division of labour, ... when the all-around development of individuals has also increased their productive powers and all the springs of cooperative wealth flow more abundantly – only then can society ... inscribe on its banner: From each according to his abilities, to each according to his needs![24]

Hence Marx considered a 'first phase' and then a 'more advanced phase' of communism. Writing in his *State and Revolution* in August 1917, Lenin referred to this passage from Marx's *Critique of the Gotha Programme* but introduced a different usage. He wanted to defend the planned Bolshevik seizure of power against the criticism that Russia was insufficiently developed economically for a radical Marxist revolution.

Lenin amended the Marxist dictionary and renamed Marx's 'first phase of communist society' as *socialism*. Under this *socialism* the means of production would be in public ownership but there would still be a struggle against bourgeois ideas and material shortages. When that struggle was completed, and after the subjugation of 'capitalist habits',

---

[22] Marx and Engels (1976b, p. 348).
[23] Marx (1978, p. 434), Marx (1976b, p. 207), Ollman (1977) and Campbell (2011).
[24] Marx (1974, p. 347).

full *communism* would be established. 'The whole of society will have
become a single office and a single factory with equality of labour and
pay.'[25]

In contrast, Marx and Engels never distinguished the terms *socialism*
and *communism* in this way. For them, *socialism* and *communism* both
meant the abolition of the private ownership of the means of production.
They wrote of lower and higher 'phases' but did not use different nouns
to distinguish them.

The Socialist International (also known as the Second International)
was a global association of socialist parties, formed in 1889. In 1919,
Lenin and the Bolsheviks broke from the Socialist International and
formed the Communist International (also known as the Third International). The difference between the Communist and Socialist Inter-
nationals was not stated in terms of ultimate objectives. Instead the
Communist International was formed because several parties in the
Socialist International had supported their national governments in
the First World War. There was no declared amendment of final goals,
although leaders of the Second International were accused of de facto
abandoning socialism.

SMALL SOCIALISM – INHIBITED BY AGORAPHOBIA

While Owen and other early socialists focused on communities of no
more than a few thousand members, Marx and Engels envisaged public
ownership and planning at the national level. This divided socialist
thought, between those that cherished the autonomy of local collective
ventures and those who sought the 'rational' organization of production
on a national scale.

Owen and others did not explain clearly in their writings how
autonomous socialist communities would relate to each other. Would they
be economically independent, or would they be allowed to trade with
each other? Complete isolation and independence would come at a price:
everything would have to be produced from within, without reaping the
benefits of lower costs due to the higher productivity of a broader
division of labour.

Alternatively, these socialist communities could sell to and buy from
other enterprises, whether they were cooperatives, sole traders or conven-
tional private firms. If they were not to be isolated and independent, then
they would have to trade on markets. The question of whether socialist

---

[25]   Lenin (1967, vol. 2, pp. 337–45).

communities were allowed to trade on markets was an enduring ideological dilemma for small-scale socialists.

Philippe Buchez was a follower of Saint-Simon. He promoted worker-owned cooperatives as early as 1831. Originally, he argued that these cooperatives should merge into a single 'universal association'. But eventually, and contrary to most contemporary socialists and communists, Buchez and his followers recognized the need for multiple, autonomous, worker cooperatives. To be autonomous, they needed rights to trade on markets.[26]

Because Buchez resisted national amalgamation and centralization, his ideas were explicitly rejected by Marx and Engels. Hence Marx in 1875 described Buchez's ideas as 'reactionary', 'sectarian', opposed to the workers' 'class movement', and contrary to the true revolutionary aim of 'cooperative production ... on a national scale'.[27]

In 1840 Pierre-Joseph Proudhon suggested a similar system of independent worker cooperatives that could freely enter into contracts. He proposed 'mutualist associations' of groups of workers who would pool their labour and their property, holding these resources in common. To distance themselves from the statist socialism of Marxists and others, Proudhon and his followers often described their philosophy as anarchism.[28]

Many socialists like cooperatives, but they dislike markets. They may support independent cooperatives, believing eventually they should merge. But if cooperatives lose the right to own and trade their property, then they lose much of their devolved power. This point is lost on many. Socialists who are opposed to markets effectively rule out genuinely autonomous worker cooperatives.

An anti-market mentality prevails among socialists. Advocates of central planning eschew markets and their alleged ills. Hence the Marxist economist Maurice Dobb objected to market socialism because it introduced 'the Trojan horse of a capitalist market mechanism into the citadel

---

[26] Gide and Rist (1915, p. 258) and Reibel (1975). Davis and Parker (2007) argue that Thomas Hodgskin, William Thompson and John Francis Bray proposed cooperatives coordinated by markets in the 1820s and 1830s.

[27] Marx (1974, pp. 353–4). Marx saw the propaganda advantages of worker cooperatives. They could show that workers were capable of managing production themselves. In his draft 'Inaugural Address of the International Working Men's Association' of 1864, Marx (1974, p. 80) praised the established producer cooperatives, but did not see them as having an autonomous future under socialism. Instead, he saw their salvation in their development 'to national dimensions ... fostered by national means'. Marx proposed that all worker cooperatives would amalgamate into nationalized industries.

[28] Proudhon (1969).

of socialist planning'.[29] There is a widespread view that markets foster competition, encourage greed, and lead to inequality and exploitation. Hence markets must be abolished. Many socialists suffer from *agoraphobia* – literally a fear of markets.

As Noel Thompson reported in his study of nineteenth-century socialism: 'The market was anathematised by almost all nineteenth century socialist writers.' Among the exceptions were John Ruskin and some of the Christian socialists. Even Fabian socialists had an 'ultimate vision of a fully planned and consciously controlled socialist economy' where markets were gradually marginalized to insignificance. Thompson concluded that 'the consequences of this determination to abandon the market were little short of disastrous for the subsequent evolution of socialist economic thinking'.[30]

There is a persistent view among socialists that markets should eventually be completely abolished. Tony Benn – a former Labour Cabinet minister in the UK – argued (rather vaguely) that 'market forces' should be opposed. Similar views are found among socialist academics. Michael Albert wrote: 'I am a market abolitionist. I know markets are going to be with us for some time to come, but I also know – or hope – that in time we will replace them entirely.' Robin Hahnel, a professor of economics at Portland State University, similarly upheld a vision of a market-less economy: 'I do not believe that markets have any role to play in a truly desirable economy ... our long run goal should be to replace markets entirely with some kind of democratic planning.' Bertell Ollman, a Marxist professor at New York University, also supported 'doing away with private ownership and market exchanges completely'.[31]

The influential Marxist and 'critical realist' philosophers Roy Bhaskar and Andrew Collier supported 'a form of socialism which is neither a market economy nor a command economy nor a mix of the two, but a genuine extension of pluralistic democracy into economic life'. The socialist philosopher John O'Neill claimed to 'puncture the case for a market economy' and argued for the money-less, market-less, international associationism, as sketched in outline by the socialist philosopher Otto Neurath.[32]

The endurance of agoraphobia helps to explain why big socialism has proved more popular than small socialism. The battle between these 'two

---

[29]   Dobb (1969, p. 188).
[30]   Thompson (1988, pp. 281, 284, 285).
[31]   Benn (1979, 1981, 1982), Albert (2004), Ollman (2004), Hahnel (2005, 2007, p. 1157).
[32]   Bhaskar and Collier (1998, p. 392), O'Neill (1998, pp. 176–7).

cultures' within socialism erupted in 1977 within the Socialist Party of France. The 'two cultures' approximate to what are described here as big socialism and small socialism. Michel Rocard led a group within the Socialist Party that criticized the centralist excesses of the statist socialism. Instead he proposed worker-owned, self-managed cooperatives, all trading within a market economy.

Rocard was then attacked for 'abandoning the very foundations of socialism and adopting fashionable individualist themes, imported from the USA'.[33] Today the critic would have accused Rocard of *neoliberalism.*

From 1988 to 1991 Rocard served as French Prime Minister under President François Mitterrand. Later Rocard remarked that 'the Socialist Party was born in 1905 with a doctrinal ambiguity that was never resolved: it still does not know whether it should accept the market economy or if it wants to smash it'.[34]

Emmanuel Macron was a protégé of Rocard. Macron broke from the Socialist party, partly because it was unable to overcome its congenital agoraphobia. Widely but misleadingly described as a *neoliberal* by the traditional Left, Macron founded a new party and was elected President of France in 2017.

NON-MARXIST SOCIALISM IN THE UK LABOUR PARTY

From the 1870s to the present day, big socialism has retained the upper hand over small socialism, among non-Marxists as well as Marxists. The majority of socialists argued for a system of comprehensive national planning based on widespread public ownership. Socialists differed more on strategy than on their goals. Some argued for gradual change, focusing on parliament. Others promoted insurrectionary violence to seize power. But almost all socialists agreed on widespread public ownership – for socialists this goal was ubiquitous, with few exceptions.

In the year that he first became Labour Prime Minister, Harold Wilson famously wrote that British socialism 'owed far more to Methodism than to Marx'. While rightly underlining the importance for socialism of Christianity in general and Methodism in particular, this statement underestimates the influence of Marx upon British thought and vice versa. But even more seriously, it overlooks the fact that state socialism

---

[33] Berstein (2003, p. 171) – translated by the present author.
[34] Reuters (2007) – translated by the present author.

was largely a Marxist invention, and notions of big socialism became dominant in the Labour Party.[35]

George Bernard Shaw was a leading Fabian. Although he was not a Marxist, in 1890 he wrote with approval: 'Socialists are trying to have the land and machinery "socialised," or made the property of the whole people'. Almost forty years later he explained in his entry on 'socialism' in the *Encyclopædia Britannica*: 'Socialism, reduced to its simplest legal and practical expression, means the complete discarding of the institution of private property by transforming it into public property'. By that time, Shaw had become an admirer of the Soviet Union under Joseph Stalin.[36]

James Keir Hardie was another Fabian socialist and he was elected to the UK parliament in 1892. He became one of the founders of the Independent Labour Party in 1893. Two years later, Hardie wrote about his socialist views and the manifesto of this party: 'State socialism is necessary ... Our platform is the creation of an industrial commonwealth upon the socialisation of land and capital.'[37]

In 1900 Hardie organized a historic meeting of various trade unions and socialist groups and they agreed to form a Labour Representation Committee. Its aim was to elect more working-class representatives to Parliament. In 1906 this was renamed the Labour Party and Hardie was elected as its leader. Although this party was devoted to obtaining power through parliament, its aim of widespread common ownership was equivalent to that of other socialists and communists. The first leader of the British Labour Party believed in big socialism, entailing widespread state ownership. In 1908 the Labour Party Conference passed a resolution, adopting the aim of 'the socialization of the means of production, distribution and exchange to be controlled by a democratic state'.[38]

The philosopher Bertrand Russell stood as a Labour Party candidate in the 1922 and 1923 general elections. He wrote in 1918: 'I think we shall come nearest to the essence of Socialism by defining it as the advocacy of communal ownership of land and capital. Communal ownership may mean ownership by a democratic State, but cannot be held to include ownership by any State which is not democratic.' Russell wrote similarly

---

[35] Wilson (1964, p. 1).
[36] Shaw (1890, p. 3), Shaw (1930, p. 3), Minney (1969) and Hollander (1998).
[37] Hardie (1895).
[38] The quotation is cited in Miliband (1961, p. 27). While the Labour Party's ideology was influenced more by Christ than by Marx, it is important not to ignore the sway of the latter. Hardie (1910, p. 13) wrote: 'The Labour Party is the only expression of orthodox Marxian Socialism in Great Britain. ... The Labour Party practices the Marxian policy of class struggle, following Marx's own example.'

in 1924: 'Socialism ... means the common ownership of land and capital, together with a democratic form of government.'[39]

When defining socialism, Russell added democratic government to common ownership.[40] Hence, contrary to many socialists at the time, he did not regard the Soviet Union as socialist. But Russell did not consider the possibility that the concentration of ownership and economic power in the hands of the state would inevitably undermine political democracy. No regime in history has combined large-scale common ownership with democratic government. Lenin promised in 1917 that the Bolshevik revolution would bring a vast expansion of democracy. But it turned out differently: the logic of big socialism undermines the socio-economic basis of democracy, irrespective of the aspirations or priorities of the leaders.

The highly influential Fabian socialists Sidney and Beatrice Webb had an ultimate vision of a fully planned economy where all markets and private ownership of the means of production were gradually marginalized to insignificance. Eventually, they wanted all private ownership of the means of production to be ended: it was a 'perversion'. They envisaged a massive, complex structure of national, regional and local committees, all involved in decision-making over details of production and distribution: 'What we wish to substitute for the present chaos is systematic co-ordination'. In 1924 Sidney Webb summarized his view of socialism as involving '(1) Collective Ownership; (2) Collective Regulation; (3) Collective Taxation; and (4) Collective Provision – the whole under the direction of Democracy, industrial and political.' Like Shaw, the Webbs became devotees of the Soviet Union under Stalin.[41]

---

[39] Russell (1918, p. 1), Griffiths (1924, p. 66).

[40] Michael Harrington was highly influential in the Democratic Socialist Organizing Committee and in its successor, the Democratic Socialists of America (DSA). Harrington (1972, 1989) insisted that socialism by definition must be democratic. Harrington (1989, p. 9) argued that capitalism itself is becoming more centralized and planned – and hence 'socialized' in his use of the term. For him, socialism meant taking power and putting that process under the 'democratic control' of the people. Both the 1972 and 1989 books attempt to rehabilitate Marx's politics, without understanding that his vision of nationally agglomerated economic power would destroy the separation of multiple politico-economic powers upon which democracy depends (Moore, 1966; Galbraith, 1952, 1969; North et al., 2009). He also fudges the question of how democratic socialism would be organized, and how resources would be valued and allocated, especially after money is 'abolished' (Harrington, 1972, pp. 421, 423, 449, 453–6).

[41] See Webb and Webb (1920, pp. 200, 342–3), Griffiths (1924, p. 80) and Webb and Webb (1935). M. Polanyi (1940, pp. 96 ff.) published a scathing review of the Webbs' apologia for the USSR.

The Webbs drafted the 1918 Constitution of the British Labour Party. Its aims included the famous Clause Four, Part Four:

> To secure for the workers by hand or by brain the full fruits of their industry and the most equitable distribution thereof that may be possible upon the basis of the common ownership of the means of production, distribution and exchange, and the best obtainable system of popular administration and control of each industry or service.

This allowed for no exception: all production would be in common ownership and there would be no private sector. The inclusive term *common ownership* satisfied both statist socialists and those who favoured other forms of common ownership, such as worker cooperatives. Big socialism and small socialism were both skilfully accommodated. Proponents of a mixed economy were not.

J. Ramsay MacDonald became the first-ever Labour Prime Minister. He led short-lived Labour minority governments in 1924 and 1929–31. He saw socialism as 'a movement to supplant Capitalism altogether, by organising communally the services which Capitalism performs or ought to perform'. He referred to 'the simple Socialist idea of communal responsibility for production and distribution'. The task of socialists was 'to transform a state of society in which capital controls labour and industry into one in which labour and industry control capital'. While stressing communal organization and control, his formulation was also consistent with wholesale common ownership.[42]

In 1923 Philip Snowden proposed the key motion in the famous 'socialism versus capitalism' debate in the UK House of Commons. This motion found the roots of economic failure 'in the private ownership and control of the means of production and distribution'. The motion called for 'an industrial and social order based on the public ownership and democratic control of the means of production and distribution'. This debate was wound up by MacDonald, who spoke in favour of the motion. It was defeated by 368 votes to 121. Labour had 142 seats at the time, and there were two Communist Party MPs, who presumably were among the 121. This suggests that about 84 per cent of the Parliamentary Labour Party voted in favour of (what could be interpreted as) 100 per cent public ownership. Snowden became the first-ever Labour Chancellor of the Exchequer in 1924.[43]

---

[42] MacDonald (1921, pp. 37, 242, 278).
[43] Griffiths (1924, p. ii).

Dan Griffiths was a schoolteacher in Wales and an active member of the Labour Party. He asked several leading British socialists to provide their definition of socialism. He received 199 publishable responses, from writers, academics, trade unionists and 59 Members of Parliament. His respondents included Clement Attlee, Fenner Brockway, G.D.H. Cole, Maurice Dobb, George Lansbury, Harold Laski, J. Ramsay MacDonald, Herbert Morrison, Bertrand Russell, Emanuel Shinwell, Philip Snowden, Sidney Webb and H.G. Wells.

Many offered sentiments or platitudes rather than clear guidance on meaning. Some interpreted his question as a request for a statement of socialist values. Others outlined what they meant by a socialist system. Several respondents saw socialism as the expression of Christian teaching. A few others were Marxists.

Notwithstanding many vague answers, as many as 85 of the 199 respondents saw socialism as bringing most or all of the means of production under some form of common ownership. This was the most prominent relevant attribute among the responses. Seven further respondents saw socialism as involving a significant public sector. Only two respondents accepted explicitly that some form of private enterprise could remain under socialism. No respondent mentioned any surviving role for competition or markets under socialism. While several respondents saw socialism primarily in terms of personal attitudes, ideals or values, none explicitly denied common ownership as a vital end or means.

For 24 respondents, socialism meant the extension of democracy from the political to the economic sphere; 77 respondents highlighted cooperation, often explicitly opposed to competition; 39 stressed production for use rather than for profit; 25 highlighted greater equality in wealth or opportunity.[44]

The survey by Griffiths shows definitively that socialism, in so far as it was defined at all, was widely (at least in the UK in the 1920s) understood as common ownership of the means of production. Among these prominent socialist politicians, intellectuals and trade unionists there was no significant support for a mixed economy and there was a complete failure to mention or defend any role for markets or the private sector.

Significantly, for Herbert Morrison, socialism meant: 'Ownership by public authorities of land and the essential means of industrial production

---

[44]   Griffiths (1924).

and distribution'.[45] Morrison became Minister of Transport during the 1929–31 Labour Government, Home Secretary in the wartime coalition of 1940–45 and Deputy Prime Minister in the Labour Government of 1945–51. He also served for a few months as Foreign Secretary before Labour's defeat in 1951. During the 1945–51 Labour Government, Morrison developed his model of the public corporation as a key form of public ownership.[46]

The Fabian G.D.H. Cole was an influential Labour Party theoretician and known as one of the famous three 'red professors', alongside Harold Laski and Richard Tawney. Cole taught Harold Wilson at Oxford, who became a Labour Prime Minister from 1964 to 1970 and 1974 to 1977. Cole was a pioneering advocate of 'guild socialism'. He saw the guilds as part of a system of national planning. He sought an integrated, national system where:

> a single authority is responsible both for the planning of the social production as a whole and for the distribution of the incomes which will be used in buying it. In other words, the remedy is some sort of Socialism – involving the socialisation of the essential means of production, distribution and exchange.[47]

In 1937 Clement Attlee wrote of the 'evils' of capitalism: their 'cause is the private ownership of the means of life; the remedy is public ownership'. Attlee then approvingly quoted the words of Bertrand Russell: 'Socialism means the common ownership of land and capital together with a democratic form of government. ... It involves the abolition of all unearned wealth and of all private control over the means of livelihood of the workers.' Apart from the exceptions noted above, the word *socialism* endured from the 1830s to the 1950s with these strong collectivist connotations, in opposition to private firms and markets.[48]

As Labour Prime Minister from 1945 to 1951, Attlee combined a measure of socialist idealism with an overriding pragmatism. Under his government, several industries were taken into public ownership, including the railways, coal, gas, steel, electricity and telecommunications. The National Health Service was founded in 1948, with strong Liberal involvement and Conservative tolerance. But with the outbreak of the

---

[45] Griffiths (1924, p. 55).

[46] Foote (1997, pp. 174–82).

[47] Cole (1935, 1948, p. 101). For evidence that Cole limited the autonomy of the guilds and saw them as subservient to the national plan see Cole (1935, pp. 332–4, 338) as quoted in Chapter 2 below.

[48] Attlee (1937, pp. 15–16).

Cold War in 1948, the Attlee government chose the side of Western capitalist democracies and NATO against Soviet Communism.

Although some Labour Party thinkers eventually began to entertain the possibility of some private enterprise in their future society, many party members remained resolutely in support of widespread common ownership. The UK Labour Party did not formally abandon its Clause Four commitment to the complete 'common ownership of the means of production, distribution and exchange' until 1995.

REVISIONIST ATTEMPTS TO SHIFT THE MEANING OF SOCIALISM

The term *revisionist* was applied to, and willingly accepted by, the prominent German socialist Eduard Bernstein. This was not because he abandoned or modified the socialist goal, although he was suspected by his severest critics of doing so. In his 1899 book *Evolutionary Socialism*, Bernstein accepted that socialism meant 'a society based on the principle of association' involving 'the socialisation of production and distribution'.[49]

Bernstein was called a revisionist because he argued that the transition from capitalism to socialism could be gradual: it would be driven by democratic reform rather than by insurrection. Bernstein argued that socialists should concentrate on positive and peaceful incremental change using democratic means, rather than by revolutionary leaps toward utopia. It is testimony to the tenacity of the original socialist goals that the famous early *revisionist* controversies concerned the path to socialism, not the final objective.

But others appropriated the name *socialism* for different purposes. Adolf Hitler founded the National Socialist German Workers' Party in 1920. Its name was chosen to draw support from the working class, who were strongly influenced by social democratic, socialist and communist ideas, as well as from anti-Semitic nationalism. For the Nazis, race was more important than social class. They rejected the goal of widespread common ownership and maintained a capitalist mixed economy, albeit under heavy state regulation and control. The Nazi adoption of the term *socialism* was a cynical propaganda ploy.[50]

The sources of a more genuine revisionism lie elsewhere. In a book published in 1909 when he was a member of the Liberal Party, Hobson

---

[49]   Bernstein (1961, pp. 96, 100).
[50]   Nolte (1965), Gregor (1974), Evans (2003, 2006).

favoured nationalization of the more routinized and standardized industries, but also made a case for retaining innovative and dynamic sectors
in private hands. Principally because of his opposition to UK participation in the First World War, Hobson left the then-governing Liberal
Party in 1916. He joined the Independent Labour Party in 1919. But he
never swallowed socialism whole. He 'never felt quite at home in a body
governed by trade union members and their finance, and intellectually by
full-blooded Socialists'. In his 1932 pamphlet *From Capitalism to
Socialism* he argued 'for a limited as against a complete socialism' and
for partial not complete public ownership. Hobson's radical revisionism
was for a mixed economy with 'socialist' components.[51]

Hobson influenced the Labour politician Douglas Jay. In his book *The
Socialist Case*, first published in 1937, Jay echoed Hobson and advocated
a mixed economy, along with redistributive taxation to alleviate economic inequality and Keynesian demand management. Jay also argued
that the meaning of socialism should be changed from common ownership to the abolition of unearned incomes. Hobson welcomed Jay's book
in a review in the *Manchester Guardian*. But Jay's cautious and
much-qualified defences of markets and consumer choice drew much
criticism from other leading figures in the Labour Party. G.D.H. Cole
castigated the 1937 volume because it was not socialist enough: Jay had
shown insufficient devotion to nationalization.[52]

Eventually Jay recoiled from his 1937 position. During the Second
World War he developed a more positive view of national planning. In
1947, after Jay had become a Labour MP, a revised edition of *The
Socialist Case* appeared with an approving Foreword by Prime Minister
Attlee. But Jay still argued that 'we must define socialism as the
abolition of private unearned or inherited incomes rather than of the
private ownership of the means of production'.[53]

Although this definition would allow some privately owned firms, it
would mean the end of all incomes from private ownership of rented land
or homes, from financial institutions and from shares in corporations. For
Jay, ending inheritance and unearned income meant 'not merely nationalization of the banking system but direct public control of investment
and of the whole range of public works'. He called for 'the transfer of
property claims and unearned incomes to the state' and 'public ownership

[51]   Hobson (1909; 1932, p. 36; 1938, p. 125). In the 1920s and 1930s, Hobson tried to
build bridges between socialism and liberalism (Clarke, 1978; Allett, 1981; Townshend,
1990).
[52]   Jay (1937, 1947), Durbin (1985, p. 150), Toye (2002).
[53]   Jay (1947, p. 194).

as well as control in all cases where the search for private profit clearly conflicts with the basic human needs of the community'. Hence social-ism would still 'extend public ownership and democratic control steadily throughout economic life'. Socialism 'in its original meaning of collect-ive ownership and collective control, is a ... true description of what we mean'. Jay's adjusted definition of socialism kept the traditional empha-sis on comprehensive planning and on extensive public ownership, but it provided a rationale for a small private sector. Nevertheless, this minimal acceptance of private enterprise was too much for many socialists, who still regarded him as a rightist and a revisionist.[54]

In the UK, reasoned revisionism found a bigger audience with the onset of the Cold War in 1948 and especially after Labour's 1951 election defeat. But strong and eloquent voices still defended traditional socialism. Aneurin Bevan was Labour Minister of Health when the UK National Health Service was founded in 1948. He warned in 1952 of the 'danger' of 'Fresh Thinkers' and of 'Socialist Revisionists': 'They suggest that an extension of public ownership is an old-fashioned and outmoded idea. ... It is essential that we should keep clear before us that one of the central principles of socialism is the substitution of public for private ownership. There is no way around this.'[55]

Bevan became the popular leader of the traditional-socialist wing of the Labour Party, against the growing attempts by 'revisionists' to dilute the mission of their movement. Bevan insisted that the 'substitution of public for private ownership' must prevail.

Then, in 1956, C. Anthony Crosland published *The Future of Social-ism*. He called for a more radical redefinition of socialism. He proposed new priorities in the face of capitalist economic growth and rising standards of living. For Crosland, public ownership was a means not an end. The true ends of socialism were greater economic equality and a welfare state that catered for basic human needs. This revisionism went much further than its predecessors.[56]

The original socialists believed that common ownership was the only way to reduce greed, inequality and social deprivation. For them, common ownership was an end as well as a means. Crosland claimed that they conceived common ownership as a means towards other ends,

---

[54]   Jay (1947, pp. xiv, 196, 261, 262, 278). Foote (1997, pp. 194–9) and Tomlinson (2014, p. 35) noted Jay's designation as a 'revisionist' or 'rightist'.

[55]   Bevan (1952, p. 2).

[56]   Crosland (1956), Foote (1997, ch. 10).

particularly welfare and equality of opportunity. He argued that capitalism had changed, and common ownership was no longer necessary to
reach these goals.

Crosland's hermetic separation of means and ends is questionable.
Means and ends interact with one another. In particular, if there is only
one means to achieve a goal, then it would logically assume the status of
an end as well. In practical circumstances a complete separation of means
from ends is impossible.[57]

In effect, Crosland had abandoned classical socialism for a version of
radical liberalism that emphasized greater economic equality and a strong
welfare state. Foreshadowed by thinkers such as Thomas Paine and John
Stuart Mill, Anglo-American liberalism had prioritized these solidaristic
goals since the 1890s. They were advanced by liberals such as John A.
Hobson, David Lloyd George, John Dewey, John Maynard Keynes,
William Beveridge and Michael Polanyi.

But instead of embracing the *liberalism* label, words such as *socialism*
and *social democracy* were ceremonially retained in post-war revisionist
circles, while there was an increasing reconciliation with markets, private
enterprise and a mixed economy. In 1959 in Continental Europe – in a
nation itself divided by the Iron Curtain – the (West) German Social
Democratic Party abandoned the goal of widespread common ownership.
In the same year, Hugh Gaitskell tried to get the British Labour Party to
follow this lead, but he met stiff resistance and he was forced to retreat.

Labour's token ideological commitment to 100 per cent common
ownership was retained while its leaders pursued policies within a mixed
economy. But this pragmatism still had to deal with Labour's ingrained
neglect or distrust of private enterprise. The historian Richard Toye noted
that the Labour Party, because of its enduring preference for public
ownership, failed to develop adequate policies to support private enterprise: 'Labour, until at least the 1950s, showed little interest in developing policies for the private sector. During the 1960s, the party
demonstrated continuing ambiguity about whether or not competition
was a good thing. This ambiguity continued at least until the 1980s.'[58]

By working within a party that had adopted the classical definition of
socialism since its inception, Labour Party revisionists were constantly

---

[57]   Dewey (1938, 1939), Hodgson (1988, pp. 93–7, 243, 285–6).
[58]   Toye (2004, p. 91).

trying to make the leopard change its spots. The German Social Democratic Party abandoned widespread common ownership only when Germany was split in two opposing camps, and the East became part of the Soviet bloc.

THE FAILURE OF REVISIONISM IN THE UK LABOUR PARTY

In the UK, while the official doctrine remained unchanged and old habits of thought remained prevalent, it took a run of four successive and decisive election defeats – 1979, 1983, 1987 and 1992 – for the British Labour Party to elect as its leader a politician with the courage and perception to challenge the mantra of 100 per cent common ownership in Labour's official aims.

Tony Blair became leader in 1994. In a short pamphlet he expressed his support for what he called 'ethical socialism'. He claimed that the ethical socialists of the past saw 'socialism' as 'defined by certain key values and beliefs' and not by common ownership. But he failed to cite any sources to confirm this. The evidence in this chapter shows that he was wrong – socialism throughout its history has generally meant common ownership.[59]

Blair claimed to be influenced by the Christian socialist John Macmurray. But Macmurray was a classical socialist who argued that the state should 'assume control of the economic and financial activities of society', which was very far from Blair's own view. As one critic put it: 'gaping chasms can be identified between the positions of Macmurray and Blair on almost every issue on which the former pronounced'. Blair played fast and loose with the history of socialist ideas.[60]

Following Crosland, Blair argued that the emphasis on common ownership or nationalization confused means with ends. Social harmony and social justice could be achieved by other means. While rejecting the overriding commitment to the common ownership of the means of production, Blair promoted 'social-ism', by which he meant recognizing individuals as socially interdependent. For Blair it also signalled social

---

[59]   Blair (1994).
[60]   Blair (1982, 1994), Hale (2002, esp. p. 193), Kirkpatrick (2005, pp. 24, 39, 157), Hodgson (2018, pp. 113–16).

justice, social cohesion, equal opportunities and the equal worth of each
citizen. But again, all of these ideas were to be found in the liberal
tradition.[61]

For Blair, social-ism is about attitudes and values, rather than institutional arrangements or modes of property ownership. It is true that
ethical statements about values have always been prominent among
socialists. But typically, their key values included a moral distaste for
competition and for profit-making from private ownership of the means
of production. Negative ethical judgements were attached to public or
private ownership of property.

Blair argued differently. He wanted ethical values such as care and
cooperation, but no moral evaluation of different systems of property
ownership. This would allow a free hand over what institutional forms
were favoured or developed, as long as some other 'core values' were
preserved. For example, privatization of nationalized industries could
occur, as long as 'social-ist' values of caring for others remained. His
value-driven revisionism meant a socialism unbounded by constraints on
the form of ownership, over the distribution of wealth or the structure of
power.

This was a very radical move. How would it be possible to persuade
the Labour Party to accept it? Interestingly, the 1918 version of Clause
Four did not include the word 'socialism'. It mentioned 'common
ownership' instead. Ironically, the revised version of 1995 declared for
the first time: 'The Labour Party is a democratic socialist party.' Perhaps
these words reassured many party members, despite the fact that Blair
wanted to eviscerate them of much of their previous meaning.

Hence Clause Four ceased to promote unalloyed common ownership.
Instead it admitted a positive role for markets and a private sector. The
new version called for a 'dynamic economy' where 'the enterprise of the
market and the rigour of competition are joined with the forces of
partnership and co-operation' and 'a thriving private sector'. But old
habits die hard. Socialist fundamentalists such as Benn wished to retain
the original wording. Benn protested: 'Labour's heart is being cut out'.[62]

The instigation of a 'democratic socialist' objective was a compromise
for those who kept much of the old intellectual baggage but recognized

---

[61]   But Blair has made some remarks that are worryingly remote from liberalism. At
his speech to the 1997 Labour Party conference Blair said that 'a decent society is not
based on rights. It is based on duty' (British Political Speech, 2018). This is redolent of
Tawney's (1921) unconvincing critique of unconditional rights. By contrast, liberals
generally stress both rights and duties.
[62]   Rentoul (1995).

that Labour's aims could be realized only through political power. For many, as R.T. Allen suspected, 'it is only the electoral failure of socialism that has motivated the creation of "New Labour" and not any appreciation of its intellectual and moral bankruptcy'.[63]

Instead of tackling the problem of Labour's old collectivist DNA more directly, Blair tried to change the meaning of *socialism* and to airbrush Labour's intellectual history. He failed to promote an adequate alternative vision to replace old-fashioned common ownership. To the traditional Left, it seemed that Blair wished to substitute capitalist compromise for cherished purity and socialist principle.

Inadvertently, Blair's endorsement of the word *socialism* gave legitimacy to those that defended socialism in its original meaning. The retention of the s-word played into the hands of the party's enduring, backward-looking Left. The 2003 invasion of Iraq helped to turn the Labour membership against Blair and his perceived compromises with capitalism and 'Western imperialism'. Collaboration with capitalism at war was seen as confirmation of Blairite 'neoliberal' collaboration with capitalism in peace. When Blair stepped down from office in 2007, he left a divided and ideologically rudderless party, which was soon to be shocked by a major crisis at the core of financial capitalism.

Eventually, as if there was an organization-level Freudian defence mechanism of developmental regression as a response to severe stress, Labour reverted to an earlier stage of its history, re-adopting its infant ideological comforts of collectivism and state control.

This theoretical, ideological and charismatic void explains why, by a large majority and with no strong rival, the Labour Party chose the retro-Marxist Jeremy Corbyn as its leader in 2015. He seized the enduring s-word in Labour's aims and claimed Labour's legacy. Classical socialism was back on the agenda. To many, Corbyn seemed to offer a new 'principled' approach to politics that broke with past compromises with capitalism. Classical socialism returned with a vengeance. Labour turned its ideological clock back to 1918.

Revisionists have a difficult choice. They may try to change the meaning of the s-word or they may drop it entirely. Both options are tricky. Dropping the word would draw accusations of betrayal from the faithful. Alternatively, changing the common understanding of a word is a formidable task.

Words sometimes shift in meaning, but rarely by command. Language is a social process and we cannot successfully redefine words at will.

---

[63] Allen (1998, pp. 2–3).

Contrary to Humpty Dumpty in *Alice through the Looking Glass*, words cannot be used to mean anything that is intended by their user. Generally, such powers are not at the behest of an individual or group. We are part of an extensive linguistic community, engaged in multiple social processes that establish evolving commonalities of meaning and understanding. We are typically obliged to accept prevalent meanings.[64]

The attempts by Jay, Crosland, Blair and others to give the word *socialism* a modernized meaning have largely failed. The strategy of Sanders, to describe himself as a socialist but to avoid being tied down by a definition, assumes that many in his audience will not consult a dictionary. But the dictionaries testify that the original meaning endures. As the Merriam-Webster online dictionary put it, socialism means the 'collective or governmental ownership and administration of the means of production and distribution'. Nothing less.

Consequently, the word *socialism* still strongly connotes its original meaning, despite the passing of almost two centuries, with multiple revisionist efforts and the existence of rival usages. It is irresponsible to declare allegiance to socialism without taking this enduring baggage into account. Radical changes in the meaning of a word can only occur if there are strong forces of change behind them. Otherwise, words kick back – as they did for Labour in 2015.

REVISIONISM WITH CHINESE CHARACTERISTICS

Mao Zedong died in 1976. Despite some positive advances in education and elsewhere, his regime had also led to about 65 million deaths and mass poverty was still widespread.[65] By 1978 the reforming wing of the Chinese Communist Party had gained power, under the leadership of Deng Xiaoping. He was bent on bringing his country out of centuries of poverty, and ending the economic disasters caused by reckless totalitarian direction from the centre.

Classical socialist doctrine clearly meant opposition to private enterprise and markets. Against this orthodoxy, Deng had to find a way of keeping the Communist Party activists on board. Consequently, he muted the meaning of socialism to mask its original opposition to private property and markets. Treating both planning and markets as possible means, not ends, Deng declared: 'The essence of socialism is liberation

---

[64] Carroll (1970, pp. 268–70). On definitions generally see Hodgson (2019a).
[65] Courtois et al. (1999). Higher estimates of the number of deaths are found in Rummel (1994).

and development of the productive forces, elimination of exploitation and polarization, and the ultimate achievement of prosperity for all ... common prosperity is the essence of socialism.' Note the switch from 'property' to 'prosperity'. But if that is socialism, then we are all socialists now.[66]

Deng's successful mobilization of platitudes opened the door to widespread markets, brought many millions of people out of poverty, and heralded explosive growth in the Chinese economy. China became a mixed economy, with an enduring strategic role for the state. Massive economic success allowed his revisionist change of meaning to endure.

To obfuscate their U-turn on markets and private ownership, official Chinese Communist Party documents today use terms like 'socialism with Chinese characteristics'. Appealing to national loyalty against enslavement to Western ideas is a clever rhetorical trick. But Marxism, Leninism, communism and socialism are all imports from the West.

In official doctrine, the eventual goal of communism with all property held in common is still preserved. Alongside revisionist formulations for the present, the old ideology has been retained for some unspecified occasion in the future. Hence the aims of the Communist Party of China still include the words: 'The realization of communism is the highest ideal and ultimate goal of the Party.' The intended meaning of *communism* here is unelaborated, allowing the Marxist faithful to retain the original meaning, while getting on with the business of building a capitalist economy and getting rich.[67]

Deng's revisionism made the word *socialism* a banality. This change of meaning could be sustained only because it opened the door for policies that led to a dramatic improvement in China's economic fortunes. At the same time, the future goal of full *communism* was retained for the faithful, even if many Chinese people ceased to believe in it. But of course, the future is always ahead: it never arrives. Such slippery formulations are possible in a one-party state, where there are the means to prevent people from asking too many awkward questions.

---

[66]   Deng (1992).
[67]   Communist Party of China (2013).

2. Small socialism requires frugality or markets

> I doubt whether those who have been comfortable and contented in their old
> mode of life, will find an increase of enjoyment when they come here.
> William Owen in 1825, from New Harmony, Indiana, USA[1]

This chapter examines the theory and practice of small-socialist experiments. It is shown that a key problem from the beginning was to establish enduring and workable rules of governance. A second issue concerned the developmental capacities of the socialist community. If it were to embrace change and engage with the outside world, then it had to overcome any ideological resistance to competition and markets. This also has been a major stumbling block.

Some argue that socialism goes against human nature – individuals are generally selfish. Against this, socialists since Robert Owen have argued that human nature is malleable, and more favourable circumstances would produce better and more moral individuals. Both these points of view are increasingly challenged by research. Owen over-stressed the possible influence of the environment and underestimated the enduring core of human dispositions and capacities. On the other hand, the purveyors of individual selfishness are also undermined by cumulative evidence concerning evolution, cooperation and human nature.

Much evidence testifies that most humans are not entirely selfish and self-regarding. We are a cooperative species. Dispositions to help others are found in all human cultures. To a degree these inclinations (or the capacity to develop them) may be inherited in our genes. These cultural and genetic traits have evolved because human groups that cohere and cooperate have been more likely to survive and procreate than others.[2]

Hunter-gatherer societies rely on norms of sharing and cooperation, which are often encoded in custom and ritual. Social cohesion is built up

---

[1] Quoted in Carmony and Elliott (1980, p. 167).

[2] For this evidence, and for discussions of the evolution of cooperation and morality in tribal communities through *group selection*, see Darwin (1871), Boyd and Richerson (1985), Sober and Wilson (1998), Henrich (2004), De Waal (2006), Bowles and Gintis (2011), Boehm (2012), Haidt (2012) and Hodgson (2013).

through face-to-face interactions that help to build trust and confidence. Contrary to worshippers of unalloyed egoism and greed, sympathy and cooperation are part of human nature. All known cultures endorse them. Measures of both egoism and altruism are ubiquitous in our species.[3]

Dispositions to help and care for others help to explain the widespread atavistic appeal of socialist ideas. But did early human communities hold property in common? In his *Origin of the Family, Private Property and the State*, Frederick Engels claimed that prehistoric bands or tribes practised a 'primitive communism' and suggested that common ownership has been the norm for much of human existence.

But adequate notions of property and ownership did not appear at least until the rise of ancient civilizations. Thorstein Veblen rightly pointed out that: 'no concept of ownership, either communal or individual, applies in the primitive community. The idea of communal ownership is of a relatively later growth.' While some resources were shared within tribes according to custom and agreement, there was no system of law that recognized individual or group property and it is misleading to talk of common ownership in these circumstances. The possibility of either individual or collective legal ownership did not emerge until systems of law developed in Ancient Mesopotamia, Greece, Rome and elsewhere.[4]

After humans moved from tribal to state-dominated societies, state autocracy provided little scope for autonomous communal living, except in some religious communities. Rare opportunities to experiment with new types of social organization arose with the occasional breakdown of central authority, or with the hazardous and infrequent possibility of emigration to new territories.

Small-scale communist experiments have been inspired by religion and later by Enlightenment rationalism. Historians estimate that there have been about three thousand experimental utopian communities in modern times, the majority of which were in North America. Many of these were set up by religious migrant groups, including the Shakers from England and the Hutterites from Germany. Others were secular and socialist, including the communities formed or inspired by Robert Owen from Britain and Charles Fourier from France.[5]

Owen and Fourier claimed that their utopian plans were based on science. Owen argued that individuals were products of their social

---

[3] Brown (1991), Schwartz (1994), Walzer (1994), Bok (1995), Haidt and Joseph (2004), Nichols (2004), Haidt (2012).

[4] Veblen (1898, p. 358). See also Fukuyama (2011, pp. 66–71). For a classic exposition of the legal concept of ownership see Honoré (1961).

[5] Oved (1997), Sosis (2000).

environment: we are all creatures of our circumstances. He saw 'the science of the influence of circumstances' as 'the most important of all the sciences'. According to Owen, the application of this behavioural 'science' would remove the need for rewards and punishments. Once people were treated with sympathy and kindness, they would respond with diligence and loyalty.[6]

Fourier's quirky human psychology proposed 12 common passions, variations of which resulted in 810 types of character. Hence the ideal community would have exactly 1620 people – one of each type from each of the sexes. Everyone would take the role most suited to his or her personality. Such arrangements would maximize social harmony.

Given our atavistic dispositions to cooperate, it might be expected that these small-scale socialist experiments would succeed. But few of the socialist communities lasted for more than ten years. Religious communities were more enduring. But this does not mean that small socialism has no staying power. In several countries, in the twentieth century, many worker-owned cooperatives have succeeded and endured. It is important to understand why some types of cooperative experiment worked and others failed. We start by looking at some of the original socialist communities, organized by Owen and his followers.

THE OWENITE COMMUNITIES

Owen acquired a cotton factory in New Lanark near Glasgow and moved there in 1800. Convinced that poor working conditions caused low productivity and anti-social behaviour, he set out on a major experiment in industrial relations. New Lanark became famous for its humane working conditions and for the quality of its cotton thread. The workers were provided with basic education and healthcare.

In 1825, with some of his profits from New Lanark, Owen purchased a large tract of land in Indiana in the US and set up the community of New Harmony. He addressed its founding settlers with these words: 'I am come to this country, to introduce an entire new state of society; to change it from the ignorant, selfish system, to an enlightened, social system, which shall gradually unite all interests into one, and remove all cause for contest between individuals.'[7]

---

6   The quoted words are from Owen (1991, pp. 277–8) – originally published in 1820.
7   Quoted in Davis (1979, p. 445).

Although he was an inspirational leader, many 'were unwilling to submit unquestioningly to his teachings, and preferred governing themselves'. Some of the Owenites in New Harmony called for the immediate establishment of common ownership, but for practical reasons Owen was reluctant to comply.[8]

Owenite communities aimed to be as self-sufficient as possible, with limited trade with the outside world. Owen believed that his communities would cohere and prosper through the powers of education and reason. Experience had taught that a workforce, if treated well, could become diligent and loyal. But Owen overestimated the powers of rational persuasion. He lacked sufficient appreciation of the conditions and time required to build trust and solidarity in close-knit groups.

His son William (who wrote the words that head this chapter) advised his father to restrict the flow of new recruits to New Harmony, so that norms of trust and cooperation could be consolidated in the community. But the father recklessly ignored this warning and issued a manifesto, inviting everyone in sympathy with his aims to proceed to New Harmony to join the new settlement. The result was a large, fragmented group that was short of key skills: there were no skilled craftsmen and insufficient farmers. For a while the community could not grow enough food to sustain itself.[9]

Partly as a result of this influx, New Harmony was divided into two, and then further subdivided several times. There was dissent over failures to establish common ownership of property. In one case it was attempted, but then the community collapsed. There were also disputes over religion and sexual behaviour. Some became disenchanted with rigid communal life. By 1828 all the Owenite communities in the New World had failed.[10]

In the UK in 1828 there were Owenite communities near Glasgow and in London. Others followed in the 1830s. Again, disputes arose on matters such as the organization of activity and the community of property. These experiments did not endure. Few Owenite communities lasted more than three years.[11] Why did they fail? Accounts by participants give several reasons: 'Again and again there is the litany of complaints of authoritarian leadership, poor financial management, a too

---

[8]   See Claeys (1991, p. xvi) and Harrison (1969, p. 76).
[9]   Erasmus (1977, p. 144), Carmony and Elliott (1980, p. 166).
[10]   See Harrison (1969, pp. 76, 164–9). There were later attempts to form Owenite communities in the USA, but without success. Several American Fourierist communities lasted a bit longer. But all had disappeared by about 1860.
[11]   See Harrison (1969, pp. 169–75).

generous "open door" policy of membership, a sublime indifference to the crushing power – as well as the seductiveness – of the outside world.'[12]

The development of community cohesion, involving the full commitment to shared rules, was crucial for communal survival. Apart from restricting inward or outward migration, how could unity be achieved? The Irish landowner John O'Driscol was a perceptive early critic of Owenism. He argued in 1823 that only 'despotic power' or 'religious zeal' would be sufficient to hold an Owenite community together. But Owenism proclaimed neither, putting their confidence in the power of reason alone. Consequently, the Owenite communities lacked strong internal ties and established rules, and they quickly fell apart.[13]

SURVIVAL IN NINETEENTH-CENTURY UTOPIAN COMMUNITIES

Research into utopian communities has confirmed O'Driscol's claim. The anthropologist Richard Sosis analysed a sample of 200 communes founded in the US in the nineteenth century. Many of them were religious. Others were secular – mainly socialist. Sosis tried to identify factors that helped to explain the survival or extinction of the communes. He noted that 'every breakdown is preceded by a loss of faith in the ideology, whether religious or secular, that originally motivated the establishment of the community'.[14]

Sosis also found major differences in the longevity of the two types. Only 6 per cent of the secular communes were still functioning 20 years after their founding, compared to 39 per cent of the religious communes. The dramatic differences are detailed in Table 2.1, which shows that on average the religious communes lasted over three times longer than the secular ones – for 25 years compared with 6 years.[15]

Data on particular types of religious and secular commune are explored in Table 2.2. Remarkably, despite their strict rules enforcing chastity, the Shaker communes lasted an average of over 56 years, compared to two or three years for the Owenite and Fourierist communities.

---

[12]   Kumar (1990, pp. 19–20).
[13]   Harrison (1969, p. 186).
[14]   Sosis (2000, p. 80).
[15]   Sosis (2000), Oved (1988).

Table 2.1   Duration of nineteenth-century secular and religious communes in the US

	n	Minimum (years)	Maximum (years)	Mean (years)	Standard Error
Secular	112	0	84	6.4	0.97
Religious	88	1	112	25.3	3.29

Source: Sosis (2000).

Table 2.2   Duration of Owenite, Fourierist and Shaker communes in the US

	n	Minimum (years)	Maximum (years)	Mean (years)	Standard Error
Owenite	14	0	10	2.1	0.67
Fourierist	37	0	16	3.2	0.67
Shaker	13	4	113	56.7	11.66

Source: Sosis (2000).

This evidence shows that religious adherence positively affected the survival rates of the communes, confirming O'Driscol's prescient assertion. Sosis argued that constraining social rules are more effective when they are made sacred. As the psychologist Jonathan Haidt put it in his discussion of Sosis's results: 'Sacredness binds people together, and then blinds them to the arbitrariness of the practice.' Ceremony and reverence resist the endless, disruptive powers of reason. Religious devotion is thus an important mechanism for establishing stable rules of governance in small communities. This has been the case for much of human history.[16]

By contrast, the secular communities appealed to utility and reason to enforce their rules, thus opening the door to endless rational challenges and arguments, based on different assessments of ethics, practicalities, costs or benefits. In his review of a study of utopian communities, Michael S. Cummings explained lucidly that secular ventures became entangled in internal disputes because intellectuals and factions 'quibble

---

[16]   Haidt (2012, p. 299). See also the discussion of the positive effects of religion on group survival in Wilson (2002) and Atran and Henrich (2010). Incidentally, these observations challenge the dichotomy between instrumental and ceremonial institutions in the writings of Ayres (1944), who was an influential figure in the post-1945 version of the original institutional economics. In some ways, the ceremonial can be instrumental.

endlessly about the best approaches to ownership and decision-making, over issues that cannot possibly put fire in the bellies of ordinary citizens on a daily basis.'[17]

By contrast, if social rules are fixed and legitimated by religion, then any criticism or dissent can be rebuffed more dramatically, by grave charges of heresy or of disrespect for the will of God. The evidence suggests that the differences of outcome are dramatic.

Sosis identified a key variable that helped to explain the degree of longevity of religious communities. It was the extent of costly sacrifice the commune demanded from its members. In many communities – secular and religious – they were asked to give up alcohol, tobacco or contacts with outsiders. But a correlation between such sacrifices and community longevity was not found in the secular communities. In contrast, in religious communities the devotion to self-sacrifice was crucial, because it had a sacred meaning. Religious devotion was tested and policed by the requirements of self-sacrifice. In turn, such devotion buttressed the rules that kept the community together.

Religiously motivated sacrifice helps explain the relative longevity of the Shaker communes. Their strict rule of chastity reduced the pro-creation rate to zero. This meant that they must endure solely by recruitment and not by breeding. But the benefits in terms of social cohesion and solidarity outweighed the disadvantages. Their simple religious culture of care, purposefulness and piety helped to integrate new recruits. Accordingly, and surprisingly, the religious devotion to chastity may have enhanced the chances of the survival of the Shaker communities.[18]

These findings are of major significance for small-scale socialism. Especially if they are secular, attention has to be given to suitable alternative mechanisms to sustain cohesion in these communities. Placing every rule and institution under the unrelenting spotlight of reason means that rules and norms are constantly challenged or overturned. If we dispense with religion, then there is a need for some authority and tradition, to avoid arguing over everything all the time.

Devotional religion worked as a social glue. It had done so previously in tribal communities, for tens of thousands of years, before the rise of states and before large-scale systems of social control. The small-scale

---

[17]   Cummings (1998, pp. 204–205).

[18]   This is an illustration of the potential force of group selection, where individual desires or interests are overridden in evolution by countervailing factors that aid the survival of the group (Darwin, 1871; Sober and Wilson, 1998; Henrich, 2004; De Waal, 2006; Bowles and Gintis, 2011; Boehm, 2012; Haidt, 2012; Hodgson, 2013).

socialist communities had no viable alternative mechanism to religion or authoritarianism. They put their faith in reason alone. That god failed.

If the Owenite and Fourierist communities had endured longer, then they would have faced additional problems. Their appeals to science were narrow, inflexible and dogmatic. There was insufficient understanding of the need for variety and experimentation in science. Consequently, if they had lasted longer, then they would have difficulties in innovating and adapting to changing circumstances. But if they had allowed scrutiny and debate over their foundational principles, then the chances of internal schism would have increased.

The greater longevity of the religious communes shows that sacred ritual and dogma may enhance coherence and the chances of survival. But once core principles are made sacred, then the capacity for innovation and adaptation is reduced. Ultimately, both the secular and religious communities faced serious problems of adaptation and survival. If they survived, then their prospect was slow change and enduring frugality.

FROM COMMUNES TO COMMERCE: THE ISRAELI KIBBUTZIM

The first kibbutz was founded in Ottoman Palestine in 1909. Most kibbutzim were ideologically socialist, including Marxists among their members. Others were religious. After the First World War, many more kibbutzim were set up and a formal association of kibbutzim was organized. By 1939, 24 105 people were living on 79 kibbutzim, comprising 5 per cent of the Jewish population of Palestine.

The kibbutz movement was tied up with the Zionist project to establish a homeland in Palestine for the Jews. As Paula Rayman explained: 'The main function of the kibbutz was to create a material base for a Jewish state in Palestine: land had to be reclaimed, new immigrants had to be supported and boundaries had to be guarded.'[19]

Because they were integral to the creation and survival of Israel, the kibbutzim saw it as their duty to supply other Israelis with food. Hence, unlike earlier communist communities, they overcame their qualms about markets and engaged in more extensive external trade. They produced agricultural products for local and eventually international markets.

A much larger wave of Jewish immigration followed the Second World War, leading to the state of Israel being formed in 1948. In 1950,

---

[19] Rayman (1981, p. 11). The use of the term *Zionism* here is not intended to be derogatory. Personally, I accept the right of the Jewish people to a homeland.

kibbutzim membership was 65 000, accounting for 7.5 per cent of the population of Israel. In 1989 the kibbutz membership peaked at 129 000. In 2010 there were 270 kibbutzim in Israel. Kibbutzim range in size from about 100 to over 1200 members. Their factories and farms accounted for 9 per cent of Israel's industrial output and 40 per cent of its agricultural output.[20]

In the original socialist kibbutzim, all property, down to kitchen implements, furniture, tools and clothing, was held in common. The defining socialist injunction to abolish private property was implemented to the extreme. Personal items such as clothing and furniture were owned collectively but distributed for personal use. Gifts and income received from outside were turned over to the community as a whole. The allocation of housing and the division of time between work, study and leisure were all determined by the community. Everyone received the same income. Medical care was made available without payment. Members ate meals together in the communal dining hall. Children were reared and housed collectively and allowed limited visits from their biological parents. Weekly general assemblies made the key decisions, which were then implemented by elected officers.[21]

The survival rates of both the secular and socialist kibbutzim proved to be much higher than the nineteenth-century Owenite and Fourierist communes. Many kibbutzim endured for decades. Did they provide an enduringly viable way forward? Sosis concluded otherwise: 'the kibbutzim have only survived economically through a combination of government subsidy, Jewish philanthropy, and debt forgiveness from Israeli banks'. Sosis also noted that the religious kibbutzim sustained a per capita productivity higher than that of the secular kibbutzim.[22]

The kibbutzim existed in a more hostile environment than the Owenite and Fourierist communes. Violent attacks from militant Arabs obliged many of the kibbutzim to form their own defence militia. A hostile enemy can help to forge communal solidarity: external threats and Israeli nationalism helped the kibbutzim to endure. The influx of money from outside sympathizers was also important.

The more the kibbutzim became embroiled in the Israeli economy, the greater the pressure to engage culturally with the modern world to relax some of their rules. Internal shortages of communal labour led to the hiring of workers from outside, on standard employment contracts.

[20] Rayman (1981), Gavron (2000), Wikipedia (2018a).
[21] Barkai (1972).
[22] Sosis (2000, p. 83).

During the 1950s and 1960s, outside employees made up between 8 and 9 per cent of the kibbutzim labour force.[23]

Periodically the kibbutzim experienced problems repaying their debts. They were helped by the Israeli government and Israeli banks. In practice the kibbutzim benefited from what János Kornai has described as 'soft budget constraints'.[24]

This changed in the 1977 elections. The previously dominant Labour Party was defeated, and public opinion became more critical of the kibbutzim. Their system of equal remuneration was criticized: it dampened individual incentives for extra effort, particularly in the larger communities where individual marginal rewards were more diluted. It was also argued that the prevalence of communal decision-making created resistance to technological and organizational experimentation.

In this more critical climate, less support was provided by the government and banks. By 1980, many kibbutzim were in economic crisis. When they turned again to the government and the banks for financial support, the national debate intensified on the efficiency and viability of the kibbutzim. Eventually most of them were obliged to restructure and change strategy.

By 2010, only a quarter of the kibbutzim still functioned as communes where all income was shared. As many as 188 out of the national total of 270 kibbutzim were run according to the 'new kibbutz' privatization model, which included differentiated salaries for its members. In many cases some kibbutz property, such as dwellings, were transferred to individual household owners. Some members were allowed to work outside the kibbutz, to bring in additional income.[25]

Most kibbutzim today are a far cry from the socialist communes that existed before 1980. The earlier model was generally less successful. Today's kibbutzim survive because of their greater commercial viability. They offer their members a relatively cohesive community life that contrasts with the more individualistic and turbulent life outside.

FROM COMMUNES TO COOPERATIVES

Producer cooperatives under worker ownership are very different from communes or kibbutzim. While both organize production cooperatively

---

[23] Barkai (1972), Erasmus (1977, ch. 6).

[24] Kornai (1992, pp. 140 ff.) developed the concept of a soft budget constraint in the context of planned, Soviet-type economies.

[25] Ashkenazi (2010).

with shared ownership of the means of production, worker-owned enterprises do not necessarily require the workers to live together communally. This is a crucial difference.

There are also retail cooperatives. Some of these were set up by Owen's followers, with the aim of making profits to fund new Owenite communities. In 1830 there were about three hundred retail cooperatives throughout Britain. By 1845 this number exceeded a thousand. Although these retail cooperatives had Owenite-socialist origins, they entered the world of trade and acquired a commercial impetus and viability.

The promotion of worker-owned producer cooperatives was not confined to socialists or anarchists. The liberal thinker John Stuart Mill endorsed worker-owned producer cooperatives in his *Principles of Political Economy*, which first appeared in 1848. The idea was also adopted by radical Catholics, among others.[26]

There are some existing large-scale worker cooperatives, such as Chèque Déjeuner and Acome enterprises in France, the Mondragón Cooperative in Spain, and the Credit Desjardins bank in Quebec in Canada. There are numerous smaller cooperatives in most capitalist countries. One study found that as many as 12 per cent of workers in the 20 most developed countries are in cooperatives. The evidence suggests that worker cooperatives can be relatively efficient in particular circumstances: they are not generally inferior in efficiency to capitalist corporations. Their performance can be enhanced if there are complementary institutions, particularly sympathetic banks making finance available. Worker participation and satisfaction are typically higher.[27]

Worker cooperatives obtain a degree of cohesion because each worker has purchased a share in the enterprise. This can deter both entry and exit, thus stabilizing the group and providing everyone with a stake in the mission and viability of the business. At the same time, the cooperative does not pervade every aspect of life and allows substantial individual autonomy outside the workplace.

Unlike the earlier utopian socialist communities discussed above, worker-owned cooperatives offer a proven way forward. They have supporters from across the political spectrum. We need to understand why this model works, where other small-scale socialist experiments have failed. We also need to appreciate why this model has proved less popular among socialists than wholesale nationalization and central planning.

---

[26]   Mill (1909, pp. 698, 772–3), Zamagni and Zamagni (2010).
[27]   Bonin et al. (1993), Dow (2003), Gagliardi (2009), Zamagni and Zamagni (2010), CICOPA (2014).

Many socialists claim to support cooperatives but retain a dislike for markets. This contradictory position is untenable. To be self-governing, worker cooperatives have to be independent legal entities with legal rights to own and trade their property. If they cannot trade and negotiate prices, then they are hobbled. Worker cooperatives require legal rights to secure their autonomy.

Tony Benn was one of the most famous UK supporters of worker cooperatives. Echoing Marx's endorsement of their propaganda value, Benn argued that cooperatives can play 'a tremendous part in boosting the self-confidence of workers by showing them the possibility of another route'. But Benn also warned of 'dangers in a naïve or emotional commitment to co-operation'. He accused the Tory enemy of having a devious plan:

> Some Conservatives would like workers to confront directly the disciplines of a market economy through co-operatives. ... This is also what lies behind 'market socialism'. Industrialists who are ready to fund co-operatives see this as a way to withdraw from their role as managers of labour ... letting the workers fight market forces alone ...[28]

Here 'market socialists' are lumped together with Tories and capitalists for their shared desire to expose workers to the onslaught of 'market forces'.

Benn often used the phrase 'market forces' to demonize rights to trade-owned property. For him, these 'forces' were hostile powers that must be 'fought'. But while markets can offer people inadequate or overly expensive choices, their removal means offering people no choice at all. For Benn, the dilemma was either wholesale common ownership or 'market forces as the sole determinant of economic activity'. For him there was no middle ground. Effectively, by banishing markets, Benn ruled out the possibility of autonomous worker cooperatives. His support for cooperatives and 'worker control' was contracted by his denial of their legal right to own and trade their property.[29]

Related shortcomings are found in the *guild socialism* of G.D.H. Cole. Although Cole said the guilds should be self-governing, he did not grant them adequate legal rights to be so. Guild socialists 'do not desire the

---

[28] Benn (1979, pp. 159–60).

[29] Benn (1982, p. 125). On a personal note, Foote (1997, pp. 320, 347) described me as a 1980s 'Bennite'. Before 1981 I had a relatively positive view of Benn. But because of my explicit acceptance of markets at that time, I was alien to the Bennite stream of thought. Consequently, Benn and his followers kept me at a distance. See Hodgson (1981, p. 206) for a contemporary statement of mine in support of a private sector and markets.

ownership of any industry by the workers employed in it'. The workers
in guilds would have the 'right of consultation' but no right to 'choose
their own foremen or managers'. Guilds would not have the legal
capacity to negotiate prices and they would be subject to the dictates of
the national plan: 'The last word in revising plans must come from the
centre ... I do not of course mean that each industry or service can be left
free to do things which militate against the success of the national plan as
a whole.'

Hence Cole supported the wholesale nationalization of industry and the
abolition of private and independent enterprise, within an overall 'single
authority'. He sought an integrated, national system 'involving the
socialisation of the essential means of production, distribution and
exchange'. Consequently, it is a mistake to regard Cole's guild socialism
as a viable model for decentralization. It is big socialism not small
socialism.[30]

If worker cooperatives (or guilds) are to have the power to sell their
products and to negotiate prices with potential buyers, then this means
they must be legal entities with the right to engage in contracts and
commodity exchange, and to sue or to be sued. If there are competing
sellers or buyers, then there are markets and 'market forces'. Devolved
property is a precondition of autonomy and markets are an outcome.

The removal of the right to engage with markets means the elimination
of the right to negotiate prices and to secure contracts for the purchase of
inputs or sale of their outputs. This prohibition means that someone else
must set the prices, such as a central or local planning authority. The
worker cooperative then loses power and autonomy; it becomes a cog in
the bigger planning machine. The agoraphobic logic of Benn and Cole
rules out autonomous, worker-managed enterprises and nullifies significant decentralization: their anti-market arguments lead to a centrally
planned economy.

THE YUGOSLAV EXPERIMENT WITH WORKER
SELF-MANAGEMENT

Viable decentralization requires the legal autonomy of small socialist
enterprises so that they may negotiate prices and trade with others. But
such toleration of commerce has been too much for most socialists.
Hence, because of this congenital socialist hostility to markets, small

---

[30]   Cole (1917; 1920a; 1920b, pp. 58–9; 1935, pp. 332–4, 338; 1948, p. 101).

socialism was in eclipse from the 1850s to the 1950s. The idea re-emerged with the Yugoslav experiment in self-management. But this system did not allow adequate legal autonomy and powers for self-managed enterprises, and that was a key reason why it failed. The experiment once again confirmed that socialism as a doctrine has enduring congenital problems with private ownership and markets.

The Yugoslav Communist Party under the leadership of Josip Tito came to power in 1945. It embarked on a programme of widespread nationalization of private enterprises. The rift with the Soviet Union in 1948, and the exacerbated difficulties with central control in a federation riven by multiple ethnic, religious and linguistic differences, caused the government to change course in 1952 and move toward a more de-centralized politico-economic system. The Yugoslav experiment did not evolve out of a market economy. Powers were delegated to enterprises from a state-owned system, overshadowed by a one-party state, and still committed to a Marxist ideology. These factors shaped its nature and destiny.

Some supporters regarded the Yugoslav system as an effective and practical socialist response to the critique of central planning developed by the Austrian economists Ludwig Mises and Friedrich Hayek.[31] For instance, Thomas Marschak wrote in the Harvard-based *Quarterly Journal of Economics*: 'The classic idea (of Hayek for example) that the burden of assembling managers' intimate technical information at one center is a major obstacle to any sort of central planning seems to lose weight in the Yugoslav context.'[32]

Branko Horvat was the leading Yugoslav economist. He too argued that a system of worker-managed firms linked by markets was a powerful answer to Mises and Hayek:

[T]he labor-managed economy achieves what Hayek considered to be impossible: an alternative form of organization in which genuine autonomy on the part of the firm is rendered compatible with *ex ante* coordination of

---

[31] 'Ludwig von Mises' leads to complications in the copy-editing process. Some copy-editors (particularly in the US) insist that the 'von' should be coupled with the 'Mises', ignoring the fact that *von* simply indicates nobility and is not part of the family name. Hence, 'von Mises' would appear under 'v' and not 'M' in the index. My suggestion henceforth is that Ludwig Mises becomes the norm. Friedrich Hayek dropped his *von*, so why shouldn't his mentor too?

[32] Marschak (1968, p. 569). Thomas was the son of Jacob Marschak, who was one of the pioneers of econometrics.

economic activities and full use is made of the existing knowledge while
losses due to market failures are avoided.[33]

Horvat suggested that the Yugoslav system was 'a promising beginning in
the development of a genuinely self-governing society'. But the Yugoslav
system provided neither genuine self-management nor enterprise
autonomy: the rights of firms to own and trade were restricted. Like
many other proponents of socialism and most orthodox economists,
Horvat paid insufficient attention to the legal structures required to
sustain a devolution of power. Also, by suggesting that the system makes
'full use ... of the existing knowledge', Horvat ignored the permanence
of layers of irretrievable tacit knowledge in any economy. His answer to
Hayek was sorely incomplete because he did not assimilate much of
Hayek's argument.[34]

Yugoslavia never developed the legal structures required for a market-
based system that could enable authentic enterprise autonomy. The
realization of genuine self-management was thwarted at the outset by
Marxist ideology. The system was still described as a 'proletarian
dictatorship' with 'social ownership', where legal and political rights
were granted only if they were deemed consistent with socialist goals.
'Social ownership' meant that ownership was by everyone and no one. It
did not mean that ownership rights were invested in self-managed groups
of workers. Academics in support of the system argued that markets
undermined rather than enabled worker self-management. Generally,
markets were tolerated but feared: they were believed to generate
inequality and instability.[35]

Because of the prevalent Marxist ideological opposition to share-
holding in particular and private ownership in general, the Yugoslav
system gave enterprises limited autonomy. Their foundation required the
approval of local government. They were not formed by workers club-
bing together as shareholders. By law, all loans had to be obtained from
state-owned banks. By 1956 the 'self-managed' enterprises had obtained
the legal right to sell their products on the open market. But all their
capital goods were owned by the state. The state granted *rights of use* of
these capital goods to the enterprises. These use-rights to capital goods

[33]   Horvat (1982, p. 208).
[34]   Horvat (1982, p. 165), Hodgson (2016a).
[35]   Erasmus (1977, p. 298) cited some anti-market views published by Yugloslav
academics. For a critique of Marxism's 'dictatorship of the proletariat' and of its
conditional view of rights see Hodgson (2018, chs 5–7). A critique of the idea that markets
necessarily lead to inequality is found in Hodgson (2015a, ch. 15).

could be sold, but only to another 'self-managed' enterprise or to a state-run firm. Hence there was a highly restrictive market for capital goods.[36]

Overall, there were incompletely devolved powers of ownership and pricing, within an economic and political system dominated by the federal and local state machines. The 'self-managed' enterprises differed from the standard model of the worker cooperative because they did not own their capital goods and they were subject to substantial and ongoing interference by the party-state. This was far from the ideals of Philippe Buchez or Pierre-Joseph Proudhon, as well as being different from the much more centralized system proposed by Marx.

This partial experiment in small socialism was impaired by the ideological prejudices of big socialism and Marxism. Fully independent enterprises and markets were mistrusted. A mild dose of small socialism existed under substantial big socialist controls within a one-party state. A dynamic, autonomous, business-orientated culture was never allowed to flourish.[37]

The prevalence of political appointments to key positions in enterprises, and the absence of adequately independent institutions to deal with grievances, led to numerous strikes by workers against their own elected managers and works councils. Striking against a system that was genuinely self-managed would be tantamount to economic hara-kiri. There would have been no motive for such strikes if the workers had felt they had an adequate voice within the enterprises and genuinely felt in a position of ownership. The existence of such strikes demonstrates that Yugoslav self-management was inauthentic.[38]

All enterprises rely on business networks with other firms, to learn from each other and to develop contractual relationships. Links with financial institutions and local government are also vital. In the Yugoslav system these networks and links were generally under Communist Party influence or control, particularly through the operation of the so-called *aktiv*. The help of the Communist Party *aktiv* units was vital to secure funds from the (publicly owned) banks and from the (Communist-run) local councils. This arrangement put major limits on enterprise autonomy, harboured corruption, and encouraged worker alienation and apathy.[39]

---

[36]   Pejovich (1966), Broekmeyer (1977), Estrin (1983), Woodward (1995).
[37]   On this point I would now modify a statement in Hodgson (2018, p. 98).
[38]   Shabad (1980).
[39]   Lydall (1986, pp. 115 ff.).

But despite all these shortcomings, there was sufficient economic devolution, flexibility and dynamism to engender substantial economic growth. Yugoslavian economic output expanded rapidly from 1952 to 1979, averaging around 6 per cent per annum with per capita consumption rising by almost 4.5 per cent per year.

But from 1974, despite economic growth, there were agoraphobic attempts by the party-state to regulate enterprise autonomy and to rein in markets: 'political or bureaucratic interference in everyday economic decision-making was rife'. Investment decisions were increasingly made by the centre. As Saul Estrin concluded: 'the Yugoslavs never fully resolved two fundamental questions: the appropriate balance of managerial and employee prerogatives in the democratically-run firm, and the decentralized capital market institutions to be associated with self-managed enterprises'.[40]

By 1980, growth in GDP per capita had ground to a halt. During the 1980s, unemployment rose, alongside bouts of severe inflation. The state made attempts to bolster the system of 'self-management', but this led to further bureaucratization and cronyism, rather than increased autonomy, new dynamic firms, more competition or renewed growth. Loss-making firms were subsidized rather than phased out. The soft budget constraint, which is familiar in centrally planned economies, became well established in Yugoslavia. Not only were inefficient firms kept on life-support by the bureaucracy, but also it was difficult to set up new firms. There was a lack of innovative entrants who might pioneer new technologies. These fatal flaws in the Yugoslav system of 'self-management' persisted because of the lack of genuine private ownership (by groups of workers or entrepreneurs) and the absence of a sufficiently independent legal system to sustain its rights.[41]

The imperfectly devolved system was ensnared by the one-party state. Both became less popular through the crisis-ridden 1980s. As loyalty to the federal state weakened and the economic crises worsened, there was a resurgence of ethnic nationalism. Tragically, the Yugoslav Federation broke up in 1991 and plunged into vicious ethnic strife and civil war.

The Yugoslav case confirms that substantial devolved ownership and legal rights are essential to decentralize power and grant autonomy to enterprises. In turn, for these legal provisions to work, there has to be a relatively autonomous legal system. For this to happen there must be political pluralism based on substantial countervailing power. Powerful

---

[40]   Estrin (1991, pp. 189, 193).
[41]   Narayanswamy (1988), Estrin (1991), Kornai (1992, pp. 140 ff., pp. 489 ff.), Uvalić (1992), Woodward (1995).

interests apart from the state are needed to keep the state in check. These in turn can help to sustain a relatively independent judiciary. But in Yugoslavia the judiciary was enmeshed in the one-party state. Hence the promises of enterprise autonomy and self-management were unfulfilled.[42]

The Yugoslav leaders chose to retain substantial central control rather than granting full legal autonomy to the worker enterprises. The temptations of central power guided by Marxist ideology remained strong. Fear of ethnic and religious fragmentation was another reason for retaining central control. These statist restrictions suffocated 'self-management': it was an unrealized promise. Excessive intervention from the centre also thwarted decentralized coordination mechanisms that could allow mutual local adjustment between enterprises on the basis of local knowledge. The centre feared those mechanisms and distrusted genuine local control.

Legal autonomy and its politico-economic preconditions are essential for lasting devolution and self-management. Yet legal structures are often underestimated in social science. Socialist scholars have often made the same mistake. Legal aspects were overlooked in the misleadingly described models of 'market socialism', developed by Oskar Lange and others. In fact, Lange-type models involve the hypothetical use of *simulated* markets – without legally enforceable contracts or trade – to try to establish prices in a centrally planned system. Lange's model was an idealized exercise in unrealistic economic theory and it was never applied in practice.[43]

In 1958 the American economist Benjamin Ward formulated a theoretical economic model of worker cooperatives in a market context. It is significant that he first described his model as 'market syndicalism', but later he described it as 'socialism' or 'market socialism'. The early title reflected the prevailing association of *socialism* with central planning, at least until the 1950s.[44]

A minority of socialists, desiring a genuine decentralization of economic and political power, began to realize that the only way to prevent over-centralization was to devolve property rights and to embrace the market mechanism. These measures are necessary to allow enterprises to make their own decisions concerning output and prices. Buchez and

---

[42] The general point about the importance of legal relations in understanding economic systems is developed in Hodgson (2015a) and Deakin et al. (2017).

[43] The blackboard models of socialism by Dickinson (1933, 1939), Lerner (1934, 1944), Durbin (1936), Lange (1936–37) and Lange and Taylor (1938) employed neoclassical general equilibrium theory, involving hypothetical iterative processes through which prices could supposedly be established. These models have been widely criticized as flawed, unrealistic and impractical (Hodgson, 2018, pp. 93–5).

[44] See Ward (1958, 1967). Models by Vanek (1970, 1972) and others followed.

Proudhon had approached similar conclusions a century earlier. But many socialists still retain their hostility to markets. This factor alone rules out any viable small socialism, as experiences in Yugoslavia and elsewhere demonstrate.

CONCLUSION: THE DILEMMAS OF SMALL SOCIALISM

This chapter has explored different versions of small socialism. It has shown that the Yugoslav system retained considerable big socialism in small socialist guise. Genuine experiments in small socialism differ on whether they involve communal living or whether they are confined to the workplace. They also differ in their degree of engagement with the outside world and in particular with markets.

Table 2.3 lays out the options for small socialism. Variations are possible along at least two dimensions. The first dimension concerns the degree of integration of work with home and family life. The Owenite and Fourierist communities of the nineteenth century, and the Israeli kibbutzim up to 1980, were mostly highly integrated in this respect, with communal organization spanning both spheres. By contrast, worker cooperatives are often organized separately from the home and family, allowing a separate autonomy in domestic and personal life.

Table 2.3   Different types of small socialism

	Integration of work with home and family life	Degree of engagement with outside markets	Examples	Comments
Largely self-sufficient communes	High	Low	Owenite and Fourierist communities	Most failed within a few years
Trading communes	High	High	Many Israeli kibbutzim before 1980	The kibbutzim were dependent on external support
Worker cooperatives	Low	High	Numerous examples in many countries	Autonomy and viability depend on legal status and markets

The second dimension concerns the degree of engagement with outside markets. For doctrinal, geographical or other reasons, many of the Owenite and Fourierist communities had little interaction with the outside world. By contrast, most Israeli kibbutzim were set up as part of the Zionist state-building project, and consequently they felt impelled to export their produce to their wider community. Also, worker cooperatives have generally been set up to trade their goods or services on markets.

Nobel Laureate Elinor Ostrom's inspirational studies of the management of common-pool resources are relevant here. She showed that resources – such as medieval common land, fisheries or agricultural irrigation schemes – can be effectively managed by relatively small communities with long historical ties of association.[45]

Within these relatively small and cohesive groups, Ostrom emphasized individual reputation, trust and targeted sanctions as mechanisms for encouraging cooperation, reciprocity and compliance with customary rules. Ostrom's case studies show that effective rules and routines evolve less by design and more by evolution and experiment in decentralized systems, over long periods of time. Even small-scale arrangements of this kind are too complex to be effectively and completely designed from above. The rules and enforcement mechanisms evolved and became ingrained in custom over many years.[46]

Can we envisage a small socialism, based on isolated, non-trading communities of less than two thousand people? New communities would find it difficult to replicate the kinds of institutional and cultural rules that had evolved over centuries in some of the communities studied by Ostrom. Without this long prior evolution of effective rules, the evidence in this chapter suggests that socialist communities must obtain cohesion via authoritarian leadership or religious zeal. But such integrative methods challenge democratic and secular ideals, and they impair the capacity of the community to adapt in the face of new challenges.

Severe isolation would come at a massive human cost. Small, independent, socialist communes would lose the huge benefits manifest since the year 1800 from the national and global divisions of labour. They would have to produce everything themselves, without the benefit of global specialization and greater returns to scale. Without the innovation and growth brought by this dynamic global market system, we

---

[45]   Ostrom (1990).

[46]   Ostrom (1990) also considered some larger scale cases, but the enforcement mechanisms are different. Reputation is an enforcement mechanism that can apply to organizations as well as individuals, but other ways of developing trust typically depend on face-to-face contact.

would be much poorer, not only in terms of wealth, but also in terms of health, life expectancy and cultural riches. Without markets, small socialism means frugality.

The alternative for small socialist communities is to engage in markets. But even here there can be problems, as illustrated by difficulties in the Israeli kibbutzim. The earlier policy of paying all kibbutz members the same wage has been largely abandoned. So too has the dissolution of the family into the community. The kibbutzim have become more flexible and less doctrinal, accepting some private property alongside greater individual and family autonomy.

This leaves us with the worker-owned cooperative, which has legal autonomy in a market economy, numerous examples of which exist in many countries. Unlike the Yugoslav model, workers in genuine cooperatives own shares and these may be saleable if the worker wishes to quit. Capital assets are owned by the cooperative itself. The co-operative can participate in markets for capital goods and financial markets that can be used to obtain loans.

Several studies show that worker cooperatives can be economically viable and relatively successful, especially when they function in the context of supportive legal, political, financial and other institutions. Market discipline provides secular incentives to install and observe robust internal rules. Cooperatives have a good track record of building ties within the local community and enhancing people's skills. Overall, this is the most realistic and satisfactory way forward for small socialism.[47]

It is also the only version of small socialism that grants some autonomy of the individual and the family from the obligations of cooperation that it retains in the workplace. It is also the only version of small socialism that would allow a relatively autonomous and diverse civil society to flourish. But there is still a need to experiment. The success hitherto of worker cooperatives has so far been within the framework of capitalism, as one among several competing forms of enterprise. So far, genuine worker cooperatives have not become the dominant form in any economy.

Genuine self-management failed in Yugoslavia because the worker enterprises had inadequate legal and practical autonomy. Viable worker cooperatives must be independent legal entities with the full legal right to engage in contracts with consumers, banks and other enterprises, with powers to negotiate contractual terms and prices. This goes too far for

---

[47]   See Marshall (2011, ch. 4). Burczak (2006) provided a well-argued proposal along these lines that accepts the force of the Hayekian critique of big socialism (Hayek, 1935, 1944, 1988).

agoraphobic socialists, many of which would not regard any system with markets as socialist at all. They opt instead for big socialism, which is discussed in the two following chapters.

3. Big socialism brings stagnation and despotism

> That, on the principle of a communion of property, small societies may exist in habits of virtue, order, industry, and peace ... I ... have seen its proofs in various small societies, which have been constituted on that principle; but I do not feel authorized to conclude from these that an extended society, like that of the United States ... could be governed happily on the same principle.
> Thomas Jefferson (1822)

> The idea of planning the whole cultural and economic life of a country from one centre has a profound appeal for the contemporary mind; it fascinates above all the intelligent, the energetic, the forward looking minds, and makes them contemptuous of traditional individual liberty.
> Michael Polanyi (1940)

Under big socialism, much of the economy is under public ownership and attempts are made to plan the economy from the centre. This bold scheme suffers from a number of fundamental problems. These difficulties are revealed by theoretical analysis and confirmed by the experience of attempts to build big socialism.

Two fundamental problems with big socialism are raised in this chapter. Further reasons why comprehensive central planning of modern, large-scale economic systems is inviable are raised in Chapter 4.

First, under big socialism there are inadequate incentives at the microeconomic level for adequate diligence, effort and innovation at work. I call this the $1/n$ problem, where n is the number of people that work collectively.

Second, there are severe political dangers inherent in big socialism's concentration of economic power in the hands of the state. Such a centralization requires and promotes a strong executive, relatively unconstrained by checks and balances. The concentration of economic power requires and reinforces political centralization. Countervailing powers are undermined because they lack their own independent resources and economic clout.

Even with the best of intentions, the temptations of concentrated power at the centre are too great. They have typically led to the curtailment of political pluralism and of freedom of expression. This process was visible in Russia, China, Cuba, North Korea and elsewhere, after big socialist governments took power. More recently, this erosion of democracy by big socialism has been dramatically illustrated in Venezuela.

The motivations of socialist revolutionaries may be caring and altruistic, but their over-confidence in their historic mission makes them intolerant of disagreement and resistance. They often use their power over the party machinery to curtail debate and suppress dissent. When they gain state power, then they may use their authority to constrain opposition in society as a whole.

Faced with the historical evidence that big socialism undermines democracy, some socialists blame the antagonism of capitalist powers or the mistakes of socialist leaders. They avoid the possibility that the authoritarian nature of these regimes might flow from the precepts of big socialism itself. The concentration of economic power in the hands of the state requires and sustains a concentration of political power in the hands of a few.

Socialists have often promised a substantial expansion and enrichment of democracy. Things always turned out differently, despite their intentions, because of the centralist logic of big socialism. The history and logic of big socialism show that democratic intentions will be overridden by the concentration of centralist power.

The two fundamental problems that are raised in this chapter do not show that big socialism is impossible. On the contrary, it has existed in Russia and China and continues to exist in Cuba and North Korea. But these regimes have never implemented the rationalist ideal of fully comprehensive planning: instead they have muddled along and conceded some space to markets. Big socialism has always led to bureaucratic ossification and political despotism. Generally, these economies have an inferior record in terms of innovation and economic growth. Universally they have curtailed democracy and diminished freedom of expression. These outcomes are not coincidental: they stem from the nature of big socialism itself.

INCENTIVES AND THE 1/*N* PROBLEM

Individual incentives are crucial to make any economy work. Incentives may range from altruism to greed. In any viable economic system there need to be 'effective stimuli to the individual wills of its members', as

John A. Hobson put it. Market or mixed economies can work more effectively because they can harness 'the play of enlightened self-interest' within institutional checks.[1]

Axel Honneth – a professor of philosophy at the University of Frankfurt and at Columbia University in New York – has challenged the argument that incentives are a severe problem for big socialism. He argued that common aims are sufficient for collective endeavour. Neither trust nor inter-personal intimacy are required for collective solidarity:

> Intimate trust is hardly necessary in order to think of oneself as a member of a community of solidarity in which each person is concerned about the needs of the others ... it is enough for the members to regard each other as sharing certain common aims, regardless of how large the given collective is and whether the members of that collective are in fact personally familiar with each other.[2]

Sure enough, we have examples in modern history of millions of people sharing and working together for common aims. Armies of millions fought against each other in the trenches of the First World War. The British people rallied in 1940 to resist the Nazi threat. The Chinese Communist Party mobilized millions of peasants to seize power in 1949.

These examples of common purpose pitted nationalist passions against perceived lethal threats. When thousands struggle together in a common cause, it is typically under the spur of nationalism, religion, fanatical ideology, or perceived threats from an adversary. There are sanctions to discourage defection. Such conditions are necessary to establish common aims on a large scale.

Common aims are insufficient to secure detailed cooperation within a complex division of labour. Honneth did not distinguish between widely shared sentiments of solidarity on the one hand, and detailed cooperation over complex projects on the other. He overlooked the detailed challenges of organizing and managing a complex venture, by dividing tasks, securing skills and monitoring outcomes. Cooperation in large-scale economies requires an extensive division of labour, breaking down tasks into organized, incentivized, modular units.

Cooperation in small-scale communities can work because of long-evolved cultural and other mechanisms to establish trust and to ensure that people carry out their tasks. These mechanisms are effective with smaller numbers, where everyone knows everyone else, and everyone is

---

[1]   Hobson (1910, p. 323).
[2]   Honneth (2017, p. 29).

trying to maintain their status and good reputation in the group. Enforcement processes may range from praise to punishment.

If benefits are shared, then selfish individuals might 'free ride' and gain from the harder work of others, while making a lesser contribution themselves. But evidence shows that in smaller communities, participants are able to monitor each other to ensure that necessary tasks are carried out: free-riding can be minimized, and the interests of the community can be served.[3]

By contrast, if everything is shared in a large collectivist system, then incentives for extra individual effort may be much less than the likely individual rewards. When thousands of people are brought together, and rewards are shared, then there is less incentive to make the extra effort, because the rewards from that additional work would be hugely diluted. Large groups are challenged by the $1/n$ problem, where n is the number of people in a collective that shares its output, and $1/n$ is the likely reward to an individual for every extra increment of his or her effort.[4]

Individual incentives to contribute to overall output are very roughly in proportion to $1/n$. As n increases, the extra effort of any single individual is rewarded less, because the output from extra effort is shared between n people. Small-scale enforcement mechanisms, which rely on trust, reputation, face-to-face contact and knowledge of everyone, cannot be relied upon in much larger groups. As the size of the collective increases, the free-rider problem can be exacerbated. Additional incentive mechanisms are required. In brief, the choice in large-scale societies is between market interactions or pressure by the state, or a combination of both.

My *Wrong Turnings* book gives examples of thinkers that recognized this crucial problem of individual incentives in large-scale economies. One of the earliest was the English Leveller John Lilburne. Lilburne accepted common ownership on a small scale, but only if it was voluntary for all parties involved. He understood that sizeable collectivization would undermine the incentive to work.[5]

---

[3]   Ostrom (1990).

[4]   The problem of incentives in large-scale organizations is also a theme of Olson's (1965) classic book. Erasmus (1977) explored the impact of scale and incentivization in utopian communities. The term '$1/n$ problem' was suggested to me by Bob Rowthorn in 1992.

[5]   See in particular the long 1652 quote from Lilburne in Hodgson (2018, pp. 20–21). The myth that the Levellers were socialists or communists was promoted by Marx and Engels (1976a, p. 461), Brockway (1980) and others. The Soviet editors of Marx and Engels (1976a) admit the error in an endnote on p. 604. See Hodgson (2018, pp. 18–22) for a refutation, citing Leveller texts.

The radical thinker Thomas Paine understood that cooperation and reciprocity could work well on a small scale, but if a larger society relied on trust and commitment alone, then people 'would begin to relax in their duty and attachment to one another'. Paine did not see collectivization of property as the solution, because incentives to contribute would dwindle. Instead he advocated voluntary cooperation between separate private enterprises.[6]

Albert Schäffle was a member of the now-neglected German historical school. He was one of the first economists to criticize big socialism and to reveal some of the severe difficulties in its implementation. In a series of works from 1870, he focused on the difficulties of organizing and planning a collectivist system. He also identified its inbuilt threat to democracy within socialism.[7]

Schäffle explained that with a large number of collectivized workers, some may slacken or shirk, knowing that they will always benefit from their share of the output of many others. How could big socialism overcome these incentive and monitoring problems? Schäffle argued that the only answer was by the imposition of a strong central authority. People would have to be bullied or forced to work.[8]

Market competition is absent or much diminished in a centrally planned economy. Instead, much of the pressure to perform comes from the state: strong state discipline would be necessary to sustain production. Consequently, big socialism means authoritarianism and bureaucracy. This authoritarianism would thwart attempts at egalitarian or democratic distributions of power. As Schäffle wrote: 'collective production without firm hands to govern it, and without immediate individual responsibility, or material interests on the part of the participators' is 'impossible for all time'. Schäffle elaborated: 'Without ... strongly deterrent drawbacks and compensatory obligations for bad and unproductive work, a collective system of production is inconceivable, or at least any system that would even distantly approach in efficiency the

---

6   See Paine (1948, p. 16), Hodgson (2018, ch. 3).

7   Schäffle (1870, 1874, 1885, 1892, 1908). See also Hodgson (2007a, 2010). Note that Schäffle's (1892) book has the title *The Impossibility of Social Democracy*. It was written at a time when *social democracy* was virtually synonymous with Marxist socialism. Schäffle's argument is that the combination of socialism and democracy is impossible. Ironically, Schäffle's own political views would be described as *social democratic* today.

8   Schäffle thus prefigured Olson's (1965, p. 71) argument concerning 'the need for coercion implicit in attempts to provide collective goods to large groups'.

capitalistic system of today. But democratic equality cannot tolerate such strong rewards and punishments.'[9]

Hence socialism administered by democratic means is unfeasible. Schäffle thus posed a choice between big socialism and democracy. We cannot have both.

Twentieth-century evidence strongly supports Schäffle's argument. After experiences in Russia, China, Eastern Europe, Cuba and elsewhere, Schäffle's stance on the threat of big socialism to democracy is highly prescient. In no case has an adequate democracy survived within a centrally planned economy. In this and other vital respects, his analysis has stood the test of time.[10]

The Soviet-type regimes in Russia, China, Eastern Europe and Cuba were not naïve enough to impose equal wages for everyone. There were production bonuses, creating incentives for people to work harder. But such systems suffered from bureaucratic corruption and a lack of transparency. A non-market system lacks meaningful prices, making the evaluation of outputs difficult. Markets can be corrupted as well. But by granting more autonomy to economic agents, markets create the possibility of countervailing politico-economic power, which can hold the corrupt to account.

Within capitalism, the $1/n$ argument concerning incentives also applies to large private corporations. With thousands of employees, how do they incentivize individual effort? Typically, they split up their organizations into divisions and work teams and give performance targets to each unit.

Could similar organizational measures be applied to nationalized industries under socialism? What is lacking under big socialism is market discipline. This missing ingredient is crucial. By contrast, capitalist corporations are subject to some degree of competition and are under constant pressure to innovate and develop new products. Planning within large capitalist corporations is symbiotic with market pressure. Markets provide the firms with benchmark prices against which planning decisions can be made. Competition for sales and finance obliges the corporate planners to seek more efficient solutions.

China's transition from a planned to a market economy shows how the $1/n$ problem was tackled in practice. Shortly after the Communist Revolution of 1949, agriculture in China was organized into large collective farms that shared their overall output among participating

---

[9]   Schäffle (1892, pp. 37, 73).
[10]   Amazingly, Schäffle also predicted the likely survival of a regulated capitalism with democratic political institutions in and beyond the year 2000 (Schäffle, 1892, pp. 416–19).

families. Mao died in 1976, opening up the possibility of reform. In 1978 some peasant farmers decided to withdraw from collective farms and take responsibility for production at the household level, where the household (instead of the collective) received the revenue from its sold output. Individual households had much greater incentives to work harder and to innovate. They overcame the $1/n$ problem.

At first, the Chinese authorities tried to confine the spread of the new 'household responsibility system' to a few provinces. But it was so successful that it spread like wildfire through the entire country. In the early 1980s the Chinese state, under the leadership of Deng Xiaoping endorsed the system and encoded it in law. With those changes, after decades of political and economic turbulence under Mao, China's economic growth began to explode. The nation produced enough food to eliminate starvation. The rural economy created surpluses, allowing workers to shift from farming to industry. As a result, half a billion people were lifted out of extreme poverty.[11]

We now consider two lengthier case studies, to show how attempts to concentrate economic power in the hands of central directing or planning authorities led to erosions of democracy and human rights. The two cases are quite different and about a century apart. But the totalitarian outcomes were similar in important respects.

THE POWER PROBLEM: THE RISE OF DICTATORSHIP IN BOLSHEVIK RUSSIA

In the early 1900s, Russia was a vast, backward country, with little industry. It had very little experience of democracy. Until the February 1917 revolution it was ruled by a repressive Tsarist regime. Writing in the summer of 1917, before the Bolshevik seizure of power, Vladimir Ilyich Lenin proclaimed in his *State and Revolution* that there would be 'an immense expansion of democracy, which for the first time becomes democracy for the poor, democracy for the people, and not democracy for the money-bags'.[12]

On 7 November 1917 the Bolsheviks overthrew the liberal-socialist government of Alexander Kerensky. Within weeks the Bolshevik government started to nationalize the banks, the land and all joint-stock

---

[11]   See Zhou (1996), Ravallion and Chen (2005) and Coase and Wang (2012).

[12]   Lenin (1967, vol. 2, pp. 334–5). See Polan (1984) for a brilliant critique of Lenin's 'democratic' vision of the dictatorship of the proletariat.

companies. On 25 November 1917 it held new elections to the Constituent Assembly (Parliament). The Assembly was convened on 18 January 1918. But no party except for the Bolsheviks and the Left Socialist Revolutionaries supported Lenin's proposal to hand over their power to the Soviets (workers' councils). So, the next day the Bolsheviks dissolved the Assembly, leaving the All-Russian Congress of Soviets as the national governing body.

Lenin declared: 'The working classes learned by experience that the old bourgeois parliamentary system had outlived its purpose and was absolutely incompatible with the aim of achieving socialism'.[13] During 1918, in the midst of a vicious civil war, all parties except the Bolsheviks were banned, and Russia became a one-party state.

Lenin's promise of an 'immense expansion of democracy' evaporated, because there was no possibility of organizing a political force to criticize Bolshevik policy. Without open debate and organized alternatives to the ruling elite, democracy became a sham.

When the exiled Kerensky spoke at a London meeting in 1921, someone in the audience claimed that the Bolsheviks were democrats. Kerensky responded: 'If it is democracy to banish your opponents, to suppress all meetings and newspapers, and to lock up people who disagree with you without trial, by what signs do you ask me to recognise tyranny?'[14]

Hence Soviet Russia became a dictatorship several years before Joseph Stalin came to power. Kerensky's testimony undermines the claim by Leon Trotsky and others that the Russian Revolution 'degenerated' only after Stalin was ascendant. On the contrary, the first roots of its dictatorship lay within Marxism and they were nurtured by Lenin, Trotsky and other Bolsheviks.[15]

Soviet Russia was immediately attacked by counter-revolutionaries and foreign powers, creating an emergency that led to the suspension of political rights and democracy. But the Bolshevik regime was itself illegal. It came to power through a coup d'état without democratic legitimacy. Some of the counter-revolutionary impetus was an attempt to restore legality and political legitimacy and to reverse that coup.

Instead of a democratic mandate, the defenders of the Bolshevik Revolution appealed to the Marxist ideology of class struggle and the historic destiny of the proletariat. Marxists do not see themselves as

---

[13]   Lenin (1967, vol. 2, pp. 525–6).
[14]   Quoted in Clarke (1978, p. 220).
[15]   Trotsky (1937). See Hodgson (2018, chs 5–7) for more on the Marxist roots of dictatorship.

required to support the wishes of the working class. As Marx and Engels wrote: 'It is not a question of what ... the ... proletariat ... *regards* as its aim. It is a question of *what the proletariat is*, and what, in accordance with this *being*, it will historically be compelled to do.' Ultimately, despite rhetoric to the contrary, Marxists decide the destiny of the working class and seek lesser guidance from democracy.[16]

TOTALITARIANISM IN RUSSIA: FROM LENIN TO STALIN

In 1918 Lenin instigated forced labour, wholesale nationalization, food rationing, the abolition of money and markets, and the requisitioning of food from the peasants. These measures were later described as 'war communism'. Scholarly admirers of the Soviet Union, such as Sidney and Beatrice Webb, E.H. Carr and Maurice Dobb, argued that these were temporary emergency measures, forced on the young Soviet regime by the exigencies of foreign invasion and civil war.[17]

On the contrary, the primary ambition behind these policies was to build full socialism. When this failed disastrously, and the Bolsheviks were obliged to change their economic policy, the retrospective story of 'war communism' as a temporary measure was invented to protect the infallibility of the Party and its leadership.

When Lenin announced the conscription of labour in January 1918, it was justified not by war but for 'the purpose of abolishing the parasitic sections of society', namely the capitalists, landowners and aristocrats. In May 1918, a few weeks after the Brest-Litovsk treaty of March 1918 between Germany and the Bolshevik regime, Lenin declared that the fragile peace gave 'an opportunity to concentrate ... on the most important and most difficult aspect of the socialist revolution' namely the 'setting up ... planned production and distribution of goods required for the existence of tens of millions of people'.[18]

---

[16]   See Marx and Engels (1975b, p. 37) and Marx and Engels (1976a, p. 88).

[17]   Webb and Webb (1935, vol. 1, p. 544), Dobb (1955), Carr (1964).

[18]   Lenin (1967, vol. 2, pp. 520, 645–6). Leftist critics accused Lenin of setting up 'state capitalism', that is, state control of enterprises, which in their view was not socialism. To which Lenin (1967, vol. 2, pp. 693 ff.) replied in May 1918 that 'state capitalism would be a *step forward*'. He repeated in June 1921: 'State capitalism would be a huge step forward' and then added 'this would be a huge success and a sure guarantee that within a year socialism would have gained a permanently firm hold' (Lenin, 1967, vol. 3, pp. 583–4 ff.). In 1922 Lenin (1967, vol. 3, pp. 683 ff., 715 ff., p. 734) saw 'state capitalism' as a transitional stage under a 'proletarian state' toward socialism 'in a few years'.

Victor Serge joined the Bolsheviks in 1919 and wrote later: 'The social system in these years was later called "War Communism". At the time it was called simply "Communism", and anyone who, like myself, went so far as to consider it purely temporary was looked upon with disdain.' Nikolai Bukharin was one of the leaders of the Bolshevik Revolution. He wrote in 1924: 'We conceived War Communism as the universal, so to say "normal" form of the economic policy of the victorious proletariat and not as being related to the war'. In other words, measures such as wholesale nationalization and the abolition of money and markets were required by Marxist dogma, not by the emergency of war. As the historian Richard Pipes put it: 'War Communism as a whole was not a "temporary measure" but an ambitious ... attempt to introduce full-blown communism.'[19]

By the abolition of money, markets and private ownership, the policy of War Communism placed absolute political and economic power in the hands of the state. The state could no longer use market incentives or prices to influence people: its only remaining means of persuasion were ideology, propaganda, and – if they failed – physical force. By 1921, as a combined result of civil war and the failure of totalitarian centralized planning, the economy was in a state of collapse and the people were starving. Overall output was about a third of 1913 levels, and heavy industry produced one-fifth of what it had done in 1913. A severe drought contributed to a famine that led to between 3 and 10 million deaths. Some peasants, workers, soldiers and sailors rebelled against the Bolsheviks.[20]

Recognizing the severe danger to the survival of his regime, in 1921 Lenin announced a 'retreat' in economic policy. As he explained in 1922 to the Fourth Congress of the Communist International, back in 1918 their 'economic offensive ... had run too far ahead ... we had not provided ourselves with adequate resources ... and the direct transition to purely socialist forms ... was beyond our available strength'. Rather than identifying the fatal flaws of a centrally planned system under complete state ownership, Lenin blamed economic deprivation for the failure. The most important economic lessons were not learned.[21]

With no feasible alternative, from 1921 the Bolsheviks allowed an extension of markets and private enterprise, known as the New Economic

---

[19]   Serge (1963, p. 115), Bukharin (1967, p. 178), Pipes (1990, pp. 671–2). See also M. Polanyi (1948, 1957, 1997, pp. 166–7), Roberts (1971), Remington (1984), Malle (1985), Boettke (1988).
[20]   Figes (2014).
[21]   Lenin (1967, vol. 3, pp. 583 ff., 715 ff.).

Policy (NEP). Requisitioning of food was ended, and farmers were allowed to sell their produce on markets. Individuals were allowed to own and operate small enterprises in the pursuit of profit, while the state continued to control finance and large industries. Central state control of the economy was relaxed, and publicly owned enterprises were allowed some autonomy to seek profits on new markets. The NEP was a success and economic output began to grow substantially.[22]

Lenin died in 1924. By 1927, Stalin had established himself as supreme leader. In 1928, in a dramatic shift in economic strategy, Stalin ended the NEP and its reliance on markets and private enterprise. Stalin perceived an eventual military threat from the West and aimed to build up heavy industry. He argued that after a period of recovery the USSR was ready for another bold leap toward socialism.[23]

The regime embarked on a rapid process of mass collectivization of agriculture, with five-year plans for the whole economy. Many construction projects involved forced labour. Hundreds of thousands of rich peasants and former entrepreneurs were imprisoned, exiled or killed.

To intimidate his opponents and consolidate his power, Stalin began a series of show trials, in which the defendants were accused of sabotage or being foreign agents. In the 1930s his reign of terror intensified. His forced famines and purges led to millions of deaths.

Stalin's deliberate concentration of economic power in the hands of the state gave him both the means and the impetus to implement policies of terror and repression. It is possible that someone else would have been less ruthless and less cruel. But kind, gentle or tolerant people are unlikely to climb to the top in revolutionary parties that have seized power illegally by force.

Even before Stalin seized absolute power, the Soviet regime had become even more punitive and oppressive than its Tsarist predecessor. In the eighty years under Tsarism from 1826 to 1905, executions averaged 17 a year. But about 11 000 were executed in the aftermath of the failed 1905 Revolution. By comparison, the Soviet secret police (Cheka) killed an average of about 28 000 people a year from 1917 to 1922, many without judicial proceedings. It is estimated that Stalin was

---

[22] Service (1997, pp. 124–5). To a degree, the NEP inspired Deng Xiaoping's post-1978 reforms in China: 'In 1985, he openly acknowledged that "perhaps" the most correct model of socialism was the New Economic Policy of the USSR' (Pantsov and Levine, 2015, p. 373).

[23] Stalin (1954).

responsible for about 15 million deaths, with between a third and a half of them dying from famine.[24]

BOLSHEVIK ENDS REQUIRE DICTATORIAL MEANS

Can we support Bolshevik ends but criticize their means? After a visit to Russia in 1920, during which he met Lenin, Bertrand Russell expressed his full support for their communist goals. But he strongly criticized their methods, including their repressive police state and their abolition of meaningful democracy.[25]

Russell understood that violent revolutionary struggles that crush parliaments throw up ruthless leaders who have little respect for democ-racy. He argued that in established democracies such as Britain and the US the transition to socialism must depend on winning over the majority of the people in the ballot box.

But Russell should have gone further with his critique. The statist economic goal of widespread nationalization dissolves the economic pluralism upon which political openness and democracy depend for support. Russell did not appreciate that the state ownership of much of industry creates the conditions for state control of political life, the erosion of civil society and the state suppression of dissent.

Russell thought that workers given 'self-government' in industry could counterbalance central power. But he did not explain how this could be achieved in an economy where all industry is owned by the state. He did not understand that adequate self-government in industry is impossible without legally independent enterprises, trading their prod-ucts on markets.

Later, writing in 1933 and reflecting to the rise of Nazism, Russell wrote: 'The fundamental cause of the trouble is that in the modern world the stupid are cocksure while the intelligent are full of doubt.' Russell admitted in the same paragraph that intelligent people can also some-times be 'just as sure of themselves'. But he failed to acknowledge that intelligent socialists, who are driven by a sense of historical destiny and

---

[24] Dziak (1988, pp. 173 ff.), Rummel (1994), Courtois et al. (1999), Ryan (2012), Conquest (2007). All these estimates are disputed, to some degree. Ryan's figure of 28 000 deaths a year under the Cheka is one of the more conservative.

[25] Russell (1920). George Orwell developed a similar stance in the 1930s, by retaining socialist ideals but distancing himself from the Soviet Union. Despite other great insights, he too did not fully understand how state-collectivist goals, perceived historical destiny and the belief in 'obvious' rational solutions can fuel fanaticism and intolerance, and thereby destroy democracy.

who believe in the 'obvious' rationality of the socialist order, can also be 'sure of themselves' to the point of intolerance.[26]

Socialists with strong and seemingly righteous convictions do not tend to acknowledge complexities or to listen to those that question their vision. Because they believe that socialism is obvious, they see defenders of the existing system as motivated not by alternative principles or priorities, but by their own self-serving interest in the status quo. The roots of dictatorial intolerance lie here. Fanaticism is not confined to insurrectionary socialists, communists or fascists. It is found among some of those claiming to be 'democratic socialists' in major leftist organizations today.

THE DEMOCRATIC SOCIALIST REVOLUTION IN VENEZUELA

They were almost a century apart: the Bolshevik Revolution and the installation of a Marxist regime in Venezuela differ radically in their terms of their inception and development. But some of the key lessons are very similar.

After 1958, during a period when much of Latin America suffered under dictatorships, Venezuela had a series of democratic governments. A country rich in oil, Venezuela still endured inequality and deprivation. The charismatic Hugo Chávez led a failed army coup in 1992 against an unpopular administration. Venezuela's experiment in radical socialism began in 1998 when Chávez was elected as President.

The Bolshevik experience demonstrates that violent revolutions require and promote ruthless and undemocratic leaders. Venezuela has been different. It shows what happens when a democratic revolution attempts to concentrate political power to extend its ownership and control of the economy, despite the commendable aim of helping the poor. The ambition of building socialism was used to justify concentrated executive power. Opposition was hobbled. Political checks and balances were neutralized or removed.

All this happened before Venezuela established a socialist economy. The private sector is still large, albeit distressed by rampant corruption and excessive government controls. Venezuela shows how centralized political and economic powers can corrupt the executive and create the

---

[26]   Russell (1998, p. 28).

conditions for tyranny, even in countries with a history of democracy, and even in the good causes of reducing inequality and eradicating poverty.

During the 1998 presidential election, Chávez called for an end to privatization of state assets, a rise in the minimum wage, a redistribution of income, constitutional reform and an end to corruption. He also sought greater independence from the dictates of global capitalism and in particular from the US. But this strategy had an obvious weakness – the Chavismo government depended on world-market revenues from Venezuela's large oil industry to finance its anti-poverty and development programmes.

Chávez used populist mobilization and repeated plebiscites. He was victorious in four presidential elections and he won four out of five referendums. He called four of these five referendums himself: all these four increased presidential powers or terms of office. Through these ballots, Chávez mobilized popular support to undermine democratic checks and balances and to increase executive power. He used the additional powers granted by these mandates to nationalize industries and to extend state control over the economy.[27]

Chávez faced a large but splintered opposition. On the one hand, there was the former political establishment, private business owners and the church. On the other hand, there were large numbers of trade unionists, liberals and leftists who were concerned about growing dictatorial powers and the erosion of human rights. Yet the regime and its supporters often lumped all these opposition groups together, describing them all as 'fascists' or 'imperialist agents'.

A national referendum was held in April 1999. The question was whether to create an elected assembly to draw up a new constitution. This process for changing the constitution was itself unconstitutional, because the standing constitution, originally enacted in 1961, had its own mechanisms to allow for modifications or replacement. This created a fateful precedent for subsequent repeated disregard of constitutional procedures and restraints.[28]

---

[27] Reuters (2012). Grandin (2013) wrote that 'Chávez has submitted himself and his agenda to fourteen national votes, winning thirteen of them by large margins'. This ignores the fact that four of these ballot victories were referendums designed to increase presidential powers. Clement Attlee famously remarked in 1945 that the referendum 'has only too often been the instrument of Nazism and Fascism' (quoted in Bogdanor, 1981, p. 35). On 11 April 1972 the leading Labour MP Roy Jenkins published a letter in *The Times* reminding people of Attlee's warning that the referendum 'is a splendid weapon for demagogues and dictators'.

[28] Brewer-Carías (2001, 2017).

While 54 per cent of the eligible electorate did not vote, 72 per cent of those voting were in favour of the referendum proposal. In July 1999 elections were held to choose delegates to the new assembly. Under an election system drawn up by the government, Chávez's slate of candidates received 52 per cent of the vote but won 95 per cent of the seats due to the non-proportional electoral system.

In August 1999 the new assembly moved to restructure the nation's judiciary and gave itself the power to fire judges. Eventually the Supreme Court was also dissolved, and new judges were appointed that were supporters of Chávez. This removed an important check on the president's growing power.

The new constitution was published in November 1999. It announced the installation of 'social human rights' to employment, housing and healthcare. The presidency and the executive branch of government were given more power, including the right to dissolve the new National Assembly. This became a unicameral body, without many of its former powers. State censorship was made easier. Chávez removed more political checks and balances, seeing them as obstacles to socialist revolution.

Elections for the new National Assembly were held in July 2000. Chávez himself stood for re-election. His supporters won two-thirds of the seats and Chávez was re-elected as president with 60 per cent of the votes. After these elections the National Assembly granted the President the right to rule by decree for one year. Chávez enacted a land tax, land reform and other measures. He expanded access to food, housing, healthcare and education, especially for the poor. Venezuela became Cuba's largest trading partner.[29]

When he came to power, Chávez encouraged the formation of worker-owned cooperatives and gave them government subsidies. Over 100 000 of these were created or converted from former enterprises that were eager to receive the state handouts. In 2005 about 16 per cent of the working population were in cooperatives. But a 2006 census showed that about half of the cooperatives were either functioning improperly or had been fraudulently created to gain access to public funds.[30]

The government encouraged citizens to form thousands of 'Communal Councils'. These had control of government funds in their local area: their decisions were binding on local government officials. In 2007 about 30 per cent of local state funds were directly controlled by Communal

[29] Nelson (2009).
[30] Wilpert (2007, pp. 77–8).

Councils. Chávez, following Castro's example, created groups of loyal supporters in communities who received military training.

Unfortunately for the regime, global oil prices were low in the first four years of Chávez's tenure. The Venezuelan economy plunged into recession and unemployment rose to 20 per cent. There was a rise in inflation and a massive flight of capital abroad. The early anti-poverty programmes faltered, with revelations of corruption among military officers.[31]

Opposition grew to Chávez's centralization of political power. Mothers protested against the use of Cuban textbooks in schools. Leftist organizations became critical. Several labour unions – over which Chávez had tried to imposed controls – joined the dissenting voices. In December 2001 a general strike was called: its leaders demanded that Chávez repeal the laws that he had imposed by decree.

In early 2002 there was a series of large protest marches, met by government sympathizers in their counter demonstrations. In April fighting and gunfire erupted, with fatalities on both sides. A group of dissident military officers seized power. But their leader, Pedro Carmona Estanga, handled things badly and alienated his own supporters. Soldiers loyal to Chávez retook the Presidential Palace and freed him from captivity. Chávez resumed his presidency. It is possible that the attempted coup had US support, but this is not proven.[32]

In 2003 Chávez launched a number of new economic programmes, aiming to end illiteracy, improve education and help indigenous peoples. Initially the Chávez regime was successful in reducing extreme poverty. With greater oil revenues due to higher global prices, there was economic growth from 2004 to 2008. But this was not to endure.

THE SLIDE TOWARD DICTATORSHIP IN VENEZUELA

Especially after the attempted coup in 2002, Chávez sought more powers to protect the 'socialist revolution' against its enemies. Since 2004, 'defamation' of the government, including 'disrespect for the authorities', has been a criminal offence.[33] In 2007 the government refused to renew the licence of the nation's most popular television station, alleging that it was involved in the 2002 coup. This led to further large protests against censorship and restrictions on freedom of speech. In early 2009 Chávez

---

[31] Nelson (2009).
[32] Vulliamy (2002).
[33] Human Rights Watch (2005).

won a referendum to eliminate term limits, allowing him to run for re-election for an indefinite period.

By 2004 Chávez had concentrated massive political power in his hands, while undermining civil liberties, press freedom and constitutional safeguards. Yet in that year a number of foreign intellectuals and politicians signed a 'manifesto' declaring that they would vote for Chávez if they were Venezuelans. The signatories included Tariq Ali, Perry Anderson, Tony Benn, George Galloway, Eric Hobsbawm, Ken Livingstone, Naomi Klein, Ken Loach, John Pilger and Harold Pinter.[34]

In 2006 Chávez announced plans for a more radical turn towards socialism. The National Assembly passed enabling legislation in 2007, allowing Chávez to nationalize more industries, and granting him some powers to rule by decree. The state increased its holdings in the oil and gas industry. Some farms and agro-businesses were nationalized. Several banks were taken over. A major glass container firm and the cement sector were nationalized.

In 2009 the Inter-American Commission on Human Rights (IACHR) published a report on human rights in Venezuela under Chávez. It recognized Venezuela's achievements, including the eradication of illiteracy, the initial reduction of poverty, and the increase in access to basic services such as healthcare. But it found that the power of the state was being used to intimidate or punish people on account of their political opinions. There were also serious shortcomings with respect to union rights as well the rights of indigenous peoples to their lands.

The IACHR report noted political intolerance, the incapacity of other branches of the state to scrutinize executive constraints on freedom of expression and peaceful protest, and a prevailing impunity affecting cases of human rights violations. It concluded that these factors were weakening the rule of law and democracy. Chávez dismissed the report as 'garbage'.[35]

In 2010 Chávez announced an 'economic war on the bourgeois owners' of supermarkets, mills, rice plants and food distribution companies. Some of these were nationalized. This was to have an enduring adverse effect on food supplies.[36]

By 2010 the economy had stalled and serious shortages of food and medicine had emerged. Poverty reached its highest levels in decades. Chávez did not reduce Venezuela's reliance on oil. He concentrated on redistributing existing resources rather than developing and diversifying

---

[34]   Ali et al. (2004).
[35]   Inter-American Commission on Human Rights (2009).
[36]   McElroy (2010).

the economy. He antagonized private investors. Corruption in business was encouraged by bureaucratic failure. The Venezuelan government became one of the most corrupt in the world.

Chávez died of cancer in 2013. One commentator declared that he left behind 'the most democratic country in the Western Hemisphere'.[37] Chávez's experiments with new grassroots social movements have impressed many observers. But these were partly designed to retain popular support for the concentration of political power in the hands of the executive. Although he was re-elected several times and he retained substantial popular support, Chávez prepared the politico-economic conditions for dictatorship. Just as sympathizers falsely declared that the Russian Bolshevik regime was democratic under Lenin, supporters of Chávez were blind to his consolidation of dictatorial power.

Chávez was replaced as President by Nicolás Maduro. The rate of inflation soared skywards, and economic output dropped dramatically. In 2015 and 2016, blaming internal 'fascists' and US intervention for the severe shortages, President Maduro declared two states of emergency. These gave him more powers to intervene in the economy. Arbitrary detentions of dissidents became more common.

By 2015, over 1200 private companies had been nationalized. Productivity did not increase. On the contrary, mis-management and corruption helped to reduce levels of production, including of food, medicine and even oil. The regimes of Chávez and Maduro wasted and misspent much of the money made in the oil boom, while over-extending the powers of their corrupt governments. The private sector was hobbled. The ultimate outcome of Venezuela's experiment with populist socialism has been authoritarianism, destitution and starvation.

In elections in late 2015, after 17 years of Chavismo policies, the opposition coalition won 112 seats in the 167-seat National Assembly, while the pro-government party retained 55 seats. Every single law approved since then by the National Assembly has been blocked by the Maduro government, or by the Chavismo appointees in the Supreme Court. The National Assembly was later dissolved.[38]

The governments of Chávez and Maduro mistrusted liberal, pluralist institutions. With effective checks and balances removed, Venezuela lurched toward dictatorship. Press freedom became highly limited and journalists and opposition leaders were jailed. A 2016 report by Human Rights Watch accumulated more evidence of abuses, including of torture

---

[37] Grandin (2013).
[38] Trombetta (2017).

and arbitrary imprisonment: 'Under the leadership of President Hugo
Chávez and now President Nicolás Maduro, the accumulation of power in
the executive branch and erosion of human rights guarantees have
enabled the government to intimidate, censor, and prosecute its critics.'[39]

Opposition and open debate were severely impaired by censorship and
arbitrary arrests. One human rights group claimed that over 11 000
people were detained from 2014 to 2017 for political reasons. Maduro
banned leading candidates from opposition parties from the 2018 presidential election.[40] Maduro won, in elections with a low turnout that were
widely boycotted.

A 2018 report by the Organization of American States found evidence
of state murders of citizens attending protests, of 8292 extrajudicial
executions since 2015, of more than 12 000 people arbitrarily detained,
imprisoned or subject to severe deprivation of physical liberty since
2013, of more than 1300 political prisoners, and of widespread and
systematic oppression.[41]

Supporters of Chávez and Maduro blame the hostility of the US for
Venezuela's economic distress, just as it was blamed for economic
problems in Cuba after its 1959 revolution. Belligerence from the West
does not help, but Chavismo Venezuela sold oil to the US and several
other countries. Chavismo Venezuela bought arms and military equipment from the UK, as well as from Russia and China. The first US
sanctions against Venezuela were in 2014, but these were targeted at
officials involved in the mistreatment of protestors. Economic sanctions
against the country as a whole did not begin until 2017.

Venezuelan GDP per capita has declined since 2008 and it shows little
sign of recovery. By 2018 there was hyper-inflation of around a million
per cent per annum, and about 3 million Venezuelans – about 10 per cent
of the population – had emigrated. One poll indicated that over half of
those still in the country desired to leave.[42]

A major cause of economic stagnation in Cuba and Venezuela has been
the unchecked concentration of excessive political, legal and economic
power in the hands of their overbearing and corrupt states. Venezuela has
enough land and resources to feed its own people. Yet government
policies, including expropriations of agro-businesses, have led to lower
food production and to famine.[43]

[39]   Human Rights Watch (2016).
[40]   Wyss (2017), *The Independent* (2017).
[41]   Organization of American States (2018).
[42]   *El Nacional* (2016), Forero (2018).
[43]   Wilson (2016).

Some still see Venezuela as a beacon of socialism. Jeremy Corbyn, the leader of the UK Labour Party, attended a 2013 vigil following the death of Chávez, hailing him as an 'inspiration to all of us fighting back against austerity and neo-liberal economics in Europe'. As late as 2015, when Venezuela was in ever-deepening crisis and human rights violations were abundant, Corbyn's enthusiasm for the regime was undiminished. He remarked: 'we celebrate, and it is a cause for celebration, the achievements of Venezuela, in jobs, in housing, in health, in education, but above all its role in the whole world ... we recognise what they have achieved.'[44]

Others have claimed that the problem with Venezuela was not too much socialism but too little.[45] They argued that the Venezuelan economy had been sabotaged by the bourgeoisie: if the remaining owners of private enterprises were expropriated then this problem would be solved. But this assumes that it is possible to run a modern developed economy without a private sector, while preserving democracy and protecting human rights. History teaches otherwise.

After two hundred years of experimentation, socialists should stop blaming their failures on their opponents. The foremost problem is that big socialist proposals are unworkable, at least in humane terms: they lead to despotism. Experiment after experiment has confirmed this. The dangers are there to see, for those who are willing to look. As one disillusioned enthusiast for the Chavismo regime put it in 2017: 'blindness is no longer an option'.[46]

Chavismo Venezuela has demonstrated to a new generation, but again at huge human cost, that big socialism requires politico-economic conditions that inevitably undermine human rights and encourage dictatorship. In the Venezuelan case these deleterious forces have been unleashed while most economic resources are still in private hands. The resolute attempt to build big socialism was enough to instigate disaster. It is again confirmed that the outcome of big socialism is dictatorship. There are other examples, from Russia and China to Cuba. Unfortunately, there is no exception.

---

[44]   Cunliffe (2015), Elgot and Asthana (2017).
[45]   Hetland (2016), Whitney (2016), Ciccariello-Maher (2017).
[46]   Cusack (2017).

DEMOCRACY AND HUMAN RIGHTS REQUIRE COUNTERVAILING ECONOMIC POWER

Impersonal relations occur in bureaucracies as well as in markets. At their worst, systems of state planning can be cesspits of human alienation and corruption, governed by disillusioned bureaucrats and dishonest state officials. Such tendencies appear in over-centralized systems with little countervailing authority.

Corruption is endemic to such systems, partly because to get anything done, people are obliged to break bureaucratic rules. Central planning is a very blunt and slow instrument, hence black markets grow up to remedy its delays and omissions. This creates a climate of illegality that has to be partly tolerated by the regime, because it provides an essential means to circumvent the unreliable and unavoidably overloaded bureaucracy. Economic illegality and corruption are inevitable consequences of the attempt to replace most commodity markets by a comprehensive system of economic planning.[47]

Big socialism undermines the rule of law in additional ways. If one political party becomes all-powerful, then the legislature becomes its pawn. The judiciary loses its capacity to hold the rulers to account. This happened after a few months in Soviet Russia and after a few years in Venezuela. In both cases the law became a cynical political instrument of a ruling caste, rather than a potential safeguard of human rights. The very notion of the rule of law was undermined.[48]

These considerations undermine an argument in favour of socialism by the eminent mainstream economist (and Nobel Laureate) Kenneth Arrow. He recognized that the 'worse problem was the possibility that socialism, by concentrating control of the economy in the state apparatus, facilitated authoritarianism or even made it inevitable'. But he then attempted to brush this aside: 'If the democratic legal tradition is strong, there are many sources of power in a modern state.' But this dubiously assumes that democracy and the rule of law can survive the state's accumulation of political and economic power. The examples of the USSR, China, North Korea, Cuba and Venezuela show otherwise. Experience shows that any separation of powers within socialist bureaucracies is always vulnerable to attempts to regain power by the centre. Contrary to Arrow, socialism cannot 'easily offer as much pluralism as capitalism' and it is not the case that 'the viability of freedom and democracy' are 'quite

---

[47] Nove (1983), Litwack (1991).
[48] Synopwich (1990), Hodgson (2018, pp. 108–11).

independent of the economic system'. Political pluralism cannot survive without economic pluralism and countervailing economic power.[49]

But obviously, as Arrow rightly pointed out, private enterprise does not guarantee democracy or the rule of law. Numerous dictatorships have been built upon market economies. Fascist regimes have retained much private enterprise. But while a large private sector is *insufficient* on its own to sustain democracy, the evidence clearly suggests that it is *necessary*. There is no case in history of a state-run economy that has remained democratic or that has adequately protected human rights.

A large body of literature exists on the socio-economic preconditions of a democratic polity. Some evidence suggests that economic development is a necessary condition for democratization. But it does not seem to be a sufficient condition: this factor alone cannot explain the widely different degrees of democratization that are found at similar levels of development. The spread of democratic ideas, the social culture and the stances of political leaders are also believed to be important.[50]

Several authors emphasize the balance of forces between competing interest groups and the degree of dispersed authority. Evidence and analysis suggest that effective countervailing power is essential to keep the modern state in check and to provide a secure foundation for democracy. Such power emanates from independent judiciaries, trade unions, employer associations, consumer associations or lobby groups.[51]

Accordingly, big socialism undermines democracy by concentrating too much political and economic power in the hands of the state. Countervailing interest groups, with their own access to resources and an ability to organize to check or influence the state, are necessary to prevent democratic abuses and over-centralization.

Additional research has added an interesting twist to the tale. At least two studies have found that the conditions most favourable to democracy are not when the Freedom House index of economic freedom is maximized. By definition, this index is inversely related to the degree of state intervention. But studies found that the optimal conditions for democracy were found in capitalist mixed economies. 'The optimal democratic state has a balance between capitalism and governmental concern for social welfare.'[52]

---

[49] Arrow (1978, pp. 476, 479–80).
[50] Lipset (1959). Vanhanen (1997) is a useful summary of the literature. See also Acemoglu et al. (2008).
[51] Galbraith (1952, 1969), Moore (1966), Whistler (1991), North et al. (2009) and Hodgson (2015a, 2018).
[52] The quote is from Burkhart (2000, p. 237). See also Brunk et al. (1987).

Several studies show a strong correlation between democracy and human rights. One found that countries with a higher level of well-being generally had fewer violations of human rights. Another confirmed a relationship between regimes with strong state control and human rights abuses.[53]

There are practical and moral limits to democracy itself. Enlightenment thinkers argued that rights are inalienable. Consequently, democracy should not undermine the rights of minorities or the human rights of the population at large. Democracies are fallible, and rights must be protected. Courts must have the power to prevent democratic decisions countering human rights. For democracy to work well, all powerful parties and interest groups must recognize its limits. It requires checks and balances based on countervailing politico-economic power.

DEMOCRATIC BIG SOCIALISM IS NOT FEASIBLE

Plentiful evidence shows that democracy is endangered by large-scale state control of the economy. But many still believe that democratic big socialism is possible. The vision of a big socialism pervaded by democratic decision-making is persistent. Fabian socialists, like Cole and the Webbs, proposed a collectivized economy run by a hierarchy of democratic councils and committees. The idea is still persistent today, often under the vague term *democratic socialism*.[54] But it has never been tried in practice. For good reasons it will never work.

Alec Nove – who was an expert on the Soviet economy – critiqued the proposal of a 'socialist democratic planning system which could dispense simultaneously with market, bureaucracy and hierarchy, based on some undefined form of mass democracy'. To him this was entirely implausible:

> Those who hold this view are usually quite unaware of the complexities of the modern industrial structure, with its innumerable complementarities and interdependencies. ... Democratic procedures are indeed essential, but these cannot be meaningfully applied to the multi-millions of micro-economic

---

[53]   Mitchell and McCormick (1988), Poe and Tate (1994).

[54]   See, for example, Hahnel (2005) and Honneth (2017). The former gives more detail than the latter, but both are vague about communication structures and on how vast amounts of information are to be handled. Honneth argued that this democratic system should satisfy everyone's needs. But needs cannot readily be discerned by democratic vote – it requires an elite of experts. Democracy cannot tell us how much vitamin C is needed for our health or how our cancer is to be cured.

decisions: an elected assembly can vote on broad priorities ... but hardly on whether three tons of constructional steel should be allocated to this or that building site, or that production of red dyestuffs should be increased by 3%.[55]

The complexity and scale of modern society create insurmountable practical problems for hyper-democracy. Making decisions and managing human interactions is immensely more complex than in early systems or in smaller organizations. There has to be some organized devolution of responsibilities to those with the specialist knowledge or skills. As Nove pointed out:

> If thousands, even millions, of interconnected and interdependent decisions must be taken, to ensure production and delivery of the items which society needs – and this must be preceded by some operationally meaningful set of decisions about what is needed – elaborate administrative machinery is required to ensure the necessary responsibilities and co-ordination.[56]

Max Weber saw bureaucracy as unavoidable in large-scale organizations and politico-economic systems. The general need for bureaucratic structures and processes is not obviated by higher levels of education or improved means of communication. These are likely to increase information inputs and to enlarge rather than diminish the need for bureaucratic regulation.[57]

Worker cooperatives are a workable alternative to capitalist corporations. But even here, only a tiny proportion of decisions can be delegated to ballots or mass meetings. The complex processes and technologies of production have to be broken up into manageable units. The advice of experts has to be relied upon.

As work becomes more complex and knowledge-intensive, even more decision-making has to be devolved. Much work today involves processing information and making judgements, even at lower management levels. Think how many assessments and decisions are made at work each day. It would be impossible to be 'democratic' and put them all to the vote.[58]

Greater industrial democracy, with worker participation in some workplace choices, can improve productivity and make work more enjoyable.

---

[55] Nove (1980, p. 7).

[56] Nove (1983, p. 34).

[57] Weber (1968, pp. 971 ff.). This argument suggests that the Internet is not the solution to the problem. It may provide a limited and useful means of increasing democratic involvement, but it cannot ensure that the whole system is subject to effective popular decision-making.

[58] Zuboff (1988).

But it is impractical to have votes on more than a tiny fraction of the important decisions that have to take place in any large, complex economy. Everyone's participation in every major question that concerned them would be a crushing burden of endless decision-making on every citizen. It would guarantee economic paralysis.[59]

Supporters of an imaginary, ultra-democratic society, where individuals make decisions throughout industry as well as the polity, fail to consider the problems of relevant knowledge and the sheer number of meetings and decisions that would be involved. That is why, contrary to the claims of many socialist ultra-democrats, private ownership and control are necessary to a large degree, so that producers and consumers can make decisions through contracts and markets, unencumbered by local or national committees and their inevitable bureaucracies.

Robert Michels was a student of Max Weber. He argued persuasively that full democratic control was impossible in large-scale, complex organizations. For individuals to coordinate and act together, sizeable organizations need leaders, who then delegate administrative tasks within complex bureaucracies. Leaders and bureaucrats manage information flows between actors inside the organization. Workers develop specialist skills: they acquire expertise and knowledge that are peculiar to their roles. People cannot become specialists in more than a few areas or take account of every piece of information in the organization. Some degree of oligarchic coordination is required in large, complex organizations.

Because of localized knowledge, specialisms, complexities, and massive amounts of information, a direct democracy, where everyone votes on everything, is not viable. It is impossible to involve everyone in every significant decision. Michels argued in detail that 'the principal cause of oligarchy in the democratic parties is to be found in the technical indispensability of leadership'.[60]

In principle, big socialist proposals for comprehensive central planning dramatically curtail the possibilities for local autonomy, democratic or otherwise. As Maurice Dobb candidly admitted: 'Either planning means overriding the autonomy of separate decisions or apparently it means nothing at all.'[61]

Whatever their other limitations, markets do not require majority agreement before a decision can be made to produce or distribute a good

---

[59] For the benefits of worker participation on productivity see, for example, Bonin et al. (1993), Poole and Whitfield (1994), Doucouliagos (1995), Hubbick (2001) and Robinson and Zhang (2005).

[60] See Michels (1915, p. 400).

[61] Dobb (1940, p. 276), Gray (1998, p. 137).

or service. Private property and contracts permit zones of partial autonomy within an interrelated system; agents may reach decisions through negotiated contracts with others.

Routinely adding the word *democratic* to *planning* or to *socialism* does not overcome any of these problems. The power problem within big socialism is always there. Democratic sentiment and practice cannot endure within such a prized monopoly of massive political and economic power.

This certainly does not mean that capitalism is without problems. But a wider distribution of power and ownership – which is feasible under capitalism but not under big socialism – makes possible the development of countervailing authority, which is essential to keep such abuses in check and to help defend the legal system from political manipulation. These countervailing mechanisms are much less effective when most property and economic power is concentrated in the hands of the state.

Specialization and hierarchy are necessary to deal with complexity in any complex, large-scale society. All hierarchies contain the seeds of oligarchy. Unless this oligarchy is checked by enforceable rights and countervailing powers, dictatorship is the likely outcome.

Despite experiences in Russia, China, North Korea, Cuba, Venezuela and elsewhere, there is a dwindling fantasy that classical socialism and meaningful democracy are compatible. This is an irresponsible delusion. It is countered by the analysis of the problem of power and by the experience of history itself.

THE IMMUNOLOGY OF BIG SOCIALISM

Socialism promises a better society. There is also a belief that socialism is the direction of history and the destiny of humankind: socialism is the next stage in human development and only reactionary, self-serving, beneficiaries of the existing system will resist it. Through such arguments, socialism has captured and retained much of the moral high ground, despite the disasters of full-blooded socialism in practice.

We can understand how the promise of socialism – of a better, more caring and more equal society – takes such a hold on people. Once it is there, it reframes perceptions radically. Awkward facts are downgraded or explained away, while positives are accentuated. A powerful immune system develops to deal with challenges from critics.

The socialist immune system is powerful because it compares an ideal socialism of the imagination, where people truly care for one another, with the grubby and exploitative reality of capitalism, as we find it in the

real world. When the defects of actually existing socialism are acknowledged, then they are treated as temporary or accidental faults, due to
hostile outside forces or flawed leaders. If the faults are too grave, then
the defective system is no longer described as socialist. We return to the
starting point, comparing idealized socialism with existing, always-
defective capitalism. With due goodwill, it is claimed, socialism will
work better next time.[62]

Hence the ongoing tragedy in Venezuela is explained away. It is the
result, not of the unavoidable politico-economic dynamics of big socialism, but of the over-reliance on oil or of the intervention and hostility of
Western powers. Market forces have conspired against favourable
exchange rates or oil prices, causing a crash in the economy that is
nothing to do with the state's grasp of the economy by the throat.

In fact, global oil prices increased dramatically from 2004 and they
peaked in 2012. Since then they have dropped, but they have still
remained above 2004 levels. Venezuela's distress cannot be blamed on
global oil markets. After all, other oil-producing countries, including
Russia and Nigeria with their highly imperfect institutions and regimes,
have not suffered the dramatic economic collapse experienced in socialist
Venezuela.

Explanations by socialists of the failure of socialism are diverse, and
sometimes bizarre. For Yanis Varoufakis, an influential Greek academic
and politician, the problem is that the Marxist texts were too potent. As a
result, they attracted devious opportunists who rode the Marxist rhetoric
for 'their own advantage. With it, they might abuse other comrades, build
their own power base, gain positions of influence, bed impressionable
students, take control of the politburo and imprison anyone who resists
them.' The problem, it seems, was that Marx and Engels were too
powerful with their prose. If only they had written more turgid texts –
then millions would have been saved from the famines and the Gulags.[63]

Seriously, the greater problem is not the power of the language, but
what it says and what it empowers and enables. Marxism hallows the
historical destiny of a rational order, where socialism is a seemingly
obvious solution to the ills of the world. It will be defied only by the rich
and their allies, whose resistance must be crushed.

Marx and Engels advocated a complete concentration of political and
economic power in the hands of the state, which always requires and
enables the very kind of people that Varoufakis warns against. Whether

[62]   Brennan (2014).
[63]   Varoufakis (2018).

the rhetoric is of shaky or of Shakespearean power, it makes no difference to the inevitable outcome: big socialism, by its concentration of state power and its obliteration of civil society, leads to despotism.

At least 90 million people have died as a result of actions and policies under big socialist regimes.[64] But even now, when we know much more about the scale of the suffering under the fateful experiments in big socialism in the twentieth century, the ideological immune system is still powerful. Even when presented with highly detrimental evidence of purges and human rights abuses under big socialism, its devotees have their explanations ready.

If excuses do not work, then the immune system has the nuclear option of total denial – denial that is that these experiments were adequately socialist, or perhaps they were not socialist at all. We can turn our heads away from history and reality, safe with the slogan that 'another world is possible'. Next time, with sufficient determination, the right leaders and the total defeat of adversaries, everything will be fine.

The deniers shun consideration of real-world experiments, by claiming that true socialism has yet to be tried. They reject pragmatic and experimental approaches. Facts alone cannot dissuade them. What is needed instead is some hard-headed politico-economic analysis of how markets, bureaucracies and states actually function. Then it is possible to understand what is feasible and what is not.

Unfortunately, mathematical mainstream economics is currently of relatively little help for this task. Understanding the great contest between capitalism and socialism, while appreciating the limits to reform of each of them, requires an economics that is informed by history, infused with the analysis of politico-economic institutions, and appreciative of the nature and functions of knowledge. These insights are dispersed across academic disciplines and largely omitted from the economics curricula in most universities.

Some powerful analytical arguments concerning the nature and role of knowledge are promoted by unconstrained-market individualists, which socialists routinely dismiss, simply because of their ideology. These important arguments require careful intellectual dissection, to strip away redundant ideology and to appreciate the important analytical core inside.

The role of knowledge is central. The development and use of knowledge is the well-spring of all economic activity. Economic systems

---

[64]   Courtois et al. (1999), Hodgson (2018, pp. 122–7). Even higher estimates of the number of deaths are found in Rummel (1994).

stand or fall according to the way they organize, access and utilize dispersed and context-dependent knowledge.

The nature and role of knowledge is addressed in the following two chapters. It will be argued that these considerations undermine the viability of big socialism and point to the need for markets. Chapter 5 retains this vital insight but bends the stick in the other direction. It argues that markets cannot organize everything, especially in a knowledge-intensive economy.

4. Knowledge, complexity and the limits to planning

> Economic accounting is unthinkable without market relations.
>
> Leon Trotsky (1933)[1]

> The rejection of market exchange as the central organizing practice of a modern economy leads inexorably to heavy reliance on state coercion.
>
> John Gray (1998)

Big socialism – whether Marxist or otherwise – makes the underlying assumption that society as a whole can be governed by the rational deliberation of leaders or committees, perhaps somehow with the input of the wider public as well. It is assumed that these bodies can bring relevant information and powers over resources to the high table in the central planning office. Then, with all the necessary information, it is possible to make sound and well-informed decisions in the pursuit of economic development and human needs.

While all Enlightenment thinkers stressed the importance of knowledge and reason, some of them overestimated the powers of human deliberation in face of the complexities involved. But other Enlightenment writers recognized some of these difficulties. Immanuel Kant argued that some unavoidable assumptions in philosophy and science might lack a rational or empirical foundation. Edmund Burke warned of the complexity of politico-economic life, while arguing that surviving institutions had evolved to cope with intricate and challenging problems over long periods of time. Hence cautious experimentation was better than bold, rational, institutional designs that could not take account of all uncertainties and complexities. Today we should take on board the enduring achievements of the Enlightenment alongside the insights of Burke, Kant and subsequent thinkers in this area.[2]

Enlightenment exaggerations of the powers of human reason and of the transmissibility of knowledge found their way into Marxism and they

---

[1]   These perceptive words, by a famous orthodox Marxist, along with further quotes from his same 1933 pamphlet, are discussed later in this chapter.

[2]   Burke (1790), Kant (1929), Levin (2014), Hodgson (2018, pp. 25–7).

inspired its goal of big socialism. These rationalist defects surface in the writings of Marx and Engels. They are most obvious in their confident assertion of the possibility of rational, comprehensive, nation-wide planning.

Over-optimism about the accessibility and transferability of knowledge is also revealed in claims by Marx and Engels that individuals can readily acquire diverse knowledge and skills, and in their repeated aspiration that the division of labour should be abolished. For example, in one of their early works, Marx and Engels wrote:

> [In] communist society, where ... each can become accomplished in any branch he wishes, society regulates the general production and thus makes it possible for me to do one thing today and another tomorrow, to hunt in the morning, fish in the afternoon, rear cattle in the evening, criticise after dinner, just as I have a mind, without ever becoming hunter, fisherman, shepherd or critic.[3]

Similarly, in 1875 Marx argued that in the future communist society 'the enslaving subordination of the individual to the division of labour' would vanish. Marx's proposal to abolish the division of labour assumed that people could acquire different skills relatively easily. His overestimation of the powers of reason and of the accessibility of dispersed knowledge led to his underestimation of the difficulties of specialized learning, and his neglect of the need for a division of labour based on differentiated skills.[4]

In reality, the high degree of specialist knowledge deployed in modern complex societies means that it often takes years to switch from one skill to another. The difficulties stem from the very nature of knowledge and expertise. Once they are understood, it becomes clear that comprehensive planning on a national scale cannot work effectively. The planners themselves cannot acquire or understand all of these skills. Some central coordination and supervision is possible – and even desirable – but it cannot bring together all the knowledge in the system. Consequently,

---

[3] Marx and Engels (1976a, p. 47).

[4] Marx (1974, p. 347). Writing in *Capital*, Marx (1976a, pp. 546–9) argued that the technical development of machinery within capitalism was reducing the time taken to acquire the specialist skills of a machine operative: 'The special skill of each individual machine-operator ... vanishes as an infinitesimal quantity.' Consequently, the development of machinery would undermine the division of labour. There is no evidence to support this assertion. On the contrary, there is evidence of a trend that *average* skill levels have increased under capitalism (Wood, 1982; Goldin and Katz, 1996; Pryor, 1996). Of course, unskilled work persists. But on the average, levels of skill have increased.

pervasive additional mechanisms of decentralized innovation, coordination and adjustment are required, including a substantial private sector and markets.

This chapter first addresses the problem that central planners can acquire and process only a tiny fraction of the vast amount of information and knowledge in a complex economy. Some elements of knowledge are irretrievably tacit – hence they are beyond full recall or codification. Consequently, planners are unable to gather together all relevant information in the centre.

Another major problem concerns pricing. Central planners require some meaningful prices to make assessments as to what is to be prioritized and what methods are to be chosen to fulfil those priorities. Without markets, such meaningful prices are unavailable. A final set of problems relate to the use of targets to manage and incentivize the performance of workers and enterprises.

THE LIMITS TO CENTRALIZED ADMINISTRATION

The brothers Michael and Karl Polanyi have both had major impacts on twentieth-century thought. While Karl's contribution is much celebrated by social scientists, Michael's is often overlooked. An accomplished physical chemist, Michael also made contributions to economics and to the philosophy of science.

Michael visited the Soviet Union in the 1930s. He rejected socialism: instead he was a Keynesian liberal. He argued that complete central planning was impossible because of the complexity of large-scale decision-making and the cognitive limits of the human brain. In this context he also developed the crucial concept of tacit knowledge.[5]

Problems with administrative coordination or planning of a large, complex organization were raised by Hayek and others, but Polanyi gives them more detailed attention, citing arguments taken from management

---

[5]   See K. Polanyi (1944) and M. Polanyi (1958, 1967). Karl's socialist views were close to those of his friend G.D.H. Cole. On Karl's socialism see Hoff (1981, pp. 242–3), Dale (2010, pp. 20–28) and Hodgson (2017b; 2018, pp. 89, 193). Despite their political differences there was some transfer of ideas. As Nye (2011, p. xviii) noted: 'Karl's stress on the role of institutions in economic systems eventually found an echo in Michael's work on the social dimensions of science.'

and administrative science. Crucial to Polanyi's argument was the distinction between an administered organization – including private corporations and state bureaucracies – and the 'spontaneous order' of the market.[6]

Polanyi drew the concept of 'span of control' from administrative science. He cited researchers who claimed that the number of subordinates that can be effectively supervised by a superior is about five. More recently it has been argued that this number depends on the degree to which face-to-face and detailed supervision is necessary, and it may be possible to increase the number slightly with the use of information technology.[7]

Nevertheless, the span of effective supervision is relatively narrow. This is one of the reasons for hierarchy. A business organization may have a CEO plus subordinates under his or her supervision. In turn, each of these subordinates could have more employees under their eye, and so on, to the bottom of the hierarchy.[8]

Polanyi placed this organization in a dynamic context, subject to exogenous shocks or internal changes. These require behavioural adjustment within the system. Communication within the organization concerning its best response is limited by the hierarchical structure.

Much of the efficacious communication in the hierarchy will be vertical, because approval of many decisions by superiors will be necessary if overall coherence of the organizational plan is to be retained. Some horizontal communication may be possible, but it will be limited by divisional compartmentalization, and any consequent action may still have to be approved by superiors in the hierarchy.

By contrast, as Polanyi pointed out, a market system allows greater horizontal communication and multiple contractual agreements. In principle, every market actor can communicate and enter into binding contracts with every other. There are still practical limits over the number of possible interactions, but a market arrangement is more flexible. While the market lacks a central command structure, it allows much more

---

6   Hayek (1935), M. Polanyi (1948).
7   M. Polanyi (1940) cited a foundational paper by A.V. Graicunas in Gulick and Urwick (1937). M. Polanyi (1948) expanded the argument. Mackenzie (1978) and Jaques (1988) addressed the issue of the span of control in management. Dunbar (1993, 2010, 2011) suggested a cognitive limit to the number of people with whom one can maintain stable social relationships. At around 150, it is larger than the span of control, but still suggests a lower and finite cognitive limit to close human interactions.
8   M. Polanyi (1948). Polanyi's emphasis on cognitive limitations is reminiscent of the work on bounded rationality by Simon (1947, 1957).

communication and interaction. This can give the market greater adaptive capacity, particularly for incremental changes.

Polanyi's key point was that the market arrangement vastly improves the scope for behavioural adjustment and adaptation in a dynamic context. Instead of a comprehensive central plan, there is a 'spontaneous order' reached by 'coordination by mutual adjustment of independent initiatives'.[9]

To illustrate the general idea of the creation of order by the mutual adjustment of elements, Polanyi used the analogy of a sack of potatoes. Imagine a committee of planners recording the unique shape of each potato and working out a satisfactory way in which these varied and irregular objects could be fitted together in a sack. Such meticulous planning would be tedious and fraught with difficulty, whereas giving the sack 'a good shaking and a few kicks will do'.[10]

This analogy not only illustrates the principle of mutual adjustment; it also reinforces another point made by Polanyi. While detailed central planning is unfeasible, some overall power or authority is necessary to hold the sack and make sure that the potatoes have settled down. Markets are often a superior mechanism, but they too require some state authority. Polanyi was more emphatic about this role of the state in a market economy than others, such as Hayek.

Although he touched on the problem, Polanyi failed to explore adequately the possible advantages of organizational planning over markets in some contexts. Without such contingent benefits, there would be no reason to have any organizations at all, and everyone would contract individually with everyone else on markets.

We can begin to remedy this omission. The Nobel Laureate Ronald Coase highlighted the transaction costs of setting up and monitoring multiple market contracts. Market transaction costs reduce the comparative efficiency of the market compared with the organization. Under specific conditions, hierarchies may also have advantages when exploiting teamwork and economies of scale.[11]

State intervention in the economy may be necessary in some cases to move from one suboptimal configuration of technology or institutions to another, such as to establish common standards, facilitate knowledge transfer and ensure adequate training in skills. State intervention is also

---

[9]   M. Polanyi (1948, 1962, p. 59).

[10]   M. Polanyi (1997, p. 168).

[11]   Note that while Coase's (1937) argument proceeds by a comparison of static cases, M. Polanyi's (1948) addresses the problem of dynamic adaptation. See also Hodgson and Knudsen (2007).

necessary to deal with major system-wide challenges such as climate change. The choice of the mix between organizations and markets depends on a complex set of factors within capitalist economy. Ultimately it is a matter of ongoing practical experimentation.[12]

Polanyi showed that the cognitive and practical demands on a centralized administration are huge. They become larger as the scale of organization increases and more serious when problems of adaptation are paramount. As organizations increase in scale, the required flow of information increases even more, but their structures restrict internal communication. Full control and planning from the centre over the entire economy is not possible.

THE NATURE OF KNOWLEDGE AND SKILLS

Consider the nature of information and knowledge. Knowledge is not the same as information or data. All knowledge depends on preconceptions and prior cognitive frameworks that cannot be established simply through reason, reflection or observation. Our minds receive sense data, but this is not the same as information or knowledge. Information is processed or interpreted data that has meaning or operational capability. Knowledge is the result of the extensive practical use of information in some context. Many of the cognitive processes that we use to process information and to form knowledge are tacit and unconscious.

All knowledge involves an irreducible tacit dimension. This consists of skills, ideas and experiences that people have, but that are not codified and may not be easily expressed. Consequently, there are aspects of knowledge that cannot be readily made subject to reflection, codification and reason. But tacit knowledge is nevertheless vital and ubiquitous. Effective transfer of tacit knowledge generally requires extensive personal contact, regular interaction and a degree of mutual understanding and trust. Its use and transmission depend on the social and physical context. This kind of knowledge is generally revealed through practice and spread by close imitation.[13]

Consider riding a bicycle. Those of us who have this skill would find it difficult or impossible to describe it fully and in detail. A cyclist learns many things – including how to use the gyroscopic forces of the front

---

[12]   OECD (2007).
[13]   As well as M. Polanyi (1958, 1967) see Nelson and Winter (1982), Dosi (1988), Neisser (1983), Reber (1993), Turner (1994), Nonaka and Takeuchi (1995), Howells (1996), Spender (1996), Leonard and Sensiper (1998), Eraut (2000), Knudsen (2002).

wheel – that have not been brought to the level of full understanding, conscious thought or rational deliberation. They are acquired through imitation, practice and trial-and-error.

As another example, we absorb many of the rules of a language by repeatedly immersing ourselves in conversation with others. Although we may consciously learn some explicit rules, the key to language acquisition is making it habitual, so we do not have to think about the rules when we are using them.

Consider the complex and opaque rules governing the use of the definite or indefinite articles in the English language – 'the', 'a' or 'an'. Many non-native English speakers have difficulty getting the usages right. Most English speakers know habitually when to use the definite or indefinite article and when not. But very few of us would be able to make these rules explicit. We know but we are unable to tell. Tacit knowledge is typically acquired by immersion in a community, by repeated imitation, and by the formation of habits.

Technology is deeply impregnated by tacit knowledge and shared habits of thought. It involves explicit and tacit knowledge, codified and uncodified rules, and organizational routines. Michael Polanyi pointed out that technology is often employed without explicit knowledge of its detailed operations. Habit, tradition and 'legendary belief' have to be relied upon in the day-to-day practice of a technology.

Furthermore, the acquisition of a technology cannot rely wholly on prescription; codified knowledge is often absent. Learning how to use a technology typically involves the formation of habit and routine by following the example of others. Technology is the accumulated tradition of experimental trial-and-error, typically with complex arrangements that cannot be dissected or fully understood in every detail.

Much learning is tacit and involves unconscious reactions to stimuli. Through a combination of conscious and unconscious processes, socialization and education help to create the cognitive apparatus to enhance deliberation and reason. As the management scientist J-C. Spender put it: 'Our explicit knowledge is but a small communicable cap of the iceberg of preconscious collective human knowledge, the vast bulk of which is tacit, unseen, and embedded in our social identity and practice.'[14]

We do not think with the brain alone: our mind works through interactions in its material and social contexts. Work by psychologists on 'situated cognition' shows that knowing is inseparable from doing and from its material and social settings. Ideas develop and play out in the

---

[14] Spender (1996, p. 54).

material and social worlds around us. Human cognitive capacities are irreducible to individuals alone: they also depend upon social structures and material cues.[15]

Knowledge is rooted in practice. For it to be accessible, conceptions and practices have to be shared. But there are limits to the extension of common or widely accessible knowledge. Learning depends on ingrained familiarity, obtained through repeated routine. For this reason, in any complex society, people have no alternative but to be specialists. There are limits to the amount of knowledge that can be understood by any individual or group.

As Ikujiro Nonaka and Hirotaka Takeuchi have demonstrated in their studies of business organizations, it is possible to codify some tacit knowledge and thereby make it non-tacit. But innovation and ongoing practice create new zones and layers of tacitness.

Crucially, it is impossible to convert all tacit knowledge into explicit knowledge. This would massively overburden decision-making with unmanageable amounts of explicit information. As Michael Polanyi put it: 'the ideal of eliminating all personal elements of knowledge would, in effect, aim at the destruction of all knowledge ... the process of formalizing all knowledge to the exclusion of any tacit knowledge is self-defeating'.[16]

Marx's idea to abolish the division of labour reflected his rationalistic failure to grasp the tacit dimension and social embeddedness of knowledge and skills. Marx did not appreciate the nature and extent of unconvertible tacit knowledge and its vital role in the economy.

TACIT AND DISPERSED KNOWLEDGE THWART COMPREHENSIVE CENTRAL PLANNING

The extent of tacit knowledge undermines the possibility of comprehensive and effective central economic planning. Tacit knowledge makes substantial decentralized coordination unavoidable. In the so-called 'socialist calculation debate' in the 1920s and 1930s, Ludwig Mises and (more forcefully) Friedrich Hayek argued that much knowledge was irretrievably dispersed throughout the economy and it could not be all

---

[15] Lave and Wenger (1991), Hutchins (1995), Lane et al. (1996), Clark (1997).
[16] Nonaka and Takeuchi (1995), M. Polanyi (1967, p. 19).

gathered together by the central planners. Hayek later made use of Michael Polanyi's insights in this area.[17]

The socialist side of this debate included economists such as Oskar Lange, Henry Dickinson, Evan Durbin and Abba Lerner. They used mainstream general equilibrium models in an effort to show that comprehensive planning could work. Unfortunately, as Hayek pointed out, their models assumed that all information was transparent and readily available. The socialist theorists had a naïve view of the availability of knowledge in socio-economic systems. They did not appreciate its nature and limited accessibility.[18]

The socialist economists assumed that all relevant knowledge and information would be readily available to the decision-makers at the centre. As Dickinson wrote naïvely: 'All organs of the socialist economy will work, so to speak, within glass walls.' As a result, the central planning authority would be the 'omnipresent, omniscient organ of the collective economy'. Similarly, Lange argued that under socialism all relevant information concerning production would be widely available, with the result that 'everything done in one productive establishment would and should also be done by the managers of each productive establishment'.[19]

Lange and Dickinson acquired this flawed view of knowledge from the mainstream economic theory that they embraced. Criticizing this theoretical approach, Hayek concluded that by depicting 'economic man' as 'a

---

[17] Oğuz (2010). M. Polanyi (1948) used the English term 'spontaneous order' before Hayek, although earlier usages stretch back to John Stuart Mill and others (Jacobs, 2000; Bladel, 2005; D'Amico, 2015; Jacobs and Mullins, 2016). It was called the *socialist calculation debate* because at its centre was the problem of calculating meaningful prices in a planned economy. But the debate also addressed other problems with socialism, such as the lack of incentives and the totalitarian dangers in the concentration of economic power in the hands of the state. Economic arguments against socialism by Albert Schäffle (going back to the 1870s) and later ones by Michael Polanyi have been relatively neglected. The *calculation debate* label is unfortunate because it concentrates on one aspect of one debate, where in fact there were more issues, more debaters and more debates.

[18] Dickinson (1933, 1939), Lerner (1934, 1944), Durbin (1936), Lange (1936–37) and Lange and Taylor (1938) tried to grapple with the challenges of Mises (1920) and Hayek (1935). Careful revaluations of the debate have overturned the preceding consensus that Mises and Hayek were on the losing side. Lange and others did not adequately answer the criticisms of Mises and Hayek, and they failed to provide a satisfactory outline of a workable and dynamic socialist system. For good accounts of this debate see Vaughn (1980), Hoff (1981), Murrell (1983), Lavoie (1985a, 1985b), Steele (1992) and Boettke (2000, 2001, 2018).

[19] Dickinson (1939, pp. 9, 191) and Lange (1987, p. 23).

quasi-omniscient individual', economics has hitherto neglected the problem that should be a major concern, namely the analysis of 'how knowledge is acquired and communicated'. The mainstream models adopted by Lange and others did not deal adequately with this central problem. Tacit and dispersed knowledge were overlooked. The widespread assimilation of technical knowledge was wrongly assumed to be unproblematic.[20]

For Hayek, the 'economic problem of society is thus not merely a problem of how to allocate "given" resources ... it is a problem of the utilization of knowledge which is not given to anyone in its totality'. All relevant knowledge 'cannot be known to the scientific observer, or to any other single brain'. Every system of comprehensive planning faces this problem of accessing dispersed information.[21]

By contrast, markets process and express information through the price mechanism. Private enterprise provides incentives for entrepreneurs to evaluate and use dispersed knowledge. Markets allow much more knowledge to be utilized – knowledge that 'exists only dispersed among uncounted persons' and is more 'than any one person can possess'.[22]

These problems are illustrated in the histories of centrally planned economies. Stalin attempted wholesale central planning from 1928, but he had to retreat because of the insurmountable problems involved. By the early 1930s, the difficulties inherent in comprehensive central planning had forced Stalin to devolve some power to sub-units in the system.[23]

But the underdevelopment of markets and the fragility of devolved powers in an overbearing political dictatorship did not allow decentralization to prosper. Decentralized authorities had limited powers to make strategic decisions and set prices. Supervision of different units was thwarted by inadequate and flawed information. Censorship and repression made critical appraisal of information impossible.

Consequently, Soviet-type economies have characteristically lurched back and forth between attempted decentralization and renewed (but inevitably incomplete) centralization. As Justin Lin reported in the case of Mao's China: 'under the planned economy there was a bizarre and repeated cycle. Decentralization led to dynamism. Dynamism led to disorder. Disorder led to retrenchment. Retrenchment led to stagnation.' In a planned economy, decentralization eventually leads to disarray

---

[20] Hayek (1948, pp. 46, 33).
[21] Hayek (1948, pp. 78–9; 1989, p. 4).
[22] Hayek (1989, p. 4).
[23] M. Polanyi (1940, pp. 36 ff.).

because possible local mechanisms of mutual adjustment, which rely on free negotiation of prices and quantities, are centrally constrained and institutionally underdeveloped. The 'bizarre cycle' thus continued.[24]

Viable local adjustment mechanisms are vital to deal with problems with fragmented and dispersed knowledge. Generally, as Michael Polanyi put it, knowledge and competent judgement are 'not held by any single human mind' but, being 'split into thousands of fragments', are 'held by a multitude of individuals, each of whom endorses the other's opinion at second hand, by relying on the consensual chains which link him to all the others through a sequence of overlapping neighbourhoods'. Markets provide a powerful and particular mechanism of 'coordination by mutual adjustment' that relies on price signals.[25]

This does not imply that markets are perfect processors of information or that they must be relied upon to the exclusion of everything else. Markets require supplementary institutions (including the legal system) and markets are not the only information-processing institutions in the economy. Organizations and legal systems also process information.

What is crucial, however, is the ability of the market to deal with dispersed, local and tacit forms of knowledge, and to signal capacities and preferences of multiple agents, over changing parameters, through the price mechanism. Other institutions do not have this ability, while they may perform better in other ways. Markets are vital to help coordinate vast amounts of complex, dispersed and tacit information.

In the absence of markets, a planning system peers into a dark room, fumbling for an understanding of what is going on. Rational appraisal of performance is thwarted by the lack of information and of meaningful general standards of evaluation. By contrast, a market provides an imperfect but powerful mechanism for setting prices and detecting under-performance. As John Gray put it: 'The fundamental problem of the centrally planned economy, is that it lacks an *error-elimination mechanism* for misconceived projects.'[26]

---

[24] Lin (2012, p. 175). See also Rutland (1985) and Kornai (1992). For evidence on early attempts at decentralization in the USSR, as discussed by M. Polanyi (1940), see Gregory and Harrison (2005).

[25] M. Polanyi (1962, pp. 57, 60).

[26] Gray (1993, pp. 207–208).

THE PRICING PROBLEM UNDER BIG SOCIALISM

Imagine that you are on the Central Planning Board in a socialist economy. You have reports on the resources that are available, and you have a number of priorities for future production and distribution. New schools and hospitals are needed as well as improvements in the transport infrastructure. The Board must develop a plan to mobilize resources and start on these needed projects.

The Central Planning Board must prioritize. There may be worries about investing in an expensive high-speed railway system if it took too many resources away from building schools and hospitals. To make evaluations of this kind, there must be some accounting system with non-arbitrary prices, to assess the relative costs of the proposed projects. This would not reduce all decisions to matters of cost, but costs must be considered. As Lenin emphasized, there is a vital need for 'accounting and control'. For accounting to take place there must be some unit of account in which prices are expressed.[27]

When the projects are prioritized, further accounting calculations are needed. The planners must allocate resources to the favoured projects in a manner that takes on board the need to use scarce resources with adequate efficiency. Otherwise the planners act wastefully, and their capacity to address human needs is weakened.

Under a centrally planned economy with minimal markets there is no meaningful method by which prices can be established. This is known as the problem of socialist calculation. Adequate accounting and well-costed assessments of alternative options are unavailable. Central planners would be unable to determine whether one alternative, by meaningful and non-arbitrary criteria, was less costly than another.

This raises the problem of how meaningful prices could be formed. Robert Owen and other socialists had proposed labour time as the unit of account under socialism. This suggestion has resurfaced several times.

---

[27]   Lenin (1967, vol. 2, p. 344) wrote in August 1917: 'Accounting and control – that is *mainly* what is needed for the "smooth working", for the proper functioning, of the *first phase* of communist society.' In April 1918, after the seizure of power, Lenin (1967, vol. 2, pp. 649, 660) still emphasized: 'The principal difficulty lies in the economic sphere, namely, the introduction of the strictest and universal accounting and control of the production and distribution of goods, raising the productivity of labour and *socialising* production *in practice*. ... In our agitation we do not sufficiently explain that lack of accounting and control in the production and distribution of goods means the death of the rudiments of socialism.' In these statements Lenin failed to acknowledge that a common unit of account cannot meaningfully be established without the existence of money and markets.

Albert Schäffle was one of the first to identify some of its insurmountable problems:

> All whose average productiveness was higher than that of their neighbours would ... come short in their share of remuneration. ... It is also quite impossible to form an accurate estimate among the labourers alone of the value of the product in proportion to the amount of revenue created by each several labour contribution.[28]

Schäffle noted the major problem that labour is variable and heterogeneous, both in terms of a large variance in types of skill between individuals (as evidenced in the division of labour) and of different and variable degrees of diligence and aptitude between individuals with similar jobs. Consequently, the reduction of all types and degrees of skill to one overall unit of labour time would be thwarted by enormous computational and practical difficulties.

Testing this idea of labour units, in the 1830s Owen established several 'labour exchanges', where artisans bought and sold their products using labour notes, reflecting the claimed number of hours of work involved. These exchanges quickly collapsed. One of the problems was that all hours of labour time were rewarded and measured as the same, when they varied hugely in terms of skill and diligence.

There is no single and obvious way in which a socialist planning authority, bent on using labour time as the common measure, could take account of different types and variable levels of skill. Attempts to do so would come up against the knowledge problem raised above. The evaluation of skills must entail some assessment of the acquired knowledge, including its tacit elements. The planners would have to rely on several highly imperfect proxy measures, such as the average number of years in training needed to acquire the skill. If used, such proxy measures are prone to abuses and distortions.

There are further problems. The capital goods (tools, machinery, raw materials and so on) must also be subject to the same metric and unit of account. The standard Marxist answer is to attempt to compute the 'socially necessary labour time' embodied in these capital goods. Engels thought that it would be an easy matter to calculate the amounts of embodied labour:

> Society can simply calculate how many hours of labour are contained in a steam-engine, a bushel of wheat of the last harvest, or a hundred square yards

---

[28] Schäffle (1892, pp. 76–8).

of cloth of a certain quality. ... The useful effects of the various articles of consumption, compared with one another and with the quantities of labour required for their production, will in the end determine the plan. People will be able to manage everything very simply ... [29]

But repeating that it is simple does not make it so. It would be necessary to standardize and calculate all the labour time involved directly in the assembly of the steam-engine, all the labour time involved in the production of its components, all the labour time involved in the production of the raw materials involved, and so on.

Because many processes produce outputs that in turn become inputs in another part of the system, this is neither a direct nor a straightforward computation. The different kinds of labour would have to be placed under one metric. Variations in other commodities would somehow have to be standardized. It would also be necessary to set up and solve thousands of simultaneous equations, reflecting all the commodities involved. A fast and copious computer would be required. Even when the results were obtained, they could be flawed, because of the numerous simplifications necessary to make the data computable.

Another problem is the lack of a time dimension involved in the use of prices based on embodied labour. Assume no accounting distinction was made between identical amounts of labour performed at different times. This would be equivalent to the assumption of zero rates of interest and time preference. At least with a growing economy, this would be suboptimal: two projects involving equal remuneration and equal investments of overall labour time, but expenditures or remunerations occurring at different times, would mistakenly be treated as equivalent. Without remedy, embodied labour time prices may bias the system excessively towards future investments. Some authors have proposed that this bias could be alleviated by the use of an assumed discount rate. But this adds yet another arbitrary and fallible assumption to the calculus.[30]

Overall, planning calculations using labour time would be subject to numerous arbitrary assumptions and simplifications. They attempt to bring different things to a common denominator without adequate interaction with consumers via markets. The arbitrariness of the assumptions involved means that accounting in terms of labour time would embody a number of difficulties and distortions.

[29] Engels (1962, pp. 424–5).
[30] Baisch (1979), Cockshott and Cottrell (1993, pp. 76–7).

CAN SIMULATED MARKETS REPLACE REAL ONES?

In the 1930s, Lange and others outlined an iterative process of price formation, based on Walrasian general equilibrium theory.[31] Although the original approach developed by Léon Walras was purportedly a representation of a market economy, it used the fiction of a single auctioneer to formalize the process by which prices are formed. The imaginary auctioneer would adjust prices up or down until an equilibrium of supply and demand was reached.

Lange suggested that this model could be used to form prices under socialism. He proposed that the central planning authority would instruct the managers of firms to expand production until marginal costs were equal to the announced price of the product. Adjustments would be made to the prices by the central planning board, which would take over the job of the Walrasian auctioneer, until an equilibrium was reached and there was no surplus or excess demand. At this point, the productive surpluses of the enterprises would be maximized, and prices would be fixed.

Lange thus claimed to demonstrate the feasibility of a planned economy with public ownership. The artificial and unrealistic Walrasian model of capitalism became the justification of socialism. But this overlooked the real processes of decision-making and the problems of knowledge involved. The economist Mark Blaug wrote with appropriate derision:

> The Lange idea of managers following marginal cost-pricing rules because they are instructed to do so, while the central planning board continually alters the prices of both producer and consumer goods so as to reduce their excess demands to zero, is so administratively naive as to be positively laughable. Only those drunk on perfectly competitive, static equilibrium theory could have swallowed such nonsense. ... in all the ... calls for reform of Soviet bloc economies, no one has ever suggested that Lange was of any relevance whatsoever. And still more ironically, Lange's 'market socialism' is, on its own grounds, socialism without anything that can be called market transactions.[32]

Consider the problem of managerial incentives. How are managers to be encouraged to take some risks, but not to be too reckless? Dickinson

---

[31] The approach of Walras (1874) was developed by Arrow and Debreu (1954), among others.

[32] Blaug (1993, p. 1571).

proposed a system of managerial bonuses to reward competent entrepreneurs. But these would provide limited encouragement for hazardous
entrepreneurship. Hayek rightly pointed out that 'managers will be afraid
of taking risks if, when the venture does not come off, it will be
somebody else who will afterward decide whether they have been
justified in embarking on it'. Unless the system gives them incentives to
take risks, managers would maximize caution, minimize personal exposure to responsibility, and stick to established routine. Hayek pointed out
that Lange and Dickinson were 'deplorably vague' about key issues,
including how competent managers were to be selected.[33]

Large capitalist corporations face related difficulties of establishing
meaningful internal prices across their multiple cost centres. But capitalism provides the external pressure of the market, which can put any
internal cost calculations to the test. Nationalized industries in centrally
planned economies are much less subject to competitive market forces.

Individuals within centrally planned hierarchies have less incentive to
develop or propose innovations. By their nature, it is often difficult to
surmise if innovations will work or be useful. Innovation is disruptive
and uncertain, so individuals tend to carry on as before. Bureaucracies
thus become routinized and tend to eschew innovation. Bureaucracies can
often manage quite well in a steady state. But with a dynamic economy
the picture changes. As the economist Richard Nelson put it: 'the
argument that centralization imposes high information and calculation
costs carries considerable weight in a dynamic context'.[34]

Consequently, the record of the former Communist countries on
technological and organizational innovation has been less impressive.
While the 'superior performance of market economies is not in doubt',
Peter Murrell presented empirical evidence that the former Soviet-type
economies were only slightly less efficient in the static allocation of their
existing resources. Their lower levels of output and consumption resulted
much more from cumulative deficiencies in innovation and transforma-
tional growth. The lack of entrepreneurial incentives under planned
economies was a major problem.[35]

---

[33]   See Dickinson (1939) and Hayek (1948, pp. 194, 199).

[34]   Nelson (1981, p. 101).

[35]   Bergson (1991), Murrell (1991, esp. p. 65), Caplan (2004). Allen (2003) argued that
the Soviet Union was relatively successful in economic terms, especially when the starting
conditions and the adverse circumstances of war are considered. Soviet policy transformed
Russia from a rural into a major industrial economy. The argument, methodology and
modelling are controversial. Even in its own terms, Allen's study offers much less succour
for socialists than may appear at first sight. It shows that the post-1928 collectivization
added little to economic growth, and the economy would have performed no worse if

Capitalism has a supreme capacity to innovate. Innovation involves taking risks. Private property provides incentives to innovate and the market offers a means of putting innovation to the test. Of course, the market is an imperfect mechanism, and market demand does not necessarily correspond to need. But bureaucracies are often sluggish and generally less conducive for innovative activity. This does not mean that the state has no role in developing and promoting innovation: it has often been vital. But successful publicly funded innovations have necessarily been tested and empowered by markets.[36]

Prices provide incentives to be economical with costs and market competition can help to bring down the price of outputs. Instead of a single overall plan, prices and markets help to coordinate multiple changing plans. With all its flaws, the price system is an indispensable communications network for the ongoing dynamic coordination of different plans by entrepreneurs and consumers in a large-scale economy.

Mises and Hayek argued that bureaucrats in a centrally planned economy could not coordinate their plans without a price system. Prices are necessary to compare plans and make basic decisions. Leon Trotsky was right: economic accounting is unthinkable without market relations.

THE TARGET PROBLEM: COMPLEXITY AND MANAGERIAL INCENTIVES

The Walrasian general equilibrium models developed by Lange and others assumed that managers will follow simple rules and they will have the information and inclination to do so. But reality is not like that. There are always problems within business organizations concerning how managers are incentivized to produce needed outputs.

---

instead the NEP had continued instead. The NEP meant a state-guided mixed economy, in some ways similar to China today. But it is questionable whether such a state-heavy arrangement is suitable for still higher levels of economic development (Hodgson, 2015a, ch. 14). The modelling also shows that growth in the USSR was facilitated by a substantial drop in birth rates, due to the education of women and their employment outside the home. Experience clearly shows that such fertility and gender outcomes are possible within capitalism.

[36] Mazzucato (2013). Potts (2019) argues that innovation is driven by institutions that govern the cooperative pooling of innovation resources and the coordination of dispersed knowledge.

In a classic paper published in 1937, Ronald Coase stressed the difference between organizations and markets. But since then this distinction has been undermined by questionable claims that 'internal markets' exist within organizations.[37]

But there cannot be legally enforceable contracts between different internal divisions of a singular legal entity. A corporation is set up in law as a singular body, with the right to make contracts with other legal entities. It can sue and be sued. Its internal divisions are not separate legal units. While a firm can take one of its contractors or employees to court for breach of contract, it cannot sue one of its own internal divisions. These legal criteria re-establish the distinction between a corporate business organization and a market.[38]

While large business corporations face problems of internal management and administration, they have advantages, including the possibility of economies of scale. Also, as Coase pointed out, a possible advantage of organized hierarchies is that they may reduce transaction costs. They can avoid the need to negotiate and monitor contracts at every internal interface.

On the down side, there are enduring problems, such as setting priorities and allocating resources, within all planned organizations. These problems can be exacerbated if competition from rival producers is limited. Even if the producers in a centrally planned economy were well-motivated and socially concerned, the lack of market engagement would bring problems.

Consider, for example, the house construction division of a planned economy. Faced with a national housing shortage, a construction team building houses might be tempted to maximize the number of dwellings built and pay less attention to the quality of each home. Of course, there is always a trade-off between quantity and quality, but even with the best will in the world, the workers and managers in the construction team would have inadequate information and would have to make poorly informed decisions on how much quality to sacrifice in favour of quantity.

---

[37] Coase (1937). Misleading claims that 'internal markets' exist within firms were made by Doeringer and Piore (1971), Cheung (1983) and even Coase (1988) in a later work. See Hodgson (2015a, ch. 8) for a critique.

[38] In an odd alliance, both Marxism and some Austrian economists (notably Mises) downplay the importance of legal forms and powers (Hodgson, 2015a, 2016a). For an authoritative statement on the legal status of the corporation see Worthington (2016). For arguments on how legal forms reveal the distinction between the firm and the market see Blair (1995, 2003), Ireland (1999), Gindis (2009, 2016), Robé (2011), Hodgson (2015a, ch. 8) and Deakin et al. (2017).

By contrast, in a market economy, competing suppliers offer rival solutions and it is possible for consumers or governments to make more meaningful calculations and decisions. (For reasons given above, the slogan of 'democratic control' is unworkable.) This is not to treat markets and competition as a panacea – they do not always work well. Instead it is a recognition of the some of the benefits of competition over national monopoly.

In a planned economy, some outputs are relatively homogeneous and hence targets are relatively easy to formulate, monitor and reward. There is little ambiguity about a kilowatt-hour of electricity. Then the planners can set meaningful targets and reward greater output with bonuses. But beyond that it gets much more complex. The vast bulk of goods and services produced today are highly complex and variegated.

Faced with product heterogeneity and complexity, directors in planned economies, such as the Soviet Union and Mao's China, had no alternative but to work with relatively simple quantitative targets. But experience showed that plants working to target-based incentives often responded by producing inferior products.

For example, planning targets in the textile sector in terms of square metres led to the production of thin, fragile cloth. Changing the target to weight led to useless, sackcloth-like material. Attempts by the planners to deal with the problem of cloth 'quality' led to its definition in terms of the absence of a particular type of imperfection. At least one enterprise responded by cutting out all the imperfections so that the cloth was dotted with holes.[39]

Plan-fulfilment targets are bound to cause such distortions when significant variations in product characteristics are typical. Nove cited an example from the Soviet Union: 'Thus when window-glass was planned in tons it was too thick and heavy; so they shifted the plan "indicator" to square metres, whereupon it became too thin.'[40] Examples of this kind abound. They are endemic to big socialism.

Eventually a centrally planned system might be able to adjust targets to eliminate the more severe distortions and misallocations. But this takes time, and success would depend on slow rates of technological change and on few changes in overall plan requirements.

---

[39] Ellman (1989, p. 45).
[40] Nove (1980, p. 6).

MORE TRADE-OFFS BETWEEN ORGANIZATIONS AND MARKETS

Related problems with targets arise in large organizations in capitalist systems. Consider the National Health Service (NHS) in the UK. It has been cited as the world's third biggest employer, after the Indian railways and Chinese army.

From its inception in 1948 until the 1980s there were relatively few attempts to restructure or reform the NHS. It remained a huge, bureaucratic, centrally planned organization. But pressures on the system increased, partly due to an ageing population and partly because of the need to deploy major improvements in diagnostic technology and drugs. These required both increased funds and changes in organization and routine.

By 1997 there was public discontent in the UK due to delays in treatment and long hospital waiting lists. The Labour Party pledged during the 1997 election to deal with this problem. After it was elected, it chose to target the maximum times on formal waiting lists, with pecuniary rewards for those hospitals that met those targets. Hospitals responded by setting up secret waiting lists to get onto their declared waiting lists.[41]

Prime Minister Blair also set up incentives in 2003 to ensure that general practitioners saw patients within 48 hours. The NHS offered monetary payments to general practices that met this target. Some general practices responded simply by refusing to make advance appointments in excess of 48 hours. Needy patients had to be among the first to make telephone contact with the appointments office immediately after it opened in the morning. Within minutes, the appointment schedules were filled up for that day and the next. The appointment time target was fulfilled by limiting the possibility of making an appointment. Such distortions are reminiscent of those in Soviet-type economies.[42]

This is not an argument for privatizing the NHS. Large public and private organizations are inevitable in modern economies. They can reap economies of scale and reduce transaction costs. This creates a crucial trade-off. A large organization is effective as long as it can bring provide net benefits that exceed those of a more fragmented system with greater market competition. It is possible that the NHS illustrates real benefits of

---

[41]   See Hansard (1997, 2002), Green and Casper (2000), BBC News (2001).
[42]   BBC News (2005).

some large organizations over their operational costs, and many of these benefits are peculiar to health service systems.

Instead of being guided solely by ideology or by overly simple economic models, the costs and benefits of large organizations have to be carefully considered in each case.

To illustrate the net gains possible within large, integrated health systems, compare the NHS in the UK with the much more fragmented market-driven health systems in the US. A recent comparison of health systems in 11 wealthy nations by the US-based Commonwealth Fund found that the US system was falling short by multiple measures, while the NHS in the UK led in several categories. Yet health spending per capita in the US is more than double that in the UK. Much of the extra expenditure in the US is on litigation and insurance. A fragmented health system creates larger transaction costs. Because of the specific complexities and uncertainties involved in health, these costs can be huge.[43]

Some advocates of market competition favour breaking up all large organizations and moving toward an economy comprised entirely of small firms. This option is unrealistic in a modern, large-scale, complex economy. Although there are legitimate worries about the power of large corporations, and it may be beneficial to split up some of them, breaking them all up into smaller pieces would in many cases mean the loss of huge economies of scale and the addition of substantial transaction costs.

Consequently, we must avoid the extremes of both big socialism and small capitalism, and search for pragmatic solutions in between. When organizations substitute for markets then (market-based) transaction costs are often reduced, because there is more reliance on management and less on contract. But on the other hand, problems with targets, monitoring and performance management increase as organizations expand. In the real world there are always trade-offs between advantages and disadvantages. Ongoing experiment is needed to discover what works.[44]

CONCLUDING REMARKS: FROM MISES TO TROTSKY

Big socialism entails large-scale organizations. But they lack market pressure to help improve performance. Also, by concentrating political and economic power in the centre, big socialism threatens democracy and critical debate, removing effective pressures of public accountability.

---

[43] Commonwealth Fund (2017), OECD (2017).
[44] For a useful discussion see Stretton and Orchard (1994, esp. ch. 7).

The powerful arguments of Mises and Hayek underline the importance of private ownership and of market competition. Mises showed that markets are vital to establish meaningful prices to make effective allocative decisions. Hayek's powerful epistemic critique of big socialism highlighted the impossibility of bringing all knowledge together to make a comprehensive overall plan.

But Mises and Hayek did not promote a mixed economy of public and private enterprises. Yet in practice all actual and successful capitalist economies are mixed economies. Experience suggests that it is possible to reconcile some public ownership with a vibrant entrepreneurial economy. Further arguments along these lines are found in following chapters.[45]

It is not a matter of dogma, but of experience and of what works in practice. The example of the NHS in the UK shows that a large bureaucratic organization, despite its downsides, can sometimes work more effectively than fragmented and more market-driven, alternatives. But any organization requires specific conditions and pressures to work effectively.

It is important to emphasize that the problems with comprehensive central planning do not simply concern the 'socialist calculation' of meaningful prices. As well as those of the Austrian school, other arguments were developed by Albert Schäffle and Michael Polanyi. There has been relatively little comparative empirical evaluation of the force of the varied arguments involved.[46]

A great deal hinges on this comparative evaluation. If Mises and Hayek were right in underlining the supreme importance of the lack of prices that adequately conveyed local knowledge, then this suggests the ubiquitous adoption of market solutions. But if, on the other hand, the problem of incentives and individual motivation are paramount, as Schäffle suggested, then this allows a mixed economy adopting management solutions to the problem of motivation, in a context of competitive pressure from imperfect markets. Further research on this issue is vital.

The reader may be perplexed by the quotation by Trotsky that heads this chapter, because it seems to endorse Mises and Hayek, yet it was written by a Marxist. This quote shows that some intelligent Marxists can

---

[45]   On the viability of real-world mixed economies see Nelson (1981, 2003), Lazonick (1991), Kenworthy (1995), Chang and Rowthorn (1995), Chang (1997, 2002a, 2002b), Evans and Rauch (1999), Vogel (2006), Reinert (2007), Martinez (2009) and Mazzucato (2013).

[46]   Murrell (1991) and Caplan (2004) are exceptions.

learn from their critics. But it also throws a market cat among the Marxist pigeons.

It is likely that Trotsky had heard of the work of Mises, or of the Russian economist Boris Brutzkus, who entered the socialist calculation debate in the 1920s and drew the admiration of Mises and Hayek. In another passage in the same 1933 pamphlet on the Soviet economy, Trotsky went further:

> If a universal mind existed, of the kind that projected itself into the scientific fancy of Laplace – a mind that could register simultaneously all the processes of nature and society, that could measure the dynamics of their motion, that could forecast the results of their inter-reactions – such a mind, of course, could a priori draw up a faultless and exhaustive economic plan, beginning with the number of acres of wheat down to the last button for a vest. The bureaucracy often imagines that just such a mind is at its disposal; that is why it so easily frees itself from the control of the market and of Soviet democracy.

Trotsky's 1933 essay criticized increasing bureaucratization in the Soviet Union under Stalin. As a remedy, Trotsky argued vaguely for a combination of three elements: 'state planning, the market and Soviet democracy'. But not only did he fail to show how this slogan could be put into practice, he also cautioned that this remedy was only for 'the correct direction of the economy of the transitional epoch'. Subsequently, 'a new and victorious revolution will widen the arena of socialist planning and will reconstruct the system'.[47]

By referring to Pierre-Simon Laplace's 1814 conjecture of an omniscient intellect, Trotsky highlighted the problem of limited cognitive capacity in the face of the huge scale and complexity of the economic system. Some have proposed that computers might eventually be able to overcome these massive information problems.[48] But even if they could, other severe impediments to comprehensive central planning, as outlined above, would still remain unresolved.

Nowhere did Trotsky identify the other major problems with comprehensive planning, such as dealing with the dispersed and tacit nature of knowledge, or how democracy can be reconciled with centralized

---

[47] Trotsky (1933). See also Nove (1983, pp. 59–60) on Trotsky's temporary tolerance of the market.

[48] Lange (1967), Bodington (1973), Cockshott and Cottrell (1993). For critiques of these arguments see Hodgson (1998, 1999).

decision-making in a complex system involving expertise and tacit knowledge, or how workers and managers could be given appropriate incentives.

Ultimately, Trotsky still believed in all-embracing socialist planning. His compromise with the market applied to the transitional economy and for a limited period, not to full-blooded socialism or communism.

We are left wondering how a widened socialist planning, after the 'victorious revolution', would cope in the absence of the omniscient Laplacian intellect. Trotsky understood why markets were unavoidable in the present, but he retained a blind faith that eventually these reasons would somehow cease to apply. Ultimately, Marxist dogma triumphed over his intelligence. He evaded the question of the feasibility of socialism.

Generally, socialists need to take the problem of the viability of socialism much more seriously than they have done so in the past. The problem can also be misunderstood. While discussing the question of feasibility, the Marxist philosopher G.A. Cohen used the analogy of a bunch of grapes:

> Suppose I see some grapes, the tastiest grapes ever. Now, suppose the grapes are out of reach – it is not feasible for me to get them. If so, it does not make them any less intrinsically desirable. It might mean that I should not attempt to pick the grapes, but their intrinsic value is independent of my ability to pick them.[49]

Here Cohen confused feasibility with accessibility. If the tasty grapes were not feasible, then they would not simply be out of reach – they would not exist. Most humane forms of socialism as envisioned by socialists are not feasible, even if people were generally kind and good to one another. They cannot work because of insurmountable problems of information, coordination and comparative evaluation, which are exacerbated in complex, large-scale societies.

Humane socialism without markets is unfeasible, not because it is out of reach, but because it cannot exist as a workable system. The grapes are not out of reach – they do not and cannot exist. A humane big socialism is an unattainable and unrealistic utopia. We must instead consider the possibility of a much better capitalism.

---

[49]   Cohen (1995, p. 256).

PART II

Towards a feasible alternative: liberal solidarity

5.   Social knowledge and freedom to choose

> Cognition is the most socially-conditioned activity of man, and knowledge is the paramount social creation.
> Ludwik Fleck (1979)

There is a prominent dilemma in the debate between supporters of capitalism and of socialism. Should the individual's choices always be sacrosanct, or sometimes would it be better for the state to make those decisions on behalf of the individual?

Market-fundamentalist libertarians argue that because of the inaccessibility of much personal knowledge, the state is ill-equipped to act on the individual's behalf. State bureaucrats serve their own interests. It would be naïve to assume that they generally act in the interests of the population at large, even if they had appropriate information about the preferences or needs of the people. Even if the individual's choice is mistaken in some way, then it is best to concede full responsibility to the chooser, giving him or her the incentive to learn from mistakes. It is wrong in principle to diminish individual choice. These libertarians conclude that individuals should be free to choose, and markets should reign.

Jeremy Bentham, the founder of utilitarianism, assumed that the individual is the best judge of his or her own well-being. This same principle is embedded in mainstream economics, where individual utility is generally the metric of welfare. Excluded is the possibility that the state or an expert may know better than what the individual prefers.[1]

---

[1]   Unlike some libertarians, Bentham advocated some government intervention in the economy and promoted equality as an ultimate aim (Hutchison, 1956). Mill (1859, bk. 5, ch. 11) added a number of important qualifications to the claim that the individual always knows best. Hayek (1948, p. 15) distanced himself from this principle, on the persuasive grounds that 'nobody can know *who* knows best'. But this unavoidable ignorance does not mean that everything should be left to individuals alone: it means nurturing institutions that help to preserve, develop and proselyte useful knowledge. Little (1950) criticized the reliance by welfare economics on individual utility as the metric of well-being. See also Hodgson (2013).

Douglas Jay was an economist who challenged this creed. He was also a Labour politician. He argued that experts should have a role in making some decisions. In some crucial areas, the state is capable of bringing all this expertise together and needs to do so for the good of society as a whole. Jay wrote: 'in the case of nutrition and health, just as in the case of education, the gentleman in Whitehall really does know better what is good for people than the people know themselves'.[2]

This statement was used in Conservative propaganda to discredit the statism and bureaucratic elitism of the Labour Party. It was slightly misquoted by Margaret Thatcher and others as 'the man in Whitehall knows best'.[3]

But does the individual always know best? John Stuart Mill worried that an individual may prefer shallow pursuits, such as the pub game of pushpin, to reading great poetry. Freedom of choice does not necessarily lead to human development or flourishing. While Bentham had treated all forms of happiness as equal, Mill argued that intellectual and moral pleasures are superior to physical and other forms of satisfaction. For Mill, education was necessary to improve our understanding of our choices and of their consequences. An uneducated individual is an imperfect judge of his or her welfare. But we are then back to the problem of who else chooses, if it is not the individual.[4]

Another line of argument is based on human needs. Needs are distinguished from wants: wants are subjective desires or whims that are not necessarily beneficial. Whether we know them or not, needs are those things that must be met to avoid sustained and serious harm. We have needs such as food, shelter, healthcare, security, a safe environment, interactions, education and autonomy. These objective and trans-cultural needs are essential for all human survival and self-realization.[5]

Some needs are complex or obscure, and they must be researched by ongoing processes of scientific investigation. For example, nutritional science has divulged our need for vitamins. Psychology has explored the various modes of human interaction that are necessary for our mental health and for our personal development. In healthcare systems, doctors try to deal with our ailments using their understanding of scientific research. Similarly, in education, while some choices are made by

---

[2] Jay (1937, p. 317; 1947, p. 258). Whitehall is a London street, lined with numerous departments and ministries, that is recognized as the centre of UK government.

[3] Thatcher (1993, p. 6).

[4] Mill (1863).

[5] Finnis (1980), Doyal and Gough (1991) and Gough (2000, 2017).

students, teachers are trusted to guide them with their superior knowledge of the subject matter.

While needs-based approaches offer a way forward, we should not underestimate the practical and ethical difficulties involved. In both the natural and social sciences, there is no single 'scientific method' that provides a royal road to truth. Sciences embody internal controversies, and to a degree these are healthy for its development. Even sciences can make big mistakes. The fruitful development of science requires a liberal devotion to its autonomy and to its own internal mechanisms of assessment and adjustment.[6]

For several reasons, people should not be subject solely to the judgements of scientific experts. Scientocracy would entail a concentration of power as dangerous as the bureaucracy of big socialism. Countervailing powers are always required to protect individual rights. Because science can make mistakes, there has to be political pluralism, combined with a climate of scepticism and free speech.

The Lysenko scandal in the Soviet Union, where a mistaken theory was promoted by Stalin to the detriment of scientific progress, shows that science itself can be derailed unless there are adequate political checks and balances.[7] As argued previously, big socialism leads to political authoritarianism. Hence a needs-based approach could falter if it endorsed big socialism.

For a needs-based approach to gain sufficient support in a pluralist democracy, there has to be adequate public education in science and ongoing dialogue between scientists and others. Trust has to be established between experts and the wider population to alleviate fears that scientists are endorsing hoaxes to promote their own political agendas. To be fruitful and serve our interests, democracy itself needs ongoing public education and scrutiny.

The development of alternatives to the idea that 'we must always assume the individual knows best' is no easy matter. Nevertheless, we should try. A good place to start is to examine the conditions under which individuals make decisions concerning their wants, needs or welfare.

COMMUNITIES OF KNOWING

How do people know? How are their preferences formed? We carry some dispositions in our genes, but almost all knowledge is acquired after birth

---

[6] M. Polanyi (1940, 1951, 1962), Laudan (1977, 1981), Kitcher (1993).
[7] Birstein (2004).

by interacting with others. As noted in the preceding chapter, much of our knowledge in these instances is tacit and cannot be readily accessed or codified. Crucially, the deployment of this submerged knowledge is triggered by interactions with people, circumstances and material objects.

Much knowledge is social and contextual because of its reliance on external cues. Psychologists distinguish between procedural memory and other, more cognitive forms of retention, such as semantic, episodic or declarative memory. Only part of our memory can be readily recalled via internal thought processes alone. In contrast, procedural memory is triggered by events and stimuli. It typically leads to behavioural responses and it has major tacit components. As confirmed by experimental evidence, it is energized by social or other cues. 'Procedural knowledge is less subject to decay, less explicitly accessible, and less easy to transfer to novel circumstances.' Procedural knowledge is triggered by social settings.[8]

Atomistic individualists dislike the notion of *social knowledge.* But it does not involve a mistaken view that society has a brain, or that society can carry knowledge independently of the brains of human individuals. It is social because it relies on individual interaction and social relations, not because it is independent of individuals.

When we rely on interactions with others to recall the knowledge that we already have, then individual interactions and social relations are necessary to make this knowledge operational. It is enabled by social practices, discourses and institutional functions. As Ian Steedman argued in an important paper, once individual development and the acquisition of beliefs about the world are considered, individual preferences are intrinsically non-autonomous.[9]

Consider the nature and role of advertising. Nobel Laureates George Stigler and Gary Becker argued in their famous 1977 paper that advertising is simply 'information'. In their account, the preference function pre-exists, and is ready to deal with unpredictable and unknowable circumstances. Mysteriously, it has already learned how to recognize and trigger desires for the commodities of the future.[10]

Research in social psychology and on situated cognition counters the Stigler–Becker view. Individuals have to learn to interpret and evaluate incoming information. Rather than supplying us with information alone, the advertisers provide the context and means to interpret and evaluate

---

[8]   Tulving and Schacter (1990), Bonini and Egidi (1999). The quote is from Cohen and Bacdayan (1994, p. 557).

[9]   Steedman (1980).

[10]   Stigler and Becker (1977). For criticisms see Hodgson (1988, 2003).

their products. As well as information, they provide the mental framing for a positive assessment of the product.[11]

Corporate advertisers exploit the social nature of knowledge by using cultural and other cues to grab attention and intensify particular desires. Advertising is not simply information. It is an interactive process that guides our choices as well. Preferences are non-autonomous. Individual interactions and social structures can lead to changes in our preferences.

Individual choice requires a conceptual framework to make sense of the world. The individual needs a cognitive scaffolding to process available information and give it meaning. We develop this cognitive apparatus through processes of socialization and education, involving extensive interaction with others. As well as language, these interactions require other, pre-existing institutions. Cognition is a social and inter-active, as well as an individual, process. Individual knowledge and choice are impossible without these institutions and interactions.[12]

Advocates of ubiquitous and unfettered markets resist such arguments. For them all coercion is evil, but somehow there is no coercion on markets. But if everything has a cause, including individual choices or preferences, then it is difficult to deny that they could in some way be 'coerced' by outside forces. They avoid this irresistible conclusion by focusing on the choosing individual as an analytical starting point, rather than on the causes of choice.[13]

This narrow focus runs against the entire history of social and behavioural psychology, and of the profitable business of advertising, upon which large corporations spend trillions of dollars. For there to be no coercion on markets, the psychologists, the advertisers and their corporate funders must all be innocent of cajoling choice.[14]

This does not mean that we should ignore individual choices. Freedom implies that, within wide limits, individual choices are respected. Any constraint on choice requires rigorous justification. Promoting individual choice is important, but so too is understanding the causes of choice. There is always the possibility that choices can be rigged or wrong.

---

[11]   Lave and Wenger (1991), Hutchins (1995), Lane et al. (1996), Clark (1997).

[12]   Cooley (1922), Dewey (1929), Mead (1934), Fleck ([1935] 1979), Wittgenstein (1953), Kuhn (1962), Neisser (1983), Burge (1986), Douglas (1986), Lave and Wenger (1991), Hutchins (1995), Lane et al. (1996), Clark (1997), Bogdan (2000), Jasanoff (2004).

[13]   Some writers adopt the ontologically untenable view that human choice, unlike anything else, is somehow uncaused. For a critique of this view see Hodgson (2004, pp. 60–62).

[14]   See the classic work on social psychology by Asch (1952) and modern behavioural economics (Thaler and Sunstein, 2008).

So where does that leave us with the questions raised earlier in this chapter? It should now be clear that *neither* the isolated individual *nor* 'the man in Whitehall' can 'know best'. If possible, we should not entrust any individual alone with such superior knowledge. Knowledge depends on context and is energized by social interaction. Victory can be granted neither to the man-in-Whitehall-trusting socialist nor to the individual-trusting libertarian.[15]

Neither big socialism nor atomistic individualism takes adequate account of the nature of knowledge and the complexities of modern economic systems. To assess what is good for us, the dilemma is not simply between individuals and the state. It is about the ongoing education of individuals and the improvement of social institutions, so that choices are ever more informed and valuable.

Problems with atomistic individualism are dramatized within contemporary capitalism. Highly complex technologies have invaded our lives. When people buy smartphones, do they know enough about them to make an informed choice between the latest varieties on offer? In making such choices, over technologies that we poorly understand, we depend on the recommendations of others. Our capacity to make such decisions effectively depends on our use of friends, peer groups or social networks, where we obtain information about what works best, or what is fashionable. We have to rely to a degree on trust, rather than purely on the specifications of a contract. Choice is never a matter of an individual acting alone, with preferences that are fixed and immutable.

Such casual enlightenment is part and parcel of living in an open society where we benefit from interactions with others. In this respect the health and autonomy of civil society is vital. Civil society is not solely about commerce. As well as trade unions and employer associations, it embraces many forms of social association (including recreation, religion and philanthropy) that are not driven by pecuniary interests. Civil society can help us form preferences and make choices.[16]

---

[15]   Wainwright (1994) argued against Hayek's market individualism on the grounds that tacit knowledge is largely social, and often held by groups of workers rather than simply by individual entrepreneurs. But in her enthusiasm for big socialism, she failed to appreciate that, while the social nature of knowledge counters aspects of individualism, it does not annul the need for private property and markets. The social nature of knowledge does not make central planning any easier. On the contrary, because it depends on dispersed contexts, much social knowledge is even more difficult to amass by the central planners.

[16]   Cohen (1982), Keane (1988, 1998), Arato and Cohen (1992), Kumar (1993), Gellner (1994), Hodgson (2019c).

Knowledge is also fostered in the institutions of science. Science works on the basis of social interactions and routinized practices. These are enabled by universities, research institutes and scientific associations. Participation in the network is screened by access to the academy. The organization of science creates mechanisms that scrutinize research while creating a division of labour among researchers. Albeit imperfect and uneven, these mechanisms provide a way in which some degree of scientific consensus can be built, involving respect for the expertise of other researchers.

For example, although few of us are experts in the science of climate change, we have enough education to understand the basic arguments and sufficient trust in the institutions of science. Consequently, we accept their consensus position that some climate change is being driven by human activity. We have formed an opinion and established policy preferences though education and engagement with a community of scientists.[17]

To understand and gain knowledge we rely on the brains of others, as structured through networks and institutions.[18] While respecting individual choices it is also important to have policies that improve the effectiveness of the institutional contexts upon which choices always rely. Individuals deciding in isolation, individuals who are egotistical, and individuals who do not listen to others, can make extremely poor decisions. There is a need for pluralist, consensus-building, evidence-driven institutions to nurture science and popular engagement with it.

INSTITUTIONS, COGNITION AND SOCIAL POWER

Robert Putnam showed how the traditional local networks and institutions of civil society in the US have been eroded, partly by the rise of television, which confines us to our homes and evacuates social space beyond the home. Even worse, in the former Soviet bloc, the institutions of both science and civil society were smothered by the overbearing

---

17   On the institutions of scientific and technological development see Hull (1988), Lundvall (1992), Kitcher (1993), Nelson (1993), Mokyr (2003), Bowler and Morus (2005), Lipsey et al. (2005), Weisberg and Muldoon (2009).
18   This is a key insight of social epistemology (Fuller, 1988; Goldman, 1999; Surowiecki, 2004; Sunstein, 2006; Goldberg, 2010).

power of the party-state. Without the freedom to discuss and express criticism, civil society cannot prosper.[19]

The health of these civil institutions is crucial. We depend upon them to obtain information, assess priorities and make choices. Such institutions have cognitive and epistemic functions for individual agents. They mould our choices and the information available to us. Through choice and action, we lay down habits that in turn affect our preferences. What becomes habitual or customary in turn appears normal, and what is deemed normal is often preferred.

By guiding choices, institutions are crucial sources of social power. This power is not limited to advertising and the media, although these are of major importance. The institutions of science and of civil society are also mechanisms of power. As Steven Lukes argued, social power has multiple dimensions and is not simply a matter of overt coercion or the threat of force. Power is often exercised more subtly, and often without conflict. Lukes thus wrote:

> To put the matter sharply, A may exercise power over B by getting him to do what he does not want to do, but he also exercises power over him by influencing, shaping or determining his very wants. Indeed, is it not the supreme exercise of power to get another or others to have the desires you want them to have – that is, to secure their compliance by controlling their thoughts and desires?[20]

The exercise of power, even in a contract-ridden economy, is largely a result of non-contractual phenomena such as 'taking things for granted' or of conformism to established custom and accepted authority. As John Westergaard and Henrietta Resler put it: 'Power is to be found more in uneventful routine than in conscious and active exercise of will.' John R. Commons noted that on those rare occasions 'when customs change … it is realized that the compulsion of custom has been there all along, but unquestioned and undisturbed'.[21]

A crucial issue in modern socio-economic systems is inequality in access to and control over information. While an information-rich society can create opportunities for education and advancement, it can also lead to dangerous concentrations of wealth, power and influence in the hands of media giants and other large corporations. This is what Ugo Pagano

---

[19]   Cohen (1982), Arato and Cohen (1992), Kumar (1993), Putnam (2000), Birstein (2004). See Hodgson (2014, 2019c) for objections to the description of these attributes of civil society by Putnam and others as 'social capital'.

[20]   Lukes (1974, p. 23).

[21]   Westergaard and Resler (1976, p. 144), Commons (1934, p. 701).

called 'intellectual monopoly capitalism' and Guy Standing ironically described as 'the most unfree market system in history'.[22]

Big socialism offers no solution to this problem. Instead it grants a monopoly over control of information to the state. Big socialism undermines the autonomy of other social institutions and in practice it has eroded the independence of civil society as well. In practice it has eroded protective and representative organizations between the individual and the state.[23]

Atomistic individualism also offers no adequate solution. It stresses the individual over the vital relations between individuals that are necessary to create networks and other vital sources of countervailing power. The power of information can be addressed only by taking both individuals and institutions into account.

PRODUCT UNCERTAINTY AND COMPLEXITY: BEYOND THE STATE–MARKET DICHOTOMY

Thousands of years ago, states established monetary units and enforced standard weights and measures. Industrialization brought new challenges. The adulteration of food became notorious in the nineteenth century. The problem did not resolve itself through the reputation of suppliers in the market. Sawdust and chalk were added to flour, and tree leaves to tea. Contemporary investigators found out that food adulteration was a lot more common than was believed and that many tainted foods were poisonous. The result was a series of acts of legislation (in the UK, US and other countries) to regulate food quality. These regulations helped the reputable producer and protected the consumer.[24]

Eventually the scope of regulation expanded to cover medicinal drugs, fuel, transport, finance, insurance, employment practices, the licensing of professional occupations, environmental protection and other matters. The twentieth century saw the massive enlargement of the regulatory state. Among the foremost causes of its expansion have been the increasing diversity and complexity of goods and services.[25]

Regulatory bodies attempt to remove dangerous products from the market and to encourage producers to consider the interests of their

[22] Pagano (2014), Standing (2017, p. 81).
[23] Cohen (1982), Arato and Cohen (1992), Kumar (1993), Hodgson (2015a, pp. 301–305).
[24] Hutt and Hutt (1984), Law and Kim (2011).
[25] Pryor (1996), Hausmann et al. (2011).

customers. Such regulation does not mean the removal of choice, but the removal of harmful choices, where the consumer does not have the means to investigate the dangers that might be inherent in all the products consumed.

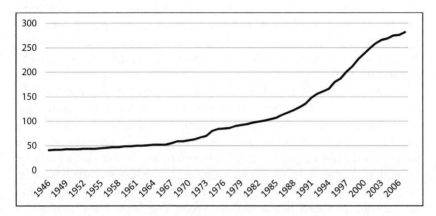

Data Source: GlobalReg Research Group (2011).

Figure 5.1   Total number of regulatory agencies in 24 OECD countries

Figure 5.1 shows the remarkable cumulative growth in regulatory agencies in developed capitalist countries. The data cover 60 years from 1946 to 2006 and include the 24 countries that constituted the Organisation for Economic Co-operation and Development (OECD) before its enlargement after 1990.[26] In this period, the overall number of regulatory agencies in these 24 countries has increased more than sixfold.[27]

The march of regulation shows little sign of having been arrested by so-called *neoliberal* attempts to 'de-regulate' since the 1970s. There has

---

[26]   Namely Australia, Austria, Belgium, Canada, Denmark, Finland, France, Germany, Greece, Iceland, Ireland, Italy, Japan, Luxembourg, the Netherlands, New Zealand, Norway, Portugal, Spain, Sweden, Switzerland, Turkey, the United Kingdom, and the United States. The kind help of David Levi-Faur is acknowledged in processing this data.

[27]   Jordana et al. (2011). They collected data on the year of establishment of regulatory agencies in 15 sectors and 48 countries for the period 1966–2007. They included all 30 OECD countries and 18 additional Latin American countries. Sectors included were competition, electricity, environment, financial services, food safety, gas, health services, insurance, pensions, pharmaceuticals, postal services, security and exchange, telecommunications, water, and work safety. Regulatory practices in major developed countries diffused after 1990 to the former Soviet bloc countries in Eastern Europe and also to Latin America. If these countries are included, then an even more remarkable rise in regulation becomes apparent after 1990.

been some removal of regulations, but the net upward trend has still been substantial. One major empirical study of attempted 'deregulation' in five major countries showed that regulations have often increased rather than diminished as an outcome.[28] In attempting to establish freer competition, new rules are necessary to encourage new entrants and promote competition. Of greater overall impact than attempted 'deregulation' has been the growth of privatization, when the state has set up agencies to regulate the privatized companies, to foster competition, maintain product quality and so on.

There are also areas where additional regulation is necessary. In particular, some corporations have grown massively and spread their power internationally. They have minimized their exposure to taxation and regulation by national governments, yet they have considerable political and economic influence. Their wealth and power can sometimes be used to influence democratic governments in corporate interests rather than in the interests of the people as a whole. International cooperation between governments is required to ensure that large corporations pay fair taxes and do not abuse their oligopolistic powers.[29]

We live in an era of increasingly regulated capitalism. The ill-defined, left-and-right rhetorics of *neoliberalism* and *free markets* mask all this. Modern capitalism is not a rebirth of the unfettered-market liberalism of the nineteenth century. The contrast is enormous: modern capitalism entails a copious and engrossing regulatory state. Regulations serve internal and external purposes. All trade requires an understanding of what is being traded. Regulations reduce the costs of verifying the nature and integrity of each good or service.

Some privatizations have improved efficiency, and some may have been necessary to deal with expanding problems of monitoring increasingly complex industries or technologies. The state cannot regulate everything from one centre. Devolved expertise is required. Some privatizations could be motivated less by so-called *neoliberal* ideology and more by the practical needs of detailed and delegated regulation.

Although big socialists and atomistic individualists regard all this as an ideological choice between the state and the market, in reality there are several intermediate combinatorial options. We should be pragmatic and experimental, to find what works best in particular contexts. Of

[28]   Vogel (1996).
[29]   Classic works on corporate power include Galbraith (1969), Lindblom (1977) and Chandler (1990).

course, regulatory agencies often fail. But so too do markets and state bureaucracies.[30]

A false dichotomy between the state and the market dominates the debate between socialism and atomistic individualism. Both sides get it wrong. In reality, the state helps to constitute the market system, by buttressing its key institutions and helping to enforce contracts and the rights of property. On the other hand, no state-run economy has ever functioned without some (legal or illegal) recourse to trade or markets. The pure extremes of a state-run or market-run economy have never existed and cannot exist.[31]

HOW INTERNATIONAL TRADE TURNS SOME LIBERTARIANS INTO NATIONALISTS

Substantial harmonization of standards and regulations is required when trade crosses international borders. Just as the separate states of the US have forged common systems of regulation and commercial law, the European Union (EU) Single Market enables large gains from trade within a harmonized system of regulation.

Any country moving outside the EU – such as the UK with Brexit – has to replace a huge apparatus of EU-wide regulation that has grown up in recent decades. This regulatory legislation is now an even more formidable burden than any increased tariff levels that may be adopted if the country leaves the EU Customs Union and Single Market.

This problem creates a dilemma for libertarians who distrust all state machines – especially large ones outside their national comfort zone. Hence, alongside nationalists and hard-left socialists, libertarians were in the intellectual forefront of the 2016 Brexit vote in the UK, chiming in with their complaints about Brussels bureaucracy.

Some of these libertarians are unable to accept that markets consist of more than individuals in isolation. They are seemingly unaware that all trade and markets must involve commonly accepted rules, as well as individuals and their assets. Markets, in short, are social institutions, where institutions are understood as systems of rules.[32]

In practice, exit from the EU Single Market means either that regulations have to be developed independently, thus reducing trade

---

[30] For a useful discussion see Stretton and Orchard (1994, esp. ch. 7).
[31] Hodgson (1984, 1988, 1999, 2015a), Martinez (2009), Eisner (2011), Marshall (2011).
[32] Hodgson (1988, 2015a), Marshall (2011).

possibilities, or that EU regulations have to be accepted for future trade, while having little say in their formation.

More generally, any contract between sellers and buyers across international boundaries requires agreement on the means of adjudication, if a dispute arises over its terms or fulfilment. Typically, it is agreed that disputes will be resolved in the courts of one nominated country. The European Court of Justice was set up to deal with contractual disputes within the EU, and between EU traders and contracting businesses located outside the EU.

In modern nations without empires, minimal-state libertarians are thus caught in a dilemma. To trade abroad, they must often accept the adjudications of a foreign court, thus dramatically violating their characteristic anti-state position, and accepting one that is outside their national homeland. The only alternative is to curtail their cherished ideological ambitions for free trade and markets across national boundaries.

Regulatory harmonization and trade dispute adjudication create problems for libertarians. Just as big socialists believe in a fantasy world where the state can do everything, some libertarians believe in the obverse fantasy of a minimal state, where trade somehow operates without an extensive state legal infrastructure. As Jamie Peck put it, these 'neoliberals' espouse 'a self-contradictory form of regulation-in-denial'.[33]

When trade crosses international boundaries, the problems of regulatory harmonization and dispute adjudication compel some libertarians to accept – especially when trading with a larger economic bloc – that disputes may have to be resolved in courts outside their national boundaries. For the more nationalistic libertarians, accepting the judgments of a foreign court is a step too far. The lenience granted to their national courts is not granted to those of foreigners.

British nationalist libertarians may imagine that Britain is still a great power, and that it has the capacity to compel that all trade disputes be resolved in British courts. In their imagination these libertarians bring back the British Empire. Imperial power makes every other country a rule-taker. This is far beyond the reality of contemporary, polycentric, global power.

---

[33]   Peck (2010, p. xiii).

CONCLUSION: REGULATION AND COMMUNITIES OF KNOWING

This chapter challenges the idea that individuals make choices with fixed preference functions that are unaffected by institutional and other circumstances. Individuals depend upon networks and institutions that do not simply provide them with information but also frame and guide their choices. This is true *a fortiori* in a market economy.

Atomistic individualists want to leave it to the individual, to choose what he or she wants. But the consequence would be to leave the individual to be swayed by powerful corporate, media and other organized interests.

But the maxim 'the individual knows best' should not be replaced by 'government knows best'. Instead it is a matter for governments, groups and individuals to build up networks and institutions that enable the individual to make fulfilling and worthwhile choices.

This problem of informed choice was addressed by the American philosopher John Dewey. Pointing to pervasive uncertainty and complexity, Dewey favoured an investigational, decentralized, process-oriented and participatory democracy. Institutional design had to be cautious and experimental. The primary role of experts is to lay out the feasible policy alternatives and their likely consequences, and to feed this information into public debate. Dewey stressed the need for an open-ended, flexible and experimental approach to dealing with human needs and welfare. He embraced a 'method of experimental and cooperative intelligence' based on democracy and science.[34]

Informed choice requires the ongoing evolution of layered, pluralist institutions, spanning the individual, civil society and the state. Neither big socialism nor atomistic individualism are capable of appreciating the complexities of modern capitalism and of embracing the pluralist and multi-layered solutions required. Big socialism uses democracy as a slogan, while its concentration of political and economic power in the hands of the state undermines both pluralism and civil society. On the other hand, atomistic individualism has insufficient trust in, or appreciation of, the institutions that are necessary to enable meaningful choice.

---

[34]   The quote is from Dewey (1935, p. 92). See also Dewey (1916, 1938, 1939). For discussions see Gouinlock (1972), Ryan (1995), Evans (2000) and Hodgson (2013, ch. 10).

Both ideologies become increasingly obsolete as capitalism becomes more knowledge-intensive and complex, depending on ever more intricate systems of regulation and scientific investigation. Just as it is increasingly difficult to gather relevant knowledge in the hands of a central planning authority, the individual relies more and more on others to make informed choices.

Our reliance on rules and regulations is dramatized even more in the world of international trade. Here we have to deal with the problem of establishing regulations and rules that can govern transnational commerce. Global trade thus poses a major challenge to both anti-state libertarians and big socialist nationalizers of industry.

The inevitable and unavoidable growth in regulation creates huge challenges for citizens, business, government and the legal system. The increasing bureaucratic burden creates new threats, such as institutional sclerosis and growing mistrust of bureaucracy or government.

These problems cannot be wished away by waving a libertarian magic wand that will somehow make markets and contracts solve all the problems. That dream world is now as unrealistic as the idealized picture of big socialism. Neither will the problems disappear with the socialist mantra of 'democratic control'. The taming of regulatory capitalism is a highly complex political problem, which will be with us for the foreseeable future.[35]

---

[35] Fukuyama (2014, pp. 473–6) noted that in the US the growing need for regulation since the 1970s, in a country with a strong mistrust of government, led to legislation that placed the burden of interpretation and dispute resolution on the courts. This greatly enlarged the scope for adversarial litigation, raising costs and undermining regulatory enforcement. By contrast, regulation in Europe was developed more by a reliance on executive power. It may be added that this has created problems within the European Union of a different kind, because regulation has crossed national boundaries and led to perceptions of loss of national control. This may have been a factor behind the Brexit vote in the UK in 2016.

6. The limits and indispensability of states and markets

> Commerce and manufactures can seldom flourish long in any state which does not enjoy a regular administration of justice, in which the people do not feel themselves secure in the possession of their property, in which the faith of contracts is not supported by law, and in which the authority of the state is not supposed to be regularly employed in enforcing the payment of debts from all those who are able to pay.
>
> Adam Smith (1776)

> In reality a *laissez-faire* economy ... cannot be reinvented. Even in its heyday it was a misnomer. It was created by state coercion, and depended at every point in its workings on the power of government.
>
> John Gray (1998)

Some economists believe that property and trade are natural human institutions: they are constituted whenever individuals freely engage with resources and each other. Hence property and contract have existed since the dawn of humanity: they are universal and ahistorical.[1]

A problem with this view is that it reduces the concept of property to that of mere possession or control.[2] At least in modern society, property rights are buttressed by institutionalized, legal authority. Property rights amount to much more than possession. They can include the rights to use, benefit from, change, sell or destroy the asset. Sometimes these rights are separable. For example, a landlord passes the right of use of an apartment, but not the rights to sell or alter the property, to the tenant in return for rent.

The full development of property rights required the rise of states with institutionalized legal systems, involving legislatures, judiciaries and mechanisms of enforcement. The state is vital for a market economy. As the institutional economist John R. Commons wrote: 'in the end, the

---

[1] Mises (1949) and Barzel (1997) are examples.

[2] Marx (1975, p. 351) also failed to acknowledge that property amounts to more than de facto possession, when he addressed 'private property' and argued that 'an object is only *ours* when we have it – ... when we directly possess, eat, drink, wear, inhabit it, etc., – in short, when we *use* it'.

actual title to property rests on the sovereign power of the state to enforce its decrees. ... There is, strictly speaking, no such thing as absolute, unlimited right of property, which law steps in as an afterthought to restrict.'[3]

A historically specific, state-related concept of property is emphasized by legal scholars. For example, the legal theorist Antony Honoré insisted that property is much more than possession or control:

> A people to whom ownership was unknown, or who accorded it a minor place in their arrangements, who meant by *meum* and *tuum* no more than 'what I (or you) presently hold' would live in a world that is not our world. ... To have worked out the notion of 'having a right to' as distinct from merely 'having' ... was a major intellectual achievement.[4]

We degrade the concept of *right* if we use the term *property right* to describe mere possession. Rights are moral entitlements, not patterns of de facto control. Rights are sustained by moral sentiments and dispositions to obey authority. The exclusive focus on control evades the potential role of property with legal title as collateral for loans for investment, which is a neglected but crucial issue in modern economic development.[5]

Property and contracts are at the core of capitalism, but capitalism entails more than property and markets. An additional defining feature of capitalism is the dominance of finance, including banks and markets for debt. Just as the state plays a crucial role in protecting property, it has also helped to develop and sustain the legal mechanisms for banking and financial markets. The state has been central to the constitution of the laws and organizations of modern financial systems.[6]

Capitalism cannot exist without this developed legal infrastructure, which supports property, contract and finance. But Marxists and some market fundamentalists deny the constitutive role of law in capitalist economies. Marxism consigns law to the 'superstructure': it is not seen as part of the economic base. In fact, the central 'economic' relations within capitalism depend on legal rules and their enforcement. Similarly, but from a different political viewpoint, some market fundamentalists

---

[3]   Commons (1893, p. 110).

[4]   Honoré (1961, pp. 107, 115).

[5]   See De Soto (2000), Cole and Grossman (2002), Steiger (2008), Fukuyama (2011, pp. 66–71), Arruñada (2012, 2017), Heinsohn and Steiger (2013) and Hodgson (2015a, 2015b, 2017a).

[6]   Commons (1924), Milhaupt and Pistor (2008) and Hodgson (2015a) emphasize the role of state law.

argue that laws and their enforcement are essentially no more than customs and can arise spontaneously, without the state. Both ideologies downplay the essential role of state law in modern capitalism.[7]

Given this basic legal role for the state within capitalism, the false dichotomy between the market and the state is further undermined. Property and markets need the state to constitute their very existence and to maintain their effectiveness.

Private property and markets are vital in any large-scale complex economy. But property and contract cannot resolve every economic problem. There are practical as well as moral limits to markets. It is immoral to trade some things, such as votes, slaves or child labour. Also, there are things that cannot be traded under capitalism, because trading them would overturn the nature of capitalism itself. This point is elaborated in the following sections.[8]

THERE CANNOT BE MARKETS FOR EVERYTHING

To function, markets involve laws and rules. Some writers propose markets for laws and rules, whereby legislative and enforcement systems are themselves traded.[9] If there are no limits to markets, then we must accept this possibility. But this would require a meta-market for the market rules that govern markets for rules, and a meta-meta-market for those rules, and so on – an infinite regress. By this logic, markets would become more than universal – they would be infinite. This of course would be impossible. We have a *reductio ad absurdum*.

In his argument against universal markets, Émile Durkheim explained that contracts require preconditions that cannot themselves be fully contracted: 'in a contract not everything is contractual'. All markets entail rules, and not all rules can be traded. Hence everything cannot be traded on markets.[10]

There are also good reasons to prevent key services of the legislature and the judiciary from being traded, including those relating to property and markets. For example, if judicial rulings were for sale to the highest bidder, then the security of property rights and their exchanges would be undermined. For a market economy to function there is a need for

---

[7]   Relevant statements are found in Marx (1971, pp. 20–21; 1976a, p. 178) and Hayek (1973, pp. 72–3). For criticisms of both see Hodgson (2015a).

[8]   On the moral limits of markets see Satz (2010) and Sandel (2012).

[9]   Benson and Engen (1988) envisage a 'market for laws'. See the critique in Hodgson (2019c).

[10]   Durkheim (1984, p. 158). See also Fox (1974).

'blocked exchanges' in some areas, excluding markets from the political, legislature and the judicial spheres.[11]

Consider the nature and use of information. It is well established that it has peculiar properties that make it different from standard commodities. For instance, once acquired by its buyer, codifiable information can often be easily reproduced in multiple copies, and possibly sold to others. But once it is sold, it also may remain in the hands of the seller. Also, the purchase is of something unknown. If we knew the information that we were going to buy, then we would no longer need to buy it. Instead, we take a leap into the dark, perhaps relying on some trusted source or authority.[12]

Consequently, in an economy involving substantial exchanges of information, it is sometimes difficult or even counter-productive to follow Friedrich Hayek's advice and establish clear 'rules which, above all, enable man to distinguish between mine and thine'. Hayek, of course, rightly emphasized the importance of information and knowledge. But such considerations also challenge the bounds of contract and market exchange.[13]

It is not always possible or efficient to break up information into discrete pieces and give each one an ownership tag. Through the use of patents, licences, copyright and so on, ideas can become intellectual property and traded on markets. But there would be problems if all information became tradeable property.

For example, the extension and subdivision of ownership in a densely interconnected knowledge economy can create an 'anti-commons' where extensively divided and interconnected rights obstruct investment and trade. This can happen with patent rights. For example, Wilbur and Orville Wright took out patents on several design features of their early aircraft, while Glenn Curtiss held patents on a superior aileron. Negotiations failed, so the government was obliged to step in and enforce the pooling of patent rights. The problem has become severe in modern, knowledge-intensive economies. Innovation in pharmaceuticals is often obstructed by the already-existing patents on the ingredients or processes involved.[14]

As market economies have become more complex, informational requirements have increased. While much information and knowledge

---

[11]   Walzer (1983). Hodgson (2019c) criticizes the non-metaphorical tendency to describe non-market phenomena as markets.
[12]   Nelson (1959), Arrow (1962).
[13]   Hayek (1948, p. 18).
[14]   Heller and Eisenberg (1998), Heller (2008), Pagano (2014), Standing (2017).

cannot readily be shared (because of tacitness, interpretative difficulty, or inaccessibility) much else can, and this can be of huge productive value. Restrictions on the shared possession of non-rivalrous informational assets can generate remarkable inefficiencies, especially when they are cheap to acquire and copy. Consequently, the benefits of private and contractual provision of some information may be much less than the overall opportunity costs of charging a price for its use. A healthy market system itself depends on the incompleteness of markets for information; some crucial data – including on prices and market rules – must be unowned and available freely.

In the early 1990s, CERN (the European Organization for Nuclear Research) developed key elements of the Internet infrastructure. To ensure that the information technology would become widespread, the ideas were released to the public without charge. Similarly, many software programs and operating systems are available free of charge. The Internet has vastly stimulated markets, but not all its components are marketed. Modern capitalism has reduced the marginal cost of many additional informational goods and services to near zero, making them nearly free, and open to non-market modes of distribution.[15]

MISSING FUTURES MARKETS FOR LABOUR

There are further reasons why under capitalism markets are always incomplete. In today's developed market economies, most people work under an employment contract. But a strange consequence of this liberty is that capitalism cannot in principle be a complete market economy. Employment contracts are for a limited period of time into the future. Enforcing detailed and extended property and contracting rights would limit the freedom of workers to quit their employment. The uncertainties involved in modern, complex, dynamic economies would also make such extensive future contracting inflexible and impractical.

For there to be full futures markets for labour, all workers must be able to enter into contracts for every future instant in their expected working life. But this would be tantamount to voluntary servitude. We cannot legally trade our life away in contracts for our whole lives. Employment contracts allow exit, subject to notice of a few weeks or months. Restrictions on the future trading of labour are important safeguards of the freedom of the employee.

---

[15]   See Rifkin (2014).

There is some future contracting for labour, such as when a student receives financial support from a company in return for a commitment to work for some years in the firm. But the time period is typically a few years, amounting to a small fraction of the student's future working life. There are sometimes 'non-compete' agreements with skilled employees, that prevent them leaving a firm and working for a rival for a while. These restrictive agreements are still far short of lifetime contracts.

For these reasons, under a market system with employment contracts, there can never be a complete set of markets for labour power. Although capitalism has meant a huge extension of property and markets, it has also, by freeing labour from servitude, sustained *missing* markets for labour futures.

Also, the future supply of labour power is not something that can be contracted at source, because babies cannot legally be farmed and sold as commodities within a system without slavery. Because they are not owned, human infants and their future labour power are not themselves produced under market arrangements. In an economy with markets and free labour, there are unavoidable missing markets for the original production of human resources.

The absence of futures markets for labour creates a problem for the employer. If he or she spends money on employee training and skill development, then this investment is lost when the worker leaves. As a result, without compensatory arrangements, employers might under-invest in human learning and education.[16]

Workers can be incentivized to remain with the employer, providing a stronger basis for training in skills. For example, employers might create a participatory culture that engenders worker commitment and loyalty to encourage 'voice' rather than 'exit' when grievances arise. The likelihood of worker exit can also be reduced by distributing company shares to employees. There may be an additional role for state aid for training. Governments have subsidized employee training (with some success) in some countries and in some US states.[17]

---

[16]   This point was made by Marshall (1920, p. 565).

[17]   On *voice* and *exit* see Hirschman (1970). On employee share ownership see Poole and Whitfield (1994), Pendleton et al. (1998), Hubbick (2001) and Robinson and Zhang (2005). On state funding of training see Holzer et al. (1993), Van Horn and Fichtner (2003) and Thelen (2004).

MISSING MARKETS AND SECOND-BEST SOLUTIONS

Capitalism can never be a 100 per cent market economy. There is an important theoretical literature in economics on missing markets, addressed within the type of general equilibrium theory developed by Nobel Laureates Kenneth Arrow and Gerard Debreu.[18] If one of the commodity-, state- and time-dependent markets is missing, then the absence of key information concerning prices on that missing market can cascade through the system and affect the overall outcome. The efficiency of other markets can be spoilt.

Accordingly, Nobel Laureate Oliver Hart showed that in 'an economy with incomplete markets ... the usual continuity and convexity assumptions are not sufficient to ensure the existence of equilibrium' and in such circumstances a market equilibrium may be Pareto suboptimal. Furthermore, 'if we start off in a situation where markets are incomplete, opening new markets may make things worse rather than better. In this respect, an economy with incomplete markets is like a typical second best situation.' Likewise, Michael Magill and Martine Quinzii showed that missing markets can lead to absent or indeterminate equilibria in existing markets.[19]

Missing markets have major implications. We enter the world of 'second-best' solutions. As Richard Lipsey and Kelvin Lancaster famously demonstrated, when one or more optimality conditions cannot be satisfied, it is possible that the next-best solution involves changing other variables away from the values that would otherwise be optimal. If it is unfeasible to introduce a well-functioning market in any part of the system, then it is possible that the introduction of further market distortions or restrictions may partially counteract that omission, and lead to a more efficient outcome. There is no 'one-size-fits-all' policy solution where the removal of market impediments always brings efficiency or welfare. On the contrary, welfare outcomes of such interventions could be positive or negative – they would be dependent on their contexts.[20]

This does not mean that the state must always step in when markets fail or where they are absent. For example, the absence of markets for child-rearing does not mean that this must be done by the state. In most

---

[18]   Arrow and Debreu (1954).

[19]   Hart (1975, p. 442). Magill and Quinzii (1996) weakened their argument by treating missing markets primarily as a result of the limitations of the human psyche, rather than also of specific social structures. Hence they overlooked the important missing markets for labour and future skills.

[20]   Lipsey and Lancaster (1956). Lipsey (2007).

societies, families care for the children. But the state may be needed elsewhere when there are major problems of overall coordination or a need for large-scale investment. Determining what the state can or cannot do well in these contexts is a matter of experimentation, and of trial and error.

In sum, markets cannot govern everything within capitalism. Capitalism, like all other systems, contains 'impurities' where the prevailing structures – including markets in the case of capitalism – are conjoined with structures of a different type. Elsewhere I have described this as the *impurity principle*: every socio-economic system must rely on at least one structurally dissimilar subsystem to function. This broad principle is supported by theoretical argument and empirical evidence.[21]

FINANCIAL MARKETS AND THE STATE

The state has been a major player in the development of capitalist financial institutions. From a historical perspective this is unsurprising, because the state has long been involved in the development of money itself. The textbook story of the spontaneous development of money from barter may have a useful heuristic function, but historically it is a myth. In the beginning, money and coinage were typically issued by the state. The development of modern financial systems was typically a response to the need of the state for finance, particularly to pay for wars.[22]

Financial markets are important to process large amounts of business information and allocate resources to different areas of economy activity. But there is no example of a modern system of large-scale finance that has not relied heavily on the state. This does not mean that financial institutions are creatures of the state alone. There is always an essential hybridity, where public and private institutions conjoin to create the modern financial powerhouses of capitalist development.

The state not only constitutes but sustains capitalist financial institutions. During the financial collapse of 2008, governments stepped in to bail out several large banks. Governments had a choice: to transfer large

[21] Hodgson (1984, 1988, 1999, 2015a). Note that the impurity principle is not functionalist. Functionalism upholds that the existence of a specific component is explained by its function. But the impurity principle does not explain why any particular subsystem exists. Alternatives are often possible. Because the impurity principle does not claim to explain the existence of any specific subsystem, it is not functionalism.

[22] Knapp (1924), Keynes (1930), Smithin (2000), Vitols (2001), Ingham (2004, 2008), Forstater (2006), Milhaupt and Pistor (2008), Graeber (2011), Fukuyama (2011), Wray (2012) and Hodgson (2015a, 2017a).

amounts of money to private banks to keep them solvent, or to let them fail. Major bank failures would have led to a disastrous economic collapse: the whole economy would have suffered even more than the massive costs of the bailouts.

Hence, paradoxically, leaving everything to the market would have had serious and long-lasting negative effects on the market economy. The survival of a buoyant market economy meant state intervention to save financial markets.

Modern capitalist finance involves a combination of state and private institutions. The system involves some market competition, but one of its functions is to create rules and set expectations for the financing of the rest of the market economy. This is why governments should not allow financial systems to topple – they embody the rules and expectations that allow other markets to function.

Capitalist finance depends on expectations of the future: these are inherently uncertain and prone to disturbing perceptions or rumours. Shocks and uncertainties always threaten to disturb an equilibrium and trigger processes where positive feedback creates speculative booms or destructive slumps. Capitalism is both dynamic and potentially unstable. For these reasons, Keynesian economists have argued for government intervention to maintain levels of aggregate demand and to minimize damaging downturns.[23]

PEOPLE AND PROFITS

'People before profits' is a prominent socialist slogan. It sounds nice. But on closer inspection it begins to unravel. It assumes that serving people and their interests is inconsistent with the profit motive and somehow the former should displace the latter. It suggests that there is a viable and humane alternative mode of economic organization that can harness different motives.

It is important that we care for others. We can care more readily for those close to us, who we know well: our family, our friends and our workmates. Extending our caring to society as a whole is trickier. It is a political project. It is a complex problem involving the use of institutions that can process information, rank priorities and provide incentives for individuals. 'People before profits' signals nothing of these complexities.

---

[23] See Keynes (1936), Minsky (1982, 1986) and Bowles et al. (2017). Reinhart and Rogoff (2009) provided 800 years of evidence that financial crises are more frequent than often believed.

We need to assess alternative forms of economic organization. Capitalism relies on profit-seeking institutions to assess priorities and incentivize individuals. Does the quest for profit go against the interests of the people? This has been a matter of protracted dispute for more than 300 years.

In 1714 Bernard Mandeville proposed in his *Fable of the Bees* that private vices can lead to public virtues. Greed for luxuries can create employment and wealth for others. Economic theory has established that this is valid under specific conditions only. The pioneering welfare economist Arthur Pigou identified circumstances where private satisfaction does not necessarily correspond with the interests or preferences of other people. For example, the use of car transport can impose pollution and congestion costs on others.[24]

Even when the profit motive helps to increase everyone's utility (or satisfaction) it does not necessarily mean that it serves the interests of the people. Interests are served by the satisfaction of needs, which may not correspond to wants. A profit-driven system is driven by consumers who maximize their satisfaction of wants at the lowest cost. It does not necessarily mean that their needs are best served.

The profit motive is far from perfect and a market economy requires some state regulation to help minimize problems and mitigate defects. For this reason, no developed capitalism has ever avoided state regulation. This is an argument against *laissez-faire*. But it is not an argument against a market economy. Fundamentally, in a modern, large-scale economy, there is no alternative to extensive private ownership and the profit motive.

If 'people before profit' means abolishing the profit motive, then how else are the needs of people to be met? We are back to the massive problems raised in the first part of this book. It turns out in practice that many human needs are not best served by public ownership and planning of the entire economy.

While big socialism can be successful in some areas, it fails in others, particularly in terms of individual self-realization and human aspiration. Cuba, for example, has a good health and education system and extreme

---

[24]   Pigou (1920). Pigou took a pragmatic and experimental approach toward the question of socialism versus capitalism. While accepting capitalism 'for the time being', he stressed the importance of 'graduated death duties and graduated income tax … with the deliberate purpose of diminishing our glaring inequalities of fortune and opportunity which deface our present civilisation'. He also favoured substantial government-promoted investment in 'the health, intelligence and character of the people' (Pigou, 1937, pp. 137–8).

poverty is rare. But, apart from the tourist sector, the economy is stagnant. Freedom of expression is highly limited.[25]

The profit motive should not govern everything, but neither should state planning. Some central allocation can be beneficial in particular areas. But the profit motive can be harnessed to great advantage. In the right circumstances, the profit motive can help drive down costs and stimulate innovation.

If some goods or services can be provided by private companies at lower cost, with no degradation of product quality, working conditions or environmental standards, then there is no reason why the private sector should not step in. But if these activities are outsourced by a public body, or government regulation is required to prevent monopolistic pricing, then the costs involved must include the costs of regulation and of monitoring and enforcing contracts.

Local and national government services are often contracted out to private companies. A private firm may be given a government contract to manage prisons, provide waste disposal services, monitor business compliance with environmental standards, and so on. Evaluation of these developments should be experimental and pragmatic, rather than crudely ideological.

A key question is whether outsourcing, while maintaining standards and the quality of service, can reduce overall costs. If costs are reduced and standards are maintained, then there should be no objection to outsourcing. But if there is no significant reduction of overall costs (including the costs of monitoring compliance with the outsourcing contract), or if standards deteriorate, then such services might be brought back into government management.

Much of the evidence is mixed. A review by Germà Bel and Mildred Warner of several studies since 1970 of the privatization of solid waste and water services found little support for a link between privatization and cost savings. Cost savings were not found in water delivery and were not systematic in waste services. The authors concluded that a less ideological and much more pragmatic and case-by-case approach was needed.[26]

A comprehensive meta-survey by William L. Megginson and Jeffry M. Netter of empirical studies of privatization in developed and developing countries since 1980 found strong evidence in many cases that the change

---

[25] Reuters (2015).
[26] Bel and Warner (2008).

from public to private ownership had resulted in substantial improvements in efficiency and productivity growth. But the effects were neither universal, immediate nor uniform. Different methods of privatization – from issuing everyone share-vouchers without charge to selling shares on the market – sometimes produced different results. If the state-owned enterprise was already facing other (private or public) competitors, then the cost-reducing benefits of privatization were often lessened. But the advantages of competition often take some time to work through.[27]

Megginson and Netter noted that one of the effects of the global wave of privatizations since 1980 has been to add massively to the scale of capital markets. This is not necessarily a deleterious outcome. But, as noted above, financial markets are inherently unstable. Hence mass privatization may lead to further problems as well as opportunities. Ironically, if privatization leads to larger capital markets with an enhanced threat of financial instability, then this puts more responsibility for maintaining financial stability on the state.

CONTROVERSIES OVER PUBLIC GOODS

The economist and Nobel Laureate Paul Samuelson established the concept of a *public good* in an academic paper in 1954, although some of the basic ideas involved had been formulated previously by others. John Stuart Mill, for example, had argued that lighthouses should be built and financed by governments. Their widespread benefits could not be financed by tolls on passing ships, hence there were insufficient incentives to construct them.[28]

By definition, public goods are non-rivalrous and non-excludable. *Non-rivalrous* means that the use or consumption of the good or service by any actor does not significantly reduce the amount available for others. *Non-excludable* means that potential users cannot practically be excluded from the use of the good or service (see Table 6.1).[29]

---

[27] Megginson and Netter (2001). While studies reveal efficiency gains from privatization, not all the empirical investigations looked out for possible deteriorations in the quality of output, environmental standards or working conditions. These too should be considered.

[28] Mill (1859, bk. 5, ch. 11).

[29] As with many such definitions, there are few, if any, pure cases. Hence a *public good* refers to a good or service where consumption by one person does not *significantly* reduce the amount available for others, and where potential users cannot *practically or generally* be excluded from the use of the good or service.

Table 6.1   Private goods, public goods, club goods and common-pool resources

	Excludable	Non-Excludable
Rivalrous	Private Goods Possible examples: food, housing, clothing, furniture, motor cars	Common-Pool Resources Possible examples: accessible pastures, forests, water resources or fisheries
Non-Rivalrous	Club Goods Possible examples: subscription television via Internet or cable, computer software, private parks	Public Goods Possible examples: lighthouses, free radio, free television, open-source information, street lighting

For example, if a town council uses local tax revenues to set up and maintain lighting on its streets, then there are widespread benefits for everyone. But it is difficult to charge people individually, according to whether they benefit from the illumination. Samuelson argued that *'no decentralized pricing system can serve to determine optimally these levels of collective consumption ...* any one person can hope to snatch some selfish benefit in a way not possible under the self-policing competitive pricing of private goods'.[30]

When elections to the town council occur, self-interested citizens will vote for candidates proposing lower taxes, assuming that they will benefit anyway from any provision of public goods. Why pay more taxes when the lighting is free at the point of use? Self-interested consumers will try to hitch a free-ride. The outcome is that the street lighting will be underfunded, while everyone would prefer streets that are well-lit.

Samuelson's argument was popularized by John Kenneth Galbraith in his 1958 book *The Affluent Society*. Galbraith argued that vital public goods would be under-provided in a market system: 'private opulence and public squalor' could coexist.[31] The combined efforts of a revered mainstream economic theoretician and of an eloquent popularizer of economic wisdom helped to pave the way for a wave of interventionist policies in the US and other developed economies.

But Ronald Coase pointed out that many early lighthouses in England were privately constructed and financed by tolls at the ports. Hence 'economists should not use the lighthouse as an example of a service

---

30   Samuelson (1954, pp. 388–9, emphasis in original).
31   Galbraith (1958).

which could only be provided by government'.[32] This and other interventions led to a widespread reaction against the Samuelson–Galbraith view that public goods necessarily require public provision or public financing.

A lighthouse is a means to an end, to help a vessel navigate from port A to port B. Coase had shown that port A or B could impose a toll, to finance the lighthouse that guided the ships that used these ports. Failure to pay the toll might mean exclusion from the port. Hence, if the lighthouse were treated as part of a service for 'getting safely into or out of a port' then its provisions would be excludable (for the ships using the ports) and the service as a whole would not be a pure public good. A lighthouse is not a pure and separable public good. Hence non-state financing is feasible.

Free radio and television broadcasts and open-source computer software are public goods. (Much software can be copied very cheaply, and it is often costly to prevent this replication.) Yet both are often provided by private companies. These examples also question the idea that public goods must be publicly financed.[33]

But as with the lighthouse there are complications. Private radio and television broadcasters often finance their broadcasts by advertising. Computer companies sometimes make software free or low cost to encourage use of their computers for which the software was designed. The software is given away to help sell the hardware, or there is a charge for support services for software users. Note that, as with lighthouses, private incentives are established in these instances by bundling services together: access to a port requires the use of a lighthouse, receiving a private broadcast means receiving adverts as well, the use of a particular computer requires use of its designated software.

Even if we exclude the cases where a public good is necessarily consumed jointly with something else, then there are still possibilities for private provision of public goods. There are many cases – as discussed above – where the state franchises out the provision of goods or services to private contractors. Such provision could include public goods. In these cases, public financing remains, but provision is private.

The claimed advantages of private franchising might include the introduction of an element of competition between potential franchisees, and the possibilities of efficiency gains through well-focused, relatively autonomous private providers. But here again the proof of the pudding is

---

[32] Coase (1974b, p. 376). But Bertrand (2006) showed that government was more involved in early British lighthouse projects than Coase had suggested.
[33] Holcombe (1997).

in the eating. Many public franchising operations have failed to deliver the promised gains. Others have been more successful.

In summary, when public goods are (nearly) pure and un-combined with other goods or services, then there may be a need for public financing, but not necessarily public provision. The existence of a public good does not necessarily imply that it has to be provided by government, particularly if it is bundled with other services, just as there is no compelling case that its private provision will always be superior or even feasible.

Accordingly, once again, we end up with a pragmatic rather than a doctrinaire conclusion. Economic systems are complex, with varied, interconnected components. Theory simplifies: it does not catch all the interactive effects. Any theory has continuously to be appraised in the light of empirical experience.

We should also address a basic assumption that is adopted by many authors on both sides of the debates surrounding public goods. The assumption is that actors act wholly out of self-interest. From evidence with humans in laboratory experiments and elsewhere, we now know that this is untrue.[34]

In a Public Goods Game, individuals in a group (of say 10) are each given (say) $10 and offered the choice of keeping the money for themselves or investing it for the benefit of the whole group. All the money invested is multiplied by (say) two and distributed equally to all the members of the group, whether they contributed or not. If everyone contributes, then each person will receive $20. If only one contributes, then she will receive $2. If no one contributes, each member gets $10. If everyone is a self-interested payoff maximizer, who assumes that everyone else is self-interested and sees the risk of non-contribution by others, then no one will invest anything, and everyone will keep $10. But in some laboratory experiments about half the participants contributed. No experimental study confirms the prediction, based on assumed self-interest, of an overall zero contribution.[35]

However, the number of participants is important. We know from the work of Elinor Ostrom and others that cooperation is possible over the use of non-excludable resources, even when usage is rivalrous, leading to possible degradation of the resource. (Non-excludable resources that have rivalrous usage are defined as *common-pool resources*, they are not

---

[34] Stretton and Orchard (1994) challenged the assumption of self-interest in public choice theory.

[35] See Dawes and Thaler (1988, p. 189), Andreoni (1995), Hoffman et al. (1998), Ostrom (1998).

public goods.) Ostrom's examples highlight the role of face-to-face interaction and the building of trust. It is doubtful that these mechanisms can be expanded to large-scale societies, at least without additional systems of control and enforcement. These crucial issues are worthy of much more research.[36]

IS EDUCATION A PUBLIC GOOD?

Careful, rational discussion of the issues surrounding vital debates over public and private provision is not simply impeded by the existence of opposing ideological extremes. There is also a growing disrespect by politicians and journalists, who should know better, for the careful use of the terms that have been established by scholars in this area.

A prominent misunderstanding of *public good* is that it means 'a good that can or should be provided by government'. This conflation of *public good* with *public provision* is mistaken. But this should not lead us to attempt to redefine *public good*. That would create even more conceptual havoc. Instead it would be more useful to look at better, empirically grounded criteria that might be used to consider whether public or private provision were superior in specific cases.

An even cruder misunderstanding is that *public good* means 'good for the public'. While anyone who has taken Econ 101 should spot this error, it is nevertheless widespread. The term 'good' in this context does not mean virtuous or worthwhile. Instead in this case it means objects of trade, including traded services. Bad things, like tobacco, heroin and personnel mines, are also *goods* in this sense.

As leader of the UK Labour Party, Jeremy Corbyn has opined that 'education is a public good' and suggested that this implies that it should all be provided by government and funded by taxation. All three leaders of the UK Green Party since 2012 – Natalie Bennett, Caroline Lucas and Jonathan Bartley – have repeated the phrase 'education is a public good'. They too implied that all education should be free of charge to the user and paid for out of taxation. Similarly, Shakira Martin, who was elected President of the UK National Union of Students in 2017, remarked: 'Education is a public good and should be paid for through taxation.'

---

[36] Ostrom (1990). Many paid-for information services have a very low marginal cost and hence can be treated as non-rivalrous and hence *club goods*. The dramatic contemporary growth of excludable information services with low marginal cost has major implications (Pagano, 2014; Rifkin, 2014; Standing, 2017).

Influential organizations are led by people who have not learned the lessons of Econ 101.[37]

Assume that education is 'good for the public' and it should be funded out of taxation and provided by public organizations. But many additional things are 'good for the public', including clothing, food and housing. By the same logic, these 'goods' should all be funded out of general taxation and distributed without further charge to their users. Influential politicians thus suggest that everything that serves basic needs should be financed, and possibly distributed, by the state. The market would simply be left for luxuries. Their logic implies a state-run economy of which Stalin and Mao would be envious.

Second, even if education were a public good (by the Econ 101 definition), then this would not imply that it should be paid for out of taxation. As noted above, radio and television broadcasting can be a public good. But little of it is paid out of taxation, and it would be difficult to make the case that it should be, unless we fancy a totalitarian state that takes over broadcasting and curtails all private radio and television stations.

Third, with the Econ 101 definition of a public good in mind, note that education is generally a rivalrous rather than a non-rivalrous service. Education services require resources, including buildings, infrastructure, equipment and trained teachers. Additional students generally require additional resources. (Although in some cases the marginal cost is low, such as with mass-distributed online courses.) Consequently, education provision is generally rivalrous.

Fourth, again with an eye on the Econ 101 definition, note that education services are mostly (but not entirely) excludable. Schools and universities can readily prevent other people from attending, while it is much more difficult to prevent any passing mariner from observing the light from a lighthouse.

Technically, by the standard definition, most education services are *private goods*, because their provision is both excludable and rivalrous. But there is no necessary reason why all private goods should be privately

---

[37]　Walker (2017), Bennett (2017), Rampen (2016), Martin (2017). This misunderstanding of the meaning of *public good* is too common among journalists and some academics, who all have a moral responsibility to use terms accurately. Standing (2017, p. 202) saw education as a 'natural' public good because 'one person having more of it does not prevent another from having more of it as well'. This criterion is unclear, inaccurately applied and insufficient. Assume that 'education' refers to services, not outcomes. Standing's statement is then inaccurate because many education services are rivalrous. It also insufficient, because even if they were non-rivalrous, then they would also need to be non-excludable to qualify as public goods.

provided. The Econ 101 distinction between public and private goods does not readily or directly correspond with public and private provision respectively.

The parts of an education system that are actually or virtually non-rivalrous, such as massive online courses, are technically *club goods*. Like radio and television broadcasting, they can feasibly be provided by public or private organizations.

POSITIVE AND NEGATIVE EXTERNALITIES

When students receive their qualifications, they often have advantages over others on the job market. They reap benefits. Nevertheless, with education there are also strong positive spill-over effects. Educated people help to raise the levels of public culture and discourse and can pass on some of their skills to others. Educated people are also vital for a healthy democracy.

The spill-over effects are important and relate to the question of public versus private provision. Another word for a spill-over is an *externality:* this is a cost or benefit that affects someone who did not choose to incur that cost or benefit. Externalities can be positive or negative. Examples of negative externalities are pollution or congestion caused by motor cars. Because a driver will suffer only a fraction of the overall pollution and congestion costs of making a car journey, negative externalities impose costs on many others with little penalty for the car user. By standard assumptions, unless compensatory measures are taken, car use will be excessive and suboptimal.

In developing the theory of externalities, Pigou argued that in the presence of negative externalities some public authority should intervene to impose taxes or subsidize superior alternatives. By such measures, motor car traffic and pollution could be reduced. Inversely, services such as education with positive externalities should receive subsidies or be provided free, to encourage more extensive participation in these activities.[38]

---

[38]   Pigou's (1920) classic analysis was developed by K. William Kapp (1950) who focused on the social costs of business enterprise. Kapp's (2016) essays show that he engaged with the socialist calculation debate, noting the failure of market prices to reflect social costs and individual needs. He seemed to assume, but did not show, that any meaningful calculation of costs or prices was possible in a planned economy. He appraised the limits of markets, but not those of planning. During their correspondence in 1941, the leading American institutional economist J.M. Clark discerned this lack of 'balance' in his analysis. Clark hinted that Kapp had compared the flaws of the real market economy with

In a famous paper, Coase dramatically changed the terms of debate with his argument that if transaction costs were zero, then all the extra costs or benefits could be subject to contractual arrangements and the externalities would disappear. For example, if the owner of every dwelling near a road had property rights in the surrounding segment of the atmosphere, then the driver of a passing and polluting car could be sued for degradation of that property. The pollution externality would be internalized.[39]

Coase's intention was to emphasize transaction costs: the existence of externalities is dependent on positive transaction costs. Coase accepted that in many cases these costs would be high. But many market enthusiasts ignored or underestimated the transaction-cost aspect of Coase's argument. Instead, their foremost claim was that Coase had undermined the case of public intervention based on externalities.[40]

Consider the positive externalities of education. It would be impossible or socially destructive for every educated person to charge a fee to participants in an intellectual dinner conversation, or to invoice the government for making a well-informed choice when casting his or her vote in the ballot box. The internalization of these positive externalities is impossible or undesirable.

The issue of missing markets is relevant here, as raised above. The prohibition of slavery means that we cannot have complete futures markets for labour. This means an enforced absence of transactions, which would be equivalent to making the transaction costs infinite.

Consequently, for reasons given above, education and training will be undersupplied through markets under capitalism. There is a rationale for some kind of public intervention. Of course, government intervention has its problems too. But markets cannot govern everything. We must experiment, and compare real-world cases, not idealized models.

There are mixtures of public and private provision of education in most countries. In higher education, many universities are private but depend on public funding. Education institutions can be local or national government organizations, charities, private not-for-profit corporations or

---

an 'ideal' planned system in his imagination. Clark asked Kapp to consider 'what sphere would be left to the market process, and what imperfections in that sphere would be tolerated in the interest of minimising central regimentation and preserving the prerequisites of liberty, both in thought and expression as well as of consumption and production?' (Berger, 2017, pp. 100 ff.).

[39] Coase (1960).

[40] See, for example, Block (1989), who proposed that the atmosphere could be fenced off with laser beams, thus reducing transaction costs and helping to enforce property rights.

private shareholder corporations. The global diversity of education systems provides an opportunity to compare them and consider what works
best.

EDUCATION AND HEALTH: SIMILARITIES AND DIFFERENCES

Like education, some health services have strong positive externalities.
For example, efforts to reduce the incidence of infectious diseases bestow
benefits for all those vulnerable to them. But in other aspects of
healthcare, such as surgery or palliative care, the positive externalities are
much lower or non-existent.

In both health and education services there are strong information
asymmetries between the providers and consumers. Teachers and doctors
know more about the issues at hand than students or patients. This means
that choice cannot be fully informed and must depend to a degree on
accreditation and trust.

Health, nutrition and education are basic needs, necessary for human
fulfilment. But general requirements for education or nutrition are more
uniformly distributed than the requirement for healthcare services. Many
healthcare requirements are specific to the individual involved. In addition, many patients are not responsible for their plight. These special
features of healthcare requirements have major motivational, moral and
policy implications, which are explored elsewhere.[41]

The complexity, variety and idiosyncrasy of healthcare services create
additional problems for market-based solutions. Market-based systems
may exacerbate the problem of transaction costs. Planned systems face
other problems of knowledge, complexity and uncertainty.

In reality we are not faced with a simple dichotomy between
market-based and planned systems. In fact, most national healthcare
systems involve a complex combination of administration and competition, of public and private provision, and of centralized and decentralized authority.

The NHS in the UK has been a mixed system since its inception.
General practitioners (GPs) are the gatekeepers for access to NHS
hospitals and other services, yet GPs are not NHS employees and their
practices are private legal entities. The development and production of
many drugs and much equipment for the NHS is conducted by private

---

[41]   Hodgson (2008; 2013, ch. 8).

companies. The NHS has been relatively successful in synergizing private and public elements.

Like other health systems the NHS faces enormous challenges in the twenty-first century, particularly concerning the funding of increasingly sophisticated services for an ageing population. Again, there is a need for careful, decentralized, organizational experimentation rather than ideological dogma.

CONCLUSION: THE BENEFITS OF AN EXPERIMENTAL MIXED ECONOMY

There never has been a pure capitalism, where everything is a commodity, and there never will be. Not only are there unavoidable missing markets, but also the state legal system is necessary to constitute those markets that exist. Furthermore, experience tells us that capitalism, at its most productive and dynamic, involves synergetic cooperation between public and private institutions. The impressive vigour of several capitalist economies shows that, while markets are necessary for economic innovation and vitality, modern economies also benefit from some economic intervention by the state.[42]

The basic functions of the state in a capitalist economy include national defence, law and order, enforcing contracts and protecting property. Without further state intervention, education and healthcare will be confined only to those that can afford them, and then society as a whole will not benefit from their positive externalities. With a minimal state, economic inequalities within capitalism are likely to become greater, with the growth of a large and only partially employable underclass.[43] Poverty and destitution would coexist alongside environmental degradation. Unless people have food, housing, healthcare and adequate education, then they cannot be players on the labour market and the market cannot work to resolve these problems. Substantial public intervention is necessary to make the market system work.

This applies also to the regulation of monopoly, the provision of essential information, and the general regulation of the rules of the game

---

[42] Nelson (1981, 2003), Lazonick (1991), Kenworthy (1995), Chang and Rowthorn (1995), Chang (1997, 2002a, 2002b), Evans and Rauch (1999), Vogel (2006), Reinert (2007), Martinez (2009) and Mazzucato (2013). This does not mean that state intervention is always beneficial (Olson, 1982; Scully, 1992; Yavas, 1998). But the experience of real-world mixed economies needs to be explored.

[43] On the mechanisms that generate economic inequality within capitalism see Galbraith (2012), Piketty (2014) and Hodgson (2015a, pp. 357–62).

in the capitalist system, including the regulation of finance, which provides its life-blood. The state intervenes to a degree in these areas in most capitalist countries, but to different extents and with varying measures of success.

Evidence in the more dynamic capitalist economies suggests that the state often takes the role of a major strategic leader. It may set priorities, support strategic sectors, promote innovation, coordinate interconnected initiatives, and provide and process vital information. But the evidence also shows that such interventions do not always work, or they have strong downsides as well as upsides. Again it is necessary to experiment and to learn from experience.[44]

The state must also redistribute some wealth from the ultra-rich, especially if capitalism is to retain legitimacy and popular support. A system that was built on the Enlightenment principle of equality under the law has helped to exacerbate inequalities in income and wealth on a massive scale. Fuller discussions of this issue, including possible policies to deal with this problem, are found elsewhere.[45] A point stressed in the present book is that different capitalist countries have had different degrees of success in ameliorating this problem, and we need to learn from these comparative experiences.

While socialists have always advocated the reduction of inequalities of income and wealth, they have often been diverted by their uppermost doctrinal goal of public ownership. They regard massive inequality as unavoidable under capitalism, and hence the task of dealing with it has been postponed to the socialist future. As Michael Polanyi put it: 'the equalisation of incomes and the curtailment of inheritance might have gone further but for the fact that progressive thought was misdirected for some time past toward the idea of nationalisation and took little interest in reforms under capitalism'. Infeasible socialist doctrine has diverted our attention from building a better capitalism.[46]

To see what may be possible, we need a comparative study of different varieties of capitalism. The following chapter is a contribution to this task.

---

[44]   See, for example, Pack and Saggi (2006), OECD (2007) and Rodrik (2008).

[45]   Ackerman and Alstott (1999), Bowles and Gintis (1999), Piketty (2014), Atkinson (2015), Hodgson (2015a, pp. 362–5; 2018, pp. 206–211).

[46]   M. Polanyi (1945, p. 146).

7. Varieties of capitalism: the realms of the possible

> The grand, leading principle, towards which every argument unfolded in these pages directly converges, is the absolute and essential importance of human development in its richest diversity.
> Wilhelm Humboldt (1854 [1792])

> The ground on which we must stand is capitalism – capitalism, however imperfect, however needful of urgent reform, but not replaceable by any fundamentally different system.
> Michael Polanyi (1945)

In terms of human development, longevity, health and prosperity, capitalism is by far the most successful economic system in history. Western European GDP per capita was about twenty times larger in 2003 than it was in 1700. World GDP per capita in 2003 was about eleven times larger than it was in 1700. In less than half the time, US GDP per capita in 2003 became about twelve times greater than it was in 1870.[1]

As a result of technological developments in medicine and the improved average standard of living, between 1800 and 2000 life expectancy at birth rose from a global average of about 30 years to 67 years, and to more than 75 years in several developed countries.[2]

Although the golden eggs of capitalism are very unequally distributed, capitalism has sometimes helped the poor, as well as massively indulging the rich. For the global poor, some of the most dramatic improvements have been recent. Many millions of people have been lifted out of poverty in China, India and elsewhere. Since 1990, the number of people living on less than $1.90 a day has halved, being reduced from 1.85 billion to 0.77 billion in 2013.[3]

This is not an apologia for trickle-down economics – the mythical idea that gains for the rich will automatically seep down to the poor. It is not an argument for complacency either. The fruits of capitalism have been

---

[1]   Maddison (2007).
[2]   Riley (2001), Fogel (2004), Deaton (2013).
[3]   World Bank (2015).

distributed very unequally. Global growth since 1700 has seen a widening gap between rich and poor nations. Capitalism has created severe problems, from inequality to global warming.[4]

But instead of killing the geese that lay the golden eggs, we should compare different geese and choose the best variety. We need to see what works best and discover where severe problems within capitalism have been alleviated. This is an argument for realist rather than reckless idealism. The search for a better world should look first among the more successful and conducive of actually existing capitalisms.

ARE CAPITALISMS CONVERGING?

Such a search would be less worthwhile if all national capitalisms were converging toward the same destination. Variety in this case would be accidental and transitory, rather than a source of permanent inspiration. There is a longstanding view – found among both advocates and critics of capitalism – that all market economies tend to gravitate toward one model and its developmental track. This view was promoted by Karl Marx and by some market fundamentalists and libertarians.[5]

The collapse of the Soviet bloc in 1989–91 changed things dramatically. Instead of the Cold War polarities of Western capitalism versus Eastern socialism, attention was focused on the divergent varieties within the capitalist camp, including the newcomers from the East. There was an explosion of literature on 'varieties of capitalism'.[6]

Driven both by empirical observation of the diversity of national capitalist systems, and by theoretical discourses on institutional complementarities and path dependence, this research on capitalist varieties countered the traditional Marxist and market-fundamentalist notions that only one model and developmental track for capitalism is feasible, normal or desirable.

For example, Bruno Amable concluded that 'no generalized pattern of convergence toward the same equilibrium model should be expected, in

---

[4]   Milanovic (2011), Gough (2017).

[5]   On Marx's view that capitalisms converge to one developmental track see Hodgson (2015a, 2016b). A similar claim from a different viewpoint is in Fukuyama (1992).

[6]   The 'varieties of capitalism approach' often signals one theoretical genre, namely that of Hall and Soskice (2001), where specific contestable explanations of why capitalisms differ were developed. By contrast, my use of the term 'varieties of capitalism' is not intended to signify a theoretical approach, but simply that there are real-world varieties of that system.

spite of "globalization"'. Despite the world integration of capitalism there would always be significant variation between national capitalisms.[7]

Some scholars pointed to institutional complementarities, where different institutions worked well when dovetailed together. Different configurations could maximize economic performance in different contexts. Other researchers considered other reasons for path dependence, where capitalist systems are locked into different developmental tracks, depending on conditions established in the past. Multiple reasons for the persistence of capitalist variety were proposed.

Critics of these arguments claimed that some earlier scholars in this area had over-emphasized the rigidities of different types of capitalist system. Internal changes and external pressures could lead to some degree of convergence. Furthermore, capitalism is a global system with supra-national dynamics. National capitalisms are expressions of this global system in different localities.[8]

After the global economic crash of 2008, some critics argued that different capitalisms had responded similarly to the crisis, imposing austerity policies and attempting to cut their public expenditures. Globalization and so-called *neoliberalism* were forcing different capitalisms toward the same destination. It was suggested that the institutional diversity in different capitalisms had been eclipsed by the common embroilment in global financial crises and the widespread imposition of austerity policies.

Commentators pointed to international evidence of deregulation and austerity, claiming that *neoliberalism* was obliging all capitalisms to move toward one developmental model, albeit at varying rates. As the journalist George Monbiot put it: 'Governments use neoliberal crises as both excuse and opportunity to cut taxes, privatize remaining public services, rip holes in the social safety net, deregulate corporations and re-regulate citizens.'[9]

Clearly, whether we call it *neoliberalism* or not, there has been a rise in market-fundamentalist, pro-privatization and anti-government thinking.

---

[7] Amable (2000, p. 645). See also Albert (1993), Hodgson (1996), Berger and Dore (1996), Crouch and Streeck (1997), Boyer (1999), Whitley (1999), Dore (2000), Amable (2000, 2003), Aoki (2001), Hall and Soskice (2001), Streeck and Yamamura (2001), Coates (2005), Crouch (2005), Hall and Gingerich (2009), Bohle and Greskovits (2012), Schneider and Paunescu (2012), Hotho (2014), Thelen (2014) and Baccaro and Benassi (2017).

[8] See Peck and Theodore (2007), Hall and Thelen (2009), Streeck (2011), Jones and Jessop (2010), Whitley (2010), Schneider and Paunescu (2012), Thelen (2014) and Baccaro and Benassi (2017).

[9] Monbiot (2016).

But to what extent has it been implemented? And to what extent is capitalist diversity being suppressed by these policies?

GLOBAL CAPITALISM AND THE PERMANENCE OF VARIETY

The extent to which variety among capitalisms has been reduced must be investigated empirically. There are theoretical reasons and strong evidence to suggest that significant national variety is likely to be maintained.

The global spread of privatization and the imposition of austerity policies in response to the Great Crash of 2008 have led to some degree of institutional convergence. But this does not mean that historical, cultural, ideological or institutional differences have been overcome. Variation between national capitalisms has not been eradicated.

Consider the prominent claim that financial systems are converging, particular toward the Anglo-American model. An empirical study of financial systems worldwide, which took in data after the 2008 Crash, found that there was slight convergence in some respects, but there was no evidence of a widespread drift toward the global homogenization of financial institutions.[10]

Globalization does not necessarily lead to uniformity. On the contrary, the enhancement of a global division of labour where countries tend to specialize and reap local economies of scale could enhance diversity rather than undermine it. For example, China has a more than average share of global manufacturing capacity and the UK has a more than average-sized financial sector. The very fact that such specialization occurs means that countries will vary in terms of institutions, workforces and economic structures.

Moreover, the fact that countries are at different levels of development means that variety will be preserved. Different levels, rates of growth and fluctuations in economic activity promote different institutional responses. For example, firms may adopt routines that are profitable in times of boom but much less so when market demand is static or falling. Some evidence suggests that the state can play a more effective economic role in the early stages of development, but as economies become more complex, central direction of the economy becomes less effective. Other evidence suggests that democracy and the rule of law become relatively

---

[10]   Maxfield et al. (2017).

more important in more complex economies. Different levels and rates of development have different institutional outcomes.[11]

Differences in rates of growth also imply structural variation. Structures and resources that are necessary for higher growth rates are different from those that are suitable for more gradual change. Fast-growing economies require much higher proportions of GDP devoted to infrastructure and other fixed assets. Consequently, the global dynamics of development are forever uneven.

Furthermore, technological and institutional innovations begin in one part of the global system and, if they are successful, spread unevenly and at different rates. Unevenness of diffusion is due to the importance and nature of tacit knowledge and varied capacities for absorption in different local contexts. Capitalism by its nature is restless: unceasingly this recreates unevenness.

Last but not least, national histories and cultures vary enormously. Once rapid and complete convergence is ruled out, there is space for a huge variety of social forms and cultures with the diversity of capitalisms. Capitalisms vary massively in their degrees of democracy, the effectiveness of law, their incarceration rates, their levels of corruption, their family forms and their economic roles, the extent and diversity of religion, and much else. Choosing capitalism does not necessarily mean choosing the dominant US model.

Also, choosing capitalism does not mean promoting markets as the universal remedy. As noted above, markets within capitalism are unavoidably incomplete. Like all socio-economic systems, capitalism always contains impurities. There are always subsystems that are dissimilar from the dominant modes of market coordination.[12]

The *impurity principle* implies that while marketization and privatization can increase, they cannot pervade everything. Capitalism is never a pure system. Some zones of the capitalist economy are market-driven. There is also the voluntary sector, where people perform unpaid work, as in the family or community. Other parts of the economy are owned or managed by the state. There is always an important residual of socio-economic life that cannot be swallowed by markets. This residual provides scope for variation, depending on history, institutions and culture.

For example, in many capitalist societies child-rearing is done within the non-capitalist institution of the nuclear family. But, in principle,

---

[11] Hodgson (2015a, pp. 339–41; 2018, pp. 127–32).
[12] See the discussions of the *impurity principle* in Hodgson (1984, 1988, 1999, 2015a).

alternative non-capitalist arrangements are possible for this purpose, such as collective households along the lines of the early Israeli *kibbutzim*. There are also important variations in the structures of families in different cultures. Another example of an optional impurity is the system of slavery that existed alongside capitalist institutions and wage labour in the US before the Civil War. History shows an immense variety of subsystemic impurities.

The particular subsystem, the nature of the combination, and the precise boundaries of the demarcation profoundly affect the nature of the specific variety of capitalist system. *A corollary of the impurity principle is the contention that an immense variety of forms of any given socio-economic system can exist.* There are limits to markets and an infinite variety of forms of capitalism is possible.

THE PERSISTENCE OF CAPITALIST VARIETY: TAXATION AND SOCIAL SPENDING

Given the rise of tax-cutting rhetoric, have taxes been reduced? There is clear evidence that taxes have been reduced for the rich in several countries, thus exacerbating the growth of inequality. Although tax revenues dipped in some countries after the 2008 crash, this was largely because of an immediate fall in income in the subsequent recession. We need to take a longer view.

Comparing tax revenues in 2005 with those in 2015, the average percentage of GDP going to taxes in developed countries has fallen only slightly and the average global tax take has actually risen. Although many people have suffered because of cuts in incomes and welfare, the *neoliberal* rhetoric of a slimmed-down public sector has not become a reality.

Figure 7.1 and Table 7.1 present data on average taxation as a percentage of GDP. In Figure 7.1 note the marked upward trend in taxation in several countries since 1975, including France and the UK. In other countries taxation has held steady or increased slightly.

Just as importantly, a large variation in tax levels has persisted, with Scandinavian countries such as Denmark and Sweden having higher and increasing levels, while tax levels in the US and elsewhere are much lower. Table 7.1 confirms this with a wider sample of countries. Average tax levels for 24 major countries from 1975 to 2000 increased significantly. There was a slight fall in average percentage tax revenues from 2000 to 2015, both globally and in 24 relatively developed countries. But these average figures are still above what they were in 1995 and in

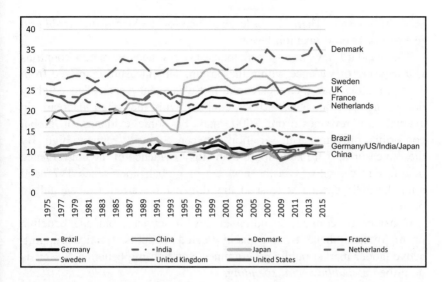

Data source: World Bank (2017).

Figure 7.1   Tax revenue as a percentage of GDP in 11 countries

Table 7.1   Tax revenue as a percentage of GDP in 24 countries and whole world

	1975	1980	1985	1990	1995	2000	2005	2010	2015
Mean of 24 Countries	16.1	17.2	17.8	18.0	18.4	19.8	19.6	18.6	19.4
Standard Deviation	5.93	6.16	6.78	6.76	7.09	7.15	7.28	6.89	6.74
World Mean	13.4	14.3	14.0	14.2	14.6	15.6	14.3	13.5	15.0

Note: The 24 countries are: Australia, Austria, Brazil, Canada, Denmark, Finland, France, Germany, Greece, India, Ireland, Italy, Japan, Mexico, the Netherlands, New Zealand, Norway, Portugal, South Korea, Sweden, Switzerland, Turkey, United Kingdom and United States. China and Russia were excluded because of the absence of data before 1999. The remaining countries are all relatively developed. Other missing data was estimated by linear interpolation or extrapolation.

Data source: World Bank (2017).

preceding years. There is little evidence of a successful *neoliberal* reversal of overall taxation levels.

The standard deviation of percentage tax revenues in the 24 countries is a measure of variance within that group. This measure increased from 1975 to 2005 and then decreased in subsequent years. This slightly decreasing variance since 2005, coupled with the small decrease in average tax revenues from 2000, may be some evidence of global conformist pressures. But variation between countries remains high. By these measures, there is no more than slight evidence of the convergence of different capitalisms in the new era of globalization since 1975 and after the 2008 Crash. At least in this dimension, varieties of capitalism persist.

Consider government spending on health services, old age benefits, unemployment benefits, incapacity-related benefits, family support, active labour market public programmes, and housing benefits. All this is described as *public social spending.*

Table 7.2 shows that most countries in the sample increased their percentage of public social spending from 1980 to 2015, during a period when the ideology of privatization and 'rolling back the state' was resurgent. The Netherlands and Sweden are the two exceptions: there the percentage allocations to public social spending have declined. But both countries were well above the mean levels in 1980 and remain significantly above the average for 2015. It has been reduced as a percentage of GDP in these two cases only, where it remains high.

Only three of the 18 countries in Table 7.2 showed decreased shares in public social spending from 2005 to 2015, namely Germany, Sweden and Switzerland. In the remaining 15 countries the percentages increased, despite the 2008 Crash. In this majority of cases, the ideology of austerity did not lead to reversals.[13]

The standard deviation in the sample in Table 7.2 fell from 1980 to 2000 and from 2000 to 2015. This may be interpreted as slight evidence for convergence. But the differences between countries remain substantial. The 2015 figures range from below 20 per cent for Australia, Canada, Switzerland and the US, to 28 per cent or above for Austria, Belgium, Denmark, Finland, France and Italy. These developed capitalist countries still show wide variations in levels of public social spending.

---

[13] Note that unemployment payments are a relatively small proportion of public social spending. As percentages of GDP from 1980 to 2015, the OECD data show few national increases in average unemployment payments.

Table 7.2   Public social spending as percentage of GDP in selected countries

	1980	2005	2015	changes
Australia	10.3	16.5	18.8	+ +
Austria	22.4	27.1	28.0	+ +
Belgium	23.5	26.5	29.2	+ +
Canada	13.7	16.9	17.2	+ +
Denmark	24.8	27.7	28.8	+ +
Finland	18.1	26.2	30.6	+ +
France	20.8	30.1	31.7	+ +
Germany	22.1	27.3	25.0	+ −
Italy	18.0	24.9	28.9	+ +
Japan	10.2	18.5	23.1	+ +
Netherlands	24.8	20.7	22.3	− +
Norway	16.9	21.6	23.9	+ +
Portugal	9.9	23.0	24.1	+ +
Spain	15.5	21.1	25.4	+ +
Sweden	27.1	29.1	26.7	+ −
Switzerland	13.8	20.2	19.6	+ −
UK	16.5	20.5	21.5	+ +
US	13.2	16.0	19.0	+ +
Mean	17.9	23.0	24.7	+ +
Standard Deviation	5.44	4.50	4.36	− −

Note: The 2015 Japan figure is for 2013.

Source: OECD (2018).

The growth of so-called *neoliberal*, unfettered-market, small-government ideology since the 1970s is indisputable. But the evidence suggests that the ideology has been borne out in practice in a few cases only. The ideology may have captured many minds, but its goal to shrink the state has not been achieved.

David Harvey – an influential Marxist critic of neoliberalism – stated that since the 1970s the 'withdrawal of the state from many areas of social provision have been all too common'. But while there have been severe cuts in several areas, the evidence suggests that overall levels of public social spending have increased rather than declined in most developed countries.[14]

Why is this so? First, it has been in the interests of administrations wedded to this ideology, and in the interests of opposition parties who resist their proposed cuts, to exaggerate the degree of governmental enthusiasm for slashing government budgets. Governments who would trim expenditures shout louder to gain approval from their ideological mentors and to reassure financial markets. Also, it is in the interests of an opposition to exaggerate the actual or potential damage (notwithstanding the fact that real damage may be done). Both sides collude in exaggerating the likely impact of *neoliberal* ideology.

Second, there is substantial inertia in government. Governments inherit irrevocable commitments from their predecessors. Consequently, policies and commitments endure from one administration to another. Changing course involves developing and testing new criteria of achievement and developing countless new routines. Shaking up the civil service is a huge and often thankless task. Some evidence suggests that change often occurs not through a new party being elected to government but as a result of changes in economic, technological or other conditions. Otherwise, countries are often locked into developmental paths formed by their unique circumstances and history.[15]

THE PERSISTENCE OF CAPITALIST VARIETY: INEQUALITIES OF INCOME AND WEALTH

Table 7.3 shows levels and changes in market income inequality in OECD countries from 2004 to 2013, measured by Gini coefficient (the higher the figure the higher the inequality). Several points are worthy of note.

From 2004 to 2013 market income (that is, before taxes and transfers) inequality within several OECD countries grew. But in a few countries market income inequality decreased, most notably in Israel and Poland. Overall, by the same measure, inequality in the OECD as a whole increased very slightly in the same period.

---

[14]   Harvey (2005, p. 3).
[15]   Rose (1990).

Table 7.3 Income inequality by Gini coefficient in OECD countries

	Before taxes and transfers				After taxes and transfers			
	2004	2007	2010	2013	2004	2007	2010	2013
Australia	0.42	0.42	0.42	0.42	0.31	0.32	0.32	0.32
Austria	0.41	0.42	0.43	0.43	0.27	0.28	0.28	0.28
Belgium	0.45	0.41	0.42	0.43	0.29	0.28	0.27	0.27
Canada	0.41	0.41	0.42	0.41	0.32	0.32	0.32	0.33
Chile	0.50	0.50	0.50	0.49		0.48	0.48	0.47
Czech Republic	0.41	0.39	0.39	0.39	0.27	0.25	0.26	0.26
Denmark	0.38	0.37	0.39	0.40		0.24	0.25	0.25
Estonia	0.44	0.38	0.43	0.45	0.34	0.31	0.33	0.36
Finland	0.42	0.42	0.42	0.42	0.27	0.27	0.27	0.26
France	0.43	0.43	0.45	0.45		0.30	0.30	0.29
Germany	0.42	0.41	0.40	0.42	0.29	0.29	0.28	0.30
Greece	0.41	0.45	0.47	0.51	0.33	0.33	0.34	0.35
Hungary		0.41	0.42	0.41		0.28	0.28	0.29
Iceland	0.33	0.34	0.36	0.34	0.27	0.29	0.26	0.25
Ireland	0.45	0.47	0.54	0.53	0.31	0.30	0.30	0.32
Israel	0.50	0.48	0.48	0.42		0.35	0.36	0.34
Italy	0.40	0.42	0.44	0.44	0.33	0.31	0.32	0.33
Japan		0.40	0.40	0.38		0.33	0.33	0.32
Latvia	0.45	0.42	0.46	0.43	0.37	0.36	0.35	0.35
Luxembourg	0.41	0.40	0.42	0.43	0.26	0.28	0.27	0.28
Mexico		0.46	0.45	0.47	0.45	0.45	0.44	0.46
Netherlands		0.39	0.38	0.40		0.30	0.29	0.28
New Zealand	0.43	0.41	0.40	0.42		0.32	0.31	0.33
Norway	0.40	0.37	0.38	0.38	0.29	0.26	0.26	0.26
Poland	0.53	0.45	0.43	0.42	0.37	0.32	0.31	0.30
Portugal	0.45	0.46	0.46	0.50	0.38	0.35	0.34	0.34
Slovakia	0.41	0.36	0.38	0.37	0.26	0.24	0.26	0.27
Slovenia	0.40	0.38	0.40	0.42	0.24	0.23	0.24	0.26
South Korea		0.32	0.32	0.31		0.30	0.30	0.28
Spain	0.39	0.40	0.46	0.48	0.32	0.31	0.34	0.35

Table 7.3 (continued)

	Before taxes and transfers				After taxes and transfers			
	2004	2007	2010	2013	2004	2007	2010	2013
Sweden	0.37	0.37	0.38	0.38	0.24	0.25	0.27	0.28
Switzerland	0.33	0.33	0.33	0.34		0.28	0.28	0.29
Turkey		0.42	0.42	0.40	0.41	0.40	0.41	0.38
United Kingdom	0.45	0.47	0.47	0.47	0.35	0.37	0.35	0.35
United States	0.46	0.46	0.47	0.48		0.37	0.37	0.39
Standard Deviation		0.042	0.046	0.049		0.055	0.053	0.053
OECD Average		0.42	0.43	0.43		0.31	0.31	0.31

Source: OECD (2016), using incomes of people of working age.

Turning to income inequality measured after taxes and transfers, it can be seen that these government measures have reduced income inequality, but by varying degrees. Chile, South Korea and Turkey were at one extreme, where taxes and transfers had only a small ameliorative effect on income inequality. But in South Korea market income inequality was already relatively low. At the other extreme, in Austria, Belgium, Finland, France, Ireland, Luxembourg and Slovenia, taxes and transfers led to much greater reductions in income inequality even if inequality after taxes and transfers increased through time. Redistributive policies seemed to work, but to different degrees. Overall, income inequality after taxes and in the OECD as a whole decreased very slightly in the same period.

The penultimate row in Table 7.3 shows data for the overall variance in these measures for 2007–2013. Despite globalization, there is no evidence in the OECD countries for convergence in levels of income inequality, before taxes and transfers. In fact, the variance increased significantly over the period.

Looking at the rightmost column in Table 7.3, which shows the Gini coefficients in 2013 after taxes and transfers, the most unequal countries were Chile, Mexico, Turkey and the United States. The most equal countries were the Czech Republic, Denmark, Finland, Iceland, Norway and Slovenia. Notably, the six most equal countries were all in Europe, and four of these nations were Nordic.

An index has been constructed to measure degrees of economic globalization in 90 countries. Economic globalization reflects the extent of cross-border trade and investment and revenue flows in relation to GDP as well as the impact of restrictions on trade and capital transactions. It is a measure of economic openness – of engagement in international markets.

By this index, derived from 2014 data, the relatively equal countries of Austria, Belgium, Czech Republic, Denmark, Finland, Luxembourg, the Netherlands, Slovakia and Sweden all were among the 18 most globalized countries in the world. All nine were more globalized economically than China, France, Germany, Japan, UK and US.[16]

As the constructors of this index explain, smaller capitalist countries are under greater pressure to trade internationally. Nevertheless, this presence of several relatively egalitarian countries among the most globalized suggests that economic globalization and involvement in international markets need not lead to higher rates of income inequality.

Fewer data are available on inequalities of wealth. Country data differ in terms of whether wealth inequality is measured using adults, families or households as the basic units. Available data are scattered over the period from 1999 to 2011. One of the most comprehensive and up-to-date sources available shows significant differences, with the richest 1 per cent owning 34.8 per cent of the wealth in Switzerland, 34.1 per cent in the United States, 15.5 per cent in Canada, and 12.5 per cent in the United Kingdom, for example.[17]

Table 7.4 shows data for the distribution of wealth. Few developed countries are as unequal as the US. Switzerland is an exception. Several developed countries – notably Japan, South Korea and Spain – have been much more equal in terms of their distributions of wealth, although this is not to claim that they are egalitarian utopias. Note generally that by the Gini measure, inequalities in the distribution of wealth are much greater than inequalities in the distribution of income.

The Nordic countries fare relatively well in terms of income redistribution, but much less well in terms of their redistribution of wealth. Nordic social democracy has been much less effective in tackling the major problem of wealth inequality. Much of the inequality of wealth found within capitalist societies results from inequalities of inheritance. Some children are born into much more fortunate circumstances than

---

16   KOF Swiss Economic Institute (2017).
17   Credit Suisse Research Institute (2012, p. 15).

others. The process is cumulative: inequalities of wealth often lead to differences in education, power and further inequalities in income.[18]

The evidence presented in this section leads us to two major conclusions. At least among the dimensions examined here, variety among capitalisms has not diminished greatly in recent decades. Despite the spread of globalization, despite the rise of minimal-state unfettered-market ideology, and despite the imposition of austerity policies since the 2008 Crash, there is little movement toward one capitalist model.

Table 7.4   Distributions of wealth in selected countries

	Year (for share data)	Unit (for share data)	Share of top					
			20%	10%	5%	2%	1%	Gini
Australia	2010	household	61.8					0.622
Brazil								0.784
Canada	2005	family	69.0	50.4	35.8		15.5	0.688
China	2002	person	59.3	41.4				0.550
France	2010	adult		62.0			24.0	0.730
Germany	2007	household	61.1					0.667
India	2002	household	69.9	52.9	38.3		15.7	0.669
Italy	2010	household	62.6	45.7	32.9	21.0	14.8	0.609
Japan	1999	household	57.7	39.3				0.547
Netherlands	2008	household	78.5	62.7				0.650
Norway	2004	household	80.1	65.3				0.633
Russia								0.699
South Korea	2011	household	63.9					0.579
Spain	2008	household	61.3	45.0	32.6	21.7	16.5	0.570
Sweden	2007	adult		67.0	49.0		24.0	0.742
Switzerland	1997	family		71.3	58.0		34.8	0.803
UK	2008	adult	62.8	44.3	30.5		12.5	0.697
USA	2010	family	86.7	74.4	60.9	44.8	34.1	0.801

Sources: Gini coefficients are from Davies et al. (2009), which are all household-based estimates for the year 2000; other data from Credit Suisse Research Institute (2012).

---

[18]   Bowles and Gintis (2002), Credit Suisse Research Institute (2012).

The Nordic countries have preserved a model that retains a strong welfare state within capitalism and is partially successful in dealing with some of its inequalities. Pragmatists looking for empirical cases of countries that have simultaneously generated prosperity while increasing welfare provision and decreasing some inequalities should look to the northern fringes of Europe for examples. We can also learn from other democratic and relatively egalitarian countries, such as Japan and South Korea.

SEARCHING FOR UTOPIA: THE NORDIC MODEL AND BEYOND

Against the shared view of supporters of Bernie Sanders and of Tea Party libertarians, the Danish Prime Minister Lars Løkke Rasmussen insisted that Denmark is a market economy and not a socialist system.[19] He is right: despite their relatively high levels of taxation and welfare provision, Denmark and other Nordic countries are capitalist.

These Nordic countries are driven by financial markets rather than by central plans, although the state does play a strategic role in the economy. They have systems of law that protect personal and corporate property and help to enforce contracts. They are stable democracies with checks, balances and countervailing powers. The Nordic countries show that major egalitarian reforms and substantial welfare states are possible within prosperous capitalist countries that are highly engaged in global markets.

In 2013 in Denmark 34.9 per cent of employees were in the public sector, in Norway it was 34.6 per cent and Sweden 28.1 per cent.[20] In all the Nordic countries a substantial majority of employees work in the private sector.

The proportions of employees who are in trade unions are higher than in most other major capitalist countries. But their unions are more inclined to participate in consensus-building toward national goals, rather than simply defending and enhancing their sectional interests.

The Nordic countries have scored highly in terms of major welfare and development indicators. Norway and Denmark have ranked first and fifth in the United Nations Human Development Index. Denmark, Finland, Norway and Sweden have been among the six least corrupt countries in the world, according to the corruption perceptions index produced by

---

[19]   Yglesias (2015).
[20]   OECD (2015).

Transparency International. By the same measure, Iceland ranks four-teenth and the US eighteenth. The four largest Nordic countries have taken up the top four positions in global indices of press freedom. Iceland, Norway and Finland took the top three positions in a global index of gender equality, with Sweden in fifth place, Denmark in fourteenth place and the US in forty-ninth place.[21]

Suicide rates in Denmark and Norway are lower than the world average. In Denmark, Iceland and Norway they are lower than in the US, France and Japan. The suicide rate in Sweden is about the same as in the US, but in Finland it is higher. Norway has ranked as the happiest country in the world, followed immediately by Denmark and Iceland. By the same happiness index, Finland ranks sixth, Sweden tenth and the US fifteenth.[22]

In terms of economic output (GDP) per capita, in 2017 Norway was 3 per cent above the US, while Iceland, Denmark, Sweden and Finland were respectively 11, 14, 16 and 25 per cent below the US. This is a mixed but still impressive performance. Every Nordic country had a GDP per capita level higher than the UK, France and Japan.[23]

Clearly, the Nordic countries have achieved very high levels of welfare and well-being, alongside levels of economic output that compare well with other highly developed countries. All economic and social policy-makers should learn from the Nordic successes. But these outcomes are not simply the results of progressive policies implemented in the twentieth century. They also result from specific historical and cultural traditions.

The Nordic countries are small and more ethnically and culturally homogeneous than most developed countries. These conditions have facilitated high levels of nationwide trust and cooperation, and con-sequently a willingness to pay higher than average levels of tax.

Consequently, all Nordic policies and institutions cannot be easily exported to other countries. Large developed countries like the US, UK, France and Germany are internally more diverse in terms of cultures and ethnicities. Their levels of unionization are lower, and in the UK and US the unions are not integrated into the corporate and state institutions as much as they are in the Nordic group.[24] Exporting the Nordic model

---

[21]   United Nations Development Programme (2016), Transparency International (2016), Reporters Without Borders (2017), World Economic Forum (2017).
[22]   Wikipedia (2018b) using World Health Organization data for both sexes for 2015, World Happiness Report (2017).
[23]   World Bank (2019).
[24]   Martin and Thelen (2007), Pontusson (2011).

creates major challenges of assimilation, integration, trust-enhancement, consensus-building and institution-formation. But it is still important to learn and experiment.

Importantly, while the Nordic countries are highly egalitarian in other respects, the data in Table 7.4 show that they do not have a lead in redistributing wealth more equally. Wealth inequality in Sweden is even higher than in France, Germany, Italy, Spain and the UK. The problem of reducing extreme inequalities in the distribution of wealth persists in the Nordic countries as well. This is a crucial unsolved problem in modern capitalism.

In summary, this chapter has established that, despite the ideology of so-called *neoliberalism*, there is only slight evidence of convergence among major capitalist countries in the last few decades and since the 2008 Crash. It has been confirmed that some countries have performed much better than others on indicators of welfare and economic equality. The Nordic states are prominent among the best performers, but some of their successes may have been facilitated by their small size and by their higher degrees of ethnic and cultural homogeneity. We need to learn from the Nordic exemplars but not apply their solutions slavishly to other cases. Yet incremental moves may be possible in their direction.

The manifest variety of structures and institutions in modern capitalism provides inspiration for cautious experimentation. Social formations are highly complex, and they cannot be constructed simply by design. Complexity, uncertainty and incomplete knowledge make complete, comprehensive planning impossible. All policies are fallible, and hence they must be provisional and practically adaptable. The search for a better future must be *evotopian*, relying more on experience than blueprints. The rich variety within existing capitalism provides its inspiration.[25]

---

[25] On evotopian approaches see Hodgson (1999, 2018). A similar focus on experimentation is found in Dewey (1916, 1935, 1938, 1939), Popper (1945) and Lindblom (1959, 1984).

8. The making of liberal solidarity

> Greed and envy must be sufficiently restrained to allow the same, or similar, principles of equity to be accepted by rich and poor. Our task is to clarify our sense of economic justice and to establish sufficient agreement with regard to its demands.
>
> Michael Polanyi (1945)

> Thus, it is a political axiom that power follows property. But it is now a historical fact that the means of production are fast becoming the monopolistic property of Big Business or Big Government. Therefore, if you believe in democracy, make arrangements to distribute property as widely as possible.
>
> Aldous Huxley (1958)

> Human beings are not the independent windowless Leibnitzian monads sometimes conjured up by libertarian theory. Society is not imposed on humans; rather, it provides the matrix in which we survive and mature and act on the environment.
>
> Herbert A. Simon (1991)

Liberalism was forged in its struggles against despotism. In the 1640s, the English Levellers fought against the absolutist ruler King Charles I before they were crushed by Oliver Cromwell. John Locke, 'the father of liberalism', was exiled under the autocratic King James II and he returned to England during the Glorious Revolution of 1688. In 1783 the American revolutionaries ended imperial rule by the British. The French revolutionaries of 1789 overthrew the repressive monarchy and ended feudal privileges. Equality under the law and individual liberty were both ends in themselves, and means towards other ends, such as happiness, prosperity and human development.

All versions of liberalism stress individual liberty and universal rights, including the rights to private property and to freedom of expression. These universal rights and liberties require equality under the law, under a competent legal system that protects rights and pursues justice. All liberals accept that democracies should not compromise individual rights, including the rights of minorities. Consequently, there have to be some constitutional limitations on the powers of all governments.

Original conservatism differs from liberalism because it stresses established or religious authority and tradition over rights. Socialism generally differs from liberalism because it downgrades the right to private property. But as John Gray and many others have pointed out, there is no historical case where personal and civil liberties have existed 'without extensive rights of private property'.[1]

Big socialism further differs from liberalism because it concentrates politico-economic power in the hands of the state, thus undermining countervailing power, which is necessary to sustain democracy and individual rights. Marxism differs from liberalism to an even greater degree, because it regards all liberal rights as *bourgeois*: it rejects the idea of universal individual rights in favour of the class rule of the proletariat.[2]

But once autocracy was pushed back, and freedom and legal equality were established, then liberalism as a whole lacked a further common purpose, other than the preservation or consolidation of those liberal gains. At this point, the wide liberal coalition divided into multiple zones, exploring different districts of their spacious common territory, and falling on different sides of several key dilemmas.

Hence the Enlightenment triumph of liberalism gave way to rival liberalisms, each stressing different priorities or visions of the future. Liberalism divided into diverse streams, made more profound by the challenges of nation-building and industrialization. While all liberals stress individual rights, some of these rights were debated. The notion of the individual, and his or her relation to others in large-scale societies, came under closer scrutiny.[3]

Liberalism is a very broad church and we need to explore its copious dimensions. Two radically different streams of liberalism are identified. One builds on an atomistic individualism, while giving less stress to the importance of solidarity, democracy and duties to others. Its leading representatives include Herbert Spencer, Ludwig Mises, Friedrich Hayek, Milton Friedman and Ayn Rand. The other stream rejects atomistic

---

[1]   Gray (1989, p. 157). For a strong philosophical defence of private property see Waldron (1988). On Marxism and rights see Hodgson (2018, chs 5–7).

[2]   See Hodgson (2018, pp. 28–9, 75 ff.).

[3]   Gray (1989) argued that the liberal project has failed to provide a convincing rational justification of its basic universal principles. But in the end, Gray (1993, pp. 314–20) still defended the core liberal notion of a flourishing and diverse civil society, under the rule of law, with protected private property. I disagree with Gray's abandonment of the notion of universal human rights and I suggest these may be defended along the ethical lines proposed by Kitcher (2011).

individualism while giving much greater stress to solidarity and democracy. It draws its inspiration from Thomas Paine, John A. Hobson, John Dewey, Michael Polanyi and others.[4] This second variety might be described as liberal social democracy, or solidaristic liberalism or liberal solidarity. The difference between the two streams is profound. While one version of liberalism extols greed, the other promotes social duty and solidarity.

Another key difference within liberalism arises on the question of democracy. Most modern liberals support democracy, at least because a democratic mandate is seen as necessary to legitimate the powers of government. Democracy, perhaps especially at the level of the community, may also be seen as a means of obtaining cooperation for mutual empowerment and fulfilment. But there are important exceptions, including Milton Friedman, Friedrich Hayek and Ludwig Mises, who defended private property rights but saw democracy, at least on occasions, as dispensable.[5]

EIGHT DIMENSIONS OF LIBERALISM

The internal differences within liberalism cover several analytical and policy issues. They range across multiple dimensions in conceptual hyperspace. They include the conception of liberty, the commitment to economic equality, the limits to markets, the role of the state, the view of the individual and the obligation to internationalism. Consider the following eight dilemmas:

1. Broad Versus Narrow Conceptions of Liberty

The narrow definition of liberty, promoted by Hayek and Friedman among others, is the absence of coercion. Other liberals – including John Stuart Mill, Michael Polanyi and Amartya Sen – argued that this is insufficient. They asked us to consider the conditions enabling the individual to appraise his or her circumstances and then to act freely, often in cooperation with others. These conditions constitute positive or public liberty, in contrast to the negative or private liberty provided by the absence of coercion. For example, against Hayek, Polanyi proposed

---

[4] On Paine see Claeys (1989), Keane (1995) and Hodgson (2018, ch. 3). On Hobson see Clarke (1978), Allett (1981) and Townshend (1990). On Dewey see Gouinlock (1972), Ryan (1995) and Evans (2000). On M. Polanyi see Allen (1998) and Nye (2011).

[5] Mirowski (2013, esp. pp. 57–8, 83–8), Hodgson (2018, pp. 181–3).

that public liberty is about social ideals and virtue, and not pure self-interest. As well as the capacities for choice and action, writers such as Mill and Sen argued that liberty is also about the opportunities for self-development and for human flourishing.[6]

2. Degrees of Commitment to Representative Political Democracy

Most liberals support representative political democracy, as long as it does not overturn basic human rights, including the rights of minorities. But some liberals, such as Mises and Hayek, have regarded democracy as dispensable under specific conditions, believing that the preservation of private property and markets is more important. The counter-argument is that representative democracy is strongly correlated with economic development, the protection of human rights, and the absence of war and famine. Hence representative democracy is vital for a healthy, tolerant and open society.[7]

3. Degrees of Emphasis on Economic Equality

Paine was a liberal who stressed the interdependence of individuals in a free society. Hence, given our debt to others, we are obliged to pay taxes for the common good. John Stuart Mill also argued there should be some redistribution of inherited wealth. Against libertarian individualists, many liberals defend responsible trade unions as a way of empowering working people and reducing inequality. These are cases of liberal solidarity rather than atomistic individualism.[8]

4. Possible Limits to Choice and Markets

While liberals generally stress the importance of individual choice, in both trade and politics, some also stress the practical and moral boundaries to contracts and to markets. For example, we condemn the

---

[6]   See M. Polanyi's (1951) stress on *public* as well as *private* liberty, Berlin's (1969) identification of the *positive* as well as *negative* freedom, and Sen's (1981) concept of capabilities. Gray (1989, p. 2) insisted that the 'vital centre' of Mill's argument in his *On Liberty* is 'in a conception of human nature and self-development'. See Gray (1989) and Allen (1998) for useful critical discussions of Berlin, Hayek and others on liberty.

[7]   The views of Mises and Hayek on democracy are discussed in Hodgson (2018, pp. 181–3). On the relationship between democracy, economic development, human rights and the prevention of famine see Hodgson (2018, pp. 124–32). Mounck (2018) and Luce (2017) discussed the contemporary global crisis of democracy.

[8]   On Mill on taxation see Ekelund and Walker (1996).

possession and trading of slaves. Against some libertarians such as
Robert Nozick, many would deny the right to sell ourselves into
slavery. Furthermore, for democracy to be incorrupt, there should not be
markets for the votes of ordinary people or of politicians. Other
market arrangements are challengeable, on moral or practical grounds,
suggesting that contracts and markets are not the solution to every
problem.[9]

5. Grounds for State Intervention and a Welfare State

Some liberals, including John A. Hobson and John Dewey, saw the
provision of adequate healthcare and education as vital for individual
self-determination and flourishing. Individuals should also be as free as
possible from the anonymous coercions of ignorance, destitution and
illness. Hence the liberals David Lloyd George and William Beveridge
built the foundations of the welfare state in the UK. John Maynard
Keynes pointed to the need for the state to intervene to prevent financial
crashes and minimize unemployment. Many modern liberals also accept
the legitimacy of judicious state action to mitigate climate change.

6. Self-interest Versus Cooperation and Morality

Several liberals have argued that social order emerges out of the
interactions of self-interested, pleasure-maximizing individuals. But this
is not a universal view among liberals. While recognizing the selfish
aspects of human nature and the importance of individual incentives,
many liberals also stress morality, justice and duty. They argue that
adequate social cohesion cannot be achieved on the basis of selfishness
alone. Adam Smith expressed this view: he was not an unalloyed
advocate of individual selfishness. Charles Darwin – who politically was
a liberal – explained how, alongside a measure of self-interest, morality
and cooperation were products of human evolution, and thus part of our
nature. Hobson took up this Darwinian view, also underlining the
importance of moral motivation. Relatedly, Keynes saw the Benthamite
utilitarian calculus of pleasure-seeking, as 'the worm which has been
gnawing the insides of modern civilisation and is responsible for the
present moral decay'. Benthamite utilitarianism reduces everything to

---

9   Fox (1974), Nozick (1974).

individual utility or pleasure, leaving no further space for transcendent moral values such as justice or duty. The motivational bases of liberal solidarity are morality, sympathy and justice, and not simply personal satisfaction or self-interest.[10]

7. Different Attitudes to the Modern Large Corporation

Business corporations became of major economic importance during the late nineteenth century. This was after the consolidation of liberal thought in the eighteenth and nineteenth centuries. Modern liberalism has to take corporate powers over markets and governments into account. By attracting capital and protecting it from shareholder retrieval, corporations have proved to be hugely advantageous over partnerships and other legal forms. They are responsible for much innovation and growth in modern capitalism. At the same time, they can bring disadvantages in terms of excessive political influence and market power. Through their lobbying activities, they can even threaten the proper functioning of democracy. But some thinkers brush these issues aside. They treat corporate power as simply the aggregation of individual influences, and hence it is neither an alarming nor novel problem for politics or economics. They obscure difficulties that must be addressed by modern liberalism. Liberal solidarity addresses the problems of the public accountability of the large corporation and its possible abuse of democracy. It sees their solution partly in terms of some judicious state regulation, and not in market forces alone.[11]

---

[10] Smith (1759), Darwin (1871), Hobson (1921, 1929), Keynes (1933, p. 445), Allen (1998), Hodgson (2013).

[11] Milton and Rose Friedman (1980, p. 40) wrote: 'The corporation is an intermediary between its owners – the stockholders – and ... the services of which it purchases. Only people have incomes ...'. But this characterization is false. Corporations are more than natural individuals: they are themselves legal persons, backed by the powers of law. They have their own incomes and expenditures and they must file their accounts with the tax authorities. Shareholders do not own the corporation, they own shares that grant them specific rights and duties according to corporate law. It is amazing that a Nobel economist can be so wrong about the nature of the corporation. On the latter see Blair (1995, 2003), Ireland (1999), Gindis (2009, 2016), Robé (2011), Hodgson (2015a, ch. 8) and Deakin et al. (2017). Good textbooks in company law confirm that the corporation is not owned, and instead it is a legal person in its own right (for example Worthington, 2016, p. 34).

8. Nationalism Versus Internationalism and Openness

Like socialism and conservatism, liberalism has been divided on questions of foreign policy. Socialists, conservatives and liberals have argued for and against specific wars, for or against imperialism or colonialism, for or against the idea of exporting favoured institutions by invading other countries. They have also been internally divided on immigration policy, advocating different degrees of restriction of free movement.

By the first five criteria above, liberal solidarity recognizes liberty as more than the absence of coercion, defends political democracy, attempts to reduce extremes of economic inequality, and conceives of a larger role for the state than small-state versions of liberalism. It promotes a mixed economy including some public ownership and a variety of forms of private enterprise. The mixture would include worker cooperatives (which are the most viable positive legacy of small socialism). Liberal solidarity counters the original liberal emphasis on minimal government. Some state intervention is necessitated by the limitations of markets and by growing complexity. Nevertheless, all liberals acknowledge the dangers of excessive bureaucracy and concentrations of state power, and they call for mechanisms of scrutiny and accountability, as well as for countervailing powers.

Addressing dimension 6, liberal solidarity emphasizes our human potential for cooperation and moral judgement, rather than focusing on self-interest alone. In regard to dimension 7, liberal solidarity recognizes problems with unaccountable huge corporations and proposes regulation and international cooperation to ensure that they serve democracy and human needs. In regard to dimension 8, liberal solidarity opposes imperialism. It stresses the importance of social inclusion and the benefits of free movement.

There are further possible political dimensions, including the differences in emphasis on rights verses (utilitarian or other) consequences. While some liberals – notably Locke – emphasized fundamental and inalienable individual rights, consequentialists such as Spencer, Mises, Hayek and Friedman sought justification in what was ultimately deemed best for individual liberty or individual satisfaction. This important division is partly (but not wholly) reflected in dimensions 1 and 6.

As they stand, the eight dimensions introduce as much complexity as we can handle here. Rather than exploring all possible zones within this hyperspace, consider some examples of famous liberals who occupy various points in this liberal cosmos.

Herbert Spencer was a prominent nineteenth-century exponent of atomistic individualism, of market competition and of a minimal state.

He became increasingly disillusioned with democracy, especially as he saw more voters and politicians endorsing growing state expenditures. He opposed compulsory education and a welfare state. In his books *Social Statics* (1851) and *The Man versus the State* (1884), Spencer complained of a tendency within liberalism to legislate and intervene in efforts to enhance the condition of the poor, improve public health and expand educational provision. He was against taxation policies to reduce inequality. But unlike many modern libertarians he defended trade unionism. For a while, he supported the nationalization of the land, to break the power of the aristocracy – but later he abandoned that view. Other than slavery, he identified few limits to contracts and markets. On the sixth dimension Spencer saw the individual as a self-interested hedonist. Consequently, on the first six dimensions, and with the exception of his positions on trade unions, Spencer took positions antithetical to liberal solidarity.[12]

In regard to the seventh dimension, Spencer noted problems with emerging large corporations but argued that they were soluble through greater competition and freedom of contract, rather than by government regulation. In the eighth dimension, Spencer's concerns about the power of the modern state made him an opponent of militarism and imperialism. In this dimension alone, Spencer was close to Hobson: they both opposed imperialism. Overall, in all eight dimensions, Spencer's position was similar to many modern thinkers who describe themselves as libertarian.[13]

The growing liberal endorsement of state intervention to redress the ills of capitalism became even more apparent after Spencer's death, when the Liberal Government of 1906 laid the foundations of the welfare state in the UK. In the US, liberalism became more interventionist, particularly in the Democratic Party. Spencerian and other minimal-state versions of liberalism were eclipsed, at least in the UK and US, for much of the twentieth century.

In the UK and US in the 1970s, when unfettered-market, minimal-state versions of liberalism again became influential, they had to find different homes. They took over the Conservative Party in the UK and the Republican Party in the US. Margaret Thatcher was elected as a Conservative Prime Minister in 1979 and Ronald Reagan as a Republican President in 1980.

---

[12] Spencer (1851, 1884).

[13] Hobson (1902). Note also Hobson's opposition to the First World War (Clarke, 1978). On Spencer see Peel (1971), Wiltshire (1978), Gray (1989, ch. 7) and Mingardi (2015).

But their adoption of unfettered-market ideology was partial, and often compromised when traditional conservative values were threatened. Supported by Thatcher, Reagan ramped up military spending. Their nationalism was heightened when it came to foreign policy and international trade. They overlooked the absence of democracy in Augusto Pinochet's Chile and in Apartheid South Africa and supported stronger military and executive powers. They retained restrictions on recreational drugs and prostitution. They stressed 'family values' as much as rampant individualism. As Andrew Gamble put it, Thatcher and Reagan promoted a 'free economy and a strong state'.[14]

The UK Conservative and US Republican parties are coalitions, involving unfettered marketeers, nationalists and traditional conservatives. The election of Donald Trump as US President in 2016 shows the strength of the conservative and nationalist strain among Republicans. Trump is no liberal: he advocates torture, attacks minorities, threatens the press, imposes tariffs and pursues a version of economic nationalism.

Thatcher and Reagan were inspired by leading intellectuals such as Hayek and Friedman, who had been working for decades to restore the influence of unfettered-market liberalism. But neither Hayek nor Friedman fits exactly into the Thatcher–Reagan mould. Friedman, for example, advocated the decriminalization of drugs and opposed compulsory military service. He also opposed the Gulf War of 1990–91 and the Iraq invasion of 2003. Hence Friedman's liberalism was closer to Spencer's.[15]

Hayek voiced partial support for a welfare state. Although he did not support redistributive taxation to reduce inequality, he advocated legislation to limit working hours, state assistance for social and health insurance, state-financed education and research, a guaranteed basic income, and other welfare measures. At least once, Hayek also accepted Keynesian-style, counter-cyclic government strategy to deal with fluctuations in economic activity. Consequently, there was some significant difference between Hayek and other libertarians and free-marketeers, at least in dimension 5 above.[16]

---

[14] Gamble (1988).
[15] Ebenstein (2007).
[16] See Hoppe (1994), Block (1996), Rodrigues (2012) and Hodgson (2015a, ch. 12) on Hayek's alleged 'social democratic' views, with relevant quotes from Hayek himself. Hayek visited Chile after Augusto Pinochet overthrew the democratically elected government of Salvador Allende in 1973. But he never criticized the human rights abuses under the Pinochet dictatorship. Thatcher was a friend of Pinochet and she praised his regime (Hodgson, 2018, pp. 182–3).

Having set out the large, eight-dimensional hyperspace and explored a few of the important positions within it, it is clear that the depiction of liberalism as a broad church is an understatement. The potential variation within liberalism is huge. That is both an asset and a problem. Each variety of liberalism faces the task of distinguishing itself from others. We need to subdivide liberalism's massive territory if we are to navigate and explore different positions. Each important position within the large space needs to be differentiated from others.

NAVIGATING LIBERALISM – LABELLING ITS REGIONS

There are several possible names for the highly varied constituent territories of liberalism. Terms such as *classical liberalism, new liberalism, social liberalism, neoliberalism* and *libertarianism* should be addressed. But all these labels have their problems.

Consider *classical liberalism*. This term is often applied to foundational liberal thought from John Locke, through Adam Smith and Jeremy Bentham to John Stuart Mill. But observers have pointed to different varieties within this broad tradition. The historian Jacob Talmon argued that two different trends emerged within Enlightenment thought in the eighteenth century. One approach 'assumes politics to be a matter of trial and error, and regards political systems as pragmatic contrivances of human ingenuity and spontaneity'. The other approach sees freedom as 'realized only in the pursuit and attainment of an absolute collective purpose'.[17]

Hayek contrasted the 'British' and 'empiricist' tradition of liberalism, including David Hume, Adam Smith and Edmund Burke, with the 'rationalist' and 'French' tradition, including the Physiocrats and Nicolas de Condorcet.[18]

Other profound divisions within classical liberalism go even further. Paine's pursuit of measures to reduce inequality was unmatched by his liberal contemporaries. Adam Smith's emphasis on the importance of 'moral sentiments' and irreducible values such as justice, contrasts with the utilitarian approaches developed by Hume and Bentham and adopted (albeit with strong reservations) by Mill.

---

[17] Talmon (1952, p. 2). Rosenblatt (2018) showed that classical liberalism was even more diverse: several prominent early liberals sought social justice and welfare, and stressed duties to society as well as individual rights.
[18] Hayek (1960, pp. 55–7).

Apart from the emphasis on individual rights including private property, the classical liberals agreed on the need for a small state. But they lived in a period when the state and its tax levels were much smaller than they became in the twentieth century. We cannot automatically assume that they would have taken the same small-state view in the present context, especially if they were responsive to practical experiment and historical experience.

Consequently, *classical liberalism* does not denote one distinctive type or phase of liberalism. The original Liberalism from the seventeenth to the mid-nineteenth century contained widely diverging variants.

A major turn in liberal thought was foreshadowed by Paine and Mill. It was developed in the later decades of the nineteenth century and the early twentieth century by Thomas H. Green, Leonard T. Hobhouse and John A. Hobson in the UK, and in the US by Lester Frank Ward, John Dewey and others. These 'new liberals' saw individual liberty as something achievable only under favourable social and economic conditions. Poverty and ignorance were barren soils for individual freedom and fulfilment. They argued that individual flourishing required the development of an education system, a welfare state and other state action to reduce unemployment and poverty.

What of the 'new liberal' label? The ideas are no longer new, and the label is in little use today. It also risks confusion with the ubiquitous, over-stretched and derogatory *neoliberalism*.[19]

Social liberalism is another term that has been used to describe the strain of liberal thinking – from Green to Dewey – that pursued greater state intervention and a welfare state. But a problem lies in the multiple meanings of the word *social*. Many used *social liberalism* to signal an emphasis on the need for cooperation between individuals through social arrangements to further human fulfilment. The word *social* here is used in a broad and inclusive sense.

An alternative understanding of *social* is as an antithesis to *economic*. This commonplace but problematic dichotomy contrasts the *economic* sphere of business, money and profit-seeking with the *social* sphere of the family, non-market relations, reciprocity and so on.[20] This enables an alternative interpretation of *social liberalism* as liberalism applied to the

---

[19] Milton Friedman originally adopted the term *neoliberalism*, then toyed with *new liberalism*, before settling on *(classical* or *old style) liberalism* (Mirowski, 2013, pp. 38–40).

[20] Karl Polanyi's (1944) problematic use of this social/economic dichotomy is criticized in Hodgson (2017b). In his 1944 book he used it to refer to different forms of motivation, but he was later to modify that view.

narrowly conceived social sphere. It would involve, for example, the promotion of homosexual rights and the decriminalization of the use of recreational drugs. Worthy as those aims may be, this is a much narrower agenda than that promoted by *social liberalism* in the broader sense.

Another option is the word *solidarism*. Contemporary with the *new liberalism* of Hobhouse and Hobson in Britain, similar ideas emerged in France, inspired by Émile Durkheim and Léon Bourgeois. The French solidarists criticized extreme *laissez-faire* and argued that individuals had a debt to society as a whole, which should be repaid through taxation and social welfare schemes. But solidarism in France put less emphasis on state intervention in the economy.

A final term considered here is *social democracy*. This has shifted more successfully in meaning than *socialism*, but originally they amounted to more or less the same thing. Many of the early *social democratic* parties were led by Marxists, including the important Social Democratic Workers' Party of Germany, founded in 1869. Although some social democrats favoured peaceful reform rather than violent revolution, at that time they mostly agreed on the goal of large-scale common ownership.

During the twentieth century the usage of the term *social democracy* shifted radically. After the Second World War it came to mean the promotion of greater economic equality and social justice within a capitalist economy. It also connoted a political strategy orientated toward the interests of the trade unions and the working class.

The term *social democracy* still carries this historical and strategic baggage. It has been eschewed by some because of its links with socialism. Others argue that its class-orientated strategy has become obsolete. Post-war social democratic policies are challenged by the fragmentation of their traditional base in the organized working class and by the heightened forces of globalization.

Consequently, while a reformed and reinvigorated *social democracy* may have some mileage, I suggest we consider the allied term *liberal solidarity* to describe an important zone within liberalism. We should examine its principles and its agenda for reform. But first it is necessary to address the tricky term *neoliberalism*.

NEOLIBERALISM VERSUS LIBERAL SOLIDARITY

Severe problems and ambiguities with the term *neoliberalism* have been raised earlier in this book. In one of the more restrained attempts to give it meaning, Philip Mirowski associated it with the Mont Pèlerin Society.

192Is socialism feasible?

But this definition is difficult to reconcile with the society's early heterogeneity and substantial internal evolution.[21]

The Mont Pèlerin Society changed in its inclusivity and direction. It began under a different name in the 1930s. When formed under its current name in 1947, it was primarily an attempt to convene different kinds of liberals in defence of individual liberty and a market economy. This was shortly after the defeat of fascist tyranny in Europe and Japan. It was during a formidable expansion of Communist totalitarianism, and a massive rise of statist socialist ideas in Western Europe and elsewhere. Liberalism was on the rocks: it needed its defenders.

At that time, the Mont Pèlerin Society was inclusive and diverse. Karl Popper, who was a friend of Hayek and a prominent Mont Pèlerin member in the early years, wrote to Hayek in 1947 that his aim was 'always to try for a reconciliation of liberals and socialists'. For other Mont Pèlerin members, such a dialogue was to be avoided.[22]

Michael Polanyi was involved in the Mont Pèlerin Society in its early years. He advocated Keynesian macroeconomics in a market economy, alongside a radical redistribution of income and wealth. He rejected a universal reliance on market solutions, seeing it as a mirror image of the socialist panacea of planning and public ownership. He did not mince his words against this 'crude Liberalism':

> For a Liberalism which believes in preserving every evil consequence of free trading, and objects in principle to every sort of State enterprise, is contrary to the very principles of civilization. ... The protection given to barbarous anarchy in the illusion of vindicating freedom, as demanded by the doctrine of *laissez faire*, has been most effective in bringing contempt on the name of freedom ...[23]

Polanyi had drifted away from the Mont Pèlerin Society by 1955. He criticized its inadequate solutions to the problems of unemployment and economic inequality. He rejected its adoption of a narrow view of liberty as the absence of coercion, which neglected the need to prioritize human self-realization and development. Rather than the negative absence of coercion, Polanyi stressed the positive institutions that were needed to sustain freedom and emancipation. Against atomistic individualism, and as R.T. Allen put it: 'Polanyi's liberalism is primarily one of institutions,

---

[21] Severe ambiguities with *neoliberalism* are pointed out by Boas and Gans-Morse (2009), Burgin (2012), Venugopal (2015), Birch (2017) and others.
[22] The quote from Popper is reported in Mirowski (2013, p. 71). See also M. Polanyi (1945, pp. 142–6).
[23] M. Polanyi (1940, pp. 57–8).

spontaneously formed and functioning, in which individuals together work out the implications of the principles which these institutions embody and serve.'[24]

In its early years, the Mont Pèlerin Society hosted debates on the possible role of the state in promoting welfare, on financial stability, on economic justice, and on the moral limits to markets. Like Polanyi and other early members of the society, Wilhelm Röpke argued that the state was necessary to sustain the institutional infrastructure of a market economy. The state should serve as a rule-maker, enforcer of competition, and provider of basic social security. Röpke's ideas were highly influential for those laying the foundations of the post-war West German economy.[25]

While Röpke's views received more sympathy from Hayek, Ludwig Mises regarded them as 'outright interventionist'. Mises became so frustrated with these arguments in favour of a major role for the state that he stormed out of a Mont Pèlerin Society meeting shouting: 'You're all a bunch of socialists.'[26]

Angus Burgin's history of the society shows how its early period of relative inclusivity was followed by schisms, departures and a narrowing of opinion. Early members like Polanyi and Röpke became inactive. Eventually the primary locus of the Mont Pèlerin Society shifted to the US, with greatly increased corporate funding under the rising intellectual leadership of Milton Friedman.

Hence the Mont Pèlerin Society evolved from a broad liberal forum to one focused on promoting a narrow version of liberalism that is more redolent of Herbert Spencer than of Adam Smith, Thomas Paine or John Stuart Mill. This ultra-individualist liberalism entails a narrow definition of liberty as the absence of coercion (dimension 1), it relegates the goal of democracy (dimension 2), it neglects economic inequality (dimension 3), it overlooks the limits to markets (dimension 4), it sees very limited grounds for state welfare provision and intervention in financial markets (dimension 5), it stresses self-interest rather than moral motivation (dimension 6) and it ignores or misunderstands the nature of the modern corporation and the possible threats that huge corporations can bring to economic progress and political democracy (dimension 7). In all of the first seven dimensions, this post-1970 *neoliberalism* is very different from liberal solidarity.

---

[24] Allen (1998, p. 154), M. Polanyi (1951), Mirowski (1998), Burgin (2012, p. 116), Jacobs and Mullins (2016).

[25] M. Polanyi (1940, pp. 35 ff.), Röpke (1960), Burgin (2012, pp. 80–86).

[26] The Mises remarks are reported in Burgin (2012, pp. 84, 121).

But along dimension 8 it tolerated a multiplicity of positions, as exemplified by Friedman's opposition to the Iraq War. Overall, the post-1970 position of the Friedman-led Mont Pèlerin Society was redolent of Spencer, but without some of the latter's Victorian idiosyncrasies.

It is only after 1970 that the Mont Pèlerin Society acquired a narrower identity, which at a pinch might be described as *neoliberalism.* Here Mirowski is onto something: '*Neoliberals seek to transcend the intolerable contradiction by treating politics as if it were a market and promoting an economic theory of democracy.*' In other words, this *neoliberalism* reduces all of politics, law and civil society as markets, which are analysed using market categories. This tendency is clearly evident in the literature.[27]

This *neoliberalism* has an odd similarity with Marxism, despite other major differences in theory and policy. Marx and Engels also reduced civil society to economic matters of money and trade. Marx wrote in 1843: '*Practical need, egoism,* is the principle of civil society ... The god of *practical need and self-interest* is *money.*' Civil society, for Marx, was the individualistic realm of money and greed. Hence Marx concluded that 'the anatomy of civil society is to be sought in political economy'. The analysis of the political, legal and social spheres was to be achieved with an economics based on the assumption of individual self-interest.[28]

Marxism made the state, law and politics under capitalism analytically subservient to its dismembered, economistic vision of civil society. Accordingly, Frederick Engels wrote in 1886 that under capitalism 'the State – the political order – is the subordinate, and civil society – the realm of economic relations – the decisive element'. Everything was deemed a matter of greed and commerce, to be understood through economic analysis.[29]

Hence in part, classical Marxism was a harbinger of modern *neoliberalism*, reducing everything to market relations. There was no defence of civil society in its own right. When attempts were made to build socialism on Marxist principles, not only were markets minimized, but also civil society was virtually destroyed. Before 1989, the restoration of

---

[27] Quote from Mirowski (2009, p. 436, emphasis in original). Coase (1974a) and Coase and Wang (2012) promoted a 'market for ideas', North (1990a, 1990b) the idea of 'political markets' and Benson and Engen (1988) 'market for laws'. There is no evidence to suggest that these particular usages were intended as metaphorical. There are several other examples. On the descriptive misuse of the term *market* and its deleterious implications see Hodgson (2019c).

[28] Quotes are from Marx and Engels (1975a, p. 172, emphasis in original) and Marx and Engels (1962, vol. 1, p. 362).

[29] Quote from Marx and Engels (1962, vol. 2, pp. 394–5).

civil society was one of the foremost demands of the dissident movements in Eastern Europe.[30]

Certainly, there are more sophisticated and less reductionist treatments by Marxists of civil society and the state, not least by Antonio Gramsci. But Marx and Engels, alongside some *neoliberals*, embraced economic reductionism. Everything turned into the economics of trade, eclipsing the autonomy of politics and law, and neglecting the vital importance of non-commercial interaction and association within civil society.[31]

On these vital issues, liberal solidarity stresses its differences from both *neoliberalism* and classical Marxism. It does not treat the individual purely as a self-interested, market-oriented maximizer. It rejects the idea that society can cohere on the basis of greed. It is committed to democracy as a distinctive source of legitimation for government, and a means of individual and social development (dimension 2), not as a marketplace for power. Liberal solidarity stresses the feasible and moral limits to markets (dimension 4). It upholds a view of the individual that combines measures of self-interest with a moral concern for justice and fairness (dimension 6). On all these points it is distinct from these other doctrines.

Liberal solidarity must emphasize its radical differences from both post-1970 *neoliberalism* and from Marxism. This is made extremely difficult in a leftist intellectual context when *any* defence of markets or private enterprise, to any extent or degree, is pushed aside as *neoliberal*. Current cavalier uses of the term do much more harm than good.

Many so-called anti-neoliberals are also anti-liberals. They prioritize neither liberty nor freedom of expression. They offer no defence of private enterprise or markets. They promote a state-dominated economy, which we know from history will always threaten freedom and human rights. They believe they are principled. But to quote from their mentor Lenin: 'The road to hell is paved with good intentions.' These anti-neoliberals fail to understand that the only principled and effective defence of human rights is some form of liberalism.

Liberalism has to be fortified, but not in all of its forms. Liberal solidarity is the radical alternative to the illiberal or undemocratic populisms of the left or right. It can address the problems created by

---

[30] Cohen (1982), Keane (1988, 1998), Arato and Cohen (1992), Kumar (1993).

[31] Gramsci (1971). See also Kumar (1993). Putnam's (2000) classic study of the erosion of American community life is highly relevant here. But the eager promotion of the language of *social capital* similarly and ironically nudges the realities of non-commercial interaction and association into the same economistic box (Hodgson, 2014, 2015a).

large corporate interests, by the power of undemocratic capitalist techno-
crats or by incipient dictatorships. It emphasizes the importance of
markets and private property, but without regarding them as universal
panaceas. It retains uppermost the importance of human rights and
human cooperation, with the ultimate goal of human flourishing and
social development.

One of the major tasks of liberal solidarity is to undo the damage done
to liberalism by the neoliberal degradation of democracy and its celebration of greed. Liberal solidarity has to show that it can provide the
politico-economic basis for human flourishing, in place of the dangerous
false claims of statist socialism. Liberal solidarity can accommodate
measures of small socialism, but only in a mixed economy subservient to
liberal-democratic rights and principles. It can embrace elements of a
Burkean experimental conservatism, but not to sanction unwarranted
privilege and gross inequality.

SOME IMPLICATIONS OF INTERDEPENDENCE: WAGES, TAXES AND JUSTICE

While defending individual rights and individual autonomy, liberal solidarity emphasizes our interdependence. Our existence and our productivity depend on the cooperation of others. Even when we seemingly work
alone, our output depends on a social infrastructure that is being
constantly maintained and enhanced by the efforts of other people. To
function we must obtain supplies of food, warmth, shelter and communication services. Our own efforts would be thwarted if these were
unavailable. Our productivity always depends on the work of others: they
too helped to contribute to our output. Consequently, our own individual
contribution is difficult to identify and often cannot be isolated.

Paine stressed our mutual dependence on others. He wrote: 'no one
man is capable, without the aid of society, of supplying his own wants,
and those wants, acting upon every individual, impel the whole of them
into society, as naturally as gravitation acts to a centre'. Similarly, Veblen
argued that 'there is no isolated, self-sufficing individual. All production
is, in fact, a production in and by the help of the community, and all
wealth is such only in society.'[32]

Consider two people working alongside but independently of each
other. They are shelling peas or knitting socks. Assume independence and

---

[32]   Paine (1945, vol. 1, p. 357; 1948, p. 192), Veblen (1898, p. 353).

negligible cooperation. The overall output of the couple is then the sum of the individual productive efforts of the two workers. If one of the two workers increases her productivity by one unit, then the overall output increases by one unit. This particular worker can claim that she was directly responsible for the increased output of the couple. Each contribution is separable.

Now consider two workers closely collaborating and interacting in some task. They are erecting the wood frame of a building or jointly producing some computer software. These jobs involve ongoing interdependence, interaction and coordination. Assume that their individual efforts can each be measured on a linear scale. Assume further that in this interactive case the overall output is determined not by the sum but by the multiplication of the two individual efforts. They both depend on each other, so if one of them does nothing, then the output is zero, even if a willing worker tries hard to get on with the job. With the other worker inactive, the willing worker is unable to increase output, despite his or her efforts.

But if the (second) inactive worker becomes active, then a positive output is possible. Any extra effort by the first worker now yields extra output. Now assume that the second worker doubles her efforts. There is a multiplication of their individual efforts. Extra effort from the first worker now yields double the extra output. Marginal outputs of one worker are directly proportional to the efforts of the other worker. Both marginal and absolute productivity depend on the efforts of others.

An output Q that is proportional to the multiplication of two individual efforts can be represented by the formula $Q = aX_1X_2$, where a is a constant. The power of multiplication can be moderated by, for instance, taking the square root of each effort. Hence $Q = aX_1^{0.5}X_2^{0.5}$. This is equivalent to a (Cobb–Douglas) version of a standard production function, as adopted in mainstream economic theory, where output Q is some function of factor inputs $X_1, X_2 \ldots X_n$.

In economics, production functions were used (or misused) in attempts to justify different individual rewards with interdependent inputs. John Bates Clark and other economists argued that under certain conditions the remuneration of each factor will be in proportion to its marginal product, which is the increment of output that is added by a marginal increase in one factor, holding the other factors constant.[33]

---

[33] To his argument that the marginal product of a factor determined its level of remuneration, Clark (1899) added an implied normative theory of entitlements. He claimed to have discovered a 'natural law' that determined shares of output. This suggested that the equilibrium wage was the remuneration to which the worker was entitled. Pullen (2010)

Milton Friedman wrote in a textbook that 'marginal productivity theory shows that each man gets what he produces' (as long as there is sufficient market competition). But, because of interdependence, the notion of one factor 'getting what it produces' is problematic. Marginal productivity theory does not say that the remuneration of an input will depend on the marginal contribution of one factor alone. In the production function, all factor inputs help to determine the output. The variable factor acts in combination with the other factors, which are held constant as this one factor varies. All the factors act causally: they are interdependent.[34]

Marginal productivity theory was originally and unconvincingly developed to support a challengeable theory of remuneration and distribution. But its core assumption of a production function may serve as a heuristic illustration of interdependence. As the above quote from Friedman shows, this interdependence can be overlooked, even by experts.[35]

The broad issue of interdependence is even more relevant today, because we are ever more dependent on many others in highly complex social institutions for our health, education and livelihood. Any business enterprise relies on a labour force that was educated and kept healthy by many other vital institutions in society. The economy depends on a massive social infrastructure, the construction and management of which typically involves the state as well as private enterprises.

The interdependence and inseparability of individual contributions to the whole output make it much more difficult, on ethical and practical grounds, to assign a 'just reward' for each separate contribution. In particular, given substantial interdependence, there is no solid case for deeming the marginal product of an input to be its ethical remuneration, because that varying product is itself affected by the inputs of others. This inseparability of inputs means that the Lockean justification of property rights does not work. The inseparability and interdependence that are assumed in standard production functions do not sustain the normative conclusions that Clark and others promoted.[36]

---

gave an excellent account of the controversy over this theory. Hobson (1900, p. 147) in particular attacked 'the fallacy which confuses mechanical composition with organic cooperation'. For the sum of marginal productivity allocations to correspond to total output, the production function must be assumed to be linearly homogeneous, which Edgeworth (1904) doubted were true in reality.

[34]   Friedman (1962b, p. 198).

[35]   It must be stressed that the production function is used here simply as a heuristic device. I do not believe that these functions are an adequate representation of the production process for analytic or predictive purposes.

[36]   Pullen (2010, esp. pp. 9, 54–5, 65, 77). Veblen (1908) argued that Clark's normative conclusions did not follow from his analysis.

There is another problem with the arguments of Clark and Friedman. As noted in Chapter 6 above, capitalism inevitably has missing markets. Consequently, capitalism can never reach the fully competitive free-for-all that their theory assumes. By implication, optimal outcomes cannot be supposed.

In such circumstances, in policy terms we are faced with a pragmatic trade-off between a net level of remuneration that retains sufficient incentives for extra effort and diligence, and a degree of shared redistribution via taxation (to a team or organization, or to society as a whole) which in part recognizes the interdependence of multiple agents.

Liberal solidarity entails a pragmatically determined mix of individual and group incentives. It appeals to social solidarity to propose some taxation for the benefit of everyone. Policies in this area have to be experimental, subject to debate and to ongoing revision in a democratic political system.

By contrast, the 'optimal taxation' approach in mainstream economics relies on the assumption of utility-maximizing individuals and utility-based standards of welfare. Instead, believing that individuals are guided by both moral sentiments and self-interest, liberal solidarity makes a moral appeal to the good of the community as a whole, while retaining incentives to work and avoiding excessive marginal rates of taxation.

Liberal solidarity opposes the prominent libertarian view that all taxation is evil – the pillage of a kleptocratic state. While the socialist left suffers from a chronic *agoraphobia* (a fear of markets), many libertarians profess a vibrant *kratophobia* (a fear of government or of the state). Liberal solidarity avoids both extremes. Alongside the need for markets, it upholds the indispensability of the state for the structural constitution and regulation of capitalism.

OUR DEBT TO PAST GENERATIONS AND OUR OBLIGATIONS FOR THE FUTURE

Chapter 3 of *Wrong Turnings* explains how Paine made a radical modification to Locke's argument concerning property rights. Locke argued that ownership becomes legitimate when it is 'mixed with' and improved by the labour of its owner. Ownership of the entire resource was justified by the beneficial improvements of labour.

While Paine accepted that private ownership of land was justified, he departed from Locke to argue that the owner does not have *full* rights to *all* the revenues from that ownership. For Paine an individual's entitlement to the benefits of an object does not extend beyond the added value that their labour has created. The mixing of labour with land or objects does not give rights to *all* the revenues from those resources. For Paine, rightful revenues derive from what labour has created anew and in addition to the original gifts of nature.

These previous gifts place obligations on the owners of such property. For Paine, uncultivated land was a gift to all from God; everyone had the right to some remuneration for this bequest. Justifiable private ownership was substantial but not absolute: there were obligations to pay taxes on inherited wealth.

Paine wanted to 'advocate the right ... of all those who have been thrown out of their natural inheritance by the system of landed property' and, at the same time, to 'defend the right of the possessor [of landed property] to the part which is his'. Because of the original gift of land to everyone, every proprietor owes the community a ground rent for the land he holds, which should be used as a right of inheritance for all.[37]

Paine then extended this argument to assets beyond land alone. Much social wealth was the work of past generations. It was achieved not by atomized individuals, but it depended on interaction and cooperation with others. This means that entitlements to the wealth that has been created spread far beyond the worker who 'mixes his labour' with other resources to produce that wealth.

But it is impossible to separate an object of property into those parts that the original private owner acquired (such as raw materials or uncultivated land), on the one hand, and those bits that were added and created by the owner, on the other. So, for obvious practical reasons, as well as the preservation of individual incentives and autonomy, Paine argued that private ownership must remain. But because the owner benefits from a bequest from the past, taxation of this wealth is morally just. Redistribution of wealth through taxation is warranted.

Infants come into the world, created and nurtured by others. We all rely on the legacy of past generations and what they built for us: language, knowledge, technology, social institutions and all the other lasting creations of past labours. All generations benefit from a legacy created by their predecessors. As well as from nature there are gifts from past generations. Millions of anonymous individuals contributed to the development of language, culture and other vital social institutions, over thousands of years.

Many of these contributions were not objects of property. Many were spill-overs (externalities) arising from technological discoveries, artistic

---

[37] Paine (1797, 1945, vol. 1, p. 612). Lamb (2010, pp. 502–506).

endeavour or participation in customs. No individual built up his or her wealth unaided and alone. Accordingly, we have reciprocal obligations to others, including the payment of taxes. These are recognition of the debts that we owe to our community and to our nation.

We also have a duty to future generations. They will inherit our world, and what we have preserved of it. If we degrade that legacy, it is to their disadvantage. Just as we have benefited from the generations before us, we must care for the natural environment and minimize the degradation of our planetary ecosystems and resources.

This raises the question of whether it is possible to reduce the reliance of the economy on scarce natural resources and on polluting technologies that threaten ecosystems and climatic stability. While this is an enormously difficult problem, there is no evidence that it is any more soluble within big socialism than a market economy. On the contrary, big socialism is incompatible with democracy. Yet democracy and a free press can help to restrain deleterious and climate-threatening emissions. Popular campaigning and protest are vital to remind governments of their obligations to safeguard our natural environment. These measures are possible only in a liberal democracy.[38]

THE PROBLEM OF ECONOMIC INEQUALITY

For liberal solidarity the reduction of economic inequality is a priority. Inequalities of wealth and income should be reduced as much as possible, while preserving incentives to work and to accumulate wealth. Initial target levels for reduced inequality might approach the lowest levels of inequality found in developed capitalist countries, as indicated in the previous chapter.

The reduction of economic inequality is important for several reasons. First it is the consummation of the Enlightenment project which first pursued equalities of rights and equality under the law. Equality of opportunity, which relies on more equal distributions of income and wealth, must follow.

Second, researchers such as Richard Wilkinson and Kate Pickett have found strong evidence of multiple deleterious effects of inequalities of income and wealth. Using data from developed countries they found negative correlations between inequality, on the one hand, and physical health, mental health, education, child well-being, social mobility, trust and community life, on the other hand. They also found positive

---

[38]   Fredriksson et al. (2005), Binder and Neumayer (2005), Li and Reuveny (2006).

correlations between inequality and drug abuse, imprisonment, obesity, violence and teenage pregnancies. They hypothesized that inequality creates adverse outcomes through stresses generated through troubled interactions in an unequal society.[39]

Much of the inequality of wealth found within capitalist societies results from inequalities of inheritance. The process is cumulative: inequalities of wealth often lead to differences in education, economic power, and further inequalities in income.[40]

To what extent can inequalities of income or wealth be attributed to the fundamental institutions of capitalism, rather than from surviving elites from the pre-capitalist past? A familiar mantra is that markets are the source of inequality under capitalism. But there is no satisfactory demonstration that competitive markets create additional inequality. Non-competitive markets can exacerbate inequality but that does not put the blame on markets as such.[41]

In my book *Conceptualizing Capitalism*, I argued that the most important generator of *additional* inequality within capitalism (above other factors such as education and inheritance) was differences in the owned amounts of collateralizable wealth. Waged employees cannot use their lifetime capacity for work as collateral to obtain money loans. By contrast, capitalists may use their property to make profits, and as collateral to borrow money, invest and make still more money. Differences become cumulative, between those with and without collateralizable assets, and between different amounts of collateralizable wealth. Even when workers become home-owners with mortgages, wealthier people in business can still race ahead. At least in this respect, capital and labour do not meet on a level playing field. This asymmetry is a major driver of inequality.

As noted previously, a consequence of missing futures markets for labour is that employers have diminished incentives to invest in the skills of their workforce. Especially as capitalism becomes more knowledge-intensive, this can create an unskilled and low-paid underclass and further exacerbate inequality, unless compensatory measures are put in place. A socially excluded underclass is observable in several developed capitalist countries.

---

[39] Wilkinson and Pickett (2009).
[40] Bowles and Gintis (2002) and Credit Suisse Research Institute (2012).
[41] Hodgson (2015a, ch. 15). Note that Marx (1976a) did not regard markets as the source of inequality. Instead, he located it in the ongoing expropriation of surplus value in the sphere of production.

Another source of inequality results from the inseparability of the worker from the work itself. By contrast, the owners of other factors of production are free to trade and seek other opportunities while their property makes money or yields other rewards. This puts workers at a disadvantage. Through positive feedbacks, even slight disadvantages can have cumulative effects.

None of these core drivers of inequality can be diminished by extending markets or increasing competition. Paine was one of the first to develop policies to reduce economic inequality within capitalism. His approach, along with recent developments in this area, were discussed in *Conceptualizing Capitalism* and in *Wrong Turnings*.[42]

The ownership of property is an important means of autonomy and self-development. As Bruce Ackerman and Anne Alstott argued: 'property is so important to the free development of individual personality that everybody ought to have some'. In particular, home ownership is of positive value, as a means of widely extending ownership of collateralizable property. But there also needs to be a substantial amount of social or private housing available for affordable rent, to cater for those unable to afford to buy their own homes.[43]

Ackerman and Alstott stressed progressive taxes on wealth rather than on income. Echoing Paine, they proposed a large cash grant to all citizens when they reach the age of majority. This grant would be repaid into the national treasury at death. To further advance redistribution, they argued for the gradual implementation of an annual wealth tax of 2 per cent on a person's net worth above an established threshold. Like Paine, they argued that every citizen has the right to share in the wealth accumulated by preceding generations. A redistribution of wealth, they proposed, would bolster the sense of solidarity and common citizenship.

Increased wealth or inheritance taxes are likely to be unpopular because they are perceived as an attack on the wealth that we have built up and wish to pass on to our children or others of our choice. But the brilliance of Paine's (1797) proposal for a cash grant at the age of majority is that it offers a quid-pro-quo for wealth or inheritance taxes at later life. People will be readier to accept wealth taxation if they have earlier benefited from a large cash grant in their youth.

Another possible wealth taxation is on land values, as Henry George argued long ago. Land is a scarce (or limited) commodity that is subject

---

42 Ackerman and Alstott (1999), Bowles and Gintis (1999) and Atkinson (2015).
43 Ackerman and Alstott (1999, p. 191). See also Waldron (1988).

to financial speculation and acquires value for those reasons. A tax on that unearned appreciation could be made politically acceptable.[44]

Employee shareholding in enterprises is a flexible strategy for extending ownership in society. In the USA alone, almost 10 000 enterprises, employing over 15 million workers, are part of employee-ownership, stock bonus, or profit-sharing schemes. Employee ownership can increase incentives, enhance personal identification with the enterprise, and improve job satisfaction for workers. Although government incentives for such schemes can be helpful, this policy does not require direct support from government. It can be progressed in any liberal-democratic society.[45]

As modern, knowledge-intensive economies, access to education and training to develop skills becomes all the more important. Those deprived of such help suffer a degree of self-perpetuating social exclusion. Widespread skill-development policies are needed, alongside integrated measures to deal with job displacement and unemployment.[46]

The need for ongoing education is one argument for a basic income guarantee. Such a basic income would be paid to everyone out of state funds, irrespective of other income or wealth, and whether the individual is working or not. It is justified on the grounds that individuals require a minimum income to function effectively as free and choosing agents. The basic means of survival are necessary to make use of our liberty, to have some autonomy, to be effective citizens, to develop ethically, and to participate in civil society. These are conditions of adequate and educated inclusion in the market world of choice and trade.[47]

Evidence suggests that economic insecurity – made worse by globalization – is a major factor behind illiberal conservatism, strident nationalism, opposition to immigration and adherence to populism. A basic income guarantee can help reduce economic insecurity and counter one major reason for the rising tide of populism and insular nationalism.[48]

A key challenge for modern capitalist societies, alongside the needs to protect the natural environment and enhance the quality of life, is to

[44] George (1879).
[45] See Bonin et al. (1993), Poole and Whitfield (1994), Doucouliagos (1995), Hubbick (2001), Robinson and Zhang (2005) and National Center for Employee Ownership (2018).
[46] See Ashton and Green (1996), Crouch et al. (1999), Goldin and Katz (2008), Acemoglu and Autor (2011, 2012) and Cowen (2013).
[47] See Van Parijs (1992, 1995), Corning (2011) and Bregman (2017).
[48] Rodrik (2017), Crouch (2018). See Norris and Inglehart (2004) on the roots of conservative religion. Evidence suggests that economic insecurity is not the only factor fuelling populism and insular nationalism. Other causes include a reaction by a disempowered section of the population to progressive change. Inglehart and Norris (2016) performed a joint test of economic and 'cultural backlash' explanations.

retain the dynamic of innovation and investment, while ensuring that the rewards of the global system are more widely distributed.

CHALLENGES TO DEMOCRACY IN THE TWENTY-FIRST CENTURY

Democratic countries tend to be richer, healthier and better educated. Human rights and the natural environment are more likely to be protected. Democracy also reduces the chances of war and famine. While the causal relationships involved are complex and multi-directional, there is substantial evidence of the positive effects of democracy on economic development, particularly for middle- and high-income countries.[49]

Because of elections, democratic governments have to take more account of the people than dictatorships. A responsive government will, for example, invest more in education and health services. Democratic legitimacy may also help sustain higher levels of taxation to help build up welfare states. Democracy allows public opinion to pressure governments to deal with grievances, including environmental problems.[50]

Effective democracy requires a separation of authority and a degree of countervailing power, within and against the state. These conditions can help protect business interests and reduce fears of arbitrary confiscation of property. Typically, the state retains some power and can intervene strategically in the market economy to help enhance human welfare.

Crucially, while some capitalist countries are or have been dictatorships, every democracy requires a market economy with a strong private sector and countervailing powers.[51] Democracy has never been sustained under a state socialist economy. This is not accidental. The concentration of economic power in the hands of the state under big socialism undermines the institutional preconditions of democracy.

Among these institutional preconditions is a healthy and vibrant civil society. As noted previously in this book, civil society is vital to guide individual choice and development. Partly through civil society we engage with our cultural legacy. It is in this sphere that political opinion is transformed and mobilized. Civil society is essential for a healthy

---

[49] See Hodgson (2018, ch. 7).

[50] Evidence that pluralist democracy can lead to improvements to policies to protect the environment is found in Binder and Neumayer (2005), Fredriksson et al. (2005) and Li and Reuveny (2006).

[51] See Galbraith (1952, 1969), Moore (1966), North et al. (2009) and Hodgson (2015a).

democracy. It is no accident that its autonomy is crushed under totalitarian regimes.

Figure 8.1 shows how the proportion of the global population living under a democratic regime has increased markedly from the beginning of

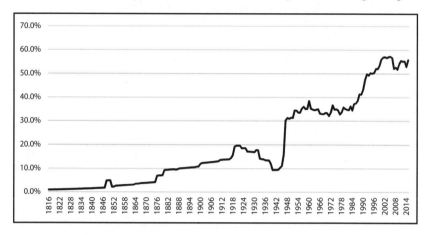

Data source: Roser (2017), using the Polity IV database (Center for Systemic Peace, 2016).

Figure 8.1   Percentage of the world population living in a democracy

the nineteenth to the end of the twentieth century. Democratization increased slowly during the nineteenth century and reached its first twentieth-century peak just after the First World War. Then the rise of fascism and other dictatorships drove democracy down to nineteenth-century levels.[52]

After 1945, the Allied victory in the Second World War brought a huge uplift in democratization. In the 1970s, dictatorships fell in Greece, Portugal, Spain and elsewhere. The 1980s and 1990s saw a second surge of democratization in the twentieth century. New democracies emerged in Latin America and the fall of the Berlin Wall in 1989 brought democracy to much of Central and Eastern Europe.

In 2015 there were 28 member states in the European Union, all of which were democracies. Just over four decades earlier, in March 1974, only 13 of these 28 countries were democracies. Although some of its own institutions have been criticized as undemocratic, one of the great

---

[52]   The data reported here categorize countries simply as democracies or non-democracies. More nuanced surveys involving degrees of democracy are clearly possible but would also involve problematic weighting assumptions.

virtues of the European Union has been to help spread and support democracy. But globally since the year 2000, democratization has peaked and come under increasing attack. Including within Europe itself.

Democracy has difficulty dealing with the growing complexity of economic systems and with establishing consensuses on challenging issues requiring technical expertise. Leading economies grew in complexity as trade expanded in the second half of the twentieth century.[53] To cope with increasing complexity, and more and more variegated products, the state has spawned numerous regulatory agencies, as noted in Chapter 5 above. These agencies, while vital, are difficult to place under close and detailed democratic control.

Growing complexity is a challenge for the state. If it ever did, it can no longer serve as the great helmsman for our future. But its function as a guardian of rights, a guarantor of basic needs and a field of just arbitration in disputes remains paramount. The state also has some responsibility for our basic needs and welfare. It must ensure that the market system works through careful regulation. It must tackle inequality and unemployment. These tasks themselves are complex and there are limits to what the state can do. The scrutinizing power of democracy is also bounded, by the degree of complexity.[54]

Among the primary functions of democracy are the legitimation of government and the safeguarding of an autonomous judiciary. But we should not assume that a globalized economy means the globalization of democracy. As John Gray put it: 'A world economy does not make a single regime – "democratic capitalism" – universal. It propagates new types of regimes as it spawns new kinds of capitalism.' Democracy is challenged by over-zealous globalization, politically powerful corporations, irresponsible media giants, reckless financial institutions, and proliferating supranational organizations that have limited democratic accountability.[55]

The erosion of democracy has become more dramatic since the economic crash of 2008. A report compiled by the Economist Intelligence Unit in 2017 noted disturbing trends throughout the world, including weaknesses in the functioning of government, declining trust in political institutions, the dwindling appeal of mainstream representative parties, widening gaps between political elites and electorates, a decline in media freedoms, an erosion of civil liberties, and growing curbs on free speech.[56]

---

53   Pryor (1996), Hausmann et al. (2011).
54   Zolo (1992).
55   Gray (1998, p. 4), Rodrik (2011), Streeck (2014).
56   Economist Intelligence Unit (2017).

In 2016 Turkey lurched towards dictatorship after a failed coup and Brazil ejected a democratically elected president. Liberal-democratic norms are now threatened in some member states of the European Union, notably in Bulgaria, Hungary and Poland. The decline in trust in mainstream parties has led to a rise in varieties of populism, including intolerant nationalists and doctrinaire socialists, each offering simplistic solutions to complex problems.

Several observers have drawn parallels with the 1930s. The threats to democracy and free speech in several countries, with an associated rise of political extremism, is alarming today as it was then. But the global extent of democracy was much higher in 2000 than it was in the preceding peak in 1920 (see Figure 8.1). By the end of the 1930s the world was threatened by the twin totalitarianisms of fascism and Soviet socialism. The credibility of democratic capitalism was undermined by the Great Depression. Progressive intellectuals saw the choice for human-kind as being between socialism and barbarism. Liberalism and other Enlightenment values were abandoned, as political thinking moved to the two extremes.

But today, the security of democracy or freedom should not be taken for granted. As Yascha Mounck and others have argued, liberal democracy and freedom are being threatened globally by illiberal democracies run by populist demagogues and by undemocratic liberalisms governed by technocratic elites. Massive corporations with strong lobbying powers can also pose a threat. As Edward Luce wrote: 'Western liberal democracy … is far closer to collapse than we may wish to believe. It is facing its greatest challenge since the Second World War.' Once again, liberal values must struggle for their survival.[57]

To defend democracy, we must be realistic about what it involves. Previous chapters of this book have noted that socialists from Lenin to Corbyn have proclaimed ultra-democratic models of participation, only to abandon these when they go against their ambitions.[58] This kind of populist rhetoric feeds a naïve, dangerous and unworkable 'folk theory of democracy', where it is imagined that people elect delegates to carry their instructions. In contrast, as Luce put it:

---

[57]   Mounck (2018), Luce (2017, p. 184).

[58]   The ultra-democracy proclaimed in Lenin's *State and Revolution* became a dictatorship a few months' later, after the Bolsheviks seized power. Corbyn pledged that under his leadership, Labour Party members would determine policy, but this idea was abandoned when the overwhelming majority of members opposed Brexit (Helm, 2018).

The sophisticated view of democracy is that it can only work if it is checked by a system of individual rights, independence of the judiciary, the separation of powers and other balances. There is no such thing as the popular will; just a series of messy deals between competing interests.[59]

Defenders of democracy must be realists. They need to be realistic about what democracy can and cannot achieve, and about its proper and effective functions, as well as being realistic enough to understand the awful consequences of its abandonment.

CONCLUSION

The economic crisis of 2008 has been followed by a growing political crisis in capitalist democracies and heightened world tensions. Especially in these circumstances, socialism has had a magnetic appeal. It harnesses our long-evolved moral sentiments to care for others. It draws on our sense of reasonableness and justice. It decries the volatility of markets and the lack of conscious control of the economy as a whole. It points to the trajectory of history, by highlighting the rise of state involvement in the economy and the growth of large-scale organizations in both public and private spheres. From this evidence it draws the conclusion that we are on the brink of a socialist transformation, if only the resistance of the rich and powerful, who benefit from the existing system, can be overcome.

This sense of historic destiny combines with a conviction that socialism is an 'obvious' solution to current problems.[60] Yet herein lie the roots of fanaticism. In politics, as in religion, people may become over-zealous when they believe that history, or the destiny of the working class, or God, is behind them. They become oblivious to argument and caution when they believe that the solutions to the problems of the world are obvious to all. These conceptions are the fuel of intolerance, which in turn can undermine democracy.

An aim of this book has been to convince the reader that we should be wary of 'obvious' solutions. Instead, because of the immense complexity of modern socio-economic systems, we have to be cautious and experimental. At the same time, we have to protect the key achievements of the Enlightenment from growing populist and extremist threats on all sides.

But it is not enough to be a liberal. We need to develop forms of democratic and solidaristic liberalism that can respond to the challenges

[59] Luce (2017, p. 120). For a critique of the 'folk theory of democracy' see Achen and Bartels (2016).
[60] Nelson (2015).

of the twenty-first century. I have used the term *liberal solidarity*. It needs to stake out its ideological territory and to debate not only with socialism and conservatism, but with other varieties of liberalism. It needs to demonstrate its vitality and importance for our era.

This is no small task, but it is an urgent one. Liberal solidarity has to counter the excesses of capitalism by preserving and enhancing the benefits of the liberal order. Basic liberal principles, such as representative democracy, equality under the law, freedom of expression, and rights to private property must be defended with enduring vigilance.

Liberalism faces further challenges that will require further reflection and intellectual development. Consider, for example, the problem of global overpopulation and our understandable aversion to the most obvious but illiberal remedies of population control. Consider also the challenges of cultural assimilation, heightened by increasing flows of people between countries, notwithstanding the benefits that immigrants often bring, in terms of skill and culture. As Isaiah Berlin and John Gray have argued, liberalism may have to entertain some kind of value-pluralism in response to the challenge of diversity.[61]

Nevertheless, as Berlin and Gray admit, even pluralism requires general organizing principles. We should not descend into an impossible cultural relativism – impossible because tolerance of anything is itself a universal claim, born itself out of some cultural specificity. The mistaken turn toward cultural relativism means an abandonment of core liberal principles.[62]

These are all pressing problems, of a theoretical and practical nature. We are also entering a world where core liberal values are under threat, from populists, intolerant nationalists and inflexible socialists, none of whom have learned the lessons of history. The challenge for liberal solidarity is to defend the liberal gains of the past as well as to tackle the pressing problems of the twenty-first century. Against the ideological extremes of *laissez-faire* capitalism and big socialism, liberal solidarity builds a better future on the ground of experience, with the goal of a better future for all humanity.

---

[61] Berlin (1990), Gray (1993).
[62] See Hodgson (2018, chs 8–9) for a critique of cultural relativism and on the need for cultural and religious assimilation.

References

Acemoglu, Daron and Autor, David H. (2011) 'Skill, Tasks and Technologies: Implications for Employment Earnings', in Ashenfelter, Orley and Card, David E. (eds) *The Handbook of Labor Economics*, vol. 4b (Amsterdam: Elsevier), pp. 1043–72.

Acemoglu, Daron and Autor, David H. (2012) 'What Does Human Capital Do? A Review of Goldin and Katz's *The Race between Education and Technology*', *Journal of Economic Literature*, **50**(2), June, pp. 426–63.

Acemoglu, Daron, Johnson, Simon, Robinson, James A. and Yared, Pierre (2008) 'Income and Democracy', *American Economic Review*, **98**(3), June, pp. 808–42.

Achen, Christopher H. and Bartels, Larry (2016) *Democracy for Realists: Why Elections do not Produce Responsive Government* (Princeton, NJ: Princeton University Press).

Ackerman, Bruce and Alstott, Anne (1999) *The Stakeholder Society* (New Haven, CT: Yale University Press).

Adaman, Fikret and Devine, Patrick (1996) 'The Economic Calculation Debate: Lessons for Socialists', *Cambridge Journal of Economics*, **20**(5), September, pp. 523–37.

Albert, Michael (2004) 'Market Madness', *Znet*. Available at http://zcomm.org/znetarticle/market-madness-by-michael-albert-1/. (Retrieved 1 October 2014.)

Albert, Michel (1993) *Capitalism against Capitalism*, trans. by Paul Haviland from the French edn of 1991 (London: Whurr Publishers).

Ali, Tariq et al. (2004) 'We Would Vote for Hugo Chávez', *Counterpunch*, 27 July. Available at https://www.counterpunch.org/2004/07/27/we-would-vote-for-hugo-chavez/. (Retrieved 24 December 2017.)

Allen, R.T. (1998) *Beyond Liberalism: The Political Thought of F.A. Hayek and Michael Polanyi* (New Brunswick, NJ: Transaction).

Allen, Robert C. (2003) *Farm to Factory: A Reinterpretation of the Soviet Industrial Revolution* (Princeton, NJ: Princeton University Press).

Allett, John (1981) *New Liberalism: The Political Economy of J.A. Hobson* (Toronto: University of Toronto Press).

Amable, Bruno (2000) 'Institutional Complementarity and Diversity of Social Systems of Innovation and Production', *Review of International Political Economy*, **7**(4), Winter, pp. 645–87.

Amable, Bruno (2003) *The Diversity of Modern Capitalism* (Oxford, UK and New York, NY, USA: Oxford University Press).

American Culture and Faith Institute (2017) 'Survey Details: How the Core Beliefs and Behaviors of Millennials Compare to Other Adults'. Available at https://www.culturefaith.com/survey-details-how-the-core-beliefs-and-behaviors-of-millennials-compare-to-those-of-other-adults/. (Retrieved 18 November 2017.)

Andreoni, James (1995) 'Cooperation in Public Goods Experiments: Kindness or Confusion?', *American Economic Review*, **85**(4), December, pp. 891–904.

Angus, Ian (2014) 'The Origin of Rosa Luxemburg's Slogan "Socialism or Barbarism"', *John Riddell: Marxist Essays and Commentary*, 21 October. Available at https://johnriddell.wordpress.com/2014/10/21/the-origin-of-rosa-luxemburgs-slogan-socialism-or-barbarism/. (Retrieved 4 May 2018.)

Aoki, Masahiko (2001) *Toward a Comparative Institutional Analysis* (Cambridge, MA: MIT Press).

Arato, Andrew and Cohen, Jean L. (1992) *Civil Society and Democratic Theory* (Cambridge, MA: MIT Press).

Arrow, Kenneth J. (1962) 'Economic Welfare and the Allocation of Resources to Invention', in Nelson, Richard R. (ed.) *The Rate and Direction of Inventive Activity: Economic and Social Factors* (Princeton: Princeton University Press), pp. 609–25.

Arrow, Kenneth J. (1978) 'A Cautious Case for Socialism', *Dissent*, **25**, Fall, pp. 472–80.

Arrow, Kenneth J. and Debreu, Gerard (1954) 'Existence of an Equilibrium for a Competitive Economy', *Econometrica*, **22**(3), pp. 265–90.

Arruñada, Benito (2012) *Institutional Foundations of Impersonal Exchange: Theory and Policy of Contractual Registries* (Chicago, IL: University of Chicago Press).

Arruñada, Benito (2017) 'Property as Sequential Exchange: The Forgotten Limits of Private Contract', *Journal of Institutional Economics*, **13**(4), December, pp. 753–83.

Asch, Solomon E. (1952) *Social Psychology* (New York: Prentice Hall).

Ashkenazi, Eli (2010) 'After 100 Years, the Kibbutz Movement has Completely Changed', *Haaretz*, 7 January. Available at https://www.haaretz.com/after-100-years-the-kibbutz-movement-has-completely-changed-1.260940. (Retrieved 23 November 2010.)

Ashton, David and Green, Francis (1996) *Education, Training and the Global Economy* (Cheltenham, UK and Northampton, MA, USA: Edward Elgar Publishing).

Atkinson, Anthony B. (2015) *Inequality: What Can be Done?* (Cambridge, MA: Harvard University Press).

Atran, Scott and Henrich, Joseph (2010) 'The Evolution of Religion: How Cognitive By-Products, Adaptive Learning Heuristics, Ritual Displays and Group Competition Generate Deep Commitments to Prosocial Religions', *Biological Theory*, **5**(1), pp. 18–30.

Attlee, Clement R. (1937) *The Labour Party in Perspective* (London: Gollancz).

Ayres, Clarence E. (1944) *The Theory of Economic Progress*, 1st edn (Chapel Hill, NC: University of North Carolina Press).

Baccaro, Lucio and Benassi, Chiara (2017) 'Throwing out the Ballast: Growth Models and the Liberalization of German Industrial Relations', *Socio-Economic Review*, **15**(1), pp. 85–115.

Badhwar, Neera K. and Long, Roderick T. (2016) 'Ayn Rand', *Stanford Encyclopedia of Philosophy*. Available at https://plato.stanford.edu/entries/ayn-rand/#Altr. (Retrieved 19 March 2018.)

Baisch, Helmut (1979) 'A Critique of Labour Values for Planning', *World Development*, **7**(10), pp. 965–72.

Barkai, Haim (1972) 'The Kibbutz: An Experiment in Microsocialism', in Howe, Irving (ed.) *Israel and Arabs: Views from the Left* (New York: Bantham), pp. 69–100. Adapted in Vanek, Jaroslav (ed.) (1975) *Self-Management: The Economic Liberation of Man* (Harmondsworth: Penguin), pp. 213–26.

Barzel, Yoram (1997) *Economic Analysis of Property Rights*, 2nd edn (Cambridge: Cambridge University Press).

BBC News (2001) 'Waiting Lists'. Available at http://news.bbc.co.uk/vote2001/hi/english/main_issues/sections/facts/newsid_1134000/1134218.stm#top, http://www.bbc.co.uk/otr/intext/20010603_whole.html. (Retrieved 8 December 2017.)

BBC News (2005) 'Blair Promises Action on GP Row'. Available at http://news.bbc.co.uk/1/hi/uk_politics/vote_2005/frontpage/4495865.stm. (Retrieved 8 December 2017.)

BBC News (2016) 'Jeremy Corbyn Outlines Labour's Vision of a "New Economics"', 21 May. Available at http://www.bbc.com/news/uk-politics-36351149. (Retrieved 19 November 2017.)

Beer, Max (1940) *A History of British Socialism*, 2 vols (London: Allen and Unwin).

Bel, Germà and Warner, Mildred (2008) 'Does Privatization of Solid Waste and Water Services Reduce Costs? A Review of Empirical Studies', *Resources, Conservation and Recycling*, **52**(12), October, pp. 1337–48.

Ben-Meir, Ilan (2015) 'Bernie Sanders Despised Democrats in 1980s, Said a JFK Speech Once Made Him Sick', *BuzzFeed News*, 16 July.

Available at https://www.buzzfeed.com/ilanbenmeir/bernie-sanders-despised-democrats-in-1980s-said-a-jfk-speech?utm_term=.wmVM4dx ppX#.trN5owqLL1. (Retrieved 19 November 2017.)

Benn, Tony (1979) *Arguments for Socialism* (London: Jonathan Cape).

Benn, Tony (1981) *Arguments for Democracy* (Harmondsworth: Penguin).

Benn, Tony (1982) *Parliament, People and Power: Agenda for a Free Society* (London: Verso).

Bennett, Natalie (2017)) '#Natalie4Sheffield – Issues: Young People'. Available at https://www.natalie4sheffield.org/issues/young-people. (Retrieved 8 January 2018.)

Benson, Bruce L. and Engen, Eric M. (1988) 'The Market for Laws: An Economic Analysis of Legislation', *Southern Economic Journal*, **54**(3), January, pp. 732–45.

Berger, Sebastian (2017) *The Social Costs of Neoliberalism: Essays on the Economics of K. William Kapp* (Nottingham: Spokesman).

Berger, Suzanne and Dore, Ronald (eds) (1996) *National Diversity and Global Capitalism* (Ithaca, NY: Cornell University Press).

Berggren, Niclas and Nilsson, Therese (2013) 'Does Economic Freedom Foster Tolerance?', *Kyklos*, **66**(2), pp. 177–207.

Berggren, Niclas and Nilsson, Therese (2015) 'Globalization and the Transmission of Social Values: The Case of Tolerance', *Journal of Comparative Economics*, **43**(2), pp. 371–89.

Bergson, Abram (1991) 'The USSR before the Fall: How Poor and Why', *Journal of Economic Perspectives*, **5**(4), pp. 29–44.

Berlin, Isaiah (1969) *Four Essays on Liberty* (Oxford: Oxford University Press).

Berlin, Isaiah (1990) *The Crooked Timber of Humanity: Chapters in the History of Ideas* (London: Murray).

Bernstein, Eduard (1961) *Evolutionary Socialism: A Criticism and Affirmation*, trans. from the German edn of 1899 (New York: Schocken).

Berstein, Serge (2003) 'Les Usages Politique de l'Autogestion', in Georgi, Frank (ed.) *Autogestion: La dernière utopie?* (Paris: Sorbonne), pp. 157–72.

Bertrand, Elodie (2006) 'The Coasean Analysis of Lighthouse Financing: Myths and Realities', *Cambridge Journal of Economics*, **30**(3), May, pp. 389–402.

Bestor, Arthur E., Jr (1948) 'The Evolution of the Socialist Vocabulary', *Journal of the History of Ideas*, **9**(3), June, pp. 259–302.

Bevan, Aneurin (1952) 'The Fatuity of Coalition', *Tribune*, 13 June, pp. 1–3.

Bhaskar, Roy and Collier, Andrew (1998) 'Introduction: Explanatory Critiques', in Archer, Margaret S., Bhaskar, Roy, Collier, Andrew,

Lawson, Tony and Norrie, Alan (eds) *Critical Realism: Essential Readings* (London, UK and New York, NY, USA: Routledge), pp. 385–94.

Binder, Seth and Neumayer, Eric (2005) 'Environmental Pressure Group Strength and Air Pollution: An Empirical Analysis', *Ecological Economics*, **55**(4), December, pp. 537–38.

Birch, Kean (2017) *A Research Agenda for Neoliberalism* (Cheltenham, UK and Northampton, MA, USA: Edward Elgar Publishing).

Birstein, Vadim J. (2004) *The Perversion of Knowledge: The True Story of Soviet Science* (Boulder, CO: Westview Press).

Bladel, John P. (2005) 'Against Polanyi-Centrism: Hayek and the Re-emergence of "Spontaneous Order"', *Quarterly Journal of Austrian Economics*, **8**(4), Winter, pp. 15–30.

Blair, Margaret M. (1995) *Ownership and Control: Rethinking Corporate Governance for the Twenty-First Century* (Washington, DC: The Brookings Institution).

Blair, Margaret M. (2003) 'Locking in Capital: What Corporate Law Achieved for Business Organizers in the Nineteenth Century', *UCLA Law Review*, **51**(2), pp. 387–455.

Blair, Tony (1982) 'Letter to Michael Foot' of July 1982. Available at http://www.telegraph.co.uk/news/uknews/1521418/The-full-text-of-Tony-Blairs-letter-to-Michael-Foot-written-in-July-1982.html. (Retrieved 22 January 2016.)

Blair, Tony (1994) *Socialism*, Fabian Pamphlet 565 (London: Fabian Society).

Blaug, Mark (1993) 'Review of D.R. Steele *From Marx to Mises*', *Economic Journal*, **103**(6), November, pp. 1570–71.

Block, Fred and Somers, Margaret (2014) *The Power of Market Fundamentalism: Karl Polanyi's Critique* (Cambridge, MA: Harvard University Press).

Block, Walter (ed.) (1989) *Economics and the Environment: A Reconciliation* (Vancouver, BC: Fraser Institute).

Block, Walter (1996) 'Hayek's Road to Serfdom', *Journal of Libertarian Studies*, **12**(2), Fall, pp. 339–65.

Boas, Taylor C. and Gans-Morse, Jordan (2009) 'Neoliberalism: From New Liberal Philosophy to Anti-Liberal Slogan', *Studies in Comparative International Development*, **44**(2), June, pp. 137–61.

Bockman, Johanna (2011) *Markets in the Name of Socialism: The Left-Wing Origins of Neoliberalism* (Stanford, CA: Stanford University Press).

Bodington, Stephen (1973) *Computers and Socialism* (Nottingham: Spokesman).

Boehm, Christopher (2012) *Moral Origins: The Evolution of Virtue, Altruism and Shame* (New York, NY: Basic Books).

Boettke, Peter J. (1988) 'The Soviet Experiment with Pure Communism', *Critical Review*, **2**(4), Fall, pp. 149–82.

Boettke, Peter J. (ed.) (2000) *Socialism and the Market: The Calculation Debate Revisited* (London, UK and New York, NY, USA: Routledge).

Boettke, Peter J. (2001) *Calculation and Coordination: Essays on Socialism and Transitional Political Economy* (London, UK and New York, NY, USA: Routledge).

Boettke, Peter J. (2018) *F.A. Hayek: Economics, Political Economy and Social Philosophy* (London, UK and New York, NY, USA: Palgrave).

Bogdan, Radu (2000) *Minding Minds: Evolving a Reflexive Mind in Interpreting Others* (Cambridge, MA: MIT Press).

Bogdanor, Vernon (1981) *The People and the Party System: The Referendum and Electoral Reform in British Politics* (Cambridge: Cambridge University Press).

Bohle, Dorethee and Greskovits, Béla (2012) *Capitalist Diversity on Europe's Periphery* (Ithaca, NY, USA and London, UK: Cornell University Press).

Bok, Sissela (1995) *Common Values* (Columbia, MO: University of Missouri Press).

Bolton, Matt and Pitts, Frederick Harry (2018) *Corbynism: A Critical Approach* (Bingley: Emerald).

Bonin, John P., Jones, Derek C. and Putterman, Louis (1993) 'Theoretical and Empirical Studies of Producer Cooperatives: Will Ever the Twain Meet?', *Journal of Economic Literature*, **31**(3), September, pp. 1290–320.

Bonini, Nicolao and Egidi, Massimo (1999) 'Cognitive Traps in Individual and Organizational Behavior: Some Empirical Evidence', Working Paper WP1999-04, University of Trento.

Bowler, Peter J. and Morus, Iwan Rhys (2005) *Making Modern Science: A Historical Survey* (Chicago, IL: University of Chicago Press).

Bowles, Samuel and Gintis, Herbert (1999) *Recasting Egalitarianism: New Rules for Markets, States, and Communities* (London: Verso).

Bowles, Samuel and Gintis, Herbert (2002) 'The Inheritance of Inequality', *Journal of Economic Perspectives*, **16**(3), Summer, pp. 3–30.

Bowles, Samuel and Gintis, Herbert (2005) 'Can Self-Interest Explain Cooperation?', *Evolutionary and Institutional Economics Review*, **2**(1), October, pp. 21–41.

Bowles, Samuel and Gintis, Herbert (2011) *A Cooperative Species: Human Reciprocity and its Evolution* (Princeton, NJ: Princeton University Press).

Bowles, Samuel, Kirman, Alan and Sethi, Rajiv (2017) 'Friedrich Hayek and the Market Algorithm', *Journal of Economic Perspectives*, **31**(3), Summer, pp. 215–30.

Boyd, Robert and Richerson, Peter J. (1985) *Culture and the Evolutionary Process* (Chicago, IL: University of Chicago Press).

Boyer, Robert (1999) 'The Variety and Dynamics of Capitalism', in Groenewegen, John and Vromen, Jack J. (eds) *Institutions and the Evolution of Capitalism: Implications of Evolutionary Economics* (Cheltenham, UK and Northampton, MA, USA: Edward Elgar Publishing), pp. 122–40.

Bregman, Rutger (2017) *Utopia for Realists* (London, UK and New York, NY, USA: Bloomsbury).

Brennan, Jason (2014) *Why Not Capitalism?* (London, UK and New York, NY, USA: Routledge).

Brewer-Carías, Allan R. (2001) 'Golpe de Estado y Proceso Constituyente en Venezuela'. Available at http://www.corteidh.or.cr/tablas/13677.pdf. (Retrieved 13 February 2018.)

Brewer-Carías, Allan R. (2017) 'Venezuela: 17 Years of Disregarding the Constitution. What to Expect?'. Available at http://allanbrewercarias.net/dev/wp-content/uploads/2017/06/1189.-conf.-ARBrewer.-Venezuela.-Final-17-years-of-contempt-for-the-Constitution-VAAUS.pdf. (Retrieved 13 February 2018.)

British Political Speech (2018) 'Speech Archive: Leader's Speech, Brighton 2017'. Available at http://www.britishpoliticalspeech.org/speech-archive.htm?speech=203. (Retrieved 12 February 2018.)

Brockway, Fenner (1980) *Britain's First Socialists: The Levellers, Agitators and Diggers of the English Revolution* (London: Quartet).

Broekmeyer, Marius (1977) 'Self-Management in Yugoslavia', *Annals of the American Academy of Political and Social Science*, **431**(1), pp. 133–40.

Brown, Donald E. (1991) *Human Universals* (New York: McGraw-Hill).

Brunk, Gregory G., Caldeira, Gregory A. and Lewis-Beck, Michael S. (1987) 'Capitalism, Socialism, and Democracy: An Empirical Inquiry', *European Journal of Political Research*, **15**(4), July, pp. 459–70.

Bukharin, Nikolai (1967) *The Path to Socialism in Russia*, trans. from the Russian edn of 1924 (New York: Omicron Books).

Burczak, Theodore (2006) *Socialism after Hayek* (Ann Arbor, MI: University of Michigan Press).

Burge, Tyler (1986) 'Individualism and Psychology', *Philosophical Review*, **95**(1), January, pp. 3–45.

Burgin, Angus (2012) *The Great Persuasion: Reinventing Free Markets since the Depression* (Cambridge, MA: Harvard University Press).

Burke, Edmund (1790) *Reflections on the Revolution in France and on the Proceedings in Certain Societies in London* (London: Dodsley).

Burkhart, Ross E. (2000) 'Economic Freedom and Democracy: Post-Cold War Tests', *European Journal of Political Research*, **37**(2), March, pp. 237–53.

Burlington Free Press (1976) 'Liberty Union Candidate Discusses His Campaign', 5 October. Available at https://www.scribd.com/document/401621724/Bernie-Interview?secret_password=ieo9zgp69wSwBvjJAnf8&campaign=VigLink&ad_group=xxc1xx&source=hp_affiliate&medium=affiliate. (Retrieved 23 May 2019.)

Cahill, Damien and Konings, Martijn (2017) *Neoliberalism* (Cambridge, UK and Medford, MA, USA: Polity Press).

Campbell, Al (2011) 'Marx and Engels' Vision of a Better Society', *Forum for Social Economics*, **39**(3), October, pp. 269–78.

Caplan, Bryan (2004) 'Is Socialism Really "Impossible"?', *Critical Review*, **16**(1), pp. 33–52.

Carmony, Donald F. and Elliott, Josephine M. (1980) 'New Harmony, Indiana: Robert Owen's Seedbed for Utopia', *Indiana Magazine of History*, **76**(3), September, pp. 161–261.

Carr, E.H. (1964) *The Russian Revolution from Lenin to Stalin, 1917–29* (London: Macmillan).

Carroll, Lewis (1970) *The Annotated Alice: Alice's Adventures in Wonderland and Through the Looking Glass*, edited with an introduction and annotations by Martin Gardner (Harmondsworth: Penguin).

Center for Systemic Peace (2016) 'The Polity Project'. Available at http://www.systemicpeace.org/polityproject.html. (Retrieved 2 February 2018.)

Chandler, Alfred D., Jr (1990) *Scale and Scope: The Dynamics of Industrial Capitalism* (Cambridge, MA: Harvard University Press).

Chang, Ha-Joon (1997) 'The Economics and Politics of Regulation: A Critical Survey', *Cambridge Journal of Economics*, **21**(6), November, pp. 703–28.

Chang, Ha-Joon (2002a) 'Breaking the Mould: An Institutionalist Political Economy Alternative to the Neo-Liberal Theory of the Market and the State', *Cambridge Journal of Economics*, **26**(5), September, pp. 539–59.

Chang, Ha-Joon (2002b) *Kicking Away the Ladder: Development Strategy in Historical Perspective* (London: Anthem Press).

Chang, Ha-Joon and Rowthorn, Robert E. (eds) (1995) *The Role of the State in Economic Change* (Oxford: Clarendon Press).

Cheung, Steven N.S. (1983) 'The Contractual Nature of the Firm', *Journal of Law and Economics*, **26**(2), April, pp. 1–21.

Ciccariello-Maher, George (2017) 'Which Way out of the Venezuelan Crisis?', *Jacobin*, 29 July. Available at https://jacobinmag.com/2017/07/venezuela-elections-chavez-maduro-bolivarianism. (Retrieved 12 February 2018.)

CICOPA (2014) 'Cooperatives Contribute to Resilient Employment, a Sustainable Economy and the Well-Being of People at Work', *CICOPA News*, 7 October. Available at http://www.cicopa.coop/Cooperatives-contribute-to.html. (Retrieved 17 February 2018.)

Claeys, Gregory (1989) *Thomas Paine: Social and Political Thought* (London, UK and New York, NY, USA: Routledge).

Claeys, Gregory (1991) 'Introduction', in Owen, Robert, *A New View of Society and Other Writings* (Harmondsworth: Penguin), pp. vii–xxxiv.

Clark, Andy (1997) *Being There: Putting the Brain, Body and World Together Again* (Cambridge, MA: MIT Press).

Clark, John Bates (1899) *The Distribution of Wealth: A Theory of Wages, Interest and Profits* (New York, NY: Macmillan).

Clarke, Peter (1978) *Liberals and Social Democrats* (Cambridge: Cambridge University Press).

Coase, Ronald H. (1937) 'The Nature of the Firm', *Economica*, **4**, New Series, November, pp. 386–405.

Coase, Ronald H. (1960) 'The Problem of Social Cost', *Journal of Law and Economics*, **3**(1), October, pp. 1–44.

Coase, Ronald H. (1974a) 'The Market for Goods and the Market for Ideas', *American Economic Review (Papers and Proceedings)*, **64**(2), May, pp. 384–91.

Coase, Ronald H. (1974b) 'The Lighthouse in Economics', *Journal of Law and Economics*, **17**(2), October, pp. 357–76.

Coase, Ronald H. (1988) *The Firm, the Market, and the Law* (Chicago, IL: University of Chicago Press).

Coase, Ronald H. and Wang, Ning (2012) *How China Became Capitalist* (London, UK and New York, NY, USA: Palgrave Macmillan).

Coates, David (ed.) (2005) *Varieties of Capitalism: Varieties of Approaches* (London, UK and New York, NY, USA: Palgrave Macmillan).

Cockshott, W. Paul and Cottrell, Allin F. (1993) *Towards a New Socialism* (Nottingham: Spokesman).

Cohen, Gerald A. (1995) *Self-Ownership, Freedom, and Equality* (Cambridge, UK and New York, NY, USA: Cambridge University Press).

Cohen, Gerald A. (2009) *Why Not Socialism?* (Princeton, NJ, USA and London, UK: Princeton University Press).

Cohen, Jean L. (1982) *Class and Civil Society: The Limits of Marxian Critical Theory* (Oxford: Martin Robertson).

Cohen, Michael D. and Bacdayan, Paul (1994) 'Organizational Routines are Stored as Procedural Memory – Evidence from a Laboratory Study', *Organization Science*, **5**(4), November, pp. 554–68.

Cole, Daniel H. and Grossman, Peter Z. (2002) 'The Meaning of Property Rights: Law versus Economics?', *Land Economics*, **78**(3), August, pp. 317–30.

Cole, George D.H. (1917) *Self-Government in Industry* (London: G. Bell).

Cole, George D.H. (1920a) *Guild Socialism Re-Stated* (London: Parsons).

Cole, George D.H. (1920b) *Chaos and Order in Industry* (London: Methuen).

Cole, George D.H. (1935) *Principles of Economic Planning* (London: Macmillan).

Cole, George D.H. (1948) *The Meaning of Marxism* (London: George Allen and Unwin).

Commons, John R. (1893) *The Distribution of Wealth* (London, UK and New York, NY, USA: Macmillan).

Commons, John R. (1924) *Legal Foundations of Capitalism* (New York, NY: Macmillan).

Commons, John R. (1934) *Institutional Economics: Its Place in Political Economy* (New York, NY: Macmillan).

Commonwealth Fund (2017) 'Mirror, Mirror 2017: International Comparison Reflects Flaws and Opportunities for Better U.S. Health Care', 14 July. Available at http://www.commonwealthfund.org/Publications/Fund-Reports/2017/Jul/Mirror-Mirror-International-Comparisons-2017. (Retrieved 8 December 2017.)

Communist Party of China (2013) *Full Text of the Constitution of the Communist Party of China.* Available at http://english.cpc.people.com.cn/206972/206981/8188065.html. (Retrieved 26 January 2018.)

Conquest, Robert (2007) *The Great Terror: A Reassessment*, 40th anniversary edn (Oxford: Oxford University Press).

Cooley, Charles Horton (1922) *Human Nature and the Social Order*, 2nd edn (New York, NY: Scribner's).

Corbyn, Jeremy (2014) 'This Belligerence Endangers Us All', *Morning Star*, 17 April. Available at http://www.morningstaronline.co.uk/a-972b-Nato-belligerence-endangers-us-all#.Vf6r4k2FOUk. (Retrieved 13 March 2018.)

Corning, Peter A. (2011) *The Fair Society: The Science of Human Nature and the Pursuit of Social Justice* (Chicago, IL: University of Chicago Press).

Council of Economic Advisors (2018) *The Opportunity Costs of Socialism* (Washington, DC: Executive Office of the President of the United States). Available at https://www.whitehouse.gov/wp-content/uploads/

2018/10/The-Opportunity-Costs-of-Socialism.pdf. (Retrieved 28 November 2018.)

Courtois, Stéphane, Werth, Nicolas, Panné, Jean-Louis, Packowski, Andrzej, Bartošek, Karel and Margolin, Jean-Louis (1999) *The Black Book of Communism: Crimes, Terror, Repression* (Cambridge, MA: Harvard University Press).

Cowen, Tyler (2013) *Average is Over: Powering America Beyond the Age of the Great Stagnation* (New York, NY: Dutton).

Credit Suisse Research Institute (2012) *Credit Suisse Global Wealth Databook 2012* (Zurich: Credit Suisse Research Institute).

Crosland, C. Anthony R. (1956) *The Future of Socialism* (London: Jonathan Cape).

Crouch, Colin (2005) *Capitalist Diversity and Change* (Oxford, UK and New York, NY, USA: Oxford University Press).

Crouch, Colin (2018) *The Globalization Backlash* (Hoboken, NJ, USA and Chichester, UK: Wiley).

Crouch, Colin and Streeck, Wolfgang (eds) (1997) *Political Economy of Modern Capitalism: Mapping Convergence and Diversity* (London, UK and Thousand Oaks, CA, USA: Sage).

Crouch, Colin, Finegold, David and Sako, Mari (1999) *Are Skills the Answer? The Political Economy of Skill Creation in Advanced Industrial Countries* (Oxford: Oxford University Press).

Cummings, Michael S. (1998) 'Review of *America's Communal Utopias* by Donald E. Pitzer', *Utopian Studies*, **9**(2), pp. 191–206.

Cunliffe, Rachel (2015) 'Why is Corbyn still Fetishising Venezuela?', *CapX*, 19 September. Available at https://capx.co/why-is-corbyn-still-fetishising-venezuela/. (Retrieved 1 December 2017.)

Cusack, Asa (2017) 'What the Left must Learn from Maduro's Failures in Venezuela', *The Guardian*, 2 August. Available at https://www.theguardian.com/commentisfree/2017/aug/02/left-learn-maduros-failures-in-venezuela-bolivarian-revolution-chavismo. (Retrieved 12 February 2018.)

D'Amico, Daniel J. (2015) 'Spontaneous Order', in Boettke, Peter J. and Coyne, Christopher (eds) *The Oxford Handbook of Austrian Economics* (Oxford, UK and New York, NY, USA: Oxford University Press), pp. 115–42.

Dahlgreen, Will (2016) 'British People Keener on Socialism than Capitalism', *YouGov*. Available at https://yougov.co.uk/news/2016/02/23/british-people-view-socialism-more-favourably-capi/. (Retrieved 18 November 2017.)

Dale, Gareth (2010) *Karl Polanyi: The Limits to the Market* (Cambridge: Polity Press).

Darwin, Charles R. (1871) *The Descent of Man, and Selection in Relation to Sex*, 2 vols (London, UK: Murray and New York, NY, USA: Hill).

Davies, James B., Sandström, Susanna, Shorrocks, Anthony B. and Wolff, Edward N. (2009) 'The Level and Distribution of Global Household Wealth', NBER Working Paper 15508 (Cambridge, MA: National Bureau of Economic Research).

Davis, David Brion (1979) *Antebellum American Culture: An Interpretive Anthology* (Lexington, MA: D.C. Heath).

Davis, Peter and Parker, Martin (2007) 'Cooperatives, Labor, and the State: The English Labor Economists Revisited', *Review of Radical Political Economics*, **39**(4), Fall, pp. 523–42.

Dawes, Robyn M. and Thaler, Richard H. (1988) 'Anomalies: Cooperation', *Journal of Economic Perspectives*, **2**(3), Summer, pp. 187–97.

De Soto, Hernando (2000) *The Mystery of Capital: Why Capitalism Triumphs in the West and Fails Everywhere Else* (New York, NY: Basic Books).

De Waal, Frans B.M. (2006) *Primates and Philosophers: How Morality Evolved* (Princeton, NJ: Princeton University Press).

Deakin, Simon, Gindis, David, Hodgson, Geoffrey M., Huang, Kainan and Pistor, Katharina (2017) 'Legal Institutionalism: Capitalism and the Constitutive Role of Law', *Journal of Comparative Economics*, **45**(1), February, pp. 188–200.

Deaton, Angus (2013) *The Great Escape: Health, Wealth, and the Origins of Inequality* (Princeton, NJ: Princeton University Press).

Debs, Eugene V. (1919) 'The Day of the People', *The Class Struggle*, **3**(1), February. Available at https://www.marxists.org/archive/debs/works/1919/daypeople.htm. (Retrieved 18 January 2018.)

Deighton, Len (1964) *Funeral in Berlin* (London: Jonathan Cape).

Democratic Socialists of America (1995) 'Where We Stand: Building the Next Left', *DSA: Democratic Socialists of America*. Available at https://www.dsausa.org/where_we_stand. (Retrieved 30 July 2018.)

Deng, Xiaoping (1992) 'Excerpts from Talks given in Wuchang, Shenzhen, Zhuhai, and Shanghai', 18 January–21 February, 1992, *People's Daily*. Available at http://www.olemiss.edu/courses/pol324/dengxp92.htm. (Retrieved 26 January 2018.) From Deng, Xiaoping, *Selected Works* (Chinese edn) (Beijing: the People's Publishing House, 1993), vol. 3, p. 360.

Devine, Patrick (1988) *Democracy and Economic Planning: The Political Economy of a Self-Governing Society* (Cambridge: Polity Press).

Dewey, John (1916) *Democracy and Education* (New York, NY: Macmillan).

Dewey, John (1929) *The Quest for Certainty: A Study of the Relation of Knowledge and Action* (New York, NY: Minton, Balch).

Dewey, John (1935) *Liberalism and Social Action* (New York, NY: G.P. Putnam's Sons).

Dewey, John (1938) *Logic: The Theory of Enquiry* (New York, NY: Holt).

Dewey, John (1939) *Theory of Valuation* (Chicago, IL: University of Chicago Press).

Dickinson, Henry D. (1933) 'Price Formation in a Socialist Community', *Economic Journal*, **43**, pp. 237–50.

Dickinson, Henry D. (1939) *Economics of Socialism* (Oxford: Oxford University Press).

Dobb, Maurice (1940) *Political Economy and Capitalism*, 2nd edn (London: Routledge and Kegan Paul).

Dobb, Maurice (1955) *On Economic Theory and Socialism: Collected Papers* (London: Routledge and Kegan Paul).

Dobb, Maurice (1969) *Welfare Economics and the Economics of Socialism: Towards a Commonsense Critique* (Cambridge: Cambridge University Press).

Doeringer, Peter B. and Piore, Michael J. (1971) *Internal Labor Markets and Manpower Analysis* (Lexington, MA: Heath).

Dore, Ronald (2000) *Stock Market Capitalism: Welfare Capitalism: Japan and Germany versus the Anglo Saxons* (Oxford: Oxford University Press).

Dosi, Giovanni (1988) 'The Sources, Procedures, and Microeconomic Effects of Innovation', *Journal of Economic Literature*, **26**(3), September, pp. 1120–71.

Doucouliagos, Chris (1995) 'Worker Participation and Productivity in Labor-Managed and Participatory Capitalist Firms: A Meta-Analysis', *Industrial and Labor Relations Review*, **49**(1), October, pp. 58–77.

Douglas, Mary T. (1986) *How Institutions Think* (London, UK: Routledge and Kegan Paul and Syracuse, NY, USA: Syracuse University Press).

Dow, Gregory K. (2003) *Governing the Firm: Workers' Control in Theory and Practice* (Cambridge, UK and New York, NY, USA: Cambridge University Press).

Doyal, Leonard and Gough, Ian (1991) *A Theory of Human Need* (London: Macmillan).

Dunbar, Robin I.M. (1993) 'Coevolution of Neocortical Size, Group Size, and Language', *Behavioral and Brain Sciences*, **16**, pp. 681–94.

Dunbar, Robin I.M. (2010) *How Many Friends does One Person Need? Dunbar's Number and Other Evolutionary Quirks* (London: Faber and Faber).

Dunbar, Robin I.M. (2011) 'Constraints on the Evolution of Social Institutions and their Implications for Information Flow', *Journal of Institutional Economics*, **7**(3), September, pp. 345–71.

Durbin, Elizabeth (1985) *New Jerusalems: The Labour Party and the Economics of Democratic Socialism* (London: Routledge and Kegan Paul).

Durbin, Evan F.M. (1936) 'Economic Calculus in a Planned Economy', *Economic Journal*, **46**(4), December, pp. 676–90.

Durkheim, Émile (1984) *The Division of Labour in Society*, trans. from the French edn of 1893 (London: Macmillan).

Dziak, John J. (1988) *Chekisty: A History of the KGB* (Lexington, MA: D.C. Heath).

Ebenstein, Alan O. (2007) *Milton Friedman: A Biography* (London, UK and New York, NY, USA: St Martin's Press).

Economist Intelligence Unit (2017) *Democracy Index 2017: Free Speech Under Attack* (London: The Economist). Available at https://www.eiu.com/topic/democracy-index. (Retrieved 5 February 2018.)

Edgeworth, Francis Y. (1904) 'The Theory of Distribution', *Quarterly Journal of Economics*, **18**, pp. 159–219.

Eisner, Marc Allen (2011) 'Beyond the Logic of the Market: Toward an Institutional Analysis of Regulatory Reforms', in Levi-Faur, David (ed.) *Handbook on the Politics of Regulation* (Cheltenham, UK and Northampton, MA, USA: Edward Elgar Publishing), pp. 129–41.

Ekelund, Robert B. Jr and Walker, Douglas M. (1996) 'J.S. Mill on Income Tax Exemption and Inheritance Taxes: The Evidence Reconsidered', *History of Political Economy*, **28**(4), pp. 559–81.

El Nacional (2016) 'Encuesta de Datincorp: 57% de los Venezolanos Quiere Irse del País', *El Nacional*, 8 December. Available at http://www.el-nacional.com/noticias/sociedad/encuesta-datincorp-los-venezolanos-quiere-irse-del-pais_11774. (Retrieved 15 February 2018.)

Elgot, Jessica and Asthana, Anushka (2017) 'Labour Speaks out on Venezuela as Pressure Mounts on Corbyn', *The Guardian*, 3 August. Available at https://www.theguardian.com/world/2017/aug/02/labour-concerns-on-venezuela-raise-pressure-on-jeremy-corbyn-to-speak-out. (Retrieved 1 December 2017.)

Elliott, Okla (2016) 'What does Sanders mean by "Democratic Socialism"?', 4 March. Available at http://thehill.com/blogs/congress-blog/presidential-campaign/271652-what-does-sanders-mean-by-democratic-socialism. (Retrieved 19 November 2017.)

Ellman, Michael (1989) *Socialist Planning*, 2nd edn (Cambridge: Cambridge University Press).

Engels, Frederick (1962) *Anti-Dühring: Herr Eugen Dühring's Revolution in Science*, trans. from the 3rd German edn of 1894 (London: Lawrence and Wishart).

Erasmus, Charles J. (1977) *In Search of the Common Good: Utopian Experiments Past and Future* (New York: Free Press).

Eraut, Michael (2000) 'Non-Formal Learning and Tacit Knowledge in Professional Work', *British Journal of Educational Psychology*, **70**(1), pp. 113–36.

ESRC (2016) *ESRC Party Members Project*, Economic and Social Research Council. Available at https://esrcpartymembersproject.org/. (Retrieved 1 May 2018.)

Estrin, Saul (1983) *Self-Management: Economic Theory and Yugoslav Practice* (Cambridge: Cambridge University Press).

Estrin, Saul (1991) 'Yugoslavia: The Case of Self-Managing Market Socialism', *Journal of Economic Perspectives*, **5**(4), Autumn, pp. 187–94.

Evans, Karen G. (2000) 'Reclaiming John Dewey: Democracy, Inquiry, Pragmatism, and Public Management', *Administration and Society*, **32**(3), July, pp. 308–28.

Evans, Peter and Rauch, James E. (1999) 'Bureaucracy and Growth: A Cross-National Analysis of the Effects of "Weberian" State Structures on Economic Growth', *American Sociological Review*, **64**, October, pp. 748–65.

Evans, Richard J. (2003) *The Coming of the Third Reich: How the Nazis Destroyed Democracy and Seized Power in Germany* (London, UK and New York, NY, USA: Penguin).

Evans, Richard J. (2006) *The Third Reich in Power, 1933–1939: How the Nazis Won Over the Hearts and Minds of a Nation* (London, UK and New York, NY, USA: Penguin).

Figes, Orlando (2014) *Revolutionary Russia, 1891–1991: A History* (New York: Metropolitan Books).

Finnis, John (1980) *Natural Law and Natural Rights* (Oxford: Clarendon Press).

Fleck, Ludwik (1979) *Genesis and Development of a Scientific Fact*, trans. by F. Bradley and T.J. Trenn from the German edn of 1935 (Chicago: University of Chicago Press).

Fogel, Robert W. (2004) *The Escape from Hunger and Premature Death, 1700–2100: Europe, America, and the Third World* (Cambridge: Cambridge University Press).

Foote, Geoffrey (1997) *The Labour Party's Political Thought: A History*, 3rd edn (London: Palgrave).

Forero, Juan (2018) 'Venezuela's Misery Fuels Emigration on an Epic Scale', *Wall Street Journal*, 13 February. Available at https://www.wsj.com/articles/venezuelas-misery-fuels-migration-on-epic-scale-1518517800. (Retrieved 15 February 2018.)

Forstater, Mathew (2006) 'Tax-Driven Money: Additional Evidence from the History of Thought, Economic History, and Economic Policy', in

Setterfield, Mark (ed.) *Complexity, Endogenous Money, and Exogenous Interest Rates* (Cheltenham, UK and Northampton, MA, USA: Edward Elgar Publishing), pp. 202–20.

Fox, Alan (1974) *Beyond Contract: Work, Power and Trust Relations* (London: Faber and Faber).

Fredriksson, Per G., Neumayer, Eric, Damania, Richard and Gates, Scott (2005) 'Environmentalism, Democracy, and Pollution Control', *Journal of Environmental Economics and Management*, **49**(2), March, pp. 343–65.

Friedman, Milton (1962a) *Capitalism and Freedom* (Chicago: University of Chicago Press).

Friedman, Milton (1962b) *Price Theory: A Provisional Text* (Chicago: Aldine).

Friedman, Milton and Friedman, Rose (1980) *Free to Choose: A Personal Statement* (Harmondsworth: Penguin).

Fukuyama, Francis (1992) *The End of History and the Last Man* (New York: Free Press).

Fukuyama, Francis (2011) *The Origins of Political Order: From Prehuman Times to the French Revolution* (London, UK and New York, NY, USA: Profile Books and Farrar, Straus and Giroux).

Fukuyama, Francis (2014) *Political Order and Political Decay: From the Industrial Revolution to the Globalization of Democracy* (London, UK and New York, NY, USA: Profile Books and Farrar, Straus and Giroux).

Fuller, Steve (1988) *Social Epistemology* (Bloomington, IN: Indiana University Press).

Gagliardi, Francesca (2009) 'Financial Development and the Growth of Cooperative Firms', *Small Business Economics*, **32**(4), April, pp. 439–64.

Galbraith, James K. (2012) *Inequality and Instability: A Study of the World Economy Just Before the Great Crisis* (Oxford, UK and New York, NY, USA: Oxford University Press).

Galbraith, John Kenneth (1952) *American Capitalism: The Concept of Countervailing Power* (Boston, MA: Houghton Mifflin).

Galbraith, John Kenneth (1958) *The Affluent Society* (London: Hamilton).

Galbraith, John Kenneth (1969) *The New Industrial State* (Harmondsworth: Penguin).

Gamble, Andrew (1988) *The Free Economy and the Strong State: The Politics of Thatcherism* (London, UK and New York, NY, USA: Palgrave Macmillan).

Gartzke, Erik (2007) 'The Capitalist Peace', *American Journal of Political Science*, **51**(1), January, pp. 166–91.

Gavron, Daniel (2000). *The Kibbutz: Awakening from Utopia* (Lanham, MD: Rowman and Littlefield).

Gellner, Ernest (1994) *Conditions of Liberty: Civil Society and its Rivals* (London, UK and New York, NY, USA: Hamish Hamilton).

George, Henry (1879) *Progress and Poverty: An Inquiry into the Cause of Industrial Depression and Increase of Want with Increase of Wealth* (London: Kegan Paul).

Gide, Charles and Rist, Charles (1915) *A History of Economic Doctrines From the Time of the Physiocrats to the Present Day* (London: George Harrap).

Gindis, David (2009) 'From Fictions and Aggregates to Real Entities in the Theory of the Firm', *Journal of Institutional Economics*, **5**(1), April, pp. 25–46.

Gindis, David (2016) 'Legal Personhood and the Firm: Avoiding Anthropomorphism and Equivocation', *Journal of Institutional Economics*, **12**(3), September, pp. 499–513.

Gintis, Herbert (2012) 'Response: Giving Economists Their Due', *Boston Review*, May/June. Available at http://bostonreview.net/archives/BR37.3/ndf_herbert_gintis_markets_morals.php. (Retrieved 10 December 2018.)

GlobalReg Research Group (2011) 'Codebook and Dataset for "The Global Diffusion of Regulatory Agencies: Channels of Transfer and Stages of Diffusion"' [Jordana, Jacint, Levi-Faur, David and i Marin, Xavier Fernández], GlobalReg, Institut Barcelona. Available at http://www.globalreg-project.net/cps-2011/. (Retrieved 20 December 2017.)

Goldberg, Michelle (2016) 'Bernie Sanders' Radical Past', *Slate*, 24 February. Available at http://www.slate.com/articles/news_and_politics/politics/2016/02/bernie_sanders_radical_past_would_haunt_him_in_a_general_election.html. (Retrieved 6 February 2018.)

Goldberg, Sanford C. (2010) *Relying on Others: An Essay in Epistemology* (Oxford: Oxford University Press).

Goldin, Claudia and Katz, Lawrence F. (1996) 'Technology, Skill, and the Wage Structure: Insights from the Past', *American Economic Review (Papers and Proceedings)*, **86**(2), May, pp. 252–7.

Goldin, Claudia and Katz, Lawrence F. (2008) *The Race Between Education and Technology* (Cambridge, MA: Harvard University Press).

Goldman, Alvin I. (1999) *Knowledge in a Social World* (Oxford, UK and New York, NY, USA: Oxford University Press).

Gough, Ian (2000) *Global Capital, Human Needs and Social Policies* (Basingstoke, UK and New York, NY, USA: Palgrave Macmillan).

Gough, Ian (2017) *Heat, Greed and Human Need* (Cheltenham, UK and Northampton, MA, USA: Edward Elgar Publishing).

Gouinlock, James (1972) *John Dewey's Philosophy of Value* (New York: Humanities Press).

Graeber, David (2011) *Debt: The First 5,000 Years* (New York: Melville House).

Gramsci, Antonio (1971) *Selections from the Prison Notebooks* (London: Lawrence and Wishart).

Grandin, Greg (2013) 'On the Legacy of Hugo Chávez', *The Nation*, 6 March. Available at https://www.thenation.com/article/legacy-hugo-chavez/. (Retrieved 24 December 2017.)

Gray, John (1989) *Liberalisms* (London: Routledge).

Gray, John (1993) *Post-Liberalism* (London, UK and New York, NY, USA: Routledge).

Gray, John (1998) *False Dawn: The Delusions of Global Capitalism* (London: Granta).

Green, David G. and Casper, Laura (2000) *Delay, Denial and Dilution: The Impact of NHS Rationing on Heart Disease and Cancer* (London: Institute for Economic Affairs).

Gregor, A. James (1974) *The Fascist Persuasion in Radical Politics* (Princeton, NJ: Princeton University Press).

Gregory, Paul and Harrison, Mark (2005) 'Allocation under Dictatorship: Research in Stalin's Archives', *Journal of Economic Literature*, **43**(3), September, pp. 721–61.

Griffiths, Dan (ed.) (1924) *What is Socialism? A Symposium* (London: Richards).

Gulick, Luther and Urwick, L. (eds) (1937) *Papers on the Science of Administration* (New York: Columbia University).

Hahnel, Robin (2005) *Economic Justice and Democracy: From Competition to Cooperation* (London, UK and New York, NY, USA: Routledge).

Hahnel, Robin (2007) 'The Case against Markets', *Journal of Economic Issues*, **41**(3), December, pp. 1139–59.

Haidt, Jonathan (2012) *The Righteous Mind: Why Good People are Divided by Politics and Religion* (London: Penguin).

Haidt, Jonathan and Joseph, Craig (2004) 'Intuitive Ethics: How Innately Prepared Intuitions Generate Culturally Variable Virtues', *Daedalus*, **133**(4), Fall, pp. 55–66.

Hale, Sarah (2002) 'Professor Macmurray and Mr Blair: The Strange Case of the Communitarian Guru that Never Was', *Political Quarterly*, **73**(2), April, pp. 191–7.

Hall, Peter A. and Gingerich, Daniel W. (2009) 'Varieties of Capitalism and Institutional Complementarities in the Political Economy: An Empirical Analysis', *British Journal of Political Science*, **39**(3), pp. 449–82.

Hall, Peter A. and Soskice, David (eds) (2001) *Varieties of Capitalism: The Institutional Foundations of Comparative Advantage* (Oxford: Oxford University Press).

Hall, Peter A. and Thelen, Kathleen (2009) 'Institutional Change in Varieties of Capitalism', *Socio-Economic Review*, **7**(1), January, pp. 7–34.

Hansard (1997) 'Hospital Waiting Lists', Hansard. Available at http://www.publications.parliament.uk/pa/cm199798/cmhansrd/vo980630/debtext/80630-04.htm. (Retrieved 8 December 2017.)

Hansard (2002) 'Column 1071', Hansard. Available at http://www.publications.parliament.uk/pa/cm200102/cmhansrd/vo020124/debtext/20124-18.htm. (Retrieved 8 December 2017.)

Hardie, James Keir (1895) 'Socialism in England', *San Francisco Call*, **87**(117), 25 September, p. 9.

Hardie, James Keir (1910) *My Confession of Faith in the Labour Alliance* (London: ILP).

Harrington, Michael (1972) *Socialism* (New York: Bantam).

Harrington, Michael (1989) *Socialism: Past and Future* (New York: Arcade).

Harrison, J.F.C. (1969) *Robert Owen and the Owenites in Britain and America* (London: Routledge and Kegan Paul).

Hart, Oliver D. (1975) 'On the Optimality of Equilibrium when the Market Structure is Incomplete', *Journal of Economic Theory*, **11**(3), December, pp. 418–43.

Harvey, David (2005) *A Brief History of Neoliberalism* (Oxford, UK and New York, NY, USA: Oxford University Press).

Hausmann, Ricardo, Hidalgo, César A., Bustos, Sebastián, Coscia, Michele, Chung, Sarah, Jimenez, Juan, Simoes, Alexander and Yildirim, Muhammed A. (2011) *The Atlas of Economic Complexity: Mapping Paths to Prosperity* (Cambridge, MA: Harvard University HKS/CDI – MIT Media Lab).

Hayek, Friedrich A. (ed.) (1935) *Collectivist Economic Planning* (London: George Routledge).

Hayek, Friedrich A. (1944) *The Road to Serfdom* (London: George Routledge).

Hayek, Friedrich A. (1948) *Individualism and Economic Order* (London, UK: George Routledge and Chicago, IL, USA: University of Chicago Press).

Hayek, Friedrich A. (1960) *The Constitution of Liberty* (London, UK: Routledge and Kegan Paul and Chicago, IL, USA: University of Chicago Press).

Hayek, Friedrich A. (1973) *Law, Legislation and Liberty; Volume 1: Rules and Order* (London: Routledge and Kegan Paul).

Hayek, Friedrich A. (1988) *The Fatal Conceit: The Errors of Socialism. The Collected Works of Friedrich August Hayek, Vol. I*, ed. William W. Bartley III (London: Routledge).

Hayek, Friedrich A. (1989) 'The Pretence of Knowledge', *American Economic Review*, **79**(6), December, pp. 1–7.

Heinsohn, Gunnar and Steiger, Otto (2013) *Ownership Economics: On the Foundations of Interest, Money, Markets, Business Cycles and Economic Development*, trans. and ed. by Frank Decker (London, UK and New York, NY, USA: Routledge).

Heller, Michael A. (2008) *The Gridlock Economy: How Too Much Ownership Wrecks Markets, Stops Innovation, and Costs Lives* (New York: Basic Books).

Heller, Michael A. and Eisenberg, Rebecca (1998) 'Can Patents Deter Innovation? The Anticommons in Biomedical Research', *Science*, **280**(5364), May, pp. 698–701.

Helm, Toby (2018) 'Corbyn faces Clash with Labour Members over Second EU Referendum', *The Guardian*, 22 September. Available at https://www.theguardian.com/politics/2018/sep/22/corbyn-under-pressure-from-labour-members-over-brexit. (Retrieved 23 November 2018.)

Henrich, Joseph (2004) 'Cultural Group Selection, Coevolutionary Processes and Large-Scale Cooperation', *Journal of Economic Behavior and Organization*, **53**(1), February, pp. 3–35.

Henrich, Joseph, Boyd, Robert, Bowles, Samuel, Camerer, Colin, Fehr, Ernst and Gintis, Herbert (2004) *Foundations of Human Sociality: Economic Experiments and Ethnographic Evidence from Fifteen Small-Scale Societies* (Oxford, UK and New York, NY, USA: Oxford University Press).

Henrich, Joseph, Boyd, Robert, Bowles, Samuel, Camerer, Colin, Fehr, Ernst, Gintis, Herbert and McElreath, Richard (2001) 'In Search of Homo Economicus: Behavioral Experiments in 15 Small-Scale Societies', *American Economic Review (Papers and Proceedings)*, **91**(2), May, pp. 73–84.

Henrich, Joseph, Ensminger, Jean, McElreath, Richard, Barr, Abigail, Barrett, Clark, Bolyanatz, Alexander, Camilo Cardenas, Juan et al. (2010) 'Markets, Religion, Community Size, and the Evolution of Fairness and Punishment', *Science*, **327**(5972), pp. 1480–84.

Hetland, Gabriel (2016) 'Why is Venezuela in Crisis?', *The Nation*, 17 August. Available at https://www.thenation.com/article/why-is-venezuela-in-crisis/. (Retrieved 12 February 2018.)

Heyward, Anna (2018) 'Since Trump's Victory, Democratic Socialists of America Has Become a Budding Political Force', *The Nation*, 15–22

January. Available at https://www.thenation.com/article/in-the-year-since-trumps-victory-democratic-socialists-of-america-has-become-a-budding-political-force/. (Retrieved 18 December 2018.)

Hirsch, Fred (1977) *Social Limits to Growth* (London: Routledge).

Hirschman, Albert O. (1970) *Exit, Voice, and Loyalty: Responses to Decline in Firms, Organizations, and States* (Cambridge, MA: Harvard University Press).

Hirschman, Albert O. (1982) 'Rival Interpretations of Market Society: Civilizing, Destructive, or Feeble?', *Journal of Economic Literature*, **20**(4), December, pp. 1463–84.

Hobson, John A. (1900) *The Economics of Distribution* (London, UK and New York, NY, USA: Macmillan).

Hobson, John A. (1901) *The Social Problem: Life and Work* (London: James Nisbet).

Hobson, John A. (1902) *Imperialism: A Study* (London: James Nisbet).

Hobson, John A. (1909) *The Crisis of Liberalism: New Issues of Democracy* (London: King).

Hobson, John A. (1910) *The Industrial System: An Inquiry into Earned and Unearned Income*, 2nd edn (New York: Longmans Green).

Hobson, John A. (1921) *Problems of a New World* (London: George Allen).

Hobson, John A. (1929) *Wealth and Life: A Study in Values* (London: Macmillan).

Hobson, John A. (1932) *From Capitalism to Socialism* (London: Hogarth Press).

Hobson, John A. (1938) *Confessions of an Economic Heretic* (London: George Allen).

Hodgson, Geoffrey M. (1981) *Labour at the Crossroads: The Political and Economic Challenge to the Labour Party in the 1980s* (Oxford: Martin Robertson).

Hodgson, Geoffrey M. (1984) *The Democratic Economy: A New Look at Planning, Markets and Power* (Harmondsworth: Penguin).

Hodgson, Geoffrey M. (1988) *Economics and Institutions: A Manifesto for a Modern Institutional Economics* (Cambridge: Polity Press).

Hodgson, Geoffrey M. (1996) 'Varieties of Capitalism and Varieties of Economic Theory', *Review of International Political Economy*, **3**(3), Autumn, pp. 381–434.

Hodgson, Geoffrey M. (1998) 'Socialism against Markets? A Critique of Two Recent Proposals', *Economy and Society*, **27**(4), November, pp. 450–76.

Hodgson, Geoffrey M. (1999) *Economics and Utopia: Why the Learning Economy is not the End of History* (London, UK and New York, NY, USA: Routledge).

Hodgson, Geoffrey M. (2003) 'The Hidden Persuaders: Institutions and Individuals in Economic Theory', *Cambridge Journal of Economics*, **27**(2), March, pp. 159–75.

Hodgson, Geoffrey M. (2004) *The Evolution of Institutional Economics: Agency, Structure and Darwinism in American Institutionalism* (London, UK and New York, NY, USA: Routledge).

Hodgson, Geoffrey M. (2005) 'The Limits to Participatory Planning: A Reply to Adaman and Devine', *Economy and Society*, **31**(1), February, pp. 141–53.

Hodgson, Geoffrey M. (2007a) '*The Impossibility of Social Democracy* by Albert E.F. Schäffle', *Journal of Institutional Economics*, **3**(1), April, pp. 113–25.

Hodgson, Geoffrey M. (2007b) 'Meanings of Methodological Individualism', *Journal of Economic Methodology*, **14**(2), June, pp. 211–26.

Hodgson, Geoffrey M. (2008) 'An Institutional and Evolutionary Perspective on Health Economics', *Cambridge Journal of Economics*, **32**(2), March, pp. 235–56.

Hodgson, Geoffrey M. (2010) 'Albert Schäffle's Critique of Socialism', in Vint, John, Metcalfe, J. Stanley, Kurz, Heinz D., Salvadori, Neri and Samuelson, Paul A. (eds) *Economic Theory and Economic Thought: Essays in Honour of Ian Steedman* (London, UK and New York, NY, USA: Routledge), pp. 296–315.

Hodgson, Geoffrey M. (2013) *From Pleasure Machines to Moral Communities: An Evolutionary Economics without Homo Economicus* (Chicago: University of Chicago Press).

Hodgson, Geoffrey M. (2014) 'What is Capital? Economists and Sociologists have changed its Meaning – Should it be Changed Back?', *Cambridge Journal of Economics*, **38**(5), September, pp. 1063–86.

Hodgson, Geoffrey M. (2015a) *Conceptualizing Capitalism: Institutions, Evolution, Future* (Chicago: University of Chicago Press).

Hodgson, Geoffrey M. (2015b) 'Much of the "Economics of Property Rights" Devalues Property and Legal Rights', *Journal of Institutional Economics*, **11**(4), December, pp. 683–709.

Hodgson, Geoffrey M. (2016a) 'Some Limitations of the Socialist Calculation Debate', *Schmollers Jarhbuch*, **136**, pp. 1–26.

Hodgson, Geoffrey M. (2016b) 'Varieties of Capitalism: Some Philosophical and Historical Considerations', *Cambridge Journal of Economics*, **40**(3), May, pp. 941–60.

Hodgson, Geoffrey M. (2017a) '1688 and All That: Property Rights, the Glorious Revolution and the Rise of British Capitalism', *Journal of Institutional Economics*, **13**(1), March, pp. 79–107.

Hodgson, Geoffrey M. (2017b) 'Karl Polanyi on Economy and Society: A Critical Analysis of Core Concepts', *Review of Social Economy*, **75**(1), March, pp. 1–25.

Hodgson, Geoffrey M. (2018) *Wrong Turnings: How the Left got Lost* (Chicago: University of Chicago Press).

Hodgson, Geoffrey M. (2019a) 'Taxonomic Definitions in Social Science, with Firms, Markets and Institutions as Case Studies', *Journal of Institutional Economics*, **15**(2), April, pp. 207–33.

Hodgson, Geoffrey M. (2019b) *Is There a Future for Heterodox Economics? Institutions, Ideology and a Scientific Community* (Cheltenham, UK and Northampton, MA, USA: Edward Elgar Publishing), forthcoming.

Hodgson, Geoffrey M. (2019c) 'How Mythical Markets Mislead Analysis: An Institutionalist Critique of Market Universalism', *Socio-Economic Review*, forthcoming.

Hodgson, Geoffrey M. and Knudsen, Thorbjørn (2007) 'Firm-Specific Learning and the Nature of the Firm: Why Transaction Costs May Provide an Incomplete Explanation', *Revue Économique*, **58**(2), March, pp. 331–50.

Hoff, Trygve J.B. (1981) *Economic Calculation in the Socialist Society*, trans. from the Norwegian edn of 1938 by M.A. Michael (Indianapolis, IN: Liberty Press).

Hoffman, Elizabeth, McCabe, Kevin A. and Smith, Vernon L. (1998) 'Behavioral Foundations of Reciprocity: Experimental Economics and Evolutionary Psychology', *Economic Inquiry*, **36**(3), July, pp. 335–52.

Holcombe, Randall G. (1997) 'A Theory of the Theory of Public Goods', *Review of Austrian Economics*, **10**(1), pp. 1–22.

Hollander, Paul (1998) *Bernard Shaw: A Brief Biography* (Philadelphia, PA: University of Pennsylvania Press).

Holzer, Harry J., Block, Richard N., Cheatham, Markus and Knott, Jack H. (1993) 'Are Training Subsidies for Firms Effective? The Michigan Experience', *Industrial and Labor Relations Review*, **46**(4), July, pp. 625–36.

Honneth, Axel (2017) *The Idea of Socialism: Towards A Renewal* (Cambridge, UK and Maldon, MA, USA: Polity Press).

Honoré, Antony M. (1961) 'Ownership', in Guest, Anthony G. (ed.) *Oxford Essays in Jurisprudence* (Oxford: Oxford University Press), pp. 107–47. Reprinted in the *Journal of Institutional Economics*, **9**(2), June 2013, pp. 227–55.

Hoppe, Hans-Hermann (1994) 'F.A. Hayek on Government and Social Evolution: A Critique', *Review of Austrian Economics*, **7**(1), pp. 67–93.

Horvat, Branko (1982) *The Political Economy of Socialism: A Marxist Social Theory* (Oxford, UK and Armonk, NY, USA: Martin Robertson and M.E. Sharpe).

Hotho, Jasper J. (2014) 'From Typology to Taxonomy: A Configurational Analysis of National Business Systems and their Explanatory Power', *Organization Studies*, **35**(5), pp. 671–702.

Howells, Jeremy (1996) 'Tacit Knowledge, Innovation and Technology Transfers', *Technology Analysis and Strategic Management*, **8**(2), pp. 91–106.

Hubbick, Elizabeth (2001) *Employee Share Ownership* (London: Chartered Institute of Personnel and Development).

Hull, David L. (1988) *Science as a Process: An Evolutionary Account of the Social and Conceptual Development of Science* (Chicago, IL: University of Chicago Press).

Human Rights Watch (2005) 'Venezuela: Curbs on Free Expression Tightened'. Available at http://pantheon.hrw.org/legacy/english/docs/2005/03/24/venezu10368.htm. (Retrieved 2 December 2017.)

Human Rights Watch (2016) 'Venezuela'. Available at https://www.hrw.org/world-report/2016/country-chapters/venezuela. (Retrieved 2 December 2017.)

Humboldt, Wilhelm (1854) *The Sphere and Duties of Government*, trans. from the German edn of 1792 (London: Chapman).

Hutchins, Edwin (1995) *Cognition in the Wild* (Cambridge, MA: MIT Press).

Hutchison, Terence W. (1956) 'Bentham as an Economist', *Economic Journal*, **66**(262), June, pp. 288–306.

Hutt, Peter Barton and Hutt, Peter Barton II (1984) 'A History of Government Regulation and Misbranding of Food', *Food Drug Cosmetic Law Journal*, **39**, pp. 2–73.

Huxley, Aldous (1958) *Brave New World Revisited* (New York: Harper and Row).

Ingham, Geoffrey (2004) *The Nature of Money* (Cambridge: Polity Press).

Ingham, Geoffrey (2008) *Capitalism* (Cambridge: Polity Press).

Inglehart, Ronald F. and Norris, Pippa (2016) 'Trump, Brexit, and the Rise of Populism: Economic Have-nots and Cultural Backlash', Harvard Kennedy School: Faculty Research Working Paper Series, August, RWP16-026 (Cambridge, MA: Harvard University).

Inter-American Commission on Human Rights (IACHR) (2009) *Democracy and Human Rights in Venezuela* (Washington, DC: Organization of American States). Available at http://cidh.org/countryrep/Venezuela2009eng/VE09.TOC.eng.htm. (Retrieved 1 December 2017.)

Ireland, Paddy W. (1999) 'Company Law and the Myth of Shareholder Ownership', *Modern Law Review*, **62**(1), January, pp. 32–57.

Jacobs, Struan (2000) 'Spontaneous Order: Michael Polanyi and Friedrich Hayek', *Critical Review of International Social and Political Philosophy*, **3**(4), pp. 49–67.

Jacobs, Struan and Mullins, Phil (2016) 'Friedrich Hayek and Michael Polanyi in Correspondence', *History of European Ideas*, **42**(1), pp. 107–30.

Jaques, Elliott (1988) *Requisite Organisation, A Total System for Effective Managerial Organization and Managerial Leadership for the 21st Century* (Gloucester, MA: Cason Hall).

Jasanoff, Sheila (ed.) (2004) *States of Knowledge: The Co-Production of Science and the Social Order* (London, UK and New York, NY, USA: Routledge).

Jay, Douglas (1937) *The Socialist Case*, 1st edn (London: Faber and Faber).

Jay, Douglas (1947) *The Socialist Case*, 2nd edn (London: Faber and Faber).

Jefferson, Thomas (1822) Letter to Cornelius C. Blatchly, 21 October. Available on https://founders.archives.gov/documents/Jefferson/98-01-02-3106. (Retrived 23 May 2019.)

Jeffries, Stuart (2012) 'Why Marxism is on the Rise Again', *The Guardian*, 4 July. Available at https://www.theguardian.com/world/2012/jul/04/the-return-of-marxism. (Retrieved 24 November 2017.)

Joas, Hans (1993) *Pragmatism and Social Theory* (Chicago: University of Chicago Press).

Jones, Martin and Jessop, Bob (2010) 'Thinking State/Space Incompossibly', *Antipode*, **42**(5), pp. 1119–49.

Jordana, Jacint, Levi-Faur, David and i Marin, Xavier Fernández (2011) 'The Global Diffusion of Regulatory Agencies: Channels of Transfer and Stages of Diffusion', *Comparative Political Studies*, **44**(10), October, pp. 1343–69.

Kant, Immanuel (1929) *Critique of Pure Reason*, trans. from the 2nd German edn of 1787 with an introduction by Norman Kemp Smith (London: Macmillan).

Kapp, K. William (1950) *The Social Costs of Private Enterprise*, 1st edn (Cambridge, MA: Harvard University Press).

Kapp, K. William (2016) *The Heterodox Theory of Social Costs*, ed. by Sebastian Berger (London, UK and New York, NY, USA: Routledge).

Kautsky, Karl (1910) *The Class Struggle (Erfurt Program)* (Chicago, IL: Charles Kerr).

Keane, John (ed.) (1988) *Civil Society and the State* (London: Verso).

Keane, John (1995) *Tom Paine: A Political Life* (London: Bloomsbury).

Keane, John (1998) *Civil Society: Old Images, New Visions* (Cambridge: Polity).

Kentish, Benjamin (2018) 'Jeremy Corbyn Supporters Launch Campaign to bring back Labour's Historic Clause IV and "End Capitalism"', *The Independent*, 27 February. Available at https://www.independent.co.uk/news/uk/politics/jeremy-corbyn-labour-party-clause-iv-4-capitalism-labour4clause4-a8231351.html. (Retrieved 18 July 2018.)

Kenworthy, Lane (1995) *In Search of National Economic Success: Balancing Competition and Cooperation* (Thousand Oaks, CA, USA and London, UK: Sage).

Keynes, John Maynard (1930) *A Treatise on Money, Vol. 1: The Pure Theory of Money* (London: Macmillan).

Keynes, John Maynard (1933) *Essays in Biography* (London: Macmillan).

Keynes, John Maynard (1936) *The General Theory of Employment, Interest and Money* (London: Macmillan).

Kirkpatrick, Frank (2005) *John Macmurray: Community beyond Political Philosophy* (Lanham, MD: Rowman and Littlefield).

Kitcher, Philip (1993) *The Advancement of Science: Science Without Legend, Objectivity Without Illusions* (Oxford, UK and New York, NY, USA: Oxford University Press).

Kitcher, Philip (2011) *The Ethical Project* (Cambridge, MA: Harvard University Press).

Knapp, Georg F. (1924) *The State Theory of Money*, trans. and abridged from the 4th German edn of 1923 (first edn 1905) (London: Macmillan).

Knudsen, Thorbjørn (2002) 'The Significance of Tacit Knowledge in the Evolution of Human Language', *Selection*, **3**(1), pp. 93–112.

KOF Swiss Economic Institute (2017) 'KOF Index of Globalization', 2017 data release. Available at http://globalization.kof.ethz.ch/. (Retrieved 19 January 2018.)

Kornai, János (1992) *The Socialist System: The Political Economy of Communism* (Oxford: Clarendon Press).

Kristol, Irving (1977) 'Socialism: An Obituary for an Idea', *Quadrant*, **21**(4), April, pp. 30–33.

Kuhn, Thomas S. (1962) *The Structure of Scientific Revolutions* (Chicago, IL: University of Chicago Press).

Kumar, Krishan (1990) 'Utopian Thought and Communal Practice: Robert Owen and the Owenite Communities', *Theory and Society*, **19**, pp. 1–35.

Kumar, Krishan (1993) 'Civil Society: An Inquiry into the Usefulness of an Historical Term', *British Journal of Sociology*, **44**(3), September, pp. 375–95.

Lamb, Robert (2010) 'Liberty, Equality, and the Boundaries of Ownership: Thomas Paine's Theory of Property Rights', *Review of Politics*, **72**(3), Summer, pp. 483–511.

Landauer, Carl A. (1959) *European Socialism: A History of Ideas and Movements from the Industrial Revolution to Hitler's Seizure of Power*, 2 vols (Berkeley: University of California Press).

Lane, David, Malerba, Franco, Maxfield, Robert and Orsenigo, Luigi (1996) 'Choice and Action', *Journal of Evolutionary Economics*, **6**(1), pp. 43–76.

Lane, Robert E. (1991) *The Market Experience* (Cambridge: Cambridge University Press).

Lange, Oskar R. (1936–37) 'On the Economic Theory of Socialism: Parts One and Two', *Review of Economic Studies*, **4**(1), pp. 53–71, and **4**(2), pp. 123–42.

Lange, Oskar R. (1967) 'The Computer and the Market', in Feinstein, C. (ed.) *Capitalism, Socialism and Economic Growth: Essays Presented to Maurice Dobb* (Cambridge: Cambridge University Press), pp. 158–61.

Lange, Oskar R. (1987) 'The Economic Operation of a Socialist Society', two lectures delivered in 1942, *Contributions to Political Economy*, **6**, pp. 3–24.

Lange, Oskar R. and Taylor, Frederick M. (1938) *On the Economic Theory of Socialism*, ed. Benjamin E. Lippincot (Minneapolis, MN: University of Minnesota Press).

Laudan, Larry (1977) *Progress and its Problems: Towards a Theory of Scientific Growth* (London: Routledge and Kegan Paul).

Laudan, Larry (1981) *Science and Hypothesis: Historical Essays on Scientific Methodology* (Dordrecht: Reidel).

Lave, Jean and Wenger, Etienne (1991) *Situated Learning: Legitimate Peripheral Participation* (Cambridge: Cambridge University Press).

Lavoie, Donald (1985a) *Rivalry and Central Planning: The Socialist Calculation Debate Reconsidered* (Cambridge: Cambridge University Press).

Lavoie, Donald (1985b) *National Economic Planning: What is Left?* (Cambridge, MA: Ballinger).

Law, Marc T. and Kim, Sukko (2011) 'The Rise of the American Regulatory State: A View from the Progressive Era', in Levi-Faur, David (ed.) *Handbook on the Politics of Regulation* (Cheltenham, UK and Northampton, MA, USA: Edward Elgar Publishing), pp. 113–28.

Lazonick, William (1991) *Business Organization and the Myth of the Market Economy* (Cambridge: Cambridge University Press).

Leacock, Eleanor and Lee, Richard (eds) (1982) *Politics and History in Band Societies* (Cambridge, UK and New York, NY, USA: Cambridge University Press).

Lenin, Vladimir Ilyich (1967) *Selected Works in Three Volumes* (London: Lawrence and Wishart).

Leonard, Dorothy A. and Sensiper, Sylvia (1998) 'The Role of Tacit Knowledge in Group Innovation', *California Management Review*, **40**(3), pp. 112–32.

Lerner, Abba P. (1934) 'Economic Theory and Socialist Economy', *Review of Economic Studies*, **2**, pp. 157–75.

Lerner, Abba P. (1944) *The Economics of Control: Principles of Welfare Economics* (New York, NY: Macmillan).

Levin, Yuval (2014) *The Great Debate: Edmund Burke, Thomas Paine, and the Birth of Right and Left* (New York, NY: Basic Books).

Li, Quan and Reuveny, Rafael (2006) 'Democracy and Environmental Degradation', *International Studies Quarterly*, **51**(4), December, pp. 935–56.

Lin, Justin Yifu (2012) *Demystifying the Chinese Economy* (Cambridge, UK and New York, NY, USA: Cambridge University Press).

Lindblom, Charles E. (1959) 'The Science of "Muddling Through"', *Public Administration Review*, **19**(1), pp. 79–88.

Lindblom, Charles E. (1977) *Politics and Markets: The World's Political-Economic Systems* (New York, NY: Basic Books).

Lindblom, Charles E. (1984) *The Policy-Making Process* (Englewood Cliffs, NJ: Prentice Hall).

Lipset, Seymour Martin (1959) 'Some Social Requisites of Democracy: Economic Development and Political Legitimacy', *American Political Science Review*, **53**(1), March, pp. 69–105.

Lipsey, Richard G. (2007) 'Reflections on the General Theory of Second Best at its Golden Jubilee', *International Tax and Public Finance*, **14**(4), pp. 349–64.

Lipsey, Richard G. and Lancaster, Kelvin (1956) 'The General Theory of Second Best', *Review of Economic Studies*, **24**(1), December, pp. 11–32.

Lipsey, Richard G., Carlaw, Kenneth I. and Bekar, Clifford T. (2005) *Economic Transformations: General Purpose Technologies and Long Term Economic Growth* (Oxford: Oxford University Press).

Little, Ian M.D. (1950) *A Critique of Welfare Economics* (Oxford: Oxford University Press).

Litwack, John M. (1991) 'Legality and Market Reform in Soviet-Type Economies', *Journal of Economic Perspectives*, **5**(4), Autumn, pp. 77–89.

Luce, Edward (2017) *The Retreat of Western Liberalism* (London: Abacus).

Lukes, Steven (1973) *Individualism* (Oxford: Basil Blackwell).

Lukes, Steven (1974) *Power: A Radical View* (London: Macmillan).

Lundvall, Bengt-Åke (ed.) (1992) *National Systems of Innovation: Towards a Theory of Innovation and Interactive Learning* (London: Pinter).

Luxemburg, Rosa (1916) *The Junius Pamphlet*. Available at https://www.marxists.org/archive/luxemburg/1915/junius/ch01.htm. (Retrieved 4 May 2018.)

Lydall, Harold (1986) *Yugoslav Socialism: Theory and Practice* (Oxford, UK and New York, NY, USA: Oxford University Press).

MacDonald, J. Ramsay (1921) *Socialism: Critical and Constructive* (London, UK and New York, NY, USA: Cassell).

Mackenzie, Kenneth D. (1978) *Organizational Structures* (Northbrook, IL: AHM Publishing).

Maddison, Angus (2007) *Contours of the World Economy, 1–2030 AD: Essays in Macro-Economic History* (Oxford, UK and New York, NY, USA: Oxford University Press).

Magill, Michael and Quinzii, Martine (1996) *Theory of Incomplete Markets* (Cambridge, MA: MIT Press).

Malle, Silvana (1985) *The Organization of War Communism, 1918–21* (Cambridge: Cambridge University Press).

Manuel, Frank E. and Manuel, Fritzie P. (1979) *Utopian Thought in the Western World* (Oxford: Basil Blackwell).

Marschak, Thomas A. (1968) 'Centralized Versus Decentralized Resource Allocation: The Yugoslav "Laboratory"', *Quarterly Journal of Economics*, **82**(4), November, pp. 561–87.

Marshall, Alex (2011) *The Surprising Design of Market Economies* (Austin, TX: University of Texas Press).

Marshall, Alfred (1920) *Principles of Economics: An Introductory Volume*, 8th edn (London: Macmillan).

Martin, Cathie Jo and Thelen, Helen (2007) 'The State and Coordinated Capitalism: Contributions of the Public Sector to Social Solidarity in Post-Industrial Societies', *World Politics*, **60**(1), October, pp. 1–36.

Martin, John (1982) 'The Meaning of Social Democracy', in Martin, John (ed.) *The Meaning of Social Democracy and Other Essays* (London: John Martin), pp. 3–19.

Martin, Shakira (2017) 'National Union of Students Responds to PM Review of Student Funding', *NUS Connect*, 1 October. Available at https://www.nusconnect.org.uk/articles/national-union-of-students-responds-to-pm-review-of-student-funding. (Retrieved 8 January 2018.)

Martinez, Mark A. (2009) *The Myth of the Free Market: The Role of the State in a Capitalist Economy* (Sterling, VA: Kumarian Press).

Marx, Karl (1971) *A Contribution to the Critique of Political Economy* (London: Lawrence and Wishart).

Marx, Karl (1973) *The Revolutions of 1848: Political Writings – Volume 1* (Harmondsworth: Penguin).

Marx, Karl (1974) *The First International and After: Political Writings – Volume 3* (Harmondsworth: Penguin).

Marx, Karl (1975) *Early Writings* (Harmondsworth: Penguin).

Marx, Karl (1976a) *Capital*, vol. 1 (Harmondsworth: Pelican).

Marx, Karl (1976b) 'Marginal Notes on Wagner', in Dragstedt, Albert (ed.) *Value: Studies by Marx* (London: New Park), pp. 195–229.

Marx, Karl (1978) *Capital*, vol. 2, trans by David Fernbach from the German edn of 1893 (Harmondsworth: Pelican).

Marx, Karl and Engels, Frederick (1962) *Selected Works in Two Volumes* (London: Lawrence and Wishart).

Marx, Karl and Engels, Frederick (1975a) *Karl Marx and Frederick Engels, Collected Works, Vol. 3, Marx and Engels: 1843–1844* (London: Lawrence and Wishart).

Marx, Karl and Engels, Frederick (1975b) *Karl Marx and Frederick Engels, Collected Works, Vol. 4, Marx and Engels: 1844–1845* (London: Lawrence and Wishart).

Marx, Karl and Engels, Frederick (1976a) *Karl Marx and Frederick Engels, Collected Works, Vol. 5, Marx and Engels: 1845–1847* (London: Lawrence and Wishart).

Marx, Karl and Engels, Frederick (1976b) *Karl Marx and Frederick Engels, Collected Works, Vol. 6, Marx and Engels: 1845–1848* (London: Lawrence and Wishart).

Maxfield, Sylvia, Winecoff, W. Kindred and Young, Kevin L. (2017) 'An Empirical Investigation of the Financialization Convergence Hypothesis', *Review of International Political Economy*, **24**(6), December, pp. 1004–29.

Mazzucato, Mariana (2013) *The Entrepreneurial State: Debunking Public vs. Private Sector Myths* (London, UK and New York, NY, USA: Anthem).

McDonald, Patrick J. (2004) 'Peace through Trade or Free Trade?', *Journal of Conflict Resolution*, **48**(4), August, pp. 211–22.

McElroy, Damien (2010) 'Chávez Pushes Venezuela into Food War', *The Telegraph*, 23 June. Available at http://www.telegraph.co.uk/news/worldnews/southamerica/venezuela/7849749/Chavez-pushes-Venezuela-into-food-war.html. (Retrieved 17 December 2017.)

Mead, George Herbert (1934) *Mind, Self and Society – From the Standpoint of a Social Behaviorist* (Chicago, IL: University of Chicago Press).

Megginson, William L. and Netter, Jeffry M. (2001) 'From State to Market: A Survey of Empirical Studies on Privatization', *Journal of Economic Literature*, **39**(2), June, pp. 321–89.

Merriam-Webster (2015) 'Gallery: Word of the Year 2015'. Available at https://www.merriam-webster.com/words-at-play/word-of-the-year-2015/-ism. (Retrieved 18 November 2017.)

Meyerson, Harold (2016) 'Why are there Suddenly Millions of Socialists in America?', *The Guardian*, 29 February. Available at https://www.theguardian.com/commentisfree/2016/feb/29/why-are-there-suddenly-millions-of-socialists-in-america. (Retrieved 18 November 2017.)

Michels, Robert (1915) *Political Parties: A Sociological Study of Oligarchical Tendencies of Modern Democracy* (New York, NY: Hearst).

Milanovic, Branko (2011) 'A Short History of Global Inequality: The Past Two Centuries', *Explorations in Economic History*, **48**(4), December, pp. 494–506.

Milhaupt, Curtis J. and Pistor, Katharina (2008) *Law and Capitalism: What Corporate Crises Reveal about Legal Systems and Economic Development around the World* (Chicago, IL: University of Chicago Press).

Miliband, Ralph (1961) *Parliamentary Socialism* (London: Allen and Unwin).

Mill, John Stuart (1859) *On Liberty* (London: John Parker & Son).

Mill, John Stuart (1863) *Utilitarianism, Liberty and Representative Government* (London: Parker, Son and Bourn).

Mill, John Stuart (1909) *Principles of Political Economy with Some of their Applications to Social Philosophy*, 7th edn (London: Longman, Green, Reader and Dyer).

Mingardi, Alberto (2015) 'Herbert Spencer on Corporate Governance', *Man and the Economy*, **2**(2), December, pp. 195–214.

Minney, Rubeigh J. (1969) *The Bogus Image of Bernard Shaw* (London: Frewin).

Minsky, Hyman P. (1982) *Can 'It' Happen Again? Essays in Instability and Finance*. (Armonk, NY: M.E. Sharpe).

Minsky, Hyman P. (1986) *Stabilizing an Unstable Economy* (New Haven, CT: Yale University Press).

Mirowski, Philip (1998) 'Economics, Science and Knowledge: Polanyi vs. Hayek', *Tradition and Discovery: The Polanyi Society Periodical*, **25**(1), pp. 29–42.

Mirowski, Philip (2009) 'Postface: Defining Neoliberalism', in Mirowski, Philip and Plehwe, Dieter (eds) *The Road from Mont Pèlerin: The Making of the Neoliberal Thought Collective* (Cambridge, MA: Harvard University Press), pp. 417–55.

Mirowski, Philip (2013) *Never Let a Serious Crisis Go to Waste: How Neoliberalism Survived the Financial Meltdown* (London, UK and New York, NY, USA: Verso).

Mirowski, Philip and Plehwe, Dieter (eds) (2009) *The Road from Mont Pèlerin: The Making of the Neoliberal Thought Collective* (Cambridge, MA: Harvard University Press).

Mises, Ludwig (1920) 'Die Wirtschaftsrechnung im Sozialistischen Gemeinwesen', *Archiv für Sozialwissenschaften und Sozialpolitik*, **47**(1), April, pp. 86–121.

Mises, Ludwig (1949) *Human Action: A Treatise on Economics* (London, UK and New Haven, CT: William Hodge and Yale University Press).

Mitchell, Neil J. and McCormick, James M. (1988) 'Economic and Political Explanations of Human Rights Violations', *World Politics*, **40**(4), July, pp. 476–98.

Mokyr, Joel (2003) *The Gifts of Athena: Historical Origins of the Knowledge Economy* (Princeton, NJ: Princeton University Press).

Monbiot, George (2016) 'Neoliberalism – The Ideology at the Root of all our Problems', *The Guardian*, 15 April. Available at https://www.theguardian.com/books/2016/apr/15/neoliberalism-ideology-problem-george-monbiot. (Retrieved 16 January 2018.)

Moore, Barrington, Jr (1966) *Social Origins of Dictatorship and Democracy: Lord and Peasant in the Making of the Modern World* (London: Allen Lane).

Moore, Michael (2009) 'Michael Moore Talks about Socialism', *YouTube*, 8 October. https://www.youtube.com/watch?v=neyMdjrbM18. (Retrieved 13 February 2018.)

Moore, Peter (2015) 'One Third of Millennials view Socialism Favourably'. Available at https://today.yougov.com/news/2015/05/11/one-third-millennials-like-socialism/. (Retrieved 18 November 2017.)

Morris, William (1973) *Political Writings of William Morris* (London: Lawrence and Wishart).

Mounck, Yascha (2018) *The People vs Democracy: Why Our Freedom is in Danger and How to Save It* (Cambridge, MA: Harvard University Press).

Murrell, Peter (1983) 'Did the Theory of Market Socialism Answer the Challenge of Ludwig von Mises? A Reinterpretation of the Socialist Controversy', *History of Political Economy*, **15**(1), Spring, pp. 92–105.

Murrell, Peter (1991) 'Can Neoclassical Economics Underpin the Reform of Centrally Planned Economies?', *Journal of Economic Perspectives*, **5**(4), Fall, pp. 59–76.

Narayanswamy, Ramnath (1988) 'Yugoslavia: Self-Management or Mismanagement?', *Economic and Political Weekly*, **23**(40), pp. 2052–4.

National Center for Employee Ownership (2018) 'A Statistical Profile of Employee Ownership'. Available at http://www.nceo.org/articles/statistical-profile-employee-ownership. (Retrieved 3 December 2018.)

Neisser, Ulrich (1983) 'Toward a Skilful Psychology', in Rogers, D. and Sloboda, J.A. (eds) *The Acquisition of Symbolic Skills* (New York, NY: Plenum Publishing), pp. 1–17.

Nelson, Brian A. (2009) *The Silence and the Scorpion: The Coup against Chávez and the Making of Modern Venezuela* (New York, NY: Nation Books).

Nelson, Nigel (2015) 'Jeremy Corbyn: If I Don't Win Labour Leadership I Can Always go Back to my Allotment', *The Mirror*, 25 July. Available at http://www.mirror.co.uk/news/uk-news/jeremy-corbyn-dont-win-labour-6138128. (Retrieved 20 December 2017.)

Nelson, Richard R. (1959) 'The Simple Economics of Basic Scientific Research', *Journal of Political Economy*, **67**(3), June, pp. 297–306.

Nelson, Richard R. (1981) 'Assessing Private Enterprise: An Exegesis of Tangled Doctrine', *Bell Journal of Economics*, **12**(1), pp. 93–111.

Nelson, Richard R. (ed.) (1993) *National Innovation Systems: A Comparative Analysis* (Oxford: Oxford University Press).

Nelson, Richard R. (2003) 'On the Complexities and Limits of Market Organization', *Review of International Political Economy*, **10**(4), November, pp. 697–710.

Nelson, Richard R. and Winter, Sidney G. (1982) *An Evolutionary Theory of Economic Change* (Cambridge, MA: Harvard University Press).

Nichols, Shaun (2004) *Sentimental Rules: On the Natural Foundations of Moral Judgment* (Oxford and New York: Oxford University Press).

Nolte, Ernest (1965) *Three Faces of Fascism: Action Française, Italian Fascism, National Socialism* (London: Weidenfeld and Nicolson).

Nonaka, Ikujiro and Takeuchi, Hirotaka (1995) *The Knowledge-Creating Company: How Japanese Companies Create the Dynamics of Innovation* (Oxford, UK and New York, NY, USA: Oxford University Press).

Norris, Pippa and Inglehart, Ronald F. (2004) *Sacred and Secular: Religion and Politics Worldwide* (Cambridge, UK and New York, NY, USA: Cambridge University Press).

North, Douglass C. (1990a) *Institutions, Institutional Change and Economic Performance* (Cambridge, UK and New York, NY, USA: Cambridge University Press).

North, Douglass C. (1990b) 'A Transactions Cost Theory of Politics', *Journal of Theoretical Politics*, **2**(4), October, pp. 355–67.

North, Douglass C., Wallis, John J. and Weingast, Barry R. (2009) *Violence and Social Orders: A Conceptual Framework for Interpreting Recorded Human History* (Cambridge: Cambridge University Press).

Nove, Alexander (1980) 'The Soviet Economy: Problems and Prospects', *New Left Review*, **119**, January–February, pp. 3–19. Reprinted in Nove,

Alec (1986) *Socialism, Economics and Development* (London: Allen and Unwin).

Nove, Alexander (1983) *The Economics of Feasible Socialism* (London: George Allen and Unwin).

Nowak, Martin A. (2006) 'Five Rules for the Evolution of Cooperation', *Science*, **314**(5805), 8 December, pp. 1560–63.

Nozick, Robert (1974) *Anarchy, State, and Utopia* (New York: Basic Books).

Nye, Mary Jo (2011) *Michael Polanyi and His Generation: Origins of the Social Construction of Science* (Chicago, IL: University of Chicago Press).

O'Neill, John (1998) *The Market: Ethics, Knowledge and Politics* (London, UK and New York, NY, USA: Routledge).

Oğuz, Fuat (2010) 'Hayek on Tacit Knowledge', *Journal of Institutional Economics*, **6**(2), June, pp. 145–65.

Ollman, Bertell (1977) 'Marx's Vision of Communism: A Reconstruction', *Critique*, **8**, Summer, pp. 4–41.

Ollman, Bertell (2004) 'Marx, Markets and Meat Grinders: Interview with Bertell Ollman'. Available at https://www.nyu.edu/projects/ollman/docs/interview02.php. (Retrieved 24 November 2017.)

Olson, Mancur, Jr (1965) *The Logic of Collective Action* (Cambridge, MA: Harvard University Press).

Olson, Mancur, Jr (1982) *The Rise and Decline of Nations: Economic Growth, Stagflation and Social Rigidities* (New Haven, CT: Yale University Press).

Organisation for Economic Co-operation and Development (OECD) (2007) *Innovation and Growth: The Rationale for an Innovation Strategy*. Available at https://www.oecd.org/sti/inno/39374789.pdf. (Retrieved 17 August 2018.)

Organisation for Economic Co-operation and Development (OECD) (2015) 'Employment in the Public Sector', *OECDiLibrary*. Available at http://www.oecd-ilibrary.org/governance/government-at-a-glance-2015/employment-in-the-public-sector_gov_glance-2015-22-en. (Retrieved 12 February 2018.)

Organisation for Economic Co-operation and Development (OECD) (2016) 'OECD Income Distribution Database', *OECD.org*. Available at http://www.oecd.org/social/income-distribution-database.htm. (Retrieved 17 January 2018.)

Organisation for Economic Co-operation and Development (OECD) (2017) 'Health Expenditure and Financing', *OECD.Stat*. Available at http://stats.oecd.org/Index.aspx?DataSetCode=SHA. (Retrieved 8 December 2017.)

Organisation for Economic Co-operation and Development (OECD) (2018) 'Social Expenditure – Aggregated Data', *OECD.Stat.* Available at https://stats.oecd.org/Index.aspx?DataSetCode=SOCX_AGG. (Retrieved 16 January 2018.)

Organization of American States (2018) 'Panel of Independent International Experts Finds "Reasonable Grounds" for Crimes against Humanity Committed in Venezuela', *OAS*, 29 May. Available at http://www.oas.org/en/media_center/press_release.asp?sCodigo=E-031/18. (Retrieved 17 June 2018.)

Ostrom, Elinor (1990) *Governing the Commons: The Evolution of Institutions for Collective Action* (Cambridge: Cambridge University Press).

Ostrom, Elinor (1998) 'A Behavioral Approach to the Rational Choice Theory of Collective Action', *American Political Science Review*, **92**(1), pp. 1–21.

Oved, Yaacov (1988) *Two Hundred Years of American Communes* (New Brunswick, NJ: Transaction Books).

Oved, Yaacov (1997) 'The Lesson of the Communes', in Leichman, D. and Paz, I. (eds) *Kibbutz: An Alternative Lifestyle* (Efal: Yad Tabenkin), pp. 159–65.

Owen, Robert (1991) *A New View of Society and Other Writings*, ed. with an introduction by Gregory Claeys (Harmondsworth: Penguin).

Pack, Howard and Saggi, Kamal (2006) 'Is There a Case for Industrial Policy? A Critical Survey', *The World Bank Research Observer*, **21**(2), October, pp. 267–97.

Pagano, Ugo (2014) 'The Crisis of Intellectual Monopoly Capitalism', *Cambridge Journal of Economics*, **38**(6), November, pp. 1409–29.

Paine, Thomas (1776) Common Sense (Philadelphia, PA: Bell).

Paine, Thomas (1797) *Agrarian Justice: Opposed to Agrarian Law and to Agrarian Monopoly* (Philadelphia, PA: Folwell).

Paine, Thomas (1945) *The Complete Writings of Thomas Paine*, ed. and introduced by Philip S. Foner (New York, NY: Citadel Press).

Paine, Thomas (1948) *The Selected Work of Tom Paine*, ed. and introduced by Howard Fast (London: Bodley Head).

Pantsov, Alexander and Levine, Steven I. (2015) *Deng Xiaoping: A Revolutionary Life* (Oxford, UK and New York, NY, USA: Oxford University Press).

Peck, Jamie (2010) *Constructions of Neoliberal Reason* (Oxford, UK and New York, NY, USA: Oxford University Press).

Peck, Jamie and Theodore, Nik (2007) 'Variegated Capitalism', *Progress in Human Geography*, **31**(6), pp. 731–72.

Peel, John D.Y. (1971) *Herbert Spencer: The Evolution of a Sociologist* (New York, NY: Basic Books).

Pejovich, Svetozar (1966) *The Market-Planned Economy of Yugoslavia* (Minneapolis, MN: University of Minnesota Press).

Pendleton, Andrew, Wilson, Nicholas and Wright, Mike (1998) 'The Perception and Effects of Share Ownership: Empirical Evidence from Employee Buy-Outs', *British Journal of Industrial Relations*, **36**(1), March, pp. 99–123.

Pigou, Arthur C. (1920) *The Economics of Welfare* (London: Macmillan).

Pigou, Arthur C. (1937) *Socialism versus Capitalism* (London: Macmillan).

Piketty, Thomas (2014) *Capital in the Twenty-First Century* (Cambridge, MA: Belknap Press).

Pipes, Richard (1990) *The Russian Revolution, 1890–1919* (New York, NY: Knopf).

Pipes, Richard (2001) *Communism: A History* (New York, NY: Random House).

Poe, Steven C. and Tate, C. Neal (1994) 'Repression of Human Rights to Personal Integrity in the 1980s: A Global Analysis', *American Political Science Review*, **88**(4), December, pp. 853–72.

Polan, Anthony J. (1984) *Lenin and the End of Politics* (London: Methuen).

Polanyi, Karl (1944) *The Great Transformation: The Political and Economic Origins of Our Time* (New York, NY: Rinehart).

Polanyi, Michael (1940) *The Contempt of Freedom: The Russian Experiment and After* (London: Watts). Part reprinted in Polanyi (1997).

Polanyi, Michael (1941) 'The Growth of Thought in Society', *Economica*, new series, **8**(32), November, pp. 428–56.

Polanyi, Michael (1945) *Full Employment and Free Trade* (Cambridge: Cambridge University Press).

Polanyi, Michael (1948) 'Planning and Spontaneous Order', *The Manchester School*, **16**, September, pp. 237–68. Reprinted in Polanyi (1951).

Polanyi, Michael (1951) *The Logic of Liberty: Reflections and Rejoinders* (London: Routledge and Kegan Paul).

Polanyi, Michael (1957) 'The Foolishness of History: November 1917–November 1957', *Encounter*, **9**(5), pp. 33–7. Reprinted in Polanyi (1997).

Polanyi, Michael (1958) *Personal Knowledge: Towards a Post-Critical Philosophy* (London: Routledge and Kegan Paul).

Polanyi, Michael (1962) 'The Republic of Science: Its Political and Economic Theory', *Minerva*, **1**, pp. 54–73.

Polanyi, Michael (1967) *The Tacit Dimension* (London: Routledge and Kegan Paul).

Polanyi, Michael (1997) *Society, Economics and Philosophy: Selected Papers* (New Brunswick, NJ: Transaction).

Pontusson, Jonas (2011) 'Once Again a Model: Nordic Social Democracy in a Globalized World', in Cronin, James E., Ross, George W. and Shoch, James (eds) *What's Left of the Left: Democrats and Social Democrats in Challenging Times* (Durham, NC: Duke University Press), pp. 89–114.

Poole, Michael and Whitfield, Keith (1994) 'Theories and Evidence on the Growth and Distribution of Profit Sharing and Employee Share-holding Schemes', *Human Systems Management*, **13**(3), pp. 209–20.

Popper, Karl R. (1945) *The Open Society and its Enemies*, 2 vols (London: Routledge and Kegan Paul).

Potts, Jason (2019) *Innovation Commons: The Origin of Economic Growth* (Oxford, UK and New York, NY, USA: Oxford University Press), forthcoming.

Proudhon, Pierre-Joseph (1969) *Selected Works* (New York, NY: Doubleday).

Pryor, Frederic L. (1996) *Economic Evolution and Structure: The Impact of Complexity on the U.S. Economic System* (Cambridge, UK and New York, NY, USA: Cambridge University Press).

Pullen, John M. (2010) *The Marginal Productivity Theory of Distribution: A Critical History* (London, UK and New York, NY, USA: Routledge).

Putnam, Hilary (1995) *Pragmatism* (Oxford: Blackwell).

Putnam, Robert D. (2000) *Bowling Alone: The Collapse and Revival of American Community* (New York: Simon and Schuster).

Rampen, Julia (2016) 'Caroline Lucas and Jonathan Bartley: "The Greens can win over Ukip Voters too"', *New Statesman*, 21 October. Available at https://www.newstatesman.com/politics/staggers/2016/10/caroline-lucas-and-jonathan-bartley-greens-can-win-over-ukip-voters-too. (Retrieved 8 January 2018.)

Rand, Ayn (2009) 'Ayn Rand – The Morality of Altruism', *YouTube*, 26 October. Available at https://www.youtube.com/watch?v=51pMod2Aaso. (Retrieved 13 February 2018.)

Ravallion, Martin and Chen, Shaohua (2005) 'China's (Uneven) Progress against Poverty', *Journal of Development Economics*, **82**(1), pp. 1–42.

Rayman, Paula M. (1981) *The Kibbutz Community and Nation Building* (Princeton, NJ: Princeton University Press).

Reber, Arthur S. (1993) *Implicit Learning and Tacit Knowledge: An Essay on the Cognitive Unconscious* (Oxford, UK and New York, NY, USA: Oxford University Press).

Reibel, R. (1975) 'The Workingman's Production Association, or the Republic in the Workshop', in Vanek, Jaroslav (ed.) *Self-Management: The Economic Liberation of Man* (Harmondsworth: Penguin), pp. 39–46.

Reinert, Erik S. (2007) *How Rich Countries Got Rich ... And Why Poor Countries Stay Poor* (London: Constable).

Reinhart, Carmen and Rogoff, Kenneth S. (2009) *This Time is Different: Eight Centuries of Financial Folly* (Princeton, NJ: Princeton University Press).

Remington, Thomas F. (1984) *Building Socialism in Bolshevik Russia: Ideology and Industrial Organization, 1917–21* (Pittsburgh, PA: University of Pittsburgh Press).

Rentoul, John (1995) '"Defining Moment" as Blair wins Backing for Clause IV', *The Independent*, 27 April. Available at http://www.independent.co.uk/news/defining-moment-as-blair-wins-backing-for-clause-iv-1611135.html. (Retrieved 27 April 2015.)

Reporters Without Borders (2017) *2017 World Press Freedom Index.* Available at https://rsf.org/en/ranking_table. (Retrieved 20 January 2017.)

Reuters (2007) 'L'ouverture Politique à Gauche se Poursuit avec Michel Rocard', 29 August. Reuters. Available at https://www.boursier.com/actualites/reuters/l-ouverture-politique-a-gauche-se-poursuit-avec-michel-rocard-28295.html. (Retrieved 5 February 2018.)

Reuters (2012) 'Factbox: Hugo Chavez's Record in Venezuelan Elections', 8 October. Reuters. Available at https://www.reuters.com/article/us-venezuela-election-ballots/factbox-hugo-chavezs-record-in-venezuelan-elections-idUSBRE89702320121008. (Retrieved 10 February 2018.)

Reuters (2015) '"There is no Money": Cash-Strapped Cuba is Forced to Cut Vital Imports', 16 October, *The Guardian*. Available at http://www.theguardian.com/world/2015/oct/16/cuba-cash-shortage-imports-oil-commodities. (Retrieved 16 October 2015.)

Rifkin, Jeremy (2014) *The Zero Marginal Cost Society: The Internet of Things, the Collaborative Commons, and the Eclipse of Capitalism* (New York, NY, USA and London, UK: Palgrave Macmillan).

Riley, James C. (2001) *Rising Life Expectancy: A Global History* (Cambridge: Cambridge University Press).

Ritchie, David G. (1891) *Principles of State Interference: Four Essays on the Political Philosophy of Mr. Herbert Spencer, J.S. Mill and T.H. Green* (London: Swan Sonnenschein).

Robé, Jean-Philippe (2011) 'The Legal Structure of the Firm', *Accounting, Economics, and Law*, **1**(1), Article 5.

Roberts, Paul Craig (1971) *Alienation and the Soviet Economy* (Albuquerque, NM: University of New Mexico Press).

Robinson, Andrew M. and Zhang, Hao (2005) 'Employee Share Ownership: Safeguarding Investments in Human Capital', *British Journal of Industrial Relations*, **43**(3), September, pp. 469–88.

Rodrigues, João (2012) 'Where to Draw the Line between the State and the Market?', *Journal of Economic Issues*, **46**(4), December, pp. 1007–33.

Rodrik, Dani (2008) *Normalizing Industrial Policy* (Washington, DC: World Bank).

Rodrik, Dani (2011) *The Globalization Paradox: Why Global Markets, States, and Democracy Can't Coexist* (Oxford, UK and New York, NY, USA: Oxford University Press).

Rodrik, Dani (2017) 'Populism and the Economics of Globalization', Discussion Paper DP12119, June (London: Centre for Economic Policy Research).

Röpke, Wilhelm (1960) *A Humane Economy: The Social Framework of the Free Market* (Chicago, IL: Henry Regnery).

Rose, Richard (1990) 'Inheritance before Choice in Public Policy', *Journal of Theoretical Politics*, **2**(3), pp. 263–91.

Rosenblatt, Helena (2018) *The Lost History of Liberalism: From Ancient Rome to the Twenty-First Century* (Princeton, NJ, USA and Oxford, UK: Princeton University Press).

Roser, Max (2017) 'Democracy', *Our World in Data*. Available at https://ourworldindata.org/democracy. (Retrieved 2 February 2018.)

Rummel, Rudolph J. (1994) *Death by Government* (New Brunswick, NJ: Transaction).

Russell, Bertrand (1918) *Proposed Roads to Freedom: Socialism, Anarchism, and Syndicalism* (London: George Allen & Unwin).

Russell, Bertrand (1920) *The Practice and Theory of Bolshevism* (London: George Allen and Unwin).

Russell, Bertrand (1998) *Mortals and Others: American Essays 1931–1935* (London, UK and New York, NY, USA: Routledge).

Rutland, Peter (1985) *The Myth of the Plan: Lessons of Soviet Planning Experience* (London: Hutchinson).

Ryan, Alan (1995) *John Dewey and the High Tide of American Liberalism* (New York: Norton).

Ryan, James (2012) *Lenin's Terror: The Ideological Origins of Early Soviet State Violence* (London, UK and New York, NY, USA: Routledge).

Sainato, Michael (2017) 'Poll Confirms that Bernie Sanders is the Most Popular Politician in the Country', *Observer*, 11 July. Available at http://observer.com/2017/07/bernie-sanders-most-popular-politician/. (Retrieved 18 November 2017.)

Samuelson, Paul A. (1954) 'The Pure Theory of Public Expenditure', *Review of Economics and Statistics*, **36**(4), pp. 387–9.

Sandel, Michael (2012) *What Money Can't Buy: The Moral Limits of Markets* (London: Allen Lane).

Satz, Debra (2010) *Why Some Things should not be for Sale: The Moral Limits of Markets* (Oxford, UK and New York, NY, USA: Oxford University Press).

Schäffle, Albert E.F. (1870) *Kapitalismus und Sozialismus: Mit besonderer Rücksicht auf Geschäfts- und Vermögensformen* (Tübingen: Laupp).

Schäffle, Albert E.F. (1874) *Quintessenz des Sozialismus* (Gotha: Perthes).

Schäffle, Albert E.F. (1885) *Die Aussichtslosigkeit der Socialdemokratie. Drei Briefe an einen Staatsmann zur Ergänzung der 'Quintessenz des Sozialismus'* (Tübingen: Laupp).

Schäffle, Albert E.F. (1892) *The Impossibility of Social Democracy: Being a Supplement to 'The Quintessence of Socialism'*, trans. from the 4th German edn of Schäffle (1885) by A.C. Morant with a preface by Bernard Bosanquet (London, UK: Swan Sonnenschein and New York, NY, USA: Charles Scribner's Sons). Excerpted in Hodgson (2007a, pp. 118–25).

Schäffle, Albert E.F. (1908) *The Quintessence of Socialism*, trans. from the 8th German edn of Schäffle (1874) under the supervision of Bernard Bosanquet (London, UK: Swan Sonnenschein and New York, NY, USA: Charles Scribner's Sons).

Schneider, Martin R. and Paunescu, Mihai (2012) 'Changing Varieties of Capitalism and Revealed Comparative Advantages from 1990 to 2005: A Test of the Hall and Soskice Claims', *Socio-Economic Review*, **10**(4), October, pp. 731–53.

Schumpeter, Joseph A. (1934) *The Theory of Economic Development: An Inquiry into Profits, Capital, Credit, Interest, and the Business Cycle*, trans. by Redvers Opie from the 2nd German edn of 1926, 1st edn 1911 (Cambridge, MA: Harvard University Press).

Schwartz, Shalom H. (1994) 'Are there Universal Aspects in the Structure and Contents of Human Values?', *Journal of Social Issues*, **50**(4), pp. 19–45.

Scully, Gerald B. (1992) *Constitutional Environments and Economic Growth* (Princeton, NJ: Princeton University Press).

Searle, John R. (1995) *The Construction of Social Reality* (London: Allen Lane).

Sen, Amartya K. (1981) *Poverty and Famines: An Essay on Entitlement and Deprivation* (Oxford: Clarendon Press).

Serge, Victor (1963) *Memoirs of a Revolutionary, 1901–1941* (Oxford, UK and New York, NY, USA: Oxford University Press).

Service, Robert (1997) *A History of Twentieth-Century Russia* (Cambridge, MA: Harvard University Press).

Shabad, Goldie (1980) 'Strikes in Yugoslavia: Implications for Industrial Democracy', *British Journal of Political Science*, **10**(3), pp. 293–315.

Shaw, George Bernard (1890) *What Socialism is*, Fabian Tract No. 13 (London: Fabian Society).

Shaw, George Bernard (1930) *Socialism: Principles and Outlook* (London: Fabian Society). Reprinted from the *Encyclopædia Britannica*, 14th edn, 1929 (New York, NY: Sears Roebuck).

Simon, Herbert A. (1947) *Administrative Behavior: A Study of Decision-Making Processes in Administrative Organization* (New York, NY: Free Press).

Simon, Herbert A. (1957) *Models of Man: Social and Rational. Mathematical Essays on Rational Human Behavior in a Social Setting* (New York, NY: Wiley).

Simon, Herbert A. (1991) 'Organizations and Markets', *Journal of Economic Perspectives*, **5**(2), Spring, pp. 25–44.

Smith, Adam (1759) *The Theory of Moral Sentiments; or, An Essay Towards an Analysis of the Principles by which Men Naturally Judge Concerning the Conduct and Character, First of their Neighbours, and Afterwards of Themselves* (London: Millar and Edinburgh: Kincaid and Bell).

Smith, Adam (1776) *An Inquiry into the Nature and Causes of the Wealth of Nations*, 2 vols (London: Strahan and Cadell).

Smithin, John (ed.) (2000) *What is Money?* (London, UK and New York, NY, USA: Routledge).

Sober, Elliott and Wilson, David Sloan (1998) *Unto Others: The Evolution and Psychology of Unselfish Behavior* (Cambridge, MA: Harvard University Press).

Socialist Party of America (1922) 'National Constitution of the Socialist Party'. Available at https://www.marxists.org/history/usa/parties/spusa/1922/0502-spa-constitution.pdf. (Retrieved 19 November 2017.)

Soros, George (1998) *The Crisis of Global Capitalism: Open Society Endangered* (New York, NY: Public Affairs).

Soros, George (2008) *The New Paradigm for Financial Markets: The Credit Crisis of 2008 and What it Means* (New York, NY: Public Affairs).

Sosis, Richard (2000) 'Religion and Intergroup Cooperation: Preliminary Results of a Comparative Analysis of Utopian Communities', *Cross-Cultural Research*, **34**(1), February, pp. 70–87.

Spencer, Herbert (1851) *Social Statics* (London: Chapman).

Spencer, Herbert (1884) *The Man versus The State* (London: Williams and Norgate).

Spender, J-C. (1996) 'Making Knowledge the Basis of a Dynamic Theory of the Firm', *Strategic Management Journal*, Winter Special Issue, pp. 45–62.

Stalin, Joseph V. (1954) *Collected Works, Volume 11: January 1928 to March 1929* (Moscow: Foreign Languages Publishing House).

Standing, Guy (2017) *The Corruption of Capitalism: Why Rentiers Thrive and Why Work Does Not Pay* (London: Biteback).

Steedman, Ian (1980) 'Economic Theory and Intrinsically Non-Autonomous Preferences and Beliefs', *Quaderni Fondazione Feltrinelli*, no. 7/8, pp. 57–73. Reprinted in Steedman, Ian (1989) *From Exploitation to Altruism* (Cambridge: Polity Press).

Steele, David Ramsay (1992) *From Marx to Mises: Post-Capitalist Society and the Challenge of Economic Calculation* (La Salle, IL: Open Court).

Steiger, Otto (ed.) (2008) *Property Economics: Property Rights, Creditor's Money and the Foundations of the Economy* (Marburg: Metropolis).

Stigler, George J. and Becker, Gary S. (1977) 'De Gustibus non est Disputandum', *American Economic Review*, **76**(1), March, pp. 76–90.

Stiglitz, Joseph E. (2008) 'The Fall of Wall Street is to Market Fundamentalism what the Fall of the Berlin Wall was to Communism', Interview with Nathan Gardels, *The Huffington Post*, 16 September. Available at http://www.huffingtonpost.com/nathan-gardels/stiglitz-the-fall-of-wall_b_126911.html. (Retrieved 10 July 2017.)

Stokes, Gale (1993) *The Walls Came Tumbling Down: The Collapse of Communism in Eastern Europe* (Oxford, UK and New York, NY, USA: Oxford University Press).

Streeck, Wolfgang (2011) 'E Pluribus Unum? Varieties and Commonalities of Capitalism', in Granovetter, Mark (ed.) *The Sociology of Economic Life*, 3rd edn (Boulder, CO: Westview), pp. 419–55.

Streeck, Wolfgang (2014) *Buying Time: The Delayed Crisis of Democratic Capitalism* (London, UK and New York, NY, USA: Verso).

Streeck, Wolfgang and Yamamura, Kozo (eds) (2001) *The Origins of Nonliberal Capitalism: Germany and Japan in Comparison* (Ithaca, NY: Cornell University Press).

Stretton, Hugh and Orchard, Lionel (1994) *Public Goods, Public Enterprise, Public Choice: Theoretical Foundations of the Contemporary Attack on Government* (London, UK: Macmillan and New York, NY, USA: St Martin's Press).

Sunstein, Cass R. (2006) *Infotopia: How Many Minds Produce Knowledge* (Oxford, UK and New York, NY, USA: Oxford University Press).

Surowiecki, James (2004) *The Wisdom of Crowds: Why the Many are Smarter than the Few and How Collective Wisdom Shapes Business, Economics, Societies, and Nations* (New York: Doubleday).

Synopwich, Christine (1990) *The Concept of Socialist Law* (Oxford: Clarendon Press).

Talmon, Jacob L. (1952) *The Origins of Totalitarian Democracy*, vol. 1 (London: Secker and Warburg).

Tawney, R.H. (1921) *The Acquisitive Society* (London: Bell).

Tawney, R.H. (1926) *Religion and the Rise of Capitalism: An Historical Study* (London: John Murray).

Taylor, Barbara (1983) *Eve and the New Jerusalem: Socialism and Feminism in the Nineteenth Century* (London: Virago).

Thaler, Richard H. and Sunstein, Cass R. (2008) *Nudge: Improving Decisions about Health, Wealth, and Happiness* (New Haven, CT: Yale University Press).

Thatcher, Margaret (1993) *The Downing Street Years* (London: Harper-Collins).

The Guardian (2017) 'Young Voters, Class and Turnout: How Britain Voted in 2017', *The Guardian*, 20 June. Available at https://www.the guardian.com/politics/datablog/ng-interactive/2017/jun/20/young-voters-class-and-turnout-how-britain-voted-in-2017. (Retrieved 22 December 2017.)

The Independent (2017) 'Venezuela Opposition Parties Banned from Election', *The Independent*, 11 December. Available at http://www.independent.co.uk/news/world/americas/venezuela-opposition-parties-banned-election-presidential-nicolas-maduro-a8102786.html. (Retrieved 11 December 2017.)

Thelen, Kathleen (2004) *How Institutions Evolve: The Political Economy of Skills in Germany, Britain, the United States and Japan* (Cambridge, UK and New York, NY, USA: Cambridge University Press).

Thelen, Kathleen (2014) *Varieties of Liberalization and the New Politics of Social Solidarity* (Cambridge, UK and New York, NY, USA: Cambridge University Press).

Thompson, Noel (1988) *The Market and its Critics: Socialist Political Economy in Nineteenth Century Britain* (London: Routledge).

Tomlinson, Jim (2014) *The Politics of Decline: Understanding Postwar Britain* (London, UK and New York, NY, USA: Routledge and Kegan Paul).

Townshend, Jules (1990) *J.A. Hobson* (Manchester: Manchester University Press).

Toye, Richard (2002) '"The Gentleman in Whitehall" Reconsidered: The Evolution of Douglas Jay's Views on Economic Planning and Consumer Choice, 1937–47', *Labour History Review*, **67**(2), pp. 187–204.

Toye, Richard (2004) 'The Smallest Party in History? New Labour in Historical Perspective', *Labour History Review*, **69**(1), April, pp. 83–104.

Transparency International (2016) *Corruption Perceptions Index 2016*. Available at https://www.transparency.org/news/feature/corruption_perceptions_index_2016#table. (Retrieved 20 January 2018.)

Trombetta, Reynaldo (2017) 'In Venezuela 82% of People Live in Poverty – Where are our Friends Now?', *The Guardian*, 5 April. Available at https://www.theguardian.com/commentisfree/2017/apr/05/venezuela-western-socialists-nicolas-maduro-abuse. (Retrieved 17 January 2018.)

Trotsky, Leon D. (1933) *The Soviet Economy in Danger* (New York, NY: Pioneer Publishers). Available at https://www.marxists.org/archive/trotsky/1932/10/sovecon.htm. (Retrieved 23 May 2019.)

Trotsky, Leon D. (1937) *The Revolution Betrayed: What is the Soviet Union and Where is it Going?* (London: Faber and Faber). Available at https://www.marxists.org/archive/trotsky/1936/revbet/ch11.htm. (Retrieved 23 May 2019.)

Tulving, Endel and Schacter, Daniel L. (1990) 'Priming and Human Memory Systems', *Science*, **247**(4940), 19 January, pp. 301–306.

Turner, Stephen (1994) *The Social Theory of Practices: Tradition, Tacit Knowledge and Presuppositions* (Cambridge: Polity Press).

Tyson, Alec and Maniam, Shiva (2016) 'Behind Trump's Victory: Divisions by Race, Gender, Education', *Pew Research Center*, 9 November. Available at http://www.pewresearch.org/fact-tank/2016/11/09/behind-trumps-victory-divisions-by-race-gender-education/. (Retrieved 22 December 2017.)

United Nations Development Programme (2016) 'Human Development Reports'. Available at http://hdr.undp.org/en/composite/HDI. (Retrieved 20 January 2018.)

Uvalić, Milica (1992) *Investment and Property Rights in Yugoslavia – The Long Transition to a Market Economy* (Cambridge, UK and New York, NY, USA: Cambridge University Press).

Van Horn, Carl E. and Fichtner, Aaron R. (2003) 'An Evaluation of State-subsidized, Firm-based Training: The Workforce Development Partnership Program', *International Journal of Manpower*, **24**(1), pp. 97–111.

Van Parijs, Philippe (ed.) (1992) *Arguing for Basic Income: Ethical Foundations for a Radical Reform* (London, UK and New York, NY, USA: Verso).

Van Parijs, Philippe (1995) *Real Freedom for All: What (if Anything) Can Justify Capitalism?* (Oxford: Clarendon Press).

Vanek, Jaroslav (1970) *The General Theory of Labor-Managed Market Economies* (Ithaca, NY: Cornell University Press).

Vanek, Jaroslav (1972) *The Economics of Workers' Management* (London: Allen and Unwin).

Vanhanen, Tatu (1997) *Prospects of Democracy: A Study of 172 Countries* (London, UK and New York, NY, USA: Routledge).

Varoufakis, Yanis (2018) 'Marx Predicted Our Present Crisis – and Points the Way Out', *The Guardian*, 20 April. Available at https://www.theguardian.com/news/2018/apr/20/yanis-varoufakis-marx-crisis-communist-manifesto?CMP=End_Tory_cLustreFck. (Retrieved 4 May 2018.)

Vaughn, Karen I. (1980) 'Economic Calculation under Socialism: The Austrian Contribution', *Economic Inquiry*, **18**, pp. 535–54.

Veblen, Thorstein B. (1898) 'The Beginnings of Ownership', *American Journal of Sociology*, **4**(3), November, pp. 352–65.

Veblen, Thorstein B. (1908) 'Professor Clark's Economics', *Quarterly Journal of Economics*, **22**(2), February, pp. 147–95.

Venugopal, Rajesh (2015) 'Neoliberalism as a Concept', *Economy and Society*, **44**(2), pp. 165–87.

Vitols, Sigurt (2001) 'The Origins of Bank-Based and Market-Based Financial Systems: Germany, Japan, and the United States', in Streeck, Wolfgang and Yamamura, Kozo (eds) *The Origins of Nonliberal Capitalism: Germany and Japan in Comparison* (Ithaca, NY: Cornell University Press), pp. 171–99.

Vogel, Steven K. (1996) *Freer Markets, More Rules: Regulatory Reform in Advanced Industrial Countries* (Ithaca, NY: Cornell University Press).

Vogel, Steven K. (2006) *Japan Remodelled: How Government and Industry are Reforming Japanese Capitalism* (Ithaca, NY: Cornell University Press).

Vulliamy, Ed (2002) 'Venezuela Coup Linked to Bush Team', *The Observer*, 21 April. Available at https://www.theguardian.com/world/2002/apr/21/usa.venezuela. (Retrieved 1 December 2017.)

Wainwright, Hilary (1994) *Arguments for a New Left: Answering the Free-Market Right* (Oxford: Basil Blackwell).

Waldron, Jeremy (1988) *The Right to Private Property* (Oxford, UK and New York, NY, USA: Oxford University Press).

Walker, Peter (2017) 'Jeremy Corbyn: UK Firms Must Pay More Tax to Fund Better Education', *The Guardian*, 6 July. Available at https://www.theguardian.com/politics/2017/jul/06/jeremy-corbyn-uk-firms-must-pay-more-tax-to-fund-better-education. (Retrieved 8 January 2018.)

Walras, Léon (1874) *Éléments d'Economie Politique Pure, ou Théorie de la Richesse Sociale* (Lausanne: Rouge).

Walzer, Michael (1983) *Spheres of Justice: A Defence of Pluralism and Equality* (New York, NY: Basic Books).

Walzer, Michael (1994) *Thick and Thin: Moral Argument at Home and Abroad* (Notre Dame, IN: University of Notre Dame Press).

Ward, Benjamin (1958) 'The Firm in Illyria: Market Syndicalism', *American Economic Review*, **48**, pp. 566–89.

Ward, Benjamin (1967) *The Socialist Economy: A Study of Organizational Alternatives* (New York, NY: Random House).

Washington Post (2015) 'The CNN Democratic Debate Transcript, Annotated', 13 October. Available at https://www.washingtonpost.com/news/the-fix/wp/2015/10/13/the-oct-13-democratic-debate-who-said-what-and-what-it-means/?tid=a_mcntx&utm_term=.d2fe0ef31955. (Retrieved 18 January 2018.)

Watt, Richard M. (1969) *The Kings Depart: The Tragedy of Germany: Versailles and the German Revolution* (London: Weidenfeld and Nicolson).

Webb, Sidney J. and Webb, Beatrice (1920) *A Constitution for the Socialist Commonwealth of Great Britain* (London: Longmans Green).

Webb, Sidney J. and Webb, Beatrice (1935) *Soviet Communism: A New Civilisation?* (London: Longmans Green).

Weber, Max (1930) *The Protestant Ethic and the Spirit of Capitalism* (London: Allen and Unwin).

Weber, Max (1968) *Economy and Society: An Outline of Interpretative Sociology*, 2 vols, trans. from the German edn of 1921–1922 (Berkeley, CA: University of California Press).

Weisberg, Michael and Muldoon, Ryan (2009) 'Epistemic Landscapes and the Division of Cognitive Labor', *Philosophy of Science*, **76**(2), 225–52.

Weissmann, Jordan (2015) 'Calling himself a Socialist was one of Bernie Sanders' Smartest Moves', *Moneybox*, 19 November. Available at http://www.slate.com/blogs/moneybox/2015/11/19/bernie_sanders_defines_democratic_socialism_it_s_not_all_that_socialist.html. (Retrieved 19 November 2017.)

Westergaard, John and Resler, Henrietta (1976) *Class in a Capitalist Society: A Study of Contemporary Britain* (Harmondsworth: Penguin).

Whistler, Donald E. (1991) 'The Mainstream Democratic Vision', *American Review of Politics*, **12**(2), Autumn, pp. 13–41.

Whitley, Richard (1999) *Divergent Capitalisms: The Social Structuring and Change of Business Systems* (Oxford, UK and New York, NY, USA: Oxford University Press).

Whitley, Richard (2010) 'Changing Competition Models in Market Economies: The Effects of Internationalization, Technological Innovations, and Academic Expansion on the Conditions Supporting Dominant Economic Logics', in Morgan, Glenn, Campbell, John L., Crouch, Colin, Pedersen, Ove K. and Whitley, Richard (eds) *The Oxford*

Handbook of Comparative Institutional Analysis (Oxford, UK and New York, NY, USA: Oxford University Press), pp. 363–97.

Whitney, W.T. (2016) 'Venezuela in Crisis: Too Much US Intervention, Too Little Socialism', *Counterpunch*, 14 July. Available at https://www.counterpunch.org/2016/07/14/venezuela-in-crisis-too-much-us-intervention-too-little-socialism/. (Retrieved 12 February 2018.)

Wikipedia (2018a) 'Kibbutz', *Wikipedia.* Available at https://en.wikipedia.org/wiki/Kibbutz#cite_note-9. (Retrieved 5 April 2018.)

Wikipedia (2018b) 'List of Countries by Suicide Rate', *Wikipedia.* Available at https://en.wikipedia.org/wiki/List_of_countries_by_suicide_rate. (Retrieved 5 April 2018.)

Wilkinson, Richard and Pickett, Kate (2009) *The Spirit Level: Why More Equal Societies Almost Always Do Better* (London: Allen Lane).

Williamson, Kevin D. (2011) *The Politically Incorrect Guide to Socialism* (Washington, DC: Regnery).

Wilpert, Gregory (2007) *Changing Venezuela by Taking Power: The History and Policies of the Chavez Government* (London: Verso).

Wilson, David Sloan (2002) *Darwin's Cathedral: Evolution, Religion, and the Nature of Society* (Chicago, IL: University of Chicago Press).

Wilson, Harold (1964) *The Relevance of British Socialism* (London: Weidenfeld and Nicolson).

Wilson, Peter (2016) 'Venezuela's Season of Starvation', *Foreign Policy*, 19 June. Available at http://foreignpolicy.com/2016/06/19/venezuela-maduro-food-shortages-price-controls-political-unrest/. (Retrieved 5 December 2017.)

Wiltshire, David (1978) *The Social and Political Thought of Herbert Spencer* (Oxford: Oxford University Press).

Wittgenstein, Ludwig (1953) *Philosophical Investigations* (Oxford: Basil Blackwell).

Wood, Stephen (ed.) (1982) *The Degradation of Work? Skill, Deskilling and the Labour Process* (London: Hutchinson).

Woodward, Susan L. (1995) *Socialist Unemployment: The Political Economy of Yugoslavia 1945–1990* (Princeton, NJ: Princeton University Press).

World Bank (2015) 'Poverty'. Available at http://www.worldbank.org/en/topic/poverty/overview. (Retrieved 23 January 2018.)

World Bank (2017) 'Tax Revenue (% of GDP)', *Databank.* Available at https://data.worldbank.org/indicator/GC.TAX.TOTL.GD.ZS. (Retrieved 16 January 2018.)

World Bank (2019) 'GDP per capita, PPP (current international $)', *Databank.* Available at https://data.worldbank.org/indicator/NY.GDP.PCAP.PP.CD?view=chart. (Retrieved 31 March 2019.)

World Economic Forum (2017) *Global Gender Gap Report 2017.* Available at https://www.weforum.org/reports/the-global-gender-gap-report-2017. (Retrieved 20 January 2018.)

World Happiness Report (2017) *World Happiness Report 2017.* Available at http://worldhappiness.report/ed/2017/. (Retrieved 20 January 2018.)

Worthington, Sarah (2016) *Sealy and Worthington's Text, Case and Materials in Company Law*, 11th edn (Oxford, UK and New York, NY, USA: Oxford University Press).

Wray, L. Randall (ed.) (2004) *Credit and State Theories of Money: The Contribution of A. Mitchell Innes* (Cheltenham, UK and Northampton, MA, USA: Edward Elgar Publishing).

Wray, L. Randall (2012) *Modern Money Theory: A Primer on Macroeconomics for Sovereign Monetary Systems* (London, UK and New York, NY, USA: Palgrave Macmillan).

Wyss, Jim (2017) 'There are 342 Political Prisoners in Venezuela this Week. Here's How We Know that', *Miami Herald*, 16 November. Available at http://www.miamiherald.com/news/nation-world/world/americas/venezuela/article184803988.html. (Retrieved 24 December 2017.)

Yavas, Abdulla (1998) 'Does too much Government Investment Retard Economic Development of a Country?', *Journal of Economic Studies*, **25**(4), pp. 296–308.

Yglesias, Matthew (2015) 'Denmark's Prime Minister says Bernie Sanders is Wrong to Call his Country Socialist', *Vox.* Available at https://www.vox.com/2015/10/31/9650030/denmark-prime-minister-bernie-sanders. (Retrieved 18 January 2018.)

Zak, Paul J. (ed.) (2008) *Moral Markets: The Critical Role of Values in the Economy* (Princeton, NJ: Princeton University Press).

Zak, Paul J. (2011a) 'The Physiology of Moral Sentiments', *Journal of Economic Behavior and Organization*, **77**(1), pp. 53–65.

Zak, Paul J. (2011b) 'Moral Markets', *Journal of Economic Behavior and Organization*, **77**(2), pp. 212–33.

Zamagni, Stefano and Zamagni, Vera (2010) *Cooperative Enterprise: Facing the Challenge of Globalisation* (Cheltenham, UK and Northampton, MA, USA: Edward Elgar Publishing).

Zhou, Kate Xiao (1996) *How the Farmers Changed China* (Boulder, CO: Westview Press).

Zolo, Danilo (1992) *Democracy and Complexity: A Realist Approach* (Cambridge: Polity Press).

Zuboff, Shoshana (1988) *In the Age of the Smart Machine: The Future of Work and Power* (Oxford: Heinemann).

Index

Acemoglu. Daron, 93, 204
Achen, Christopher H., 209
Ackerman, Bruce, 162, 203
Adaman, Fikret, 21
advertising, 129–30, 133, 154
Africa, ix
agoraphobia, viii, 4, 32–5, 39, 40, 62, 66, 70–71, 199
Albert, Michael, 34
Albert, Michel, 165
Ali, Tariq, 88
Allen, R.T., 47, 182–3, 185, 192
Allen, Robert C., 116
Allende, Salvador, 188
Allett, John, 42, 182
Alstott, Anne, 162, 203
altruism, 5–6, 15, 51, 73
Amable, Bruno, 164–5
anarchism, 33, 60
Anderson, Perry, 88
Andreoni, James, 155
Angus, Ian, 20
anthropology, 54
anti-commons, 144
anti-Semitism, 15, 41
Aoki, Masahiko, 165
Arato, Andrew, 131, 133–4, 194
Arrow, Kenneth J., 92–3, 115, 144, 147
Asch, Solomon E., 130
Ashkenazi, Eli, 59
Ashton, David, 204
Atkinson, Anthony B., 162, 203
Atran, Scott, 55
Attlee, Clement, 3, 4, 39–42, 85
Australia, 135, 169–71, 173, 176
Austria, 135, 169–75

Austrian school of economics, 21, 63, 118, 122
Ayres, Clarence E., 55

Babeuf, Gracchus, 27
Baccaro, Lucia, 165
Bacdayan, Paul, 129
Badhwar, Neera K., 5
Barkai, Haim, 20, 58–9
Barmby, John Goodwyn, 27–8
Bartels, Larry, 209
Bartley, Jonathan, 156
Barzel, Yoram, 141
Becker, Gary S., 129
Beer, Max, 26
Bel, Germà, 151
Belgium, 135, 170–75
Benassi, Chiara, 165
Ben-Meir, Ilan, 8
Benn, Tony, 20, 34, 46, 61–2, 88
Bennett, Nathalie, 156–7
Benson, Bruce L., 143, 194
Bentham, Jeremy, 15, 126–7, 189
Berger, Sebastian, x, 158
Berger, Suzanne, 165
Berggren, Niclas, 6
Bergson, Abram, 116
Berlin Wall, 1, 206
Berlin, Isaiah, 183, 210
Bernstein, Eduard, 41
Berstein, Serge, 35
Bertrand, Elodie, 36, 39–40, 83, 153
Bestor, Arthur E., Jr, 13, 26–8
Bevan, Aneurin, 43
Beveridge, William, 19, 44, 184
Bhaskar, Roy, 34
Binder, Seth, 201, 205

Birch, Kean, 18, 191
Birstein, Vadim J., 128, 133
Bladel, John P., 109
Blair, Margaret M., 118, 185
Blair, Tony, 16, 45–8, 120
Blaug, Mark, 115
Block, Fred, 16
Block, Walter, 159, 188
blocked exchanges, 143–4
Boas, Taylor C., 18, 191
Bockman, Johanna, 17
Bodington, Stephen, 123
Boehm, Christopher, 5, 15, 50, 56
Boettke, Peter J., 81, 109
Bogdan, Radu, 130
Bogdanor, Vernon, 85
Bohle, Dorethee, 165
Bolsheviks, 8, 31–2, 37, 78–84, 89,
    208
Bolton, Matt, 4
Bonin, John P., 60, 96, 204
Bonini, Nicolao, 129
Bourgeois, Léon, 190–91
Bowler, Peter J., 132
Bowles, Samuel, 5, 6, 15, 50, 56, 149,
    162, 176, 202–3
Boyd, Robert, 50
Boyer, Robert, 165
Bray, John Francis, 33
Brazil, 169, 176, 207
Brennan. Jason, 22, 98
Brewer-Carías, Allan R., 85
Brexit, 137, 140, 208
British Empire, 138
broadcasting, radio and television,
    157–8
Brockway, Fenner, 39, 75
Broekmeyer, Marius, 65
Brown, Donald E., 51
Brunk, Gregory G., 93
Brutzkus, Boris, 123
Buchez, Philippe, 33, 65–8
Bukharin, Nikolai, 81
Burczak, Theodore, 70
bureaucracy, 4, 66, 73, 76–7, 89,
    92–6, 99, 104, 117, 120–23,
    126–8, 137, 140, 186
Burge, Tyler, 130

Burgin, Andrew, 18, 191–3
Burke, Edmund, 101, 189
Burkhart, Ross E., 93

Cabet, Étienne, 26–9
Cahill, Damien, 16
Campbell, Al, 31
Canada, 60, 135, 169–76
Canning, Paul, x
capitalism, vi–x, 1–49, 60, 70, 73, 77,
    92–9, 102, 106, 115–17, 120–26,
    131, 135, 139–50, 159–79, 185,
    187, 191, 194–5, 198–210
  democratic, viii, x, 20
  financial, 149
  global, 85
  inequality under, vi–x, 5, 19, 161–2
  intellectual monopoly, 133–4
  regulatory, 134–6
  state, 10, 80
  varieties of, 163–79
Caplan, Bryan, 116, 122
Carmony, Donald F., 50, 53
Carr, E.H., 80
Carroll, Lewis, 48
Casper, Laura, 120
Catholicism, 29, 60
censorship, 86–7, 90
central planning, vii, 1, 6–10, 17, 19,
    21, 26, 31–7, 43, 59–63, 66–7,
    72–3, 76–7, 80–81, 92, 96,
    101–24, 131, 140, 151, 158, 160,
    179
Chandler, Alfred D., Jr, 136
Chang, Ha-Joon, 122, 161
Chávez, Hugo, 84–91
Chen, Shaohua, 17, 78
Cheung, Steven N.S., 118
Chicago, 7
Chile, 173–4, 187–8
China, 1–2, 10, 17, 48–9, 73–4, 77–8,
    82, 90–92, 97, 110, 116, 119–20,
    163, 166, 169, 175–6
Christianity, 13, 25, 27, 34, 39, 45
civil society, 6, 10, 70, 83, 99, 131–4,
    139, 181, 194–5, 204–5
Claeys, Gregory, 53, 182

Clark, Andy, 108, 130
Clark, John Bates, 197–8
Clark, John Maurice, 158
Clarke, Peter, 42, 79, 182, 187
Clause Four, 11, 38, 41, 46
climate change, ix, 106, 132, 164, 184, 201
Clinton, Bill, 16
Clinton, Hillary, 4, 16
Coase, Ronald H., 78, 105, 118, 153–4, 159, 194
Coates, David, 165
Cobden, Richard, 6–7
Cockshott, W. Paul, 114, 123
coercion, 14, 76, 101, 130, 133, 141, 182, 184, 186, 192–3
Cohen, G.A., 22, 124
Cohen, Jean L., 131–4, 194
Cohen, Michael D., 129
Cold War, 40–41, 43, 164
Cole, Daniel H., 142
Cole, G.D.H., 20, 39–42, 61–2, 94, 103
Collier, Andrew, 34
common ownership, vi, 8–12, 19–20, 25–30, 36–47, 51, 53, 61, 75, 191
    see also nationalization; public ownership
common-pool resources, 69, 153–6
Commons, John R., 38, 133, 141–2
communism, ix, 1, 3, 25–33, 36, 38, 41, 48–51, 57, 63, 65, 74–84, 102, 112, 116, 124, 192
    primitive, 51
    war, 80–81
Communist International, 32, 81
Communist Party (China), 48–9
Communist Party (UK), 38
competition, 5, 6, 10, 34, 39, 44, 46, 50, 66, 76–7, 117–22, 135–6, 149, 152, 154, 160, 186–7, 193, 197–8, 203
complexity, vii, 84, 94–7, 101, 103, 119, 121–3, 131–4, 139, 149, 160, 186, 207, 209
Condorcet, Nicolas de, 189
Conquest, Robert, 83

conservatism, 12, 181, 185, 196, 204, 210
Conservative Party, 40, 127, 187–8
Cooley, Charles Horton, 130
cooperation, vi, 5–7, 15, 21–2, 26, 39, 46, 50–53, 69–70, 74, 76, 136, 155, 161, 178, 182, 184, 186, 190, 195–7, 200
    evolution of, 5, 50
cooperatives, viii, 11, 19–20, 32–5, 38, 52, 59–62, 68–70, 86, 95, 186
coordination by mutual adjustment, 105, 111
Corbyn, Jeremy, viii, 3, 4, 7, 10–12, 47, 91, 156, 208
corporations, 9, 14, 42, 60, 77, 95, 104, 116, 118, 121, 130, 133, 136, 159–60, 165, 185–7, 193, 207–8
corruption, 7, 13, 65, 77, 84–92, 167, 178
Cottrell, Allin F., 114, 123
Council of Economic Advisors, 4
countervailing power *see* power, countervailing
Courtois, Stéphane, vii, 48, 83, 99
Credit Suisse, 175–6, 202
Cromwell, Oliver, 180
Crosland, C. Anthony, 43–5, 48
Crouch, Colin, 165, 204
Cuba, 1, 73, 77, 86, 90–92, 97, 150–51
cultural relativism, 210
culture, 3, 56, 65, 93, 146, 158, 167, 200, 210
Cummings, Michael S., 55–6
Curtiss, Glenn, 144
Czech Republic, 173–5

D'Amico, Daniel J., 109
Dahlgreen, Will, 3
Dale, Gareth, 103
Darwin, Charles R., 5, 15, 50, 56, 184–5
Davis, David Brion, 52
Davis, Peter, 33

De Soto, Hernando, 142
De Waal, Frans, 5, 15, 50, 56
Deakin, Simon, 67, 118, 185
Deaton, Angus, 163
Debreu, Gerard, 115, 147
Debs, Eugene, 4, 8
decentralization, vii–viii, 8, 20, 23,
    62–3, 66–9, 103, 108–11, 139,
    153, 160–61
decentralized coordination
    mechanisms and systems,
    vii–viii, 67
Deighton, Len, 25
democracy, vi–x, 4, 7–13, 18–23, 30,
    34–43, 46, 66, 69, 73, 76–80,
    83–5, 88–97, 119–24, 128, 136,
    139–40, 158, 166–7, 177,
    180–88, 191–6, 199, 201,
    204–10
  and planning, 94–5
  preconditions of, 93
Democratic Party (US), viii, 187
democratic socialism *see* socialism,
    democratic
Democratic Socialists of America, 4,
    37
Deng, Xiaoping, 17, 48–9, 78, 82
Denmark, 9, 135, 168–78
deskilling, 102
Devine, Pat, 21
devolution, 66
Dewey, John, 19, 44, 130, 139, 179,
    182, 184, 190
Dezamy, Théodore, 26, 27
Dickinson, Henry D., 67, 109, 115–16
dictatorship, 19, 64, 78–9, 89, 91, 97,
    110, 188, 207–8
Diggers, 25
division of labour, 22, 31–2, 74, 102,
    108, 113, 166
  scientific, 132
Dobb, Maurice, 33–4, 39, 80, 96
Doeringer, Peter B., 118
Dore, Ronald, 165
Dosi, Giovanni, 106
Doucouliagos, Chris, 96, 204
Douglas, Mary T., 130
Dow, Gregory K., 60

Dunbar, Robin I.M., 104
Durbin, Elizabeth, 42
Durbin, Evan F.M., 67, 109
Durkheim, Émile, 143, 190–91

Ebenstein, Alan O., 188
economic calculation, 103, 109–12,
    123
economics, 5, 15, 63–4, 76, 109, 118,
    141, 149, 153, 197
  Austrian school of, 21, 63, 118,
    122
  institutional, 55, 141, 158
economics, heterodox, vii–viii
economies of scale, 105, 118–21, 166
Edgeworth, Francis Y., 197
education, 3, 16, 48, 52–3, 86–7, 91,
    95, 107, 116, 127–33, 146,
    150–51, 156–61, 176, 184, 186,
    188, 190, 198, 201–5
Egidi, Massimo, 129
Eisenberg, Rebecca, 144
Eisner, Marc Allen, 137
Ekelund, Robert B., Jr, 183
Elliott, Josephine M., 50, 53
Elliott, Okla, 9
Ellman, Michael, 119
employment, 3, 11, 59, 77, 104, 118,
    146, 160, 177, 202–4
Engels, Frederick, ix, 20, 26–33, 51,
    75, 80, 98, 102, 113–14, 194
Engen, Eric M., 143, 194
English Civil War, 25
Enlightenment, viii, 13–14, 51, 94,
    101–2, 162, 181, 189, 201,
    208–9
entrepreneurship, 16, 66, 82, 110,
    116–17, 122, 131
Erasmus, Charles J., 25, 29, 53, 59,
    64, 75
Eraut, Michael, 106
Estanga, Pedro Carmona, 87
Estrin, Saul, 65–6
ethics *see* morality
EU, 137–40, 206, 208
Europe, 1, 2, 27, 29, 44, 91, 137–40,
    174, 177, 192, 206, 208

Eastern, 77, 135, 194, 206
European Court of Justice, 138
Evans, Karen G., 139, 182
Evans, Peter, 122, 161
Evans, Richard J., 41
externalities, 6, 158–61, 200

Fabian Society, 30, 34–7, 40, 94
families, 6, 63, 68, 70, 149, 167–70,
   176, 188, 190
famines, vii, ix, 81–3, 90, 98, 183,
   205
fascism, 13, 85, 206, 208
feudalism, 12
Fichtner, Aaron R., 146
Figes, Orlando, 81
Finland, 135, 169–75, 178
First World War, 32, 42, 57, 74, 187,
   206
Fleck, Ludwik, 126, 130
Fogel, Robert W., 163
food adulteration, 134
Foote, Geoffrey, 40, 43, 61
Forero, Juan, 90
Forstater, Mathew, 12, 148
Fourier, François Marie Charles,
   26–7, 51–2
Fourierism, 28, 53–8, 68–69
Fox, Alan, 143, 184
France, ix, 3, 27–9, 34–5, 51, 60, 135,
   168–79, 190–91
franchising, 154–5
Fredriksson, Per G., 201, 205
freedom *see* liberty
free-rider problem, 153
French Revolution, viii, 180
Friedman, Milton, 14, 18, 181–90,
   193, 197–8
Friedman, Rose, 185
Fukuyama, Francis, 51, 140, 142, 148,
   164
Fuller, Steve, 132

Gagliardi, Francesca, 60
Galbraith, James K., 161
Galbraith, John Kenneth, 37, 93, 136,
   153–4, 205

Galloway, George, 88
Gamble, Andrew, 188
Gans-Morse, Jordan, 18, 191
Gartzke, Eric, 7
Gavron, Daniel, 58
Gekko, Gordon, 5
Gellner, Ernest, 131
general equilibrium theory, 67, 109,
   115, 117, 147
George, Henry, 203
Germany, ix, 3, 8, 21, 25–9, 41, 44–5,
   51, 76, 80, 135, 169–93
Gide, Charles, 13, 26, 33
Gindis, David, 118, 185
Gingerich, Daniel W., 165
Gintis, Herbert, 5–6, 15, 50, 56, 162,
   176, 202–3
Glasgow, 52–3
global warming *see* climate change
globalization, 2, 164–5, 170, 174–6,
   191, 204, 207
   index of, 175
Glorious Revolution, 180
Goldberg, Michelle, 8
Goldberg, Sanford C., 132
Goldin, Claudia, 102, 204
Goldman, Alvin I., 132
Gough, Ian, 127, 164
Gouinlock, James, 139, 182
Graeber, David, 12, 148
Graicunas, A. V., 104
Gramsci, Antonio, 194–5
Grandin, Greg, 85, 89
Gray, John, 1, 3, 96, 101, 111, 141,
   181, 183, 187, 207, 210
Great Crash of 2008, vi, 2, 148,
   165–70, 176, 179, 207, 209
Greece, 25, 51, 135, 169, 173, 206
greed, vi, 5–7, 34, 43, 51, 73, 182,
   194–6
Green Party (UK), 156
Green, David G., 120
Green, Francis, 204
Green, Thomas H., 190
Gregory, Paul, 111
Greskovits, Béla, 165
Griffiths, Dan, 37–40
Grossman, Peter Z., 142

group selection, 50, 56
Gulick, Luther, 104

Hahnel, Robin, 34, 94
Haidt, Jonathan, 5, 15, 50–51, 55–6
Hale, Sarah, 45
Hall, Peter A., 164–5
happiness index, 178
Hardie, James Keir, 36
Harrington, Michael, 37
Harrison, J.F.C., 26–7, 29, 53–54
Harrison, Mark, 111
Hart, Oliver D., 147
Harvey, David, 16–18, 171–2
Hausmann, Ricardo, 134, 207
Hayek, Friedrich A., 13, 15, 21, 63–4,
    70, 103–5, 108–10, 116–17,
    122–3, 126, 131, 143–4, 181–3,
    186, 188–9, 192–3
healthcare, 9, 52, 86, 88, 127, 160–61,
    184
Heinsohn, Gunnar, 142
Heller, Michael, 144
Helm, Toby, 208
Henrich, Joseph, 5–6, 15, 50, 55–6
Hirsch, Fred, 6
Hirschman, Albert O., 6–7, 146
historical school, 21, 76
Hitler, Adolf, 41
Hobhouse, Leonard T., 190
Hobsbawm, Eric, 88
Hobson, John A., 6–7, 14–15, 19,
    41–4, 73–4, 182–7, 190, 197
Hodgskin, Thomas, 33
Hoff, Trygve J.B., 103, 109
Hoffman, Elizabeth, 155
Holcombe, Randall G., 154
Hollander, Paul, 36
Holzer, Harry J., 146
Honneth, Axel, 26, 74, 94
Honoré, Antony M., 51, 142
Hoppe, Hans-Hermann, 188
Horvat, Branko, 63–4
Hotho, Jasper J., 165
Howells, Jeremy, 106
Hubbick, Elizabeth, 96, 146, 204
Hull, David L., 132

human evolution, 21
human rights, 5, 21, 78, 85–94, 99,
    181, 183, 188, 195
Humboldt, Wilhelm, 163
Hume, David, 189
Hungary, 17, 173, 208
Hutchins, Edwin, 108, 130
Hutchison, Terence W., 126
Hutt, Peter Barton, 134
Hutt, Peter Barton II, 134
Hutterites, 51
Huxley, Aldous, 180

Iceland, 135, 173–4, 178
imperialism, 4, 85
impurity principle, 148, 167–8
incentives, vii, 21–2, 59, 70–78, 81,
    103, 109, 110, 115–20, 122, 124,
    146, 149–50, 152, 154, 184,
    199–204
Independent Labour Party (UK), 36,
    42
India, 163, 169, 176
individual rights, 14, 128, 180–81,
    186, 189, 196, 208–9
    see also human rights
individualism, vi, 6, 13–16, 23, 26,
    99, 131, 134, 137, 139, 181–3,
    186, 188
    and rights, 14
    atomistic, 13–16, 19, 23, 129, 131,
        136, 139, 181, 183, 192
    methodological, 14
    ontological, 14
inequality, vi–x, 2, 5, 7, 10–11, 13,
    17, 19–20, 34, 42–3, 64, 84–5,
    133, 161–4, 168, 172, 174–5,
    179, 183, 186–9, 192–3, 196,
    201–3, 207
Ingham, Geoffrey, 12, 148
Inglehart, Ronald F., 204
inheritance, 42, 162, 175, 200, 202
inheritance taxes *see* taxation,
    redistributive
innovation, 77–8, 116–17, 167
institutional complementarities, 164–5

institutional economics *see*
economics, institutional
institutions, 2–3, 6, 13–15, 22, 42, 60,
65–6, 70, 77, 89, 98–105, 111,
117, 126, 130–34, 137, 139, 141,
148–50, 159, 161, 165–8, 178–9,
185, 192, 198, 200, 202, 206–7
ceremonial, 55
educational, 160
financial, 148
of science, 132
international trade, 6, 140, 187
International Working Men's
Association, 33
Internet, 95, 145, 153
Iraq, 47, 188, 193
Ireland, 135, 169
Ireland, Paddy W., 118, 185
Israel, 20, 57–70, 168, 172–3
Italy, 3, 27, 135, 169–71, 173, 176,
179

Jacobs, Struan, 15, 109, 192
Japan, ix, 135, 169, 171, 173, 175–8,
192
Jaques, Elliott, 104
Jasanoff, Sheila, 130
Jay, Douglas, 42–3, 48, 127
Jefferson, Thomas, 72
Jeffries, Stuart, 2
Jenkins, Roy, 85
Jessop, Bob, 165
Joas, Hans, x
Jones, Martin, 165
Jordana, Jacint, 135
Joseph, Craig, 51
justice, 45, 141, 180, 184–5, 189, 192,
195, 209

Kant, Immanuel, 101
Kapp, K. William, 6, 158
Katz, Lawrence F., 102, 204
Kautsky, Karl, 20
Keane, John, 131, 182, 194
Kentish, Benjamin, 11
Kenworthy, Lane, 122, 161
Kerensky, Kerensky, 78, 79

Keynes, John Maynard, 1, 12, 19, 44,
148–9, 184–5
Keynesianism, 18, 21, 42, 103, 149,
188, 192
kibbutzim, 20, 57–70, 168
Kim, Sukko, 134
Kirkpatrick, Frank, 45
Kitcher, Philip, 128, 132, 181
Klein, Naomi, 88
Knapp, George F., 12, 148
knowledge, vii, 11–12, 21–2, 64, 67,
75, 95–117, 122–32, 140, 144–5,
160–67, 179, 200–204
tacit, vii, 12, 21, 64, 103, 106–13,
123–4, 129, 131, 144–5, 167
Knudsen, Thorbjørn, 105–6
Konings, Martijn, 16
Kornai, János, vii, x, 59, 66, 111
Kristol, Irving, 1–2, 5
Kumar, Krishan, 54, 131, 133–4,
194–5

Labour Governments (UK), 40, 120
Labour Party (UK), viii, 3, 11, 36–47,
91, 120, 127, 156, 208
Labour Party (Israel), 59
labour-value pricing, 112–14
Lamb, Robert, 200
Lancaster, Kelvin, 147
Landauer, Carl A., 26
Lane, David, 108, 130
Lane, Robert E., 15
Lange, Oskar R., 67, 109–10, 115–17,
123
Lansbury, George, 39
Laplace, Pierre-Simon, 123–4
Laski, Harold, 39–40
Latvia, 173
Laudan, Larry, 128
Lave, Jean, 108, 130
Lavoie, Donald, 109
law, 14–15, 20, 22, 26, 36, 51, 61–70,
78, 86–94, 97, 111, 118, 137–43,
160–62, 166–7, 177, 180–81,
185, 194–5, 201, 207–10
Law, Mark T., 134
Lazonick, William, 122, 161

Leacock, Eleanor, 5, 6
Lee, Richard, 5, 6
Lenin, Vladimir Ilyich, 17, 31–2, 37,
    49, 78–83, 89, 112, 195, 208
Leonard, Dorothy A., 106
Lerner, Abba P., 67, 109
Leroux, Pierre, 26
Levellers, 75, 180
Levi-Faur, David, x, 135
Levine, Steven I., 17, 82
Li, Quan, 201, 205
liberal solidarity, 18–19, 22–3, 44,
    182–7, 191, 193, 195–6, 199,
    201, 210
liberalism, x, 10–15, 18–23, 40–46,
    60, 78, 85, 89, 91, 103, 128,
    136, 180–210
  classical, 189
  social, 190
libertarianism, x, 16, 22, 126, 131–40,
    164, 177, 180, 183–4, 187–9,
    199
liberty, ix, 14–16, 19, 72–3, 87–93,
    127, 130, 133, 145, 151, 158,
    178–83, 186–95, 204, 207–10
  as absence of coercion, 15, 182,
    186, 192–3
  public, 183
Liebknecht, Karl, 8
lighthouses, 153–4, 157
Lilburne, John, 75
Lin, Justin Yifu, 110–11
Lindblom, Charles E., 136, 179
Lipset, Seymour Martin, 93
Lipsey, Richard G., 132, 147
Little, Ian M.D., 126
Litwack, John M., 92
Livingstone, Ken, 88
Lloyd George, David, 19, 44, 184
Loach, Ken, 88
Locke, John, 180, 186, 189, 199
Logan, Vinny, x
London, 26, 27, 53, 79, 127
London Communist Propaganda
    Society, 27
Long, Roderick T., 5
Lucas, Caroline, 156
Luce, Edward, 183, 208–9

Lukes, Steven, 13, 133
Lundvall, Bengt-Åke, 132
Luxemburg, 135, 174–5
Luxemburg, Rosa, 8, 20
Lydall, Harold, 65
Lysenko scandal, 128

MacDonald, J. Ramsay, 38–9
Mackenzie, Kenneth D., 104
Macmurray, John, 45
Macron, Emmanuel, 16, 35
Maddison, Angus, ix, 163
Maduro, Nicolás, 89–90
Magill, Michael, 147
Malle, Silvana, 81
Mandeville, Bernard, 150
Maniam, Shiva, 3
Manuel, Frank E., 25–6
Manuel, Fritzie P., 25–6
Mao, Zedong, 48, 78, 110, 119, 157
marginal productivity, 197
market abolitionism, 34
market fundamentalism, x, 15–16,
    126, 142–3, 164–6
markets, vi–x, 1–23, 30–50, 57,
    61–85, 92–106, 110–26, 130–53,
    157–61, 164–77, 182–209
  as social institutions, 15
  financial, 10, 66, 152
  for ideas, 194
  for laws or rules, 143, 194
  internal, 118
  labour, 145–6
  missing, 143–7, 161
  political, 194
  simulated, 115
Marschak, Jacob, 63
Marschak, Thomas A., 63
Marshall, Alex, 16, 70, 137
Marshall, Alfred, 146
Martin, Shakira, 156–7
Martinez, Mark A., x, 122, 137, 161
Martinez-Alier, Joan, x
Marx, Karl, ix, 2, 4, 15, 26–37, 61,
    65, 75, 80, 98, 102, 108, 141,
    143, 164, 194, 202

Marxism, 2–8, 15–18, 25–36, 47–9, 63–7, 76, 79–81, 84, 98, 101–2, 113, 118, 122–4, 142–3, 164, 171, 181, 194–5
Mazzucato, Mariana, 117, 122, 161
McCormick, James M., 94
McDonald, Patrick J., 7
McDonnell, John, 3–4
McElroy, Damien, 88
Mead, George Herbert, 130
Megginson, William L., 151–2
Methodism, 35
Mexico, 169, 173–4
Meyerson, Harold, 3
Michels, Robert, 96
Milanovich, Branko, 164
Milhaupt, Curtis J., 142, 148
Miliband, Ed, 3
Miliband, Ralph, 36
Mill, John Stuart, 27–8, 44, 60, 109, 126–7, 152, 182–3, 189–90, 193
Mingardi, Alberto, 187
Minney, Rubeigh J., 36
Minsky, Hyman P., 149
Mirowski, Philip, 16–18, 182, 190–94
Mises, Ludwig, 15, 21, 63, 108, 109, 117–18, 122–3, 141, 181–3, 186, 193
Mitchell, Neil J., 94
Mitterrand, François, 35
mixed economy, 10–11, 19, 38–44, 49, 116, 122, 186, 196
Mokyr, Joel, 132
Monbiot, George, 165
Mondragón, 60
money, 9–12, 34, 37, 58, 78–81, 89, 112, 120, 134, 146–9, 155, 190, 194, 202–3
Mont Pèlerin Society, 18, 191–3
Montesinos-Yufa, Hugo, x
Moore, Barrington, Jr, 37, 93, 205
Moore, Michael, 9
Moore, Peter, 3
moral sentiments, 15, 142, 189, 199, 209
morality, 5–7, 15–16, 23, 45–7, 50, 94, 97, 127–8, 142–3, 157, 160, 181–6, 192–5, 198–200, 209

More, Thomas, 25
Morris, William, 30
Morrison, Herbert, 39–40
Morus, Iwan Rhys, 132
Mounck, Yascha, 183, 208
Muldoon, Ryan, 132
Mullins, Phil, 15, 109, 192
Müntzer, Thomas, 25
Murrell, Peter, 109, 116, 122

National Health Service, 10, 40, 43, 120–22, 160–61
nationalism, 2, 6, 20, 41, 58, 66, 74, 138, 185–8, 204
nationalization, 33, 41–6, 60, 63, 77–85, 88–9, 187
  see also public ownership
NATO, 4, 41
Nazism, 41, 74, 83, 85
needs, human, x, 42–3, 101, 112, 127, 139, 150, 186
Neisser, Ulrich, 106, 130
Nelson, Brian A., 86–7
Nelson, Nigel, 7, 209
Nelson, Richard R., 106, 116, 122, 132, 144, 161
neoliberalism, 16–18, 35, 47, 135–6, 165, 166–72, 179, 189–96
Netherlands, 135, 169–76
Netter, Jeffry M., 151–2
Neumayer, Eric, 201, 205
Neurath, Otto, 34
New Economic Policy (in Soviet Union), 17, 81–2, 116
New Harmony (US), 50–53
New Zealand, 135, 169, 173
Nichols, Shaun, 51
Nilsson, Terese, 6
Nonaka, Ikujiro, 106, 108
Nordic countries, vi, 4, 9–10, 23, 169–79
Norris, Pippa, 204
North Korea, 1, 73, 92, 97
North, Douglass C., 37, 93, 194, 205
Norway, 9, 135, 169–78
Nove, Alexander, 92–5, 119, 123
Nowak, Martin A., 6

Nozick, Nozik, 184
Nuti, D. Mario, x
Nye, Mary Jo, 103, 182

O'Driscol, John, 54–5
O'Neill, John, 34
Ocasio-Cortez, Alexandria, 4
Oğuz, Fuat, 109
Ollman, Bertell, 31, 34
Olson, Mancur, Jr, 75–6, 161
one-over-n problem, 72–8
Orchard, Lionel, 15, 121, 137, 155
Orwell, George, 83
Ostrom, Elinor, 69, 75, 155–6
Oved, Yaacov, 51, 54
Owen, Robert, 20, 26–7, 30, 32,
    50–53, 60, 112–13
Owen, William, 50, 53
Owenism, 26–9, 53–60, 68–9

Pack, Howard, 162
Pagano, Ugo, 133–4, 144, 156
Paine, Thomas, 1, 6–7, 19, 44, 76,
    182–3, 189–90, 193, 196,
    199–200, 203
Palestine, 57
Pantsov, Alexander, 17, 82
Paris, 26–7
Parker, Martin, 33
patents, 144
path dependence, 164–5
Paunescu, Mihai, 165
Peck, Jamie, 138, 165
Pejovich, Svetozar, 65
Pendleton, Andrew, 146
Perez, Carlota, x
Pickett, Kate E., 2, 201–2
Pigou, Arthur C., 6, 150, 158
Piketty, Thomas, 2, 161–2
Pilger, John, 88
Pillot, Jean–Jacques, 26–7
Pinochet, Augusto, 187–8
Pinter, Harold, 88
Piore, Michael J., 118
Pipes, Richard, 25, 81
Pistor, Katharina, 142, 148
Pitts, Frederick Harry, 4

Plehwe, Dieter, 17–18
pluralism, 19, 21, 66–7, 72–3, 77, 83,
    89, 92–4, 109, 128, 132, 139,
    181, 205, 210
    economic, 19, 21, 66–7, 72, 77,
        92–4, 109, 181, 205
Poe, Steven C., 94
Polan, Anthony J., 78
Poland, 172–3, 208
Polanyi, Karl, 20, 103, 190
Polanyi, Michael, vii–viii, 15, 19, 21,
    37, 44, 72, 81, 103–11, 122, 128,
    162–3, 180–83, 192–3
Pontussen, Jonas, 179
Poole, Michael, 96, 146, 204
Popper, Karl R., 179, 192
populism, x, 7, 85, 89, 204, 208–9
Portugal, 135, 169, 171, 173, 206
poverty, ix, 1, 7, 11, 17, 48–9, 78,
    85–8, 150–51, 163, 190
power, 2, 10, 13, 18–21, 31–7, 46–8,
    52, 54, 62–7, 72–99, 105, 110,
    112, 121, 128, 132–42, 146, 176,
    180–81, 185–7, 195, 197, 202,
    205–8
    corporate, 136
    countervailing, 21, 66–7, 72, 77,
        92–4, 97, 109, 128, 134, 177,
        181, 186, 205
pragmatism, x, 40, 44
private enterprise, vi–vii, 1, 10–11,
    16–17, 38–46, 48, 61, 81–4, 89,
    91, 93, 103, 151, 177, 186, 195,
    205
private property, x, 7, 13, 16, 22,
    25–8, 30, 32, 34, 36–43, 46,
    48–9, 58, 63–6, 70, 81, 85, 96,
    120, 122, 131, 136, 141, 150–52,
    165–7, 170, 180–83, 189, 195,
    199, 200, 210
privatization, x, 46, 59, 85, 120, 136,
    151, 152, 165–7, 170
procedural memory, 129
production function, 197–8
profits, 5, 7–8, 17, 39, 42–3, 46, 82,
    149–51, 159, 190, 203–4
property rights, 16, 22, 67, 141, 143,
    145, 159, 182, 198–9

Proudhon, Pierre-Joseph, 33, 65–8
Pryor, Frederic L., 102, 134, 207
psychology, 26, 52, 129–30
public goods, 152–7
Public Goods Game, 155
public ownership, vi, x, 1, 4, 8–9,
    19–20, 31–2, 35, 38, 40, 42–4,
    64, 72, 115, 122, 150, 162, 186,
    192
    see also nationalization
Pullen, John M., 197–8
Putnam, Hilary, x
Putnam, Robert D., 132–3, 195

Quinzii, Martine, 147

Rampen, Julia, 157
Rand, Ayn, 5, 181
Rasmussen, Lars Løkke, 9, 177
Rauch, James E., 122, 161
Ravallion, Martin, 17, 78
Rayman, Paula M., 57–8
Reagan, Ronald, 16, 187–8
Reber, Arthur S., 106
reciprocity, 6, 69, 76, 190
referendums, 85–8
Reibel, R., 33
Reinert, Erik S., 122, 161
Reinhart, Carmen, 149
religion, 13, 25–8, 51–8, 63, 67, 69,
    74, 131, 167, 181, 204, 209–10
Remington, Thomas F., 81
Rentoul, John, 46
Resler, Henrietta, 133
Reuveny, Rafael, 201, 205
revisionism, 2, 17, 25, 41–9
Richerson, Peter J., 50
Rifkin, Jeremy, 145, 156
Riley, James C., 163
Rist, Charles, 13, 26, 33
Ritchie, David G., 14–15
Robé, Jean-Philippe, 118, 185
Roberts, Paul Craig, 81
Robinson, Andrew M., 96, 146, 204
Rocard, Michel, 35
Rodrigues, João, 188
Rodrik, Dani, 162, 204, 207

Rogoff, Kenneth S., 149
Rome, Ancient, 51
Röpke, Wilhelm, 192–3
Rose, Richard, 172
Rosenblatt, Helena, 189
Roser, Max, 206
Rowthorn, Robert E., 75, 122, 161
Rummel, Rudolph J., vii, 48, 83, 99
Ruskin, John, 34
Russell, Bertrand, 36–40, 83–4
Russia, 2, 8, 17, 21, 31, 73, 77–9, 83,
    89–92, 97–8, 116, 123, 169, 176
    see also Soviet Union
Rutland, Peter, 111
Ryan, Alan, 139, 182
Ryan, James, 83

Saggi, Kamal, 162
Sainato, Michael, 4
Saint–Simon, Claude Henri de, 26–7,
    33
Samuelson, Paul A., 152–4
Sandel, Michael, 143
Sanders, Bernie, viii, 4, 7–12, 48, 177
Satz, Debra, 143
Schacter, Daniel L., 129
Schäffle, Albert E.F., 21, 76–7, 109,
    113, 122
Schneider, Martin R., 165
Schumpeter, Joseph A., 10
Schwartz, Shalom H., 51
science, vii, 51, 52, 57, 67, 101,
    103–4, 127–8, 132–3, 139
Scully, Gerald B., 161
Searle, John R., 12
second best (Lipsey and Lancaster),
    147
Second World War, 42, 57, 191, 206,
    208
self-interest, 5–6, 15, 26, 50, 52,
    74–5, 153, 155, 183–6, 193–5,
    199
Sen, Amartya K., 182–3
Sensiper, Sylvia, 106
Serge, Victor, 81
Shabad, Goldie, 65
Shakers, 51, 54–6

Shaw, George Bernard, 36–7
Shinwell, Emanuel, 39
Simon, Herbert A., 104, 180
slavery, 146, 159, 168, 184, 187
Slovakia, 173, 175
Slovenia, 173–4
Smith, Adam, 141, 184–5, 189, 193
Smithin, John, 12, 148
Snowden, Philip, 38–9
Sober, Elliott, 5, 15, 50, 56
social capital, 133, 195
social democracy, vi, x, 1–2, 4, 9–10,
    18–19, 25, 29, 44–5, 76, 175,
    182, 188, 191
Social Democratic Party (Germany),
    44–5
Social Democratic Workers' Party
    (Germany), 191
social justice, 45–6, 189, 191
social ownership *see* public ownership
socialism, vi–140, 149–50, 158, 162,
    164, 177, 181, 185–6, 191–4,
    196, 199, 201, 205, 208–10
  big, viii, 2, 4, 10, 19–40, 62, 65,
    68, 72–100, 121, 124, 128,
    131–6, 140, 181, 201
  death of, 1, 5
  deaths under, vii, 48, 83, 99
  democratic, viii, 7–11, 37, 46, 84,
    94, 97
  guild, 40
  small, viii, 4, 19–22, 33–5, 38,
    50–71, 196
  utopian, 26, 29, 51
social-ism, 45–46
socialist calculation *see* economic
    calculation
Socialist International, 32
Socialist Party (France), 34–5
Socialist Party of America, 4,
    7–8
Socialist Workers' Party (US), 8
soft budget constraint, 59, 66
solidarism, 190–91
Somers, Margaret, 16
Soros, George, 16
Sosis, Richard, 51, 54–6, 58
Soskice, David, 164–5

South Africa, 187
South Korea, 169, 173–7
Soviet Bloc, 1, 45, 59, 77, 115, 132,
    135, 164
Soviet Union, 1, 8, 17, 21, 25, 36–7,
    41, 63, 75–83, 92, 94, 103,
    110–11, 116, 119–20, 123, 128,
    132, 164, 208
Spain, 60, 135, 171, 173, 175–6, 179,
    206
span of control, 104
Spencer, Herbert, 14, 181, 186–8, 193
Spender, J.-C., 106–7
spontaneous order, 104, 105, 109
Stalin, Joseph, 36–7, 79, 82–3, 110,
    123, 128, 157
Standing, Guy, 134, 144, 156–7
state planning *see* central planning
Steedman, Ian, 129
Steele, David Ramsay, 109
Steiger, Otto, 142
Stigler, George J., 129
Stiglitz, Joseph E., 16
Stojanović, Aleksandar, x
Streeck, Wolfgang, 165, 207
Stretton, Hugh, 15, 121, 137, 155
Sunstein, Cass R., 130, 132
Surowiecki, James, 132
Sweden, 9, 135, 168–79
Switzerland, 27, 135, 169–76
sympathy, 51–2, 184–5
syndicalism, 67
Synopwich, Christine, 92

tacit knowledge, vii, 12, 21, 64, 103,
    106–13, 123–4, 129, 131, 144–5,
    167
Takeuchi, Hirotaka, 106, 108
Talmon, Jacob, 189
target problem, 119–21
Tate, C. Neal, 94
Tawney, R. H., 13, 40, 46
taxation, 10, 16, 19, 23, 37, 42, 85,
    88, 136, 156–7, 168, 170, 174–5,
    177, 183, 188, 187–92, 199–200,
    203, 205

redistributive, 19, 85, 88, 162, 174–5, 179, 183, 188, 192, 199–200, 203
Taylor, Barbara, 27
Taylor, Frederick M., 67, 109
technology, 104–105, 107, 120, 145, 200
Thaler, Richard H., 130, 155
Thatcher, Margaret, 16, 127, 187–8
Thelen, Kathleen, 146, 165, 179
Theodore, Nik, 165
Thompson, Noel, 34
Thompson, William, 33
Tito, Josip, 63
Tlaib, Rashida, 4
Tomlinson, Jim, 43
torture, 89–90, 188
Townshend, Jules, 42, 182
Toye, Richard, 42, 44
trade unions, 14, 16, 18, 36, 87, 93, 131, 177–9, 183, 187, 191
transaction costs, 105, 118–21, 159–60
Trotsky, Leon, 79, 101, 117, 122–4
Trotskyism, 1, 8
Trump, Donald, 16, 188
trust, 6, 21, 50–53, 69, 74–6, 106, 131–2, 139, 156, 160, 178–9, 201, 207–8
Tulving, Endel, 129
Turkey, 135, 169, 174, 207
Turner, Stephen, 106
Tyson, Alec, 3

UK, viii–ix, 3, 10, 27, 29, 34–45, 51, 53, 60–61, 83, 90–91, 120–22, 127, 134–40, 156, 160, 166–71, 174–9, 184, 187–8, 190
unemployment, 2, 66, 87, 161, 170, 184, 190, 192, 204, 207
Urwick, L., 104
US, viii, 2–4, 8–13, 16–20, 23, 27, 29, 44, 52–5, 63, 67, 72, 83, 85, 87, 89–90, 121, 132, 134–5, 137, 140, 146, 153, 163, 166–75, 178–80, 187–90, 193, 195
USSR *see* Soviet Union

utilitarianism, 126, 184–6, 189
Uvalić, Milica, 66

Vahabi, Mehrdad, x
Van Horn, Carl E., 146
Vanek, Jaroslav, 67
Vanhanen, Tatu, 93
Varoufakis, Yanis, 98
Vaughn, Karen I., 109
Veblen, Thorstein, 51, 196, 198
Venezuela, 21, 73, 84–92, 97–8
Venugopal, Rajesh, 18, 191
Vidal, Matt, x
Vitols, Sigurt, 148
Vogel, Steven K., 122, 136, 161
Vulliamy, Ed, 87

wage labour, 13, 168
Wainwright, Hilary, 131
Waldron, Jeremy, 181, 203
Walker, Douglas M., 183
Walker, Peter, 157
Walras, Léon, 115
Walrasian models, 115–17
    see also general equilibrium theory
Walzer, Michael, 51, 144
Wang, Ning, 78, 194
war, ix, 81, 148, 168, 185, 188, 193
Ward, Benjamin, 67
Ward, Lester Frank, 190
Warner, Mildred, 151
Webb, Beatrice, 37–8, 80, 94
Webb, Sidney, 37–9, 80, 94
Weber, Max, 13, 95–6
Weisberg, Michael, 132
Weissmann, Jordan, 10
welfare state, x, 10, 18–20, 23, 43, 44, 177, 184–90, 205
Wells, H.G., 39
Wenger, Etienne, 108, 130
Westergaard, John, 133
Whitehall, man in, 127, 131
Whitfield, Keith, 96, 146, 204
Whitley, Richard, 165
Wilkinson, Richard, 2, 201–2
Williamson, Kevin D., 10

Wilpert, Gregory, 86
Wilson, David Sloan, 5, 15, 50, 55–6
Wilson, Harold, 35–6, 40
Wilson, Peter, 90
Wiltshire, David, 187
Winter, Sidney G., 106
Wittgenstein, Ludwig, 130
Wood, Stephen, 102
Woodward, Susan L., 17, 65–6
working class, 2–3, 29, 41, 64, 78–81,
    181, 191, 209
Worthington, Sarah, 118, 185
Wray, L. Randall, 12, 148
Wright brothers, 144
Wyss, Jim, 90

Yamamura, Kozo, 165
Yavas, Abdulla, 161
Yglesias, Matthew, 9, 177
Young People's Socialist League
    (US), 7
Yugoslavia, viii, 17, 20, 62–70

Zak, Paul J., 6
Zamagni, Stefano, 60
Zamagni, Vera, 60
Zhang, Hao, 96, 146, 204
Zhou, Kate Xiao, 78
Zionism, 57, 69
Zolo, Danilo, 207
Zuboff, Shoshana, 95